"We Get What We Vote For ... Or Do We?"

The Impact of Elections on Governing

Edited by Paul E. Scheele

PRAEGER

Westport, Connecticut
London

147133

Library of Congress Cataloging-in-Publication Data

"We get what we vote for . . . or do we?" : the impact of elections on
  governing / edited by Paul E. Scheele.
      p.   cm.
    Includes bibliographical references (p.   ) and index.
    ISBN 0–275–96602–X (alk. paper).— ISBN 0–275–96603–8 (pbk. : alk. paper)
    1. Elections—United States.   2. Electioneering—United States.   3.
  Voting—United States.   4. Political planning—United States.   I.
  Scheele, Paul E., 1934–
  JK1967.W4   1999
  324.973—dc21   99–21596

British Library Cataloguing in Publication Data is available.

Library of Congress Catalog Card Number: 99–21596
ISBN: 0–275–96602–X
        0–275–96603–8 (pbk.)

First published in 1999

Praeger Publishers, 88 Post Road West, Westport, CT 06881
An imprint of Greenwood Publishing Group, Inc.
www.praeger.com

Printed in the United States of America

The paper used in this book complies with the
Permanent Paper Standard issued by the National
Information Standards Organization (Z39.48–1984).

10 9 8 7 6 5 4 3 2 1

Copyright Acknowledgments

The author and publisher gratefully acknowledge permission for use of the following material:

Portions of Daniel M. Shea's article appeared in "The Advent of Realignment and the Passing of
the 'Base-Less' Party System," *American Politics Quarterly* 27(1): 1999; pp. 33–57. Reprinted
with permission.

Gerald M. Pomper's article appeared in John C. Green and Daniel M. Shea, eds., *The State of the
Parties: The Changing Role of the Contemporary American Parties*, 3rd edition. Lanham, MD:
Rowan & Littlefield Publishers, 1998.

Contents

Preface

This volume of readings on the linkage (or lack of it) between American elections and governing grew out of a conference (with the same name as the book) at SUNY College at Oneonta shortly before the 1996 elections. To the delight of both organizers and participants, the conference elicited a wide array of scholarly presentations that led to two days of spirited discussion.

The genesis of the conference was a conversation one March 1996 Sunday morning among the editor, his daughter Carla Scheele, and her husband, Harold Augenbraum. We had just read another of what seemed to be endless accounts about a new law that suited American industries and political contributors but ran directly contrary to what the president, his party, and a majority of Congress had said they stood for in recent elections and polls showed the public favored.

"Have elections no meaning?" was our anguished question. "Why not write a book?" asked Harold. "My expertise isn't wide enough," I responded. But I knew that expertise existed, and a conference might be the vehicle to tap it. So the conference grew out of the convention, and now this reader, with articles updated to late 1998, results from the conference. If the reader elicits thought, discussion, and action, the effort will indeed have been worth it.

Special thanks in preparation of this volume go to the twenty-one contributors who have worked thoughtfully to present the best of current scholarship;

SUNY College at Oneonta for essential logistical support; my secretary, Sue DeJoy, for excellent work and cheerful cooperation through many months of efforts; and my friend, Susan R. Hughson, for her strong encouragement and gentle suggestions.

Introduction

Elections in modern mass societies are extraordinarily complex phenomena. Obviously, in any aspiring democracy, elections are the indispensable link between citizens and government. But how close a link? At base, elections allow citizens to "throw the rascals out," to change governments "by ballots rather than bullets." However, elections carry a deeper meaning for democracy, as explained by William Riker. "Democracy is self-respect for everybody," he wrote, an understanding of one's dignity. Self-respect "is a function of [man's] self-direction and self-control, of the choice and living of the life he thinks best" (Riker 1965: 17).

But how can people control their lives if government, which potentially controls so much of life, is beyond them? Clearly, *popular* government is essential. In Riker's words, "Everybody must help govern: The knowledge of self-direction is acquired in no other way than the having of it in the important affairs of life" (18).

Thus, to (small "d") democrats, self-government is an ideal of the highest significance. But it is more than an ideal. Democracy is also a method, and the method is voting in popular, free, competitive, meaningful elections. Again, Riker: "Truly responsible government is only possible when elections are so conducted that a choice of men is a decision on policy, that a decision on policy is soon transformed into action, and that action taken is popularly supervised" (84–85).

These are extraordinarily high demands. But if popular government becomes a reality, not a mere myth, with it come ennobled, self-directing, self-respecting citizens who recognize their "indispensability to society" (Riker 1965: 17). No wonder the promise of democracy has attracted people for ages!

That's a brief theory of democracy and elections. What of the reality? Modern democracies assume that elections not only choose government leaders, they set policy directions as well. Does this assumption hold in today's America? Many critics argue that elections today are largely symbolic, having little if any impact on government. Is such skepticism justified? The answers to these questions are largely what this book is about. We can however lay out some initial observations.

America has one of the oldest traditions of popular elections in the world. Most remarkably, *every government* since the adoption of the Constitution in 1789 has stood or fallen based on the results of popular elections (mediated, of course, through the idiosyncratic and occasionally undemocratic Electoral College).

Second, with its federal system including national, state, and local governments, America elects more officers than any other nation, and through the direct primary involves more people in the nominating process than any other country.

Third, elections have occasionally produced major policy shifts. In this century, FDR's victory in 1932 led directly to the monumental domestic policy initiatives known as the New Deal, Lyndon Johnson's Great Society programs grew out of the landslide of 1964, and a significant conservative shift followed Ronald Reagan's election in 1980. In addition, all general elections produce *some* policy changes, even when, as in the succession by George Bush to Reagan, the same party controls the government.

America also has the most open electoral system in the world, in two senses: it has the freeest exercise of the underlying rights of speech, press, and association, and it is more open to candidates from fields other than politics and government.

On the other hand, the combination of America's unique system of "separated institutions sharing power" (Richard Neustadt's phrase 1960: 33) with increasing voter independence of party and split-ticket voting has produced since World War II a new norm of divided government. By 1998, in thirty-four of the fifty-two years (more than 65 percent) since 1946 the presidency and at least one house of Congress have been controlled by different parties, a practice unheard of in most other countries.

It is not that divided governments cannot make public policy; they can. But so can dictatorships. Two of democracy's key assumptions are that (a) one party representing a popular majority controls the government and thus has not only the responsibility but also the power to govern, and (b) at the next election voters can readily reward policy successes or punish policy failures. But under divided government, neither assumption holds: the "government" does not actually control policy making, and voters cannot readily determine whom to reward or punish.

America also has the doubtful distinctions of having *the longest election cycle in the world*, *the most expensive election campaigns*, and *the lowest voter turnout* of any industrialized nation. Each of these points will be expanded in the articles to follow.

On the other hand, many nations share our election problems. Increasingly in mass societies, the attention of citizens is eroded by their concerns as consumers and employees and by the distractions and entertainments of modern life—television, motion pictures, the Internet, etc. Thus, to be effective, political communication must increasingly be via mass media. In the words of Hal Malchow, Al Gore's campaign manager for his first U.S. Senate run in 1984, "You can't retail politics anymore" (Malchow 1985). Politics today can only be wholesaled, and that means using TV and mass mailings, both of which are very expensive.

That expense in turn drives campaigns and candidates to thrash about for contributions, the larger the better. Witness former senator Bill Bradley's report of a colleague who claimed he had to spend *80 percent* of his time in fundraising! Witness as well Bill Clinton's frantic efforts to raise cash after the 1994 Republican sweep of Congress. The Federal Election Commission increasingly has deferred since 1980 to private fund-raising of "soft money" beyond the substantial federal subsidies. Some of these contributions, to each party, exceeded $1 million and allowed George Bush to accumulate $111 million in 1992 beyond the $55 million federal subsidy, while Clinton garnered $86 million (Arterton 1993: 84). Clinton feared that the Republicans' superior fund-raising abilities would swamp him in 1996, and he encouraged and allowed extraordinary (perhaps illegal) fund-raising efforts.

The danger here is that policy making will be subordinated to financial interests instead of the interests of citizens. The charge is even made (proven in some past administrations) that policy positions are traded directly for campaign contributions. Robert Reich, former secretary of labor, makes the further point that when both major parties receive most of their large contributions from the wealthy, there may be no one to represent the interests of the non-wealthy or the poor.

In fact, analyses of voter participation in elections raise the question, "Can democratic politics function without voters?" (Lowi and Ginsberg 1995: 585). How can the 51 percent who did not vote in 1996, or the 61 percent in 1994 and 1998, be represented? Or, what of the persistent nonparticipation of the poorest and least educated fifth of the population, most of whom never vote? Have they no interests worth considering? Are they to have no voice in policy? To return to Riker, are they never to enjoy the self-respect that comes from democratic participation and control? Or is this simply a hopeless dream? Is self-respect something only campaign contributors can aspire to?

Finally, what of the role of political parties? Without political organizations, a society of 265 million people (or 180 million voters) will probably find that it has millions of different interests: perfect representation of interests, and not a prayer for self-government. Democracy requires more than representation; it also demands the formation of majorities on the basis of which decisions about officers and policies must legitimately rest. Throughout the past two centuries, the indispensable institution to assist in majority formation is the competitive political party system. When it functions well, such a system identifies and gives voice to people's significant policy concerns, and develops proposals to address those concerns and turn them into public policy.

The place of parties as major influences in American politics is increasingly being taken by the mass media and political interest groups. The great difficulty with these organizations is that neither has the interest of the public as its *primary* concern and may give no thought to any sort of public interest. Most of the mass media is primarily interested in profits, which leads them to build mass audiences, who in turn are most attracted by entertainment and sensation, by "gotcha" stories. Balanced reporting, background information, and "good news" stories are all unfashionable today, leaving voters angry and ill informed.

Interest groups, like the media, are vital to a functioning democracy, but their interests are generally narrow. Moreover, they represent society's "haves," those with discretionary money and time to spend on interest groups, and the education to understand that groups can expand their political influence. If it is the *public* interest we wish to maximize, the media and interest groups are weak reeds on which to rely.

In America, however, both party and politics have become pejorative terms. Voter identification with the two major parties is less than 70 percent, fewer people than ever identify strongly with either party, and ticket splitting is widespread. Under those circumstances, it should not be surprising that

- George Bush wins the presidency with only 53 percent of the vote, carries neither house of Congress with him, and finds significant policy success rare;
- Bill Clinton wins the presidency with only 43 percent of the vote (1992), carries only a nominal Democratic edge in Congress, and finds significant policy success rare;
- Newt Gingrich leads Republicans to narrow majorities in 1994 with 51 percent of the 39 percent of citizens who voted, tries to govern from his twin roles as Speaker and Republican party leader, and finds significant policy success rare; and
- Bill Clinton wins reelection with a 49 percent plurality, is opposed in both Houses by Republican majorities, and finds significant policy success rare.

This nation has significant problems, problems for which most polities would find government an apt instrument. But the nation is very large, both in population and geography; it has more (and more diverse) interests than anywhere in the world; our governmental and political systems are highly complex, difficult to understand and even harder for the public to make work for them; and courageous political leadership is scarce. Under these circumstances, a book of readings such as this examining "The Impact of Elections on Governing" would seem to be very apt and very timely.

The message of this volume is positive: the contributors value democracy as a system to link people and policy and wish to maximize it. Their descriptions and prescriptions will enlighten and challenge, will heighten citizens' understanding and appreciation of the system while alerting them to its shortcomings. Mostly, I believe, readers will want to become more involved in that system.

The articles are organized into three sections: How American Elections Work, The Impact of Elections on Specific Policies, and Rethinking Election Theories and Practices. This structure has the advantage of first establishing a solid base of information and data by examining and critiquing the main elements affecting elections (the political communications of candidates; TV, advertising, and polling; campaign finance; and political parties); turns then to consider the specific policy impacts elections have had on women's issues, welfare, and the Supreme Court; and concludes with five broadly conceived pieces devoted to questions of electoral reform.

The contributors join the editor in hoping that our efforts enhance Americans' ability to "get what we vote for," and to realize the human self-respect that is democracy's highest goal.

Paul E. Scheele
December 18, 1998

REFERENCES

Arterton, F. Christopher. 1993. "Campaign '92: Strategies and Tactics of the Candidates." In Gerald M. Pomper, ed., *The Election of 1992*. Chatham, NJ: Chatham House.

Lowi, Theodore, and Benjamin Ginsberg. 1995. *American Government*, 4th ed. New York: W. W. Norton.

Malchow, Hal. 1985. Lecture. Washington, D.C., March.

Neustadt, Richard. 1960. *Presidential Power*. New York: Wiley.

Riker, William. 1965. *Democracy in the United States*. New York: Macmillan.

PART ONE

HOW AMERICAN ELECTIONS WORK

We begin with eleven articles that lay the groundwork for our study, articles that examine in detail the key elements of, and influences upon, American elections as we approach the millennium. The first three report on candidates' political communication: the platforms of presidential *candidates* (as opposed to the more familiar *party* platforms), a case study of candidate communication (the rhetoric of George Bush in the 1988 campaign and its effect on his presidency), and the sources of political ambiguity (sources other than the mendaciousness of candidates).

Earlier in our history, the significant linkages between voters and officials were provided by political parties (and elections), but today's mass society more often employs television, advertising, and polling for those connections. Their role in elections is explored in the next three articles.

Modern technology is extraordinarily expensive, raising campaign finance to a level of prominence and concern not before seen. We offer three articles on this crucial topic, one studying public financing in New York City, a second tracing the connections between campaign financing and public policy in New York state government, and the last reporting on the tortured life (and eventual death) of the McCain-Feingold campaign finance reform bill in Congress the last few years.

We conclude our "primer on election practices" with two papers on the role of the modern political party. One describes the politically relevant values of today's political party activists; the other, the role of the Democratic and Republican national committees in elections.

Taken together, these eleven articles will provide readers the understanding needed for the subsequent sections that detail the impact of elections in specific policy areas and suggest changes in the way we conduct and think about elections.

A. CANDIDATES' POLITICAL COMMUNICATION

1

Political Accountability in a Post-Party Era: An Examination of Candidate and Specialized Platforms in 1992 and 1994

Joseph Cammarano

INTRODUCTION

A major concern of political scientists is the ever increasing atomization of American politics. The combined effects of our Constitution—which eschews direct democracy in favor of an indirect, representative form—and the rise of individualistic political campaigning, raise serious concerns about the ability of our political system to successfully ensure that citizens exert effective control over their government. Separated national institutions sharing political authority (a phenomenon mimicked by most state governments as well) makes democracy difficult except in the most unusual of times.

Despite this, the United States has been able to survive by using the nearly two-hundred-year-old solution to political fragmentation: the political party. Since 1800 or so, parties have been used to provide the linkage between the individual votes of citizens and democratic accountability that is made problematic by our constitutional system. Such a linkage occurred both inside and outside of government. For citizens, parties provided coherent agendas, information on political matters, candidates for office, and clear choices for government policy. In government, parties provided a segue for leadership coordinating the actions of members from disparate regions and interests, and bridging the constitutional gap between the executive and legislative branches. By ordering elections and providing control for governmental actions, parties, for all their historical faults, assured a level of accountability otherwise unattainable.

In the past fifty years, however, the ability of political parties to achieve democratic accountability has diminished, and the focus has shifted significantly away from parties to interest groups and toward our increasingly individualistic candidate-centered campaign system. Such disaggregation from party to individual has coincided with many troubling trends in American politics, such as diminished voter turnout, declining trust in government, increased costs of political campaigning, the increasingly common condition of divided control of government, and an increased personalization of politics.

Most observers of American politics believe that the best solution to the individualistic politics of recent generations is a return to strong political parties. Indeed, some argue that parties have never been quite so weak as has been pronounced (see Maisel 1991; Herrnson 1988). By adapting and responding to the fiscal realities of contemporary campaigns, parties continue to provide substantial assistance to candidates even if they do not have complete control over who carries their party banner. Once elections are over, parties exert an impressive amount of influence over their members in legislative institutions. Still, most discussion in political science has been over whether parties are currently strong or how we can make them stronger. Implicit in both arguments is that parties are the best way to provide for accountability by government to citizens.

This article takes issue with such an assumption. Putting aside the propriety of strong political parties, the purpose here is to assess the possibilities for political accountability within the current system of individualistic politics. Contrary to the view that our system becomes less accountable as we move further toward fragmentation, some recent elections have provided a glimpse at how elections can be and are linked consistently to government action without a party-centered electoral system. The national elections of 1992 and 1994 provide evidence that our politics can indeed tolerate campaigns controlled by individuals while also providing direction for government action.

The remainder of this article will examine how political campaigns have adapted to the contemporary electoral dynamics without abandoning political accountability. A detailed examination of candidate-centered platforms in 1992 and 1994 will illustrate how political candidates, as part of deliberate campaign strategies, have provided voters with detailed, specific promises for government action, promises that became the center of governing agendas in 1993 and 1995.

POLITICAL CAMPAIGNING IN A POST-PARTY ERA

The United States has been moving toward a post-party political system since the 1950s, when candidates at the presidential level began to make or break their own political fortunes. By the 1970s, presidential politics was almost completely candidate-centered, followed quickly by gubernatorial, congressional, and, to some degree, state legislative campaigns. Such a movement has been well presented by others (see Wattenberg 1990) and is not the central concern of this article. Still, the evolution of this system is significant because of the change in the locus of control over elections that has resulted from the shift from party- to candidate-centered campaigns. Although current campaigns are a complex mixture of political forces, candidates ultimately control the themes, strategies, and tenor of their own campaigns. Of course parties can provide an umbrella for candidates, significant financial support and expertise, and a base of supporters for campaigns, but candidates themselves have to win elections. This means that they must find ways to reach and activate a sufficient number of people to win a plurality of votes. Increasingly, then, candidates must make clear their stands on important public issues, and they must do so in a precise enough manner to convince voters that they are the better candidate.

This movement toward using specific policy pronouncements can best be seen on the presidential and gubernatorial levels, where the connections between electoral victory and government policy are most obvious. However, we have also seen a similar movement in legislative politics, although in a slightly different form. In both arenas we have seen an attempt by candidates to develop and utilize specific platforms for their own purposes. Such platforms are as specific as party platforms, but they relate only to the individual context in which they occur. On the presidential level, they are called *candidate platforms*, as they relate to the actions of an individual candidate, while the congressional level has seen the rise of *specialized platforms*. Such platforms, introduced in 1992 and 1994, have served to increase the burden on public officials, as they have had to work harder to fulfill the specific promises made during the campaigns.

The use of candidate platforms, or, in the case of 1994, a "contract" with voters, must be seen as more than simply a campaign tool aimed at garnering votes. In fact, there is little evidence that the documents presented below had any direct impact on voting behavior in elections. Instead, such documents are best understood as ways for political candidates to distinguish themselves from their opposition, and for them to advertise themselves as having coherent agendas for governmental action. Once in office, they provide a guide for elected officials in organizing the governmental agenda. In addition to providing coherence for public officials, they provide guidance for evaluating the effectiveness of public officials' tenure in office, in much the way that party platforms served as a mechanism for accountability in the era of party-centered politics.

CANDIDATE PLATFORMS IN THE 1992 CAMPAIGN

The 1992 presidential campaign was notable for its several unique features. In the general election, there were three well-funded candidates rather than the standard two. Also, the candidates in primaries and the general election made extensive use of so-called *new media,* such as radio and television talk shows. Two candidates made use of a toll-free telephone number to solicit donations and volunteers. Electronic mail and fax machines became a central feature of campaigns rather than an afterthought. These and other innovations permitted candidates to engage in a form of political communication called *narrowcasting,* that is, unique appeals to specific segments of voters as opposed to sending broadcast messages to larger groups of supporters.

Although not the first to exploit the various innovations in 1992, the Clinton campaign embraced most of them, because the use of such technologies and tactics fit well with the desire of the Clinton campaign to focus on voters without clear political affiliations, voters who could and would be persuaded by a moderate message from a centrist Democrat (Arterton 1993). The tactics also fit well with the campaign of Ross Perot, the first independent presidential candidate in the candidate-centered era to have the enormous bank account needed to engage in contemporary political communication.

The combination of available technology and strategic imperatives significantly changed the way campaigns conducted business in 1992. This new environment led Perot, Clinton, and, later, George Bush, to make use of candidate platforms. These platforms took the form of trade books in the instance of Perot and Clinton, and a free forty-page booklet by Bush, all of which contained detailed discussions of issues, including many specific policy promises by the candidates. Although such policy pronouncements are not new—position papers by campaigns have been around presidential campaigns for decades—the form and meaning of these documents made them more important to both the campaigns and, after victory, to the Clinton administration.

I refer to these documents as *candidate platforms* to imply that they signify the continuance of candidate-dominated presidential campaigns and the decline of political parties as the grounding elements of campaigns. In 1992, candidate platforms eclipsed the party platforms, which were relegated to general expressions of the core beliefs of party activists. In the past, party platforms have been important for the agendas of winning candidates (Pomper and Lederman 1980; Fishel 1985), but in 1992, the introduction of Clinton's platform displaced this role for the Democratic party platform.

Presidential candidates have long produced books for public consumption. Every aspiring president produces at least one autobiography or memoir. Among the many produced are Nixon's *Challenges We Face,* Barry Goldwater's *Conscience of a Conservative* and *Either/Or, A Self-Portrait Based Upon His Own Words,* and Jimmy Carter's *Why Not the Best?* These and other books by presidential hopefuls were used as springboards to candidacies, and thus they fit well within our presidential system, where rank-and-file voters control the nomination of party candidates. Still, these books differ from candidate platforms in that they serve to introduce the individual to voters and not to delineate explicit pronouncements of positions on public policy. In other words, traditional books published by presidential candidates served an important public relations function for the individuals, whereas candidate platforms emerged in 1992 as campaign documents.

The 1992 candidate platforms merit study for several reasons. First, they are an indicator of the increasing separation of candidate from party. Second, they offer a very clear indication of presidential agendas in much the same way that party platforms have done. Third, they help to portray the images of candidates that campaigns wish to express to voters. Fourth, they reveal the different personalities involved; a detailed study of the platforms tells us much about the candidates themselves, not just their specific policy positions. Finally, the 1992 candidate platforms are important because they were part of a return to issue-based political campaigning, a generally welcome change from the 1988 presidential campaign.

The use of candidate platforms in 1992 was started by Paul Tsongas, a candidate in the Democratic primaries. The earliest and perhaps least well-known entry into the Democratic nomination contest, Tsongas based his campaign on his claim that he was a unique candidate, one with real, detailed solutions to many of the current problems in the United States. To advertise both the claim and the details of these solutions, he published *A Call to Economic Arms: Forging a New American Mandate* long before the official campaign began. When Tsongas, a former U.S. senator from Massachusetts, won the primary in neighboring New Hampshire, his issue-focused appeal was given legitimacy, and the other candidates for the Democratic nomination followed Tsongas's lead. In the midst of the New Hampshire primary campaign, the Clinton campaign responded to Tsongas with a pamphlet of their own entitled *Putting People First*, an outline of the detailed version published later in book form.

This concern with issues in the 1992 Democratic primaries was intensified by the candidacy of Ross Perot, and a candidate platform was the ideal medium for an independent candidate like Perot. *United We Stand: How We Can Take Back Our Country* enabled Perot to present himself as being driven not by personal motives but by a concern with steering the nation in a direction consistent with "fixing" our political and social ills. In the midst of the general election campaign, the book spent several weeks at the top of the *New York Times* best-seller list and served as the focal point for United We Stand, his campaign organization. This connection was an important part of the effort to get Perot's name on the ballot in every state (Bernstein 1992; Sweeney 1992; Holmes 1992). Published after Perot dropped out of the race in July, the book helped the movement Perot started to survive his departure, and it provided a rationale for Perot to reenter the race in early October.

The Clinton campaign was the third presidential campaign to develop a candidate platform. The early response to Tsongas's platform provided the basis for the full-blown platform, *Putting People First: How We Can All Change America*, released by the campaign in late September. As the title indicates, the book was intended to highlight two of the major themes of the Clinton/Gore campaign: that they would change government and that they were concerned with people who, in the words of candidate Clinton, "work hard and play by the rules." The publication of the book received little attention from the press but was noticed by the Bush campaign, which quickly filed a complaint with the Federal Elections Commission asserting that Clinton's use of a commercial publisher, Times Books, was an attempt to circumvent campaign laws (Bernstein 1992). The sales of the book increased with the fortunes of the Clinton/Gore campaign, remaining on the *New York Times* best-seller list through October 1992. With more than two-hundred thousand copies sold before the November election, *Putting People First* bolstered the Clinton campaign's contention that they, not the Bush campaign, had a detailed plan for the next presidential administration.

President Bush's reelection campaign responded to the challenge, but only after the commercial success of the Perot and Clinton books. Bush's *Agenda for American Renewal* was produced, distributed and paid for by the Bush campaign in early October. Unlike the Clinton and Perot books (which were book length, if only through repetition of the same arguments and promises), the Bush platform was closer in appearance and length to Tsongas's pamphlet, the result of Bush's late entry into the candidate platform market. Since the book was self-produced, the Bush campaign bore all costs of production and distribution. This put Bush at a disadvantage: interested voters had to first know about the book, and then call a toll-free phone number and request a copy from the Bush campaign. Of course, Bush had less need for a candidate platform since he had four years as president to produce a public record of his agenda and performance in office.

ANALYSIS OF THE 1992 CANDIDATE PLATFORMS

The argument here is that candidate platforms provide an alternative to parties for making government accountable to citizens. To this end a content analysis was conducted on each of the three candidate platforms in the 1992 general election. A complete report of the content analysis is available elsewhere (Cammarano and Josefson 1995), but for the purpose of this article there are some important findings that point to the promise of candidate platforms for augmenting accountability. Each paragraph of the candidate platforms was coded for the presence and type of pledge. The coding scheme used is the same as that used by Gerald Pomper in his landmark study of party platforms (Pomper and Lederman 1980). Pledges, when made, fall into one of six categories: rhetorical, general pledges, pledges of continuity, expression of intentions to meet goals, pledges of action, and detailed pledges (for a detailed description of each category, see Pomper and Lederman 1980: 236–37). The two major party platforms were also analyzed, using the same coding scheme. Table 1.1 presents the results.

Table 1.1
Type of Pledge Made by Presidential Candidates and Political Parties

	Republican		Democratic		Independent
	Agenda for American Renewal	Republican Party Platform	Putting People First	Democratic Party Platform	United We Stand
Type of Pledge					
No Promise	43%	27%	11%	20%	59%
Rhetorical	2	9	6	12	2
General	6	10	11	24	2
Continuity	5	19	2	0	1
Goal	23	18	26	30	16
Action	9	9	22	12	6
Detailed	13	8	23	2	9
(N)	(218)	(91)	(827)	(451)	(446)

The degree to which these platforms provided guidance for voters is impressive. As reported in Table 1.1, the Clinton platform was saturated with pledges (many of them repeated several times), many quite specific. Clinton was far more specific in what he would do than was his party. This is consistent with the reputation that Clinton had for being a "policy wonk," and with the need of the party to make a more generalized appeal that would satisfy the various parts of its coalition. Despite the differences in specificity, the Clinton and Democratic platforms were complementary in content, reflecting the degree of control the Clinton campaign had over the construction of the party platform.

The Bush platform was far less detailed than the Clinton platform in making pledges but was as specific as the Republican party platform. In many ways it is a reflection of the context Bush found himself in during the 1992 campaign. By the time Bush produced his platform, the fallout from the 1992 Republican National Convention had been felt. The Bush campaign saw a need to distinguish their candidate's record and agenda from that of his party, which then was seen as hurting Bush's chances for victory (Baker 1993). The Bush campaign had allowed party activists to control the content of the Republican platform, and this prompted his advisers to exercise a second chance to communicate more specifically through Bush's candidate platform.

For all his protestations about substance, the Perot platform is the least specific in terms of promises. This is consistent with Perot's campaign in general, a campaign that raised questions and presumed to have answers, just not at that moment. *United We Stand* was, as would be expected, far more critical of government than the other platforms, but it actually offered fewer promises than any other 1992 platform.

Overall, the introduction of candidate platforms appears to have increased the potential for accountability through elections. Once victorious, President Clinton had a clear agenda upon which he would be judged by other members of the Washington political establishment and by voters. The success of the Clinton campaign in making their policy stands clear became a model for several subsequent political battles. The Clinton administration continued to publish their ideas in book form, including a summary of Clinton's proposal for health care reform and of the Vice-President's Commission on Reinventing Government. This direct marketing of policy ideas was copied by John Chretien in his party's victorious campaign in the 1993 Canadian elections, by many candidates for the United States Senate in 1994, and by the British Labour Party in 1997. But perhaps the most famous of the platforms in this genre comes from the House Republican leadership in 1994.

THE CONTRACT WITH AMERICA

The 1994 elections provided an opportunity for House Republicans to put their own twist on candidate platforms. That year, the chance to offer a clear plan was enticing for several reasons. First, the clarity with which the Clinton campaign spelled out the candidate's agenda gave the House Republicans the chance to offer stark comparisons between themselves and the Democrats (through Clinton). Second, there were several reasons to believe that President Clinton's performance made the Democrats in Congress vulnerable. Clinton's popularity had plummeted faster than traditional models of presidential approval predicted (Brace and Hinckley 1992), and although his success rate with Congress was fairly high, there were some very visible and highly significant failures. Third, there was increasing voter hostility toward the national government. By 1994, public approval of Congress was at an all-time low and there was growing skepticism about the ability of government to address the concerns of most Americans. This was not new in 1994, as Clinton and Perot both exploited voter skepticism in 1992, but in 1994 the focus of public frustration was on those who controlled the government: the Democrats. Finally, the drive and energy of several Republican leaders in the House, most notably Newt Gingrich, made the development of a coherent set of campaign promises by most Republican House candidates possible.

Much of the 103rd Congress was focused on the agenda enunciated by Bill Clinton in the 1992 presidential campaign. Democrats in Congress welcomed an ally in the White House, and they quickly worked to implement those portions of *Putting People First* and the Democratic platform that had broad support within the party. The Family and Medical Leave Act, the Motor-Voter

Law, national service, and other highly visible pieces of legislation were quickly enacted into law. Within the first two months, the Clinton administration issued a press release outlining all the campaign promises that had already been fulfilled. Still, there were early signs of trouble for the Clinton agenda. A bruising fight over the North American Free Trade Agreement (NAFTA), outcry over the proposal to change the policy regarding homosexuals in the military, the inability to pass an economic stimulus package, and a razor-thin victory on the 1994 budget all suggested that Clinton might not be able to achieve the more difficult promises he made in 1992.

Adding to Clinton's troubles was the emergence of a solidly unified Republican party in Congress. Although NAFTA passed with bipartisan support, most issues in the 103rd Congress fell along partisan lines. Of the major Clinton initiatives in 1993, only NAFTA garnered more than a few Republican votes in either chamber of Congress. This partisan division served to increase the already partisan environment on Capitol Hill, and it increased the amount of conflict that ensued in legislative politics. As the session progressed, House Republicans frequently argued that President Clinton was not keeping the promises that candidate Clinton had made. Although, as Gerald Pomper has reported, Clinton was able to keep or try to keep about two-thirds of the specific promises he made, every time one was not kept, his book provided evidence for his critics that he was not following through on his promises.

Several times during the 103rd Congress, House Republicans attacked the Clinton agenda by using *Putting People First*. The presence of the 1992 document assisted Newt Gingrich and his allies in their attempt to provide a contrasting view to Clinton's (Gimpel 1996). In the major legislative battles of 1993, Republican House members frequently referred to the Clinton promises. During the budget battle of 1993, Rep. Gerald Solomon, GOP floor leader, cited chapter and verse from his own dog-eared copy of *Putting People First* to provide evidence that the Clinton administration was not keeping its word to the American people. In other words, Clinton, by producing his platform in 1992, indirectly assisted the Republicans in two ways: first, by giving them a highly publicized document they could use as evidence of his failure; and second, by giving them an innovative idea that they could use for their own electoral fortunes.

The Contract with America emanated from the opportunities presented by the political environment in 1994. House Republicans met early in 1994 to develop a victory plan for November. Although some argued that the best strategy would be an anti-Clinton and antigovernment one, Republican leaders, particularly Newt Gingrich, saw the creation of a clear policy agenda as an opportunity to present a comprehensive alternative to sixty years of national and Democratic dominance of government. In Gingrich's assessment, 1994 was a major showdown between the two dominant views of government. As early as February 1994, Gingrich proposed a national platform on which House Republicans would run in the midterm elections. Long a proponent of symbolic politics, Gingrich even planned to have an event to express the unity and clarity of the Republican alternative before the actual set of proposals was compiled (Gimpel 1996).

The Contract was the result of extensive research done by House Republican leaders, studying the views of both incumbent members and Republican challengers. Both groups were polled to find areas where there was sufficient unity among Republicans. The ideas that had the broad support of candidates and incumbents were included in the Contract, while any issues that divided them were left out. The end result was ten policy proposals specifically intended to appeal to all Republicans and many independent and Democratic voters who were upset with the current state of affairs in Washington. The focus of the Contract with America was primarily on regulatory relief, fiscal reform, and the scaling back of some of the laws enacted in the 103rd Congress (ironically, the same laws that were promised in the Clinton platform in 1992).

Unlike the Clinton and Perot platforms in 1992, the Contract with America was more than an individual agenda of one candidate. Instead, it reflected the policy agenda not of the Republican party, but of Republican candidates for House seats. The Contract did not relate to senatorial candidates or to Republican candidates for state and local elections. In this sense, it can be seen as a middling document, somewhere between a party platform and a candidate platform. But the key to understanding the Contract is in its primary purposes and effect. The document was first and foremost a tool for the 1994 campaign, one that provided a basis for Republicans running against the record of the Democrats. Second, it made explicit promises, but only within the relevant institutional setting: the House of Representatives. Those promises related only to a vote in the House on each contract item in the first 100 days of the 104th Congress. There were no explicit promises beyond the taking of these votes, and, although voters and reporters might have assumed that the goal was to enact the promises into law, there was nothing in the actual document that promised as much. Given this, the Contract was an attempt to offer a specific alternative to the Clinton and Democratic party agenda, and was the opening salvo in what was to become a long and divisive debate over the basic role of the national government.

Despite being less comprehensive and less ambitious than party platforms, the Contract with America is part of a continuing trend that emerged in 1992. In the era of candidate-centered campaigns, questions of substance and direction of government are being addressed through explicit promises made to voters by candidates. The promises made by Republican candidates were certainly specific. Each of the ten items was outlined in enough detail to be easily translated into legislation. Also, by making a collective commitment to the platform, but keeping the scope of that commitment narrowed to one subunit of government, the Contract assured an accountability to voters that was as direct as the Clinton platform in 1992.

As with *Putting People First*, there is little direct empirical evidence that the Contract with America reached and influenced many voters in 1994. But the codifying of promises had important meaning to those running for office. Republican candidates in nearly every congressional district used both the premise of the Contract (that, unlike Clinton and the Democrats, House Republicans were committed to a clear, explicit agenda, one that could be achieved) and the details of the ten items in the Contract as important elements of their campaigns. In an election where there was enormous negative sentiment among voters, it provided a focal point for Republican candidates, one that allowed them to contrast that focus with the inability of the Democrats in Washington to agree on issues. It also helped to nationalize congressional elections in 1994, which furthered the cause of making 1994 a referendum on unified Democratic control of the government.

Following the 1994 elections, the Contract with America became the center of attention in the 104th Congress. As promised, the Republican leadership scheduled and held votes on each of the ten items in the Contract. The exact promise made was simply to vote on each item, and in so doing, Republicans could boast that they had kept the promises they made to the American people. Although less than half of the Contract was actually passed and only a small portion of it became law, the fact that votes were taken on all items within the first 100 days of the 104th Congress provided evidence that incumbent Republicans could use in their 1996 reelection campaigns. Therefore, like Clinton's platform, the Contract with America provided a direct link between the substance of campaigns and the actions of government, one that displaces to some degree the promises made in party platforms.

THE CONSEQUENCES OF INDIVIDUALIZED PLATFORMS

Political scientists have written extensively about the need for strong political parties, and most agree that without strong parties our system of government cannot be maintained. Advocates of strong parties have been heartened by the reappearance of strong party organizations and party line voting in Congress. Still, the ability of political parties to rally the electorate is elusive, and there is little indication that voters are becoming more partisan; most evidence points to the opposite. Given the continued decline of importance of partisanship for voters, there is considerable concern that elections cannot serve as mandates for government action, since voters are not voting for parties but for individual candidates. In this context, the emergence of individualized campaign platforms seems to be both an important and welcome innovation, part of a continuing evolution of the relationship between politicians, government, and citizens.

Specialized campaign platforms are useful in the current political climate for several reasons. First, and most important, they provide information to voters in a manner that conforms to the realities of modern campaign politics. Candidates can send out and voters can receive relatively detailed information on issue stands, information that is tailored to the specific context of the race at hand. Such appeals remove the diffusing effects of two political filters: political parties and the mass media. Therefore voters can get a clear idea of what happens if a particular person gets elected. Second, specific issue appeals can assist candidates in challenging the stereotypes that voters have about them based upon party affiliation. When information challenges or bypasses the conventional wisdom about a Republican or Democrat, voters tend to seek out more information about the candidates. Such a search is likely to better inform voters about those running for public office.

Perhaps the most important reason why specialized platforms are a welcome addition to campaigns, however, relates to the question of political accountability. In the past, party platforms have proved to be good indicators of presidential agendas. Presidents and parties try to make good on the promises they make to voters (Pomper and Lederman 1980; Fishel 1985). This is also true of *Putting People First*, two-thirds of which was either implemented or attempted. With the nationalizing of the 1994 elections, the Contract with America became the bellwether for the 104th Congress. In a fragmented political system with divided control of government, such specific promises allow for an accountability that is difficult under the use of party platforms. If a party agenda is not implemented under a system of divided government, there is a ready excuse. If, however, the Clinton administration or the Republicans in Congress fail to follow through on their promises, then voters can hold them accountable for their failure. In this sense, specialized platforms are a benefit to democratic accountability.

Of course, there are problems with this adjustment, the most significant being the disparity between making explicit promises and the ability to fulfill them. Presidents, constitutional outsiders in the development of public policy, are bound to fail, and failure to fulfill promises inevitably leads to diminished reputation, popularity, and power (Lowi 1985; Brace and Hinckley 1992). On the congressional side, the inherent nature of congressional politics includes the bargaining process, and the bargaining away of promises made in campaigns can have dire consequences come election time. Also, the inability to control the entire legislative process means that any explicit promises made by individuals or the majority party within a chamber of Congress are bound to provide campaign bytes for political opponents. This means that politicians will be more vulnerable to political attack as they compromise away various promises or change their minds about the propriety of pledges made in campaigns.

Still, the problem for politicians is not a problem for democratic accountability. If the pressure is increased on politicians to do what they promise, the linkage between elections and governing can only be strengthened. If politicians make irresponsible, thoughtless, or superficial promises in elections, they will be punished accordingly. If voters make choices based upon explicit pledges made by candidates, then they can expect to receive what the candidates promised. The desirability of such a mechanism of accountability is obvious. Since they help to strengthen the link between campaigns, elections, and government actions, specialized political platforms are a desirable and welcome addition to political campaigns.

REFERENCES

Arterton, Christopher. 1993. "Campaign '92: Strategies and Tactics." In Gerald Pomper, ed., *The Elections of 1992: Reports and Interpretations.* Chatham, NJ: Chatham House.

Baker, Ross K. 1993. "Sorting Out and Suiting Up: The Presidential Primaries." In Gerald Pomper, ed., *The Elections of 1992: Reports and Interpretations.* Chatham, NJ: Chatham House.

Bernstein, Amy. 1992. "Making Book." *U.S. News and World Report* (October 16): 12.

Brace, Paul, and Barbara Hinckley. 1992. *Follow the Leader.* New York: Basic Books.

Cammarano, Joseph, and Jim Josefson. 1995. "Putting It in Writing: An Examination of Presidential Campaign Platforms in the 1992 Election." *Southeastern Political Review* 15 (June): 187–204.

Fishel, Jeff. 1985. *Presidents and Promises.* Washington, DC: Congressional Quarterly Press.

Gimpel, James. 1996. *Legislating the Revolution: The Contract With America in its First 100 Days.* Boston: Allyn and Bacon.

Herrnson, Paul. 1988. *Party Campaigning in the 80s.* Cambridge: Harvard University Press.

Holmes, Stephen. 1992. "No New Plans? Read My Book, Perot Says." *New York Times,* August 22: A8.

Lowi, Theodore. 1985. *The Personal President: Power Invested, Promised, Unfulfilled.* Ithaca, NY: Cornell University Press.

Maisel, L. Sandy, ed. 1991. *The Parties Respond.* Boulder, CO: Westview Press.

Pomper, Gerald, with Susan Lederman. 1980. *Elections in America: Control and Influence in American Politics,* 2nd ed. New York: Longman.

Sweeney, Louise. 1992. "Perot's Troops Are Still on the Move." *Christian Science Monitor* (January 18): 8.

Wattenberg, Martin. 1990. *The Rise of Candidate-Centered Politics.* Cambridge: Harvard University Press.

2

Presidential Campaign Rhetoric in 1988: Its Significance for George Bush's Presidency

Jean-Philippe Faletta

INTRODUCTION

On November 3, 1992, George Bush, the forty-first president of the United States, failed in his quest for a second term. In any other presidential election year the political pundits would have noted that this was just another example of an incumbent incurring the wrath of the electorate. However, in 1992 Bush's loss was somewhat surprising and unique. In February 1991, the president's polling numbers reached a historic high of 91 percent. As a result, most political observers agreed that George Bush would easily win reelection. Even many Democrats saw this as a foregone conclusion, as first-tier politicians such as Richard Gephardt and Mario Cuomo decided not to seek the Democratic presidential nomination.

That the commander in chief who led the nation through the Persian Gulf crisis would lose twenty-one months later to a relatively unknown governor of a small southern state is astounding in terms of the historic precedent it set. One of the only other similar occurrences with which it can be compared is Winston Churchill's eviction from office following World War II. How did this happen? What factors could have accounted for this fall from grace in the eyes of the American electorate?

Many factors could be pointed to as major reasons for Bush's inability to win reelection, such as the perceived state of the economy; his "read my lips, no new taxes" pledge; or the contention that George Bush really did have a vision but he was merely ineffective at articulating it to the American people, unlike his predecessor Ronald Reagan. The one strand that can be argued as connecting all of these disparate elements is campaign rhetoric. This article examines the 1988 Bush campaign, the subsequent Bush administration, and the unsuccessful 1992 effort from this perspective.

THE BUSH/DUKAKIS PRESIDENTIAL CAMPAIGN

In 1988, George Bush's campaign had been very effective at erasing the extensive lead which Michael Dukakis had built up following the Democratic National Convention in July. They accomplished this for the most part by casting Dukakis as the classic example of a Massachusetts liberal. By the 1980s, "liberal" had taken on several connotations, including association with "big government, high taxes, a leftist position in foreign affairs, and social engineering" (Drew 1989: 264).

Bush's handlers believed that they had found a formula for negative campaigning that was acceptable. While much of the campaign message consisted of negative ads and personal attacks, Bush sprinkled his speeches with a positive spin throughout the election cycle. Therefore, Bush was not only able to cast himself as the candidate who would be "the environmental president," "the education president," etc., but could also deflect criticism for the negative manner in which he was conducting his election bid.

No one in the Dukakis camp could foresee that seemingly irrelevant issues in a presidential campaign, such as the Pledge of Allegiance and a prison furlough program, would have the effect they did. Bush's campaign would decide on a theme of the week, stay with it, and then "measure the impact of each point every night, to see if it was working or needed reinforcement" (Drew 1989: 267).

Bush's most powerful themes were based on Dukakis's alleged liberalism, identified as such "by nearly half of Bush supporters." When specific themes were measured, issues such as "the Pledge of Allegiance and the prison furlough program in Massachusetts were cited by almost 40 percent of these supporters." Though the Bush team emphasized negative campaigning, Bush was also more successful with respect to specific policy issues than Dukakis, especially in terms of "national defense, abortion, crime, foreign trade, and taxes" (Quirk 1989: 83).

The origin of the campaign strategy adopted by Bush's handlers could be traced to a focus group conducted by Roger Ailes, Lee Atwater, and Bob Teeter in Paramus, New Jersey, on May 19, 1988. Analysis of the focus group found that Michael Dukakis was extremely vulnerable in specific areas such as: "the Pledge of Allegiance, his membership in the American Civil Liberties Union (ACLU), and a Massachusetts prison furlough program" (Blumenthal 1991: 259–60).

"Wedge issues" such as race had become the weapon of choice of political consultants such as Lee Atwater. Through its use, they could splinter an already creaking Democratic coalition, while appealing to a mass cross section of the electorate. Bush's extremely high negative ratings as compared with Dukakis in May 1988 drove the strategy. At the time of the focus group, those ratings were at "41 [Bush] and 15 percent [Dukakis]" (Goldman et al. 1989: 418). Bush's handlers convinced him that a negative campaign would be necessary in order to reverse the situation.

As mentioned, many of the issues raised by the Bush campaign seemed trivial. Bush attacked Dukakis for his veto of a Massachusetts law which would have required school children to recite the Pledge of Allegiance as proof of which of the two candidates was 100 percent American. Dukakis was cast as being strange, different, and out of the mainstream (Blumenthal 1991: 263).

As if he were a card-carrying member of the Communist party, Dukakis was attacked for being a card-carrying member of the American Civil Liberties Union (ACLU). Dukakis said that his membership was proof of his belief in the Bill of Rights, while the Bush people charged that it was equal to "taking the Fifth Amendment" (Goldman et al. 1989: 185). In addition, the furloughing of a felon, Willie Horton, by a Massachusetts prison board was used as solid evidence of "Dukakis's weakness, incompetence, lack of compassion for victims of crime, and as a symbol of ideological extremism" (418).

Bob Teeter had discovered that certain feelings were invoked by the Willie Horton issue. Perception of being soft on criminals was on the same level as being soft on communism (Goldman et al. 1989: 418). Public safety was seen in the same context as national security. In order to reinforce this connection, Clifford and Angela Barnes, two of Horton's victims, were put on a four-state tour to "speak about their experience and criticize Dukakis for never apologizing to them" (Drew 1989: 305).

On August 25, in a speech in Texas, Bush summed up his attacks on Dukakis in the now infamous "L-word" (Blumenthal 1991: 266), or liberalism, speech. All of his other themes were also found in that speech. "I can't help feel that his fervent opposition to the Pledge is symbolic of an entire attitude best summed up in four little letters: ACLU," Bush said (Germond and Witcover 1989: 402). Throughout this period, George Bush insisted that "it wasn't negative campaigning to try and help the American people understand the differences between the candidates" (Blumenthal 1991: 292).

Bush for the first time gained a lead on Dukakis that he would never relinquish. In an Associated Press poll conducted on September 6, Bush led Dukakis 45 to 32 percent (Associated Press poll, September 6, 1988), in contrast to Dukakis's 15 to 20 point lead over Bush following the Democratic National Convention in Atlanta in July (Patterson 1989: 107). Every day from the beginning of September there came a new charge. Various state Republican parties, independent expenditure committees, and pro-Bush political action committees (PACs) spent large amounts of money on television ads, pamphlets, and brochures.

Dukakis's impersonal monotone voice along with his technical answer to Bernard Shaw's question in the second presidential debate as to whether or not he would favor the death penalty if Kitty Dukakis were raped and murdered solidified the image of him projected by George Bush as weak and unfeeling. The vice president was now free to do and say almost anything that he wanted; almost nothing stood between him and the presidency. On Election Day, November 8, George Bush won the presidency, 54 to 46 percent, with 426 votes in the Electoral College to 112.

The negative advertising of the 1988 presidential campaign was powerful and controversial because "it played on the fears and prejudices of the American people, stretched the truth, and created false impressions" (Jamieson 1988: C1–2). The negative ads seemed to have an effect. Unfavorable perceptions of Dukakis increased, while those of Bush remained constant.

If one examines these perceptions over the course of the campaign in terms of favorable/unfavorable ratings, the shift in opinion is evident. Prior to the Democratic National Convention, Dukakis had "a 57 percent favorable rating as compared with 52 percent for Bush." This increased "to 61 percent for Dukakis following the convention. However, he dropped to 48 percent following the Republican National Convention, and was down to 40 percent by November 1" (Goldman et al. 1989: 420–22). Meanwhile, Bush hovered around the mid-50s during the same period.

Though it is undeniable that George Bush's victory in 1988 was due significantly to the favorable retrospective evaluation of the Reagan administration of which Bush was a part, examination of polling data reveals a correlation between the dates that the Bush campaign began its negative campaign tactics and Dukakis's decline in the polls. For example, a CBS News/*New York Times* poll conducted on October 31 found that "over 32 percent of respondents had made up their mind in terms of voting earlier in the fall, while 29 percent stated that their decision had been made in late summer" (CBS News/*New York Times* poll, October 31, 1988).

Bush's strategy allowed him to leave a deep early impression of Michael Dukakis in the mind of the electorate. This, together with an almost total lack of discussion of public policy differences between the Democratic and Republican nominees left Dukakis with an uphill battle in his attempts to change his image and to focus attention on potential shortcomings in George Bush.

The 1988 presidential campaign shows that the distorted presentation of candidate positions, reliance on emotional and misleading appeals, and lack of serious policy debate made it virtually impossible for voters to make meaningful choices about major issues facing the country. Despite this, Bush contended in his first post-election news conference, "[T]he American people are wonderful in understanding when a campaign ends, and the work of business begins" (Blumenthal 1991: 319). However, George Bush's presidential campaign had not laid the groundwork for presidential policies.

THE ADMINISTRATION OF GEORGE BUSH

George Bush did have several options in governing. He could have extended the Reagan themes with the hope that the still significant fear of reform would influence the thinking in the polity; he could have modified the conservative argument by incorporating some public concerns; or he could have defined his administration through major shifts in public concerns and international relationships. He chose not to adopt any of the three.

As in any administration, presidential concerns can be divided into two distinct spheres, foreign and domestic. These two areas would prove to be somewhat of a paradox for George Bush. In the realm of foreign policy, the president would come across as being steadfast, committed, comfortable, and visionary—that is, calling for a "New World Order." However, in domestic affairs, Bush would be perceived by the American people as lacking the "vision thing," being out of touch with the realities of daily life in America, and even lacking in compassion.

As mentioned, Bush had in part been elected due to a retrospective thumbs up to the Reagan administration, especially in terms of its Cold War foreign policy, but also to the public perception that the economy was strong. However, by the end of Bush's first year in office, the Cold War themes that had dominated the American political scene for the entire post-1945 period lost their importance and guiding influence. George Bush himself called 1989 one of "the singular moments in history" that "divided all that goes before from all that comes after" (Bush 1990: 129–34). The end of the Cold War would have a profound impact on how the American public would view the relative importance of foreign affairs.

The crisis in the Persian Gulf (1990–91) momentarily shifted this perception and drove George Bush's approval rating up to a historic high of 91 percent. This would in the end have a damaging effect on the perception of his handling of domestic affairs. President Bush was able to successfully construct a multinational coalition under the United Nations flag. But shortly thereafter, the American polity would demand action on the economy, on which the president was seemingly not able to deliver. In many respects, he brought this on himself in asking that Americans use the same spirit and determination shown in Desert Storm to tackle domestic concerns.

Though the Bush administration had some notable domestic legislation, such as the Clean Air Act Amendments of 1990, the Americans with Disabilities Act of 1991, and the reenactment of the Civil Rights Act, his presidency will always be remembered for two domestic events: the Budget Act of 1990 and the recession. In the budget deal cut with congressional Democrats for the

1991 fiscal year, Bush rescinded his "read my lips, no new taxes" pledge of the 1988 campaign.

Many scholars argued that the budget deal was good policy and governance at the expense of a campaign promise. It is pointed out that the result was "the setting of tight limits on discretionary spending, which was not matched by congressional policy vis a vis entitlements" (Ippolito 1997) and the beginning of deficit reduction in 1990. Duane Windsor hypothesizes that even if it was good policy, it was not good timing or politics. A coherent policy on Bush's part would have taken one of two approaches: eliminate the deficit by raising taxes, or veto every tax increase and leave it in Congress's lap. Instead, "his policy was in between the two avenues" (Windsor 1997).

Despite the seeming differences between the two schools of thought, many believe that the economic recovery that followed was two parts Bush and only one part Clinton. However, the problem with these various analyses from the perspective of this article is that these factors had absolutely no bearing on Bush's ability to be reelected in 1992. The president in his public statements reiterated that Reagan's economic expansion had only been temporarily interrupted.

His response to this "temporary interruption" (Bush 1992: 74–79) was to propose tax-free savings accounts, penalty-free withdrawals from individual retirement accounts (IRAs) for first-time home buyers, and a reduced tax for long-term capital gains to increase jobs and growth. However, Bush was just not very good at communicating how these initiatives would help people who were experiencing economic dislocation. In the first two years of his administration, Bush talked of a "time of change" (Denton 1994: 137), yet to the American public, he seemed to offer no vision for the future. Where Bush seemed resolute in the area of foreign policy, he resonated a lack of self-confidence in the domestic arena.

The president's job approval rating which had climbed "from 52 percent in late 1990 to 91 percent" (Denton 1994: 138) following the Gulf War, declined rapidly as 1991 progressed. This disparity became even more apparent when domestic and foreign policy were tracked in separate polls. In October 1991, Bush received "a 63 percent approval rating in his handling of foreign policy, but only a 30 percent approval rating" (138) on domestic policy.

Many analysts agreed that the economy bottomed out in March 1991, and that it was then that the recovery began (Edwards 1997). Despite this, the economy emerged in late 1991 above all others as the main issue. Economic pain was a perceived daily reality since there "was a lag effect in terms of the economic recovery. Unemployment is always the last thing to recover" (Ostrander 1997). In addition, a Kettering Foundation study conducted in 1990 and 1991 found that Americans believed that "elected officials, lobbyists, PACs, and the media responded only to their own interests" (Goldman and Mathews 1992: 20–23).

In his 1992 State of the Union address, George Bush outlined what would become the foundation of his 1992 bid for reelection. He attempted to put national problems in an international frame, arguing that the world and nation were interconnected and interdependent. He also made "character" and "trust" central points by which one could evaluate his presidency.

However, to many Americans Bush still seemed unable to articulate a vision, a domestic agenda, or a coherent budget policy. In a *Hotline* poll at the end of January 1992, 46 percent of Americans responded that they had "not much of an idea where Bush planned to lead the country" (*Hotline* 1991–1992: 68). Just ten months before the general election, the American people could neither identify specific policies or a vision on Bush's part. The perceived failure to articulate a bold new direction for his administration opened the door for any challenger promising to act on the electorate's call for change.

THE 1992 PRESIDENTIAL CAMPAIGN

While the Bush campaign struggled to find a consistent, on-target message, in contrast the Democratic challenger, Bill Clinton, offered an optimistic vision and a reassurance that the American people could take back their government and their destinies. It seemed to the Bush campaign that a bold new domestic blueprint would not have been taken seriously by the American public, since less than a year before the White House had given the impression that no change in direction was necessary.

Their strategy therefore was to try to raise enough doubts about what Clinton would be like as president by running a campaign based on "character, trust and experience" (Denton 1994: 151). Bush's campaign staff emphasized not so much what direction he planned to take the country, as what would happen "if the Democrats were in control of both the executive and legislative branches of government" (Bush 1992: 1445–1634). This strategy had two facets: that the United States was a victim of a global slowdown, and that the lack of any substantive domestic policy could be attributed to Congress.

Bush stressed that a new Congress was what was needed. However, "it seemed unlikely that Congress would change drastically, and if it did, the voting public needed reassurance that President Bush could lead a new Congress" (Denton 1994: 154). The Bush campaign's strategy was analogous to a double-edged sword. Though he was able to formulate a line of attack on Clinton, that attack focused the public's attention on one of the clearest perceptions of Bush, that his global perspective prevented him from recognizing and attending to domestic issues, real or perceived.

Bush's handlers tried also to extend doubts about Clinton's private character to his public character. However, it seems that Bush failed to gauge the definitional shift in the public's mind of what constituted character. The character the public found relevant was "political character" (Goldman and Mathews

1992: 20–23). There seemed to have been a shift between 1988 when character had been defined as life experiences, a candidate's personal past a barometer for voters, and 1992 when the focus was on exactly what a candidate said he would do. Clinton "offered clear plans, while Bush did not" (Denton 1994: 158).

CONCLUSIONS

On November 3, 1992, more then 104 million voters went to the polls. When the polls closed, George Bush had lost his bid for reelection and Bill Clinton had won. Clinton had based his campaign on a promise of sharp policy change and seemed to win with a mandate for change. This was in sharp contrast to the campaign of candidate Bush in 1988. The Clinton/Gore campaign, with its promise of concrete legislative action, contrasted sharply with the Bush campaign, which was full of symbolism and based on a promise of continuity and a lack of substantive change.

It would seem that the Bush campaign in 1992 was convinced that it could use the same smoke and mirror tactics that were so successful in 1988. However, the president's seeming inability to establish a clear and concrete agenda led to "a nebulous presidential image" (Fairhurst and Wendt 1995: 101). Many see George Bush as a transactional leader and not an individual who was concerned with transformation.

As mentioned, Bush did have some major legislative accomplishments in his administration. However, with respect to the top three major events that came to dominate the American public's impression of George Bush—the Persian Gulf War, the 1990 budget deal, and the economic recession of 1990–91—he was perceived as a president who governed by reaction to whatever his staff and events put in front of him. Bush therefore seemed to fail in defining himself to the American electorate.

The 1988 campaign was built on the premise that a presidential candidate could win mainly through the use of symbols or images, as opposed to concrete policy proposals. However, once in the White House, George Bush was unable to articulate an agenda or vision effectively enough for the American electorate to know what he stood for. Instead, Bush felt that, as in 1988, he could rely on slick packaging to bypass the vision problem and win reelection in 1992. The ultimate lesson for future administrations may be the main theme in Richard Neustadt's *Presidential Power* (1990) that neither a president's prestige nor his decision making should be placed in the hands of or at the disposal of others.

REFERENCES

Associated Press Poll. 1988. (September 6).

Blumenthal, Sidney. 1991. *Pledging Allegiance: The Last Campaign of the Cold War*. New York: HarperCollins Publishing.

Bush, George. 1990. "Address before a Joint Session of the Congress on the State of the Union." In *Public Papers of the Presidents*, 1. Washington, DC: U.S. Government Printing Office.

Bush, George. 1992. "Address before a Joint Session of the Congress on the State of the Union." In *Public Papers of the Presidents*, 28. Washington, DC: U.S. Government Printing Office.

CBS News/*New York Times* Poll. 1988 (October 31).

DeFrank, Thomas M. 1992. "A Silver Bullet." *Newsweek* (November): 82–85.

Denton, Robert E. 1994. *The 1992 Presidential Campaign: A Communication Perspective*. Westport, CT: Praeger Publishing.

Drew, Elizabeth B. 1989. *Election Journal: Political Events of 1987–1988*. New York: William Morrow and Company, Inc.

Edwards III, George C. 1997. "Public Opinion Polls and the Bush Presidency." Paper presented at the Tenth Presidential Conference, George Bush, 41st president of the United States. Hofstra University, April 17–19.

Fairhurst, Gail T., and Ronald F. Wendt. 1995. "Looking for 'The Vision Thing': The Rhetoric of Leadership in the 1992 Presidential Election." In Kathleen E. Kendall, ed., *Presidential Campaign Discourse: Strategic Communication Problems*. Albany: State University of New York Press.

Germond, Jack, and Jules Witcover. 1989. *Whose Broad Stripes and Bright Stars? The Trivial Pursuit of the Presidency 1988*. New York: Warner Books.

Goldman, Peter, Tony Fuller, and Tom Mathews. 1989. *The Quest for the Presidency: The 1988 Campaign*. New York: Touchstone.

Goldman, Peter, and Tom Mathews. 1992. "America Changes the Guard." *Newsweek* 120 (November/December): 20–23.

Hotline. 1991–1992. 4, no. 224; 6, no. 68.

Ippolito, Dennis. 1997. "Governance versus Politics: The Budget Policy Legacy of the Bush Administration." Paper presented at the Tenth Presidential Conference, George Bush, 41st president of the United States. Hofstra University, April 17–19.

Jamieson, Kathleen Hall. 1988. "For Televised Mendacity, This Year's Race is the Worst Ever." *Washington Post*, October 30, C1, 2.

Neustadt, Richard. 1990. *Presidential Power*. New York: Free Press.

Ostrander, Dan L. 1997. "Read My Lips: Political Pragmatism, an Essential Ingredient for Presidential Leadership." Paper presented at the Tenth Presidential Conference, George Bush, 41st president of the United States, Hofstra University, April 17–19.

Patterson, Thomas E. 1989. "The Press and Its Missed Assignments." In Michael Nelson, ed., *The Elections of 1988*. Washington, DC: Congressional Quarterly Press.

Quirk, Paul J. 1989. "The Election." In Michael Nelson, ed., *The Elections of 1988*. Washington, DC: Congressional Quarterly Press.

Windsor, Duane. 1997. "The 1990 Deficit Reduction Deal." Paper presented at the Tenth Presidential Conference, George Bush, 41st president of the United States, Hofstra University, April 17–19.

3

Clarity or Ambiguity: What Should We Expect From Candidates in American Politics?

William C. Pink

A seemingly constant complaint concerning political candidates in American politics is that they either equivocate or simply avoid important policy stands. A good example of what people fear was the outlook of Boise Penrose, Republican boss of Philadelphia, concerning the 1920 campaign of candidate Warren G. Harding. Penrose is reputed to have said, "Keep Warren at home. If he goes on tour, somebody's sure to ask him questions, and Warren's just the sort of damn fool that'll try and answer them" (Polsby and Wildavsky 1996: 221–22). More recently, pundits have noted President Clinton's "nifty obfuscation" on policy towards affirmative action in the 1996 campaign as he proposed the following: "Mend it, don't end it" (Gigot 1996: 12).

Yet, there are also many examples in American politics where candidates both advertise and maintain clear policy positions. As Page notes, "Despite all the possible expectations of inconsistency or change, . . . constancy of policy stands is the rule. Most candidates take a single stand on each issue they deal with, and stick to it, or at least do not contradict it" (Page and Shapiro 1978: 109). For instance, in 1968, Richard Nixon was emphatic that he took stands on 227 specific policy issues, and he published a book to prove the point (178).

This empirical phenomenon leads to the following question: What is the rationale behind candidates choosing to send either ambiguous policy messages or clear policy stands? This is the question that this paper will explore. To do so, I will first present and defend a series of assumptions and stylized arguments about candidates and voters in American elections. The assumptions and arguments will be used as tools to generate predictions concerning the behavior of candidates and voters. Following each prediction, I will present evidence that shows how these predictions conform to the behavior of actual candidates and voters in American elections.

STYLIZED ARGUMENTS

Given the existence of the two-party system, the vast majority of general elections (not the primary elections) in American politics involve only two candidates with a legitimate chance of gaining office: the current Democrat or Republican officeholder and the challenger from the other party. Accordingly, *A1: Assume that an election has only two candidates: an incumbent (I) and a challenger (C).*

Next, one must ask exactly what it is that motivates both officeholders (incumbents) and office-seekers (challengers). In his study of congressional committees, Fenno finds that committee members are motivated by three primary goals: reelection, power and influence within the House, and good public policy (1973: 1). A plausible case can be made for each of these goals as sources of political motivation. However, the electoral goal "has an attractive universality to it. It has to be the *proximate* goal of everyone, the goal that must be achieved over and over if other ends are to be entertained" (Mayhew 1987: 18). Indeed, there is overwhelming evidence that both incumbents and challengers are primarily concerned with winning elections (King 1997). As Fiorina notes, there is the occasional "electoral gamble because some other goal is sufficiently valued. President John F. Kennedy put his name on a book recounting a number of such examples. But if they were frequent, let alone the norm, there would have been no reason (for Kennedy) to write the book at all, let alone reason to entitle it *Profiles in Courage*" (1989: 103).[1] Hence, *A2: Assume that both candidates are primarily concerned with winning elections and that both candidates are rational.*

The above assumption that both candidates are "rational" signifies that the candidates will calculate the most reasonable way to achieve their goal of election (or reelection) and will choose this most reasonable way. No living person perfectly behaves in accordance with this standard. However, "Some such simplification is necessary for the prediction of behavior, because decisions made at random, or without any relation to each other, do not fall into any pattern. Yet only if human actions form some pattern can they ever be forecast or the relations between them subject to analysis" (Downs 1957: 4). Thus, to make predictions about both candidate and voter behavior, the rationality assumption is necessary.

The next question concerns voters: how do voters determine who to vote for? First, since there are only two candidates, it will always be in the voter's interest to vote for the candidate that he or she prefers. In other words, *A3: Assume that each voter chooses "sincerely" (i.e., votes for the candidate that he or she prefers)*. Consequently, one must ask the following question: On what basis is this choice made? In previous research on presidential voters, three leading forces emerge that shape voter choice: issues, party identification, and candidate attributes (Lewis-Beck and Rice 1992: 25). However, since this analysis is an attempt to grasp the rationality of political ambiguity, it makes sense to focus on issues, which are the potential subject of ambiguity or clarity. Also, issues seem to have risen to prominence. While party identification is still a very strong determinant of voter choice, empirical evidence shows that voters are becoming less motivated by partisanship. For instance, in a 1986 survey by Larry Sabato, 92 percent of the respondents agreed with the statement, "I always vote for the person who I think is best, regardless of what party they belong to." On the other hand, only 14 percent of the respondents in the same survey agreed with the statement, "I always support the candidates of just one party" (Wattenberg 1990: 163; Sabato 1988: 133). Further, candidate attributes such as "honesty" and "integrity" are clearly important; "Nearly everyone wants such qualities as honesty, intelligence, prudence, and energy in government leaders" (Page and Shapiro 1976: 749). Of course, all candidates claim to possess such qualities. No candidate willingly equivocates when asked whether he is honest or intelligent. However, if a candidate is perceived as equivocating, barring some scandal, it is likely because of some confusion about his or her issue positions. Accordingly, issues will be the focus of our assumption concerning voter choice. *A4: Assume that each voter chooses the candidate whose issue positions are "closer" to the issue positions of the voter.*

To understand the concept of "closer," consider the Figure 3.1. I and C are the two candidates, and V is the lone voter. The scale represents their issue positions for a policy area. In this example, the policy area is abortion. The left extreme of the scale represents the full legalization of abortion, the right extreme represents outlawing all abortions. In between are all the possible variations of policy between these two extremes. In this scale, if the voter is solely voting according to a candidate's abortion policy, V chooses I because the distance between I and V is smaller than the distance between V and C. In other words, V is closer to I, so V votes for I.[2]

Next, one must determine how these issue positions are known by the voters. The obvious case occurs when a candidate directly announces a policy position on an issue and maintains that position over time. By keeping this consistency, voters know the candidate's issue position with "certainty." However, if a candidate changes his position on an issue, the voters are "uncertain" about where the candidate stands. Thus, in the previous figure, if C recognizes that his announced policy position is further away from the policy position of V than I is, C will change his policy and move closer to V to get V's vote. However, since V knows C's previous announcement, he is less sure whether to believe C because of this movement. In effect, C's movement creates political

Figure 3.1
A Representation of Voter and Candidate Issue Positions

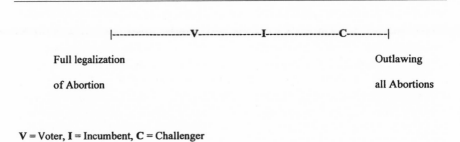

|---------------------V----------------I-------------------C-----------|

Full legalization   Outlawing

of Abortion   all Abortions

V = Voter, **I** = Incumbent, **C** = Challenger

ambiguity, or the condition of not knowing a candidate's issue position with confidence (Brams 1978: 29). Therefore, *A5: Assume that voters know a candidate's issue position with certainty if he does not change his announced position and that voters are uncertain about a candidate's issue position if he changes his issue position (i.e., the candidate's issue position becomes ambiguous). The more a candidate changes that position, the more uncertain voters are about his actual position.* Thus, candidate movement in an issue area is the source of political ambiguity.

For this kind of ambiguity to emerge, voters need to have known the previous issue position of the candidate. From previous research on national elections, it is clear that "while voters generally lack specific factual knowledge about issues and events, through years of political experience and socialization, they do acquire some information about parties and candidates" (Ansolabehere and Iyengar 1994: 335). And, as one would expect, campaign advertising is designed to play on this preexisting knowledge that voters possess: "The imagery of campaign advertising serves to remind voters about what they already 'know' about the candidates' positions on issues. Most Americans are socialized to believe, for example, that Democrats favor jobs programs and that Republicans favor balanced budgets. Advertising on the issues evokes these stereotypic beliefs about the candidates. In effect, political advertising informs voters both by providing new information and by refreshing their existing store of knowledge" (Ansolabehere and Iyengar 1995: 60).

To capture this preexisting knowledge of candidate issue positions, the following assumption will be made: *A6: Assume that each candidate has a "reputation" for an issue position on all of the issue areas and that his reputation is known by the voters.* Thus, political ambiguity is effectively "bound" by candidate reputations (Bernhardt and Ingberman 1985). If a candidate chooses an issue position that is the same as his reputation, then voters are certain about the candidate's position. However, the more a candidate moves from his reputation on an issue, the more uncertain voters become concerning that candidate's actual issue position.

Given the above assumptions, a final question emerges: Since voters choose candidates based upon policy preferences, how does a candidate choose which policies to announce or emphasize? Clearly, he will choose to emphasize the issue positions on which he will garner the most votes. In other words, he will emphasize the issues on which his position is closer to the position of a majority of voters than the position of his opponent. In fact, this is one of the basic decisions of campaign strategists: to maximize votes "by setting the political agenda in the way most favorable to its own candidates" by raising the visibility of issues that are advantageous to the candidate (Arterton 1992; Paleologos 1997; Popkin 1994: 216). As political consultant Dick Morris states, "The key is to advertise your positions only if the public agrees with them. If the public won't accept your basic premise, it doesn't matter how much you spend or how well your ads are produced; they won't work" (1997: 152). Thus, *A7: Assume that candidates strategically choose to emphasize the issues on which their issue positions are closer to the issue positions of a majority of the voters.*

In addition, empirical evidence demonstrates that political advertising on certain policy areas actually changes the basis for voters' choices:

Simply by focusing on one issue to the exclusion of others, candidates alter the criteria on which voting choices are based and, indirectly, change voting intentions. For example, when campaign advertisements emphasize economic issues, voters' beliefs about the economy and the candidates' abilities to deal with economic problems become especially important determinants of voting preferences. When candidates focus on women's issues, opinions on sexual harassment or reproductive rights or gender equality take on added importance as criteria for judging candidates. (Ansolabehere and Iyengar 1995: 72)

In other words, "Citizens do not reach their electoral decisions in a vacuum. Instead, they make choices within the confines of the options presented by leaders" (West 1993: 31). Therefore, *A8: Assume that the issues chosen for emphasis by the candidates are the issues that the voters base their votes upon.*

Logically, the above assumption can only make sense if one also assumes that issues are separable—that is, that issue positions in one policy area are unrelated to issue positions in another policy area. Of course, this is not always the case. However, the assumption is necessary for two reasons. First, if one conceives of candidates choosing among policy areas to find the most electorally advantageous, then one must also conceive of these areas as separable or distinguishable. Otherwise, how will the candidate make that choice? Without separability of issue areas, candidates cannot effectively distinguish and utilize issues for increasing votes. And, second, if issues are not separable, how will the issue gain in importance in the voter's decision-making process with respect to the other issues, as they have been observed to do? Therefore, *A9: Assume that the issue areas are separable.*

PREDICTIONS AND EVIDENCE

Given these assumptions concerning candidate and voter behavior, the following predictions can be made:

Prediction 1: Assuming a stable distribution of voter preferences in many issue areas, the incumbent candidate will emphasize his issue positions that are the same as the positions he is known for in his reputation and the same he used in the prior election(s). The challenger, in this situation, will have to attempt to match the incumbent's issue positions, which means that he will be perceived as the more ambiguous candidate. The incumbent will win the election.

"A stable distribution of voter preferences" signifies that the desired or preferred issue positions of the voters has remained the same. Since the incumbent has already been elected once (or more) by the same voters on the issue positions that he espoused, he has a clear advantage over the challenger. The incumbent has no incentive to announce a new position. Instead, he will maintain the same issue positions as in the prior election(s), which implies that these positions will be extremely similar to the positions he is known for in his reputation. Thus, the voters will be confident that the incumbent actually stands for these positions. The challenger, on the other hand, will realize that the distribution of voter preferences has remained the same and that the incumbent's issue positions are what the voters desire. Consequently, his only chance to win will be to match these positions. However, this means that he may have to move from his reputation. If he does, voters will be less confident about the challenger's positions; the challenger will be perceived as ambiguous. The incumbent will win the election, and there will be no ambiguity as to which issue positions he represents.

This prediction is well supported by empirical evidence. First, the assumption about the stability of the distribution of voter preferences accurately reflects collective public opinion as measured in survey data. Over time, the American public has remained remarkably stable in its policy preferences (Page and Shapiro 1992). And, in this setting of stable voter preferences, incumbent candidates typically adopt the same issue positions. In Congress, incumbents remain particularly consistent in the policy preferences that they espouse (Poole and Rosenthal 1997). And at the presidential level, only in the "exceptional cases" of ideologically extreme challengers are there a number of substantial changes of issue stands (Page and Shapiro 1978: 118).

Second, in this setting of stable voter preferences and stable incumbent issue positions, incumbents usually win reelection. For example, the very members of Congress that Poole and Rosenthal find to be so consistent in their issue preferences also win reelection to the U.S. House of Representatives at incredible rates. Between 1946 and 1994, on average fewer than 7 percent of incumbents in the House lost in general elections (Jacobson 1997: 20).[3] This enables one to understand the frequently noted "incumbency advantage" simply as a logical implication of the constraints of a stable distribution of preferences among the voters and the incumbent's possession of electorally effective issue reputations. Thus, high incumbent reelection rates are an anticipated feature of the electoral process, given the condition of stable policy preferences among the voters.

Third, Prediction 1 complies with the observation that candidates stress the consistency of their public record, while frequently attacking the inconsistencies of their opponent.

> Indeed, in almost any election . . . much of the discussion revolves around the question of what each candidate is likely to do in office. Each candidate attempts to demonstrate how his current position is consistent with his record (and therefore represents his "true preferences") while impugning the consistency of his opponent's record. In other words, candidates attempt to make the voters uncertain about their opponents' intentions while simultaneously offering evidence as to their own sincerity. (Bernhardt and Ingberman 1985: 59)

Given a stable distribution of preferences, this is exactly how Prediction 1 expects the incumbent to behave.

As can be inferred from above, a large change in the distribution of preferences among the electorate is potentially disastrous for an incumbent. The change implies that the preferred issue positions of a majority of the electorate have moved away from the positions that were successful for the incumbent in the prior election(s). This leads to the following prediction:

Prediction 2: Assuming a change in the distribution of voter preferences in many issue areas, the incumbent will have to change his issue positions to accommodate the change in the distribution of preferences, which means that he will have to move from the issue positions of his reputation. Therefore, voters will be uncertain concerning the incumbent's actual policy stances; he will be perceived as an ambiguous candidate. This leaves two possible outcomes:

a) First, if the challenger's reputation matches the changes of issue positions that have taken place among a majority of the electorate, he will simply emphasize the issue positions he is known for. In this situation, the challenger will win the election.

b) On the other hand, if the change in voter preferences results in the electorate's preferred positions corresponding with neither the positions of the incumbent nor the positions of the challenger, then both candidates will have to change their positions toward the majority preferred positions. In this situation, both candidates will be perceived as ambiguous candidates. Accordingly, the candidate who had to move less from his reputation will be the candidate who will win the election.

The change in the distribution of preferences removes the incumbent's ability to run on the issue positions that previously enabled him to get elected. Thus, the incumbent loses his electoral advantage and, instead, has strong incentives to switch his issue positions to accommodate the changes in preferences that have taken place among the voters. These changes, when viewed in comparison with the incumbent's distinct reputation, will cause the voters to be uncertain about what the incumbent truly stands for. Now, the incumbent will be perceived as ambiguous.

As noted in Prediction 2, this leaves two possible outcomes. One possible situation provides an opportunity for the challenger. In this scenario, a majority of voters have changed their policy preferences to issue positions that correspond with the challenger's reputation. Here, the challenger will simply emphasize these issue positions and the voters will be confident that the challenger truly represents these policy stances. The voters will compare an incumbent and a challenger with very similar issue positions, but they will be uncertain whether to believe the incumbent. The challenger will win the election.

However, it is also possible that the change in the preferences of the voters does not correspond with the issue positions of the reputation of either the incumbent or the challenger. Now, both candidates will have strong incentives to change their policy stands toward the new majority-preferred position. Because of their respective shifts, both candidates will be perceived by the voters to be ambiguous. The voters with the majority-preferred issue positions will engage in the following two-step decision process. First, they will determine which of the two candidates moved less from his reputation to accommodate their new preferences and which of the candidates moved further from his reputation. After making this determination, they will vote for the candidate who moved less from his reputation since they can be more confident of his new issue stance than that of his opponent (who had to move further from his reputation).

For Prediction 2 to materialize, a majority of the electorate must have changed its opinions on many issues. This is not typical of American public opinion. However, such changes have occurred from time to time, and the electoral results of such times reflect the expected outcomes of Prediction 2. A good example of such an occasion was the presidential election of 1992. While it would be inaccurate to maintain that the distribution of voter preferences changed in 1992 in many issue areas, it is accurate to claim that the distribution changed in the issue areas that emerged as the decisive areas of voter choice in that election. Particularly, as will be shown below, the public's perspective on the need for government intervention in the economy had significantly changed since the prior presidential election of 1988.

As the 1992 campaign began, President Bush maintained that the economy was healthy and that no action was necessary to help it recover from an earlier recession before the November elections. In fact, President Bush continually insisted that the preexisting social programs were sufficient to reenergize the economy (Popkin 1994: 247). Such a stance squared nicely with his reputation as someone who believed in the free market and opposed "social engineering." However, the distribution of preferences among the electorate had clearly changed from this position. The public believed that the country was in the midst of a recession (a term Bush was reluctant to even utter until later in the campaign) and that the government ought to be taking action to restore jobs and prosperity (Trent and Trent 1995: 72). Consequently, when Bush finally announced a changed position on the economy, the voters perceived the new position in relation to his reputation and previously held position. And, due to the great distance between these two positions, voters were uncertain about Bush's economic policy stance. In essence, on this crucial issue dimension, he became the ambiguous candidate.

The challenger, Governor Clinton, saw a clear opportunity to utilize this change in the distribution of preferences to gain voter support. In fact, Clinton's polltaker, Stan Greenberg, noted as early as December 1991 that Clinton would gain support in New Hampshire if he campaigned upon middle-class economics and sought to put "Main Street before Wall Street and Washington" (Greenberg 1991: 623). Fred Steeper, Bush's polltaker, found similar results from his studies of focus groups, and he warned Bush that he was viewed as the "absent president" on all domestic issues, including the economy (Steeper 1992). In the general election, as one would expect, Clinton capitalized on the change of preferences of the electorate by emphasizing this crucial issue area in which his position and the position of a majority of the electorate's were the same. Statistical analysis has revealed the success of Clinton's strategy; the probability of voting for either Clinton or Bush was strongly affected by voters' beliefs about the economy (Alvarez and Nagler 1995: 737). And, as Prediction 2 expects, Clinton won the election.

Interestingly, because Clinton's reputation and issue positions were not as well known as Bush's reputation and issue positions before the campaign began, this example does not perfectly comply with the assumptions behind Prediction 2. However, Clinton purposefully advertised his record in Arkansas to show how it conformed to his current issue positions regarding the economy. For example, he advertised the training program he developed for moving women off the welfare roles and finding new jobs. Also, he used commercials featuring Nobel laureates in economics and hundreds of business executives who endorsed his economic plan (Murray 1992: 1; Popkin 1994: 258–59). Thus, he established his reputation among the voters through his campaign advertising. And once he established that his reputation and his current issue position were consistent, the voters were able to accept his popular economic policy stance with certainty.

DISCUSSION

As can now be seen, the rationale behind candidates choosing to send either clear policy stands or ambiguous policy messages to the electorate stems from both the distribution of preferences of the voters and how well that distribution of preferences conforms to the candidate's reputation. During times of a stable distribution of voter preferences, the challenger is the only candidate who is likely to send ambiguous policy messages. And, during times of a changing distribution of voter preferences, the incumbent is always likely to send ambiguous policy messages while the challenger will occasionally send ambiguous policy messages. Again, the challenger's decision simply depends upon how well the challenger's reputation matches up with the new distribution of voter preferences.

Clearly, this is a highly simplified representation of the electoral process and it cannot account for other kinds of political ambiguity. For example, the public relations theme of the 1984 Reagan campaign was "Morning Again in America," and the candidate's messages were a combination of "Ronald Reagan, apple pie, and the American dream" (Ceaser 1988: 195). This is a distinct kind of political ambiguity that is difficult to fit into our understanding of issue positions. This kind of ambiguity emerges from candidates trying to win reelection by appealing to symbolic values, instead of stating what policies they propose (Stokes 1992).

However, the existence of other forms of political ambiguity does not refute the findings of this analysis. Of course, the real world of elections and campaigns appears more complicated than the representation provided here by the assumptions and stylized arguments. Yet, this appearance of complexity may simply be a lack of comprehension. The patterns of constancy and ambiguity among candidates' policy stands noted at the outset of the paper remain as regularities in American elections. And, to grasp the process underlying these patterns, the following question needs to answered: How might American elections be structured so that these regularities are anticipated features of these elections?[4] This analysis provides an answer to that question based upon the distribution of voter preferences and candidate reputations on issue positions. In doing so, it becomes clear that a candidate's decision to send either clear or ambiguous policy messages is simply a rational choice, operating within the aforementioned constraints of the electoral process, to win either election or reelection to office.

NOTES

The author wishes to thank Steven J. Brams, Josep Colomer, Michael Gilligan, H. Mark Roelofs, Paul E. Scheele, and Alexander A. Schuessler for comments and suggestions on earlier versions of this paper. The responsibility for any errors that remain is my own.

1. President Kennedy's book featured brave and unpopular political deeds by U.S. senators.

2. For fuller and more sophisticated discussions of this type of analysis of voting, see Downs (1957), Black (1958), Enelow and Hinich (1984), and Miller, Grofman, and Feld (1989).

3. In fact, even in 1994, the Democrats' worst electoral year since 1946, 84 percent of the House Democrats who sought reelection still won.

4. For a full elaboration of this perspective, see Fiorina and Shepsle (1982).

REFERENCES

Alvarez, Michael R., and Jonathan Nagler. 1995. "Economics, Issues, and the Perot Candidacy: Voter Choice in the 1992 Presidential Election." *American Journal of Political Science* 39 (August): 714–44.

Ansolabehere, Stephen, and Shanto Iyengar. 1994. "Riding The Wave And Claiming Ownership Over Issues: The Joint Effects Of Advertising And News Coverage in Campaigns." *Public Opinion Quarterly* 58 (fall): 335–57.

———. 1995. *Going Negative. How Political Advertisements Shrink and Polarize the Electorate*. New York: The Free Press.

Arterton, Christopher F. 1992. "The Persuasive Art in Politics: The Role of Paid Advertising in Presidential Campaigns." In Mathew D. McCubbins, ed., *Under the Watchful Eye, Managing Presidential Campaigns in the Television Era*. Washington, DC: Congressional Quarterly Press.

Bernhardt, M. Daniel, and Daniel E. Ingberman. 1985. "Candidate Reputations and the 'Incumbency Effect.'" *Journal of Public Economics* 27 (June): 47–67.

Black, Duncan. 1958. *The Theory of Committees and Elections*. Cambridge: Cambridge University Press.

Brams, Steven J. 1978. *The Presidential Election Game*. New Haven: Yale University Press.

Ceaser, James W. 1988. "The Reagan Presidency and Public Opinion." In Charles O. Jones, ed., *The Reagan Legacy. Promise and Performance*. Chatham, NJ: Chatham House.

Downs, Anthony. 1957. *An Economic Theory of Democracy*. New York: HarperCollins Publishers, Inc.

Enelow, James M., and Melvin J. Hinich. 1984. *The Spatial Theory of Voting. An Introduction*. Cambridge: Cambridge University Press.

Fenno Jr., Richard R. 1973. *Congressmen in Committees*. Boston: Little, Brown.

Fiorina, Morris P. 1989. *Congress: Keystone to the Washington Establishment*. 2nd ed. New Haven: Yale University Press.

Fiorina, Morris P., and Kenneth A. Shepsle. 1982. "Equilibrium, Disequilibrium, and the General Possibility of a Science of Politics." In Peter C. Ordeshook and Kenneth A. Shepsle, eds., *Political Equilibrium*. Boston: Kluwer-Nijhoff Publishing: 49–64.

Gigot, Paul A. 1996. "Potomac Watch: Clinton Campaign Is in a Class All by Itself." *The Wall Street Journal*, November 1, A12.

Greenberg, Stan. 1991. "To: The Clinton Campaign. Re: New Hampshire Update." In Peter Goldman, Thomas M. DeFrank, Mark Miller, Andrew Murr, Tom Mathews, eds., with Patrick Rogers and Melanie Cooper. 1994. *Quest for the Presidency. 1992*. College Station: Texas A & M University Press.

Jacobson, Gary C. 1997. *The Politics of Congressional Elections*. 4th ed. New York: Longman.

Kennedy, John F. 1955. *Profiles in Courage*. New York: Harper and Row.

King, Anthony. 1997. *Running Scared. Why America's Politicians Campaign Too Much and Govern Too Little*. New York: The Free Press.

Lewis-Beck, Michael S., and Tom W. Rice. 1992. *Forecasting Elections*. Washington DC: CQ Press.

Mayhew, David R. 1987. "The Electoral Connection and the Congress." In Mathew D. McCubbins and Terry Sullivan, eds., *Congress: Structure and Policy*. Cambridge: Cambridge University Press: 18–29.

Miller, Nicholas R., Bernard Grofman, and Scott L. Feld. 1989. "The Geometry of Majority Rule." *Journal of Theoretical Politics* 4 (October): 379–406.

Morris, Dick. 1997. *Behind the Oval Office. Winning the Presidency in the Nineties*. New York: Random House.

Murray, Alan. 1992. "Campaign '92—Defining Differences; Clintonomics." *Wall Street Journal*, October 19, A1.

Page, Benjamin I., and Robert Y. Shapiro. 1992. *The Rational Public. Fifty Years of Trends in Americans' Policy Preferences*. Chicago: University of Chicago Press.

———. 1976. "The Theory of Political Ambiguity." *American Political Science Review* 70 (September): 742–52.

———. 1978. *Choices and Echoes in Presidential Elections. Rational Man and Electoral Democracy*. Chicago: University of Chicago Press.

Paleologos, David A. 1997. "A Pollster on Polling." *American Behavioral Scientist* 40: 1183–89.

Polsby, Nelson W., and Aaron Wildavsky. 1996. *Presidential Elections. Strategies and Structures of American Politics*, 9th ed. Chatham, NJ: Chatham House Publishers, Inc.

Poole, Keith T., and Howard Rosenthal. 1997. *Congress: a Political-economic History of Roll Call Voting*. New York: Oxford University Press.

Popkin, Samuel L. 1994. *The Reasoning Voter. Communication and Persuasion in Presidential Campaigns*, 2nd ed. Chicago: University of Chicago Press.

Sabato, Larry J. 1988. *The Party's Just Begun: Shaping Political Parties for America's Future*. Glenview, IL: Scott, Foresman.

Steeper, Fred. 1992. "Memorandum RE: Implications of the April Focus Groups." In Peter Goldman,Thomas M. DeFrank, Mark Miller, Andrew Murr, and Tom Mathews, eds., with Patrick Rogers and Melanie Cooper. 1994. *Quest for the Presidency. 1992*. College Station: Texas A & M University Press: 674–75.

Stokes, Donald. 1992. "Valence Politics." In Dennis Kavanagh, ed., *Electoral Politics*. Oxford: Clarendon Press: 141–64.

Trent, Jimmie D., and Judith S. Trent. 1995. "The Incumbent and His Challengers. The Problem of Adapting to Prevailing Conditions." In Kathleen E. Kendall, ed., *Presidential Campaign Discourse. Strategic Communication Problems*. Albany: State University of New York Press.

Wattenberg, Martin P. 1990. *The Decline of American Political Parties 1952–1988*. Cambridge: Harvard University Press.

West, Darrell M. 1993. *Air Wars. Television Advertising in Election Campaigns, 1952–1992*. Washington DC: Congressional Quarterly Press.

B. THE ROLE OF TELEVISION, ADVERTISING, AND POLLING IN AMERICAN ELECTIONS

4

The Image of Democracy: Television's Effect on the American Political System

Marc A. Triebwasser

The first live national television hookup occurred in 1950 for a press conference by President Harry Truman. Up to that point, live television coverage had been strictly local. The prospect of national television changed the landscape of political campaigning. Now, one TV ad could reach millions of potential voters. At first, television advertising was used only to a limited extent. Many of the ads ran for a full minute, and most of them were quite simple.

THE EVOLUTION OF CAMPAIGN ADS

In the 1952 presidential election, Walt Disney Studios prepared a cartoon ad for the Eisenhower campaign that presented a simple jingle in favor of Eisenhower. It was generally reminiscent of the cartoons that had been used in movie theaters and elsewhere to support some of Franklin Roosevelt's campaigns. In the 1960 election, Kennedy ran another simple jingle advertisement with a montage of graphics and still photographs depicting Democratic political heroes and Kennedy in various appealing poses. By today's standards these ads were not only simplistic, they would be considered by many to be naive. Many of these ads reflected the advertising philosophy of getting a product's (candidate's) name etched indelibly in the viewer's mind.

At first, television was used more by the Republicans. Ad agencies, whose major clients were large corporations, were loath to produce advertisements for Democrats since this might offend their clients. However, this soon changed.

By the 1964 election, some advertisements took a different tack, playing on popular prejudices. These ads only hinted at a theme and let the viewers draw their own conclusions. The most famous political commercial of that campaign, and perhaps of any campaign, depicted a young girl counting the petals on a daisy. The video remains, but audio fades to a countdown. Then the screen erupts into a nuclear explosion with a voice-over by Lyndon Johnson suggesting that we must avoid nuclear war. Although it is never mentioned in the ad, the obvious import was that if elected, Goldwater might get us into a nuclear war. The advertisement was so stark that it only appeared once and was immediately pulled, but its effect was long remembered. It has, in fact, become a classic in television political advertising.

By the 1988 presidential campaign, television advertising had become a fine art. It was used to great advantage by the Bush forces; the Dukakis campaign lagged considerably in its use of television. During that campaign Willy Horton became a major issue. Willy Horton was a black convict who had been let out of prison on furlough, and while on furlough raped a woman. The Bush campaign created an ad featuring a revolving door through which men were being let out of prison. A voice-over suggested that under Dukakis's governorship of Massachusetts, many imprisoned criminals were allowed to go on furlough. Few, if any, of the prisoners depicted in the ad were African Americans. However, because the ad was taped in black and white it appeared that many were black. Although Willy Horton's name was never mentioned, this ad became known as the Willy Horton ad. Clearly, this advertisement was meant to play on people's fear of violent crime, as well as on their racial prejudice.

It is important to note that in television advertising, it is not only the actual language used that can be misleading. The way an ad is filmed—that is, its production value—and the music and sounds that may seem incidental can also induce in the viewer very specific emotional effects. Of course, most viewers are unaware of these techniques and their consequences. The Dukakis campaign did produce an effective ad refuting the Bush revolving door ad. It noted that the prisoner furlough program had been started by a Republican governor and stopped by Governor Dukakis. It also pointed out that a federal prisoner furlough program was being carried out while George Bush was vice president. The ad suggested that the Bush campaign was "taking a furlough from the truth." However, this ad appeared too late in the campaign to be useful.

Another Bush ad was called "The Harbor." It suggested that Dukakis had failed to clean up Boston harbor. The ad of course did not mention that the funds for this cleanup were held up by the Reagan administration in which George Bush served as vice president. Such a misleading verbal statement may be considered par for the course in political campaigns. What television added to this misleading presentation was that in the beginning of the ad the video is clearly of Boston harbor, but later in the ad the video of a polluted harbor site was most likely *not* Boston harbor. Of course, the ad never claimed it was: the ad was simply titled "The Harbor." The viewer was, however, led to conclude that the final footage was Boston harbor because of the voice-over message. Thus, we are dealing here not simply with verbal misrepresentation which has long been used in politics, but with more subtle forms of video and aural audience manipulation which had originally been developed for entertainment purposes in movies and television programs.[1]

During the 1992 campaign between George Bush and Bill Clinton, the Bush forces tried to use the same tactics they used in the 1988 campaign. However, the Clinton campaign was very sophisticated in the use of television and was able to counter the Bush efforts effectively. Increasingly important in political campaigns is expertise in using television and television commercials to manipulate the public. To understand the effect of all this on American politics, we need to examine the effect television has had on our political parties and on the development of public policy.

THE EMERGENCE OF MASS SOCIETY

As people began to pay more attention in the 1950s and 1960s to what was happening on TV than to what was going on in their own neighborhoods, the television screen became most people's *window on the world*. At the same time, many of the community institutions and organizations that had traditionally served as buffers for communication between the individual and society at large were dissolving. In other words, television—as the major means of communication—led to the development of a *mass society* in which the individual related directly to society as a whole, without the intervention of intermediary community institutions.

As political campaigns for presidential, senatorial, congressional, and statewide office focused more heavily on television, the role of the political party changed markedly. Television advertising proved very expensive. Not only was there the expense of buying television time from the networks and local television stations, there was also the tremendous cost of hiring media experts to help shape images and develop the most effective television spots. Opinion polling is also expensive. In developing a campaign message, it is critical to know which issues are important to potential voters, and which *phrases* in particular capture their interest. It is therefore important to conduct regular opinion polls among voters and to use such techniques as focus groups and continuous polling to find out which phrases work the best. In the words of former Senator Frank Church, we have moved from the politics of *substance* to the politics of *style*.

As candidates needed both more money and greater media expertise to run their campaigns, they found the traditional party organizations less relevant to their needs. Traditionally, these party organizations were able to supply volunteers for Get-Out-the-Vote campaigns. This was important when campaigning was done door-to-door, or when it was necessary to maintain large phone banks to contact potential voters. These Get-Out-the-Vote efforts are still very important today for *local* elections, where broadcast television has not been able to focus effectively on local constituencies. However, for *statewide* and *national* office the move to television campaigning has been very significant. As traditional local party structures became irrelevant to television campaigns where money played the key role, candidates depended on their own fundraising mechanisms and paid less attention to their own political parties. This caused some to see a diminishing role for political parties, and led to the publication of such books as David Broder's *The Party's Over* (1971).

The parties, however, responded to these changes (Maisel 1994). At first this could be seen most significantly in the Republican party, which had always relied more heavily on large financial contributions. However, by the 1980s the Democratic party began to catch up. This phenomenon led to a shift from a *labor intensive* role and structure in political parties to a more *capital intensive* structure and role. As a new type of political party emerged, the spirit of these renewed party organizations was captured in such books as Larry Sabato's *The Party's Just Begun* (1988). However, although the political party emerged as a stronger organization, its character had changed totally. Many of the functions the party had previously fulfilled as a conduit for bringing the voice of the masses into the system and integrating them into the political process no longer operated effectively.

Machine politics, which had dominated the early part of this century, was dying out by the 1950s and 1960s. Some of this was due to reforms put in place by the Progressive movement. Much had to do with the fact that the immigrant populations—serviced by these political bosses—had finally been assimilated into American society and were becoming more middle class in both prosperity and increased opportunities after World War II.

When people's attention had been focused on their local communities, neighborhood opinion makers were important in the political process and were sought out by political organizations. Reaching these people, whom Robert Dahl and others called *subleaders*, often served to gain the support of entire neighborhoods (Dahl 1961). In this mode of organization, having enough people to do door-to-door campaigning—even for national office—was very important. Campaigning at the time was thus very labor intensive.

With the development of television, it became more important to get one's message on the air. In order to do this, one needed heavy finances. As money became more important, other structures emerged to finance political campaigns. As a result of the 1971 Federal Election Campaign Act and its 1974 amendments—and subsequent Supreme Court and Federal Election Commission decisions—political action committees or PACs became increasingly important. This was especially true of PACs related to corporations, trade organizations, and labor unions—although labor unions were diminishing in strength by this period.

At first, the Republicans thought corporate PACs, being ideologically closer to them, would support Republican candidates. However, the trend that emerged was that these PACs more heavily supported *incumbents*—no matter the political party to which they belonged. Since the Democrats at that time held the majority in the House and Senate, PACs tended to support Democratic candidates.

In the 1994 elections, the Republicans gained the majority in both the House and Senate for the first time in decades. As a result, they became the incumbents and have enjoyed a substantial advantage over the Democrats in receiving PAC contributions. In fact, they now have a far greater advantage in terms of PAC contributions than the Democrats ever enjoyed when they were the incumbents.

Other fund-raising organizations that emerged later were congressional campaign committees (CCCs) and legislative campaign committees (LCCs). Since candidates needed increasing funds for their races as well as more television expertise, they tended to turn to these organizations more than to their political parties.

In response to these developments, the parties reinvented themselves *as fund-raising organizations.* In this process, such mechanisms as soft money and independent expenditures became increasingly important. Since much of the money raised in this process involved *national* rather than *local* organizations, a major portion of the fund-raising took place in the Washington, D.C., area, and national political party organizations for the first time took on major importance. Political parties were transformed from bottom-up mechanisms in which local and statewide parties dominated, to top-down organizations in which the national organization played the major role. What had once been structured as decentralized webs of local volunteer party organizations became centralized professional/service organizations that could offer funds and expertise in fund-raising, television advertising, and polling (Appleton and Ward 1996).

Although this is not meant to be a quantitative presentation, some figures might be useful to see the increased importance of money in national races. In 1925, the Federal Corrupt Practices Act had attempted to cap spending on congressional races at $5,000 and on senatorial races at $25,000. However, by 1996, it was estimated that unless a challenger raised at least $200,000 for a congressional race, there would not be enough funds available simply to achieve name recognition—and thus the challenger would not be a viable candidate.

Furthermore, in 1996 the various party and other committees spent over $2 *billion* on the congressional, senatorial, and presidential races as well as on the national conventions. This figure was something like $650 million more than they spent in 1992. On the other hand, candidates for the House and Senate raised over $659 million in 1996, about 8 percent over what they raised in the 1994 election. Moreover, 1996 spending represents more than a 30 percent increase over 1992.

In 1996 congressional races involving Republican incumbents, the median receipts of these incumbents were $648,000 and in races involving Democrat incumbents, $522,000. Judging from these figures it seems that to win reelection, *most congresspersons have to raise at least half a million dollars every two years.* How they can do this without becoming beholden to monied interests is anybody's guess.[2]

How some of these campaign funding figures have changed in recent decades may be seen in Figures 4.1 through 4.4.

These changes in campaign financing represent a major transformation in the role of parties in our political process. They have moved from structures through which the public could speak and offer input into the political system, from organizations that could integrate the masses into the political process, to ones that only speak *at* the public in *one-way* communications, from the top downward. The eroding effect on democracy is immeasurable.

Figure 4.1
Party Spending for National Offices

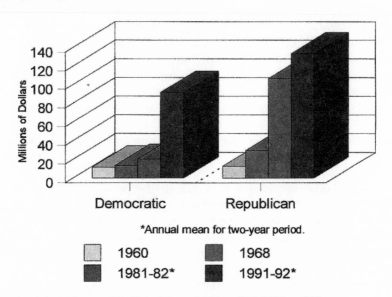

Source: Statistical Abstract of the United States, 1977, p. 513; 1995, p. 295.

Figure 4.2
Party Spending for Congressional Races

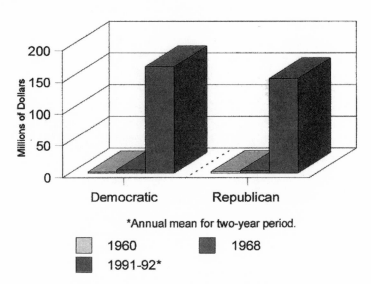

Source: Statistical Abstract of the United States, 1977, p. 513; 1995, p. 294.

Figure 4.3
PAC Contributions to House Races

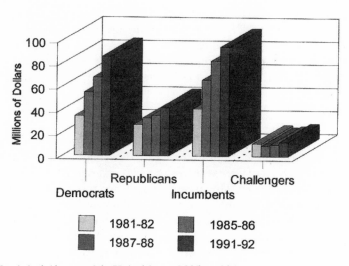

Source: Statistical Abstract of the United States, 1995, p. 294.

Figure 4.4
PAC Contributions to Senate Races

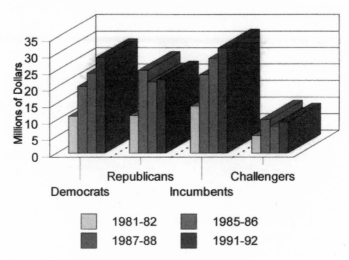

Democrats   Republicans   Incumbents   Challengers

1981-82   1985-86
1987-88   1991-92

Source: Statistical Abstract of the United States, 1995, p. 294.

EFFECTS ON PUBLIC POLICY

Not only have television and the ascendancy of money changed the structure and role of our political parties, they have also affected the process of public policy formation. A classic model of the dominant relationships in the policy-making process is the Iron Triangle. One side of this triangle is made up of congressional committees and subcommittees. A second side consists of executive agencies and regulatory commissions. The third side is made up of lobbyists and the interest groups and organizations (largely corporate) whom they represent.

The special interests—mainly economic—whom the lobbyists represent tend to give campaign contributions specifically to the members of those congressional committees and subcommittees that have jurisdiction over their particular industries. These committees in turn determine the jurisdiction, and sometimes the budgets, of the executive agencies and regulatory commissions that deal with that industry. The executive agencies and regulatory commissions in turn give out government contracts and promulgate regulations that affect that industry. It is to the advantage of everyone in this symbiotic relationship to cooperate with one another. Note, however, that the general public is not usually involved in the operation of these iron triangles.

An iron triangle (or subgovernment) relationship exists in every functional area with which the government deals—be it military, education, housing, banking, telecommunications, etc.

In studying the votes of Congress, citizens and the mass media usually pay attention to general issues rather than to details. However, the *details* are often of most concern to particular industries. A bill that seems to serve the general public on a specific issue *can be molded in its details* to contain large amounts of corporate welfare for a specific industry. Or, it can contain loopholes that provide substantial tax or regulatory benefits for that industry. Generally these benefits are contained in the specific details of the bill as it is worked out in committee, or later in conference committee. With individual pieces of legislation that are often several hundred pages long, it is difficult for the general public or the news media to focus on these details. Often our representatives and senators are themselves unaware of most of these detailed provisions.

The addition of a detail here or there may help a specific politician gain campaign funding and foster the development of a large enough coalition to get a bill approved. These individual concessions all seem rather small when compared to the total process. However, the *cumulative* effect of all of these details may cost the American public *tens or hundreds of billions of dollars*. The devil is indeed in the details.

The cumulative effect of these special benefits often leaves little money for programs that might benefit the general public. And in an age when the importance of a balanced budget is stressed, programs that might solve problems about which the general public is very concerned cannot be financed with the small amount of money left over. The public is then left with politicians who spout *slogans* that do little but sound catchy in political campaigns, instead of with campaigns that deal with significant *issues*.

When political parties depended on statewide networks of grassroots party organizations, the subleaders involved in these local organizations paid attention to the political process after the elections had taken place. Promises made to them during election campaigns were usually concrete ones that would benefit their local constituencies and thus elevate the reputation of these subleaders. It was therefore very important to them that these promises were fulfilled, and that programs were enacted and administered to provide the promised benefits. In other words, the subleaders tended to keep an eye on the shop. With television campaigning and the erosion of community-based political campaigns, there is no longer anyone to keep an eye on the shop as far as the general public is concerned. Politicians can therefore make vague promises during campaigns that sound good but mean little.

And when policies are announced, they are often promulgated on television in the same stylistic manner in which election campaigns are conducted. With each party having its own television studio on Capitol Hill, and each orchestrating its own press conferences, the public is most often treated to news reporting by press release. After presenting a few sound bites from these staged conferences, television news programs seldom provide their own independent analysis of what is actually going on. With few subleaders available today to check up on the details, and even fewer having access to television, the public is often unaware of the specific effects of new policies. The lobbyists, however, are present and very aware of the specifics of the policies and programs being adopted; and they do indeed make sure that their clients' special interests are being addressed. Thus television has enhanced not only *politics* as style more than as substance but has fostered *policy* as style as well.

THE IMPACT ON DEMOCRACY

In the 1950s, there was a debate in political science as to whether America was indeed a democracy. C. Wright Mills suggested in *The Power Elite* that public policy was being formulated to meet the interests of the top few (Mills 1956). Some studies of local communities, such as Floyd Hunter's research on Atlanta in *Community Power Structure,* came to the same conclusion (Hunter 1953). In contrast, Robert Dahl and Charles E. Lindblom of Yale University proposed a theory of democratic pluralism. They argued that although not everyone participated in the political process, as suggested by the classical model of democracy, people did belong to groups whose leaders participated in the policy making process. In some policy areas, one group's leaders would dominate; in other policy areas, those at the head of other groups would take the lead. They suggested what has been called a theory of *circulating* elites: that different groups of leaders dominate different areas of policy-making. In other words, there was a *plurality* of leadership groups in America—both locally and nationally—and people participated in politics through their membership in various groups (Dahl and Lindblom 1953).

In tracing the history of New Haven in his book, *Who Governs?* (1961), Dahl noted that in colonial days there had been an elite. Those who held social power also held economic and political power. He called this a situation of *cumulative inequalities.* However, Dahl suggested that by the 20th century, those who held social power were different from those who had economic power, and both of these groups of leaders were different from those who held political power. Different power structures were operating in society in Dahl's view, and the benefits that might accrue from one's social, economic, or political status would not reinforce each other. Dahl pointed out, for example, that the old Yankee factory owners had a great deal of economic power at the turn of the twentieth century but that the new immigrant laborers held political power because of the size of the voting block they represented.

In other words, although there might be different groups of leaders or elites in society, the advantages they enjoyed were not *cumulative,* but *dispersed.* In fact, these leaders were often at odds with each other. Dahl's idea was that through the tension between various leadership groups in society, everyone's needs would be represented and some form of dynamic balance would be maintained.

This description certainly applies to *labor intensive* politics based on local volunteer organizations in which the masses participate. Through these organizations the masses were able to exercise political clout. However, the situation is markedly different in the *capital intensive* political organizations of today in which money plays such a dominant role. In this case, political leaders are beholden to the economic elites rather than to the masses, and the political and economic elites become intertwined or *cumulative*.

This deterioration in democracy can be seen even more strikingly by reference to our constitutional foundations. In order to avoid tyranny, our constitutional forebears constructed a mixed system of government with checks and balances. The idea was that each branch of government would represent a different constituency. As originally formulated, the president would represent the nation, the Senate the states, and the House of Representatives the people. With three different branches of government and three different constituencies, each would check the other.

Unfortunately, television and the rapidly growing need for money in political campaigns has changed all this. If candidates for the presidency, the Senate, and the House must depend on the same monied interests for political campaign funds, then in fact each branch has the *same cash constituency*. Where then is our traditionally touted system of checks and balances? It would seem that television and the consequent need for million-dollar campaign budgets has transmuted this idea today into a system in which those who pay the *checks* get the *balance* shifted in their favor.

THE NEED FOR CAMPAIGN FINANCE REFORM

The use of television in politics has thus made far more urgent the need for campaign finance reform. The issue of campaign finance was first brought into the national spotlight some 100 years ago in the 1896 election between William McKinley and William Jennings Bryan. Corporations poured millions of dollars into the McKinley campaign, alerting the public to the need for reform.

Several pieces of legislation were passed in succeeding years, such as the Publicity Act, attempting to limit the role of money in political campaigns, but none were really successful. Perhaps the most sweeping act passed during this period was the Federal Corrupt Practices Act of 1925, which not only limited campaign *contributions* but campaign *spending* as well. If it had actually been enforced, it would have reformed campaign financing. The fact is, unfortunately, that this law did not contain effective enforcement provisions and was never really carried out.

The Federal Election Campaign Act of 1971 and its post-Watergate amendments of 1974 again attempted to deal with campaign finance but was substantially weakened by the *Buckley v. Valeo* Supreme Court decision (434 U.S. 1 [1976]). This decision ruled unconstitutional all limitations on campaign *spending* unless some form of public campaign financing was involved.

After the savings and loan debacle that wound up costing American taxpayers *hundreds of billions* of dollars, campaign finance reform was again attempted. A rather strong measure was passed by the Democratic-dominated 102nd Congress in 1990 but was vetoed by Republican President George Bush. When the Democrats gained control of both the 103rd Congress and the presidency in the 1992 election, campaign finance legislation similar to that passed by Congress two years earlier was again attempted but never made it past conference committee. This time, President Clinton had promised to approve such legislation (although he did little to support it), so Congress was no longer interested in passing it. After all, it really might become a law.

The experience of the last 100 years clearly demonstrates that effective campaign finance reform is *not* possible simply through *legislative* means. The public must, in one way or another, be much more directly involved. Certainly, our representatives and senators—who benefit from the current campaign finance situation—are not likely to act to change it *unless* forced to do so. They may talk the talk, but 100 years of experience tells us they are not willing to walk the walk.

Measures such as mandatory free television time given in large enough blocks so candidates will actually have to say something would be an important step in congressional, senatorial, and presidential races. Unless we are willing to amend the Constitution to allow campaign spending limits, it will also be necessary to enact some form of public campaign financing because of the *Buckley v. Valeo* decision. It is simply much better to have candidates beholden to the general public than to special monied interests. What we spend on political campaigns out of the general treasury would more than be made up for by what we would save on many of the provisions enacted in current laws on behalf of these special monied interests. There is also a great need to revitalize grassroots political organizations and better inform the public of the specific effects of legislation being passed and policies being adopted.

CONCLUSION

Much of this situation was predicted thirty years ago by Robert F. Kennedy, then senator from New York. In his prophetic speech, he said that Marshall McLuhan's dictum that "the medium is the message" provided a "disturbing" insight into modern politics:

For more and more, as our population increases, as the problems of our society become more complex, and as the cost of political campaigns continues to mount, it becomes more and more clear that the package is more important than the product. And that the perceived image of a candidate is often more important than what he actually has to say.

This is one reason, I believe, the political parties are turning to the pre-packaged, pre-sold candidate. . . . The cost of campaigning really has become so high, that to make a candidate and his views well enough known in a state like California or New York is impossible without either a well-known personality or enormous sums of money. . . .

This situation is rapidly becoming intolerable for a democratic society where the right to vote and to become a candidate is the ultimate political protection. We are in danger of creating a situation in which our candidates must be chosen only from the rich, the famous, or those willing to become beholden to others who will pay their bills. (Kennedy 1986)

Unless the public acts to correct the present situation both with regard to campaign financing and to the current top-down nature of our political parties, television will not only have replaced politics as a system in which real issues are discussed with politics by sound bite but will have left us with only the *image of democracy* instead of democracy itself.

NOTES

I would like to thank my colleagues Paul Petterson, Brian Janiskee, and Scott Olson for their helpful comments on this chapter and their assistance in researching some of the statistics used in it.

1. For a fuller analysis of this, see for example: Kathleen Hall Jamieson, *Packaging the Presidency: A History and Criticism of Presidential Campaign Advertising* (New York: Oxford University Press, 1996); and Kathleen Hall Jamieson, *The Interplay of Influence: News, Advertising, Politics, and the Mass Media* (Belmont, CA: Wadsworth Publishing, 1997).

2. The statistics in the preceding paragraphs were taken from Corrado, 1997: 135–71.

REFERENCES

Appleton, Andrew M., and Daniel S. Ward. 1996. *State Party Profiles: A 50-State Guide to Development, Organization, and Resources.* Washington, DC: Congressional Quarterly Press.

Bennett, W. Lance. 1988. *News: The Politics of Illusion.* New York: Longman.

Broder, David. 1971. *The Party's Over: The Failure of Politics in America.* New York: Harper & Row.

Corrado, Anthony. 1997. "Financing the 1996 Elections." In Gerald M. Pomper, ed., *The Election of 1996: Reports and Interpretations.* Chatham, NJ: Chatham House Publishers, Inc.: 135–71.

Dahl, Robert A. 1961. *Who Governs? Democracy and Power in an American City.* New Haven: Yale University Press.

Dahl, Robert A., and Lindblom, Charles E. 1953. *Politics, Economics, and Welfare.* New Brunswick, NJ: Transaction Publishers.

Edsall, Thomas Byrne. 1984. *The New Politics of Inequality.* New York: W. W. Norton & Company.

Graber, Doris A. 1993. *Mass Media and American Politics.* Washington, DC: Congressional Quarterly Press.

Greider, William. 1994. *Who Will Tell the People?* New York: Simon & Schuster.

Hofstadter, Richard. 1969. *The Idea of a Party System.* Los Angeles: University of California Press.

Hunter, Floyd. 1953. *Community Power Structure: A Study of Decision Makers.* Garden City, NJ: Doubleday.

Jamieson, Kathleen Hall. 1997. *The Interplay of Influence: News, Advertising, Politics, and the Mass* Media, 4th ed. Belmont, CA: Wadsworth.

———. 1996. *Packaging the Presidency: A History and Criticism of Presidential Campaign Advertising*, 3d ed. New York: Oxford University Press.

Kennedy, Robert. 1986. "Robert Kennedy Discusses Campaign Spending—1967." *Video Encyclopedia of the Twentieth Century.* Chapter 19. Video Disc 21, Side A (Reference No. 1218). New York: CEL Educational Resources. (A collection of several dozen laser video discs with accompanying printed reference manuals.)

Maisel, L. Sandy. 1994. *The Parties Respond: Changes in American Parties and Campaigns*, 2nd ed. Boulder, CO: Westview Press.

Mills, C. Wright. 1956. *The Power Elite.* London: Oxford University Press, Inc.

Parenti, Michael. 1986. *Inventing Reality: The Politics of the Mass Media.* New York: St. Martin's Press.

Reiter, Howard L. 1993. *Parties and Elections in Corporate America.* New York: Longman.

Sabato, Larry J. 1988. *The Party's Just Begun: Shaping Political Parties for America's Future.* Boston: Scott, Foresman and Company.

United States. Bureau of the Census. 1977. *Statistical Abstract of the United States, 1977*, 98th ed. Washington, DC: U.S. Government Printing Office.

———. 1995. *Statistical Abstract of the United States, 1995: The National Data Book*, 115th ed. Washington, DC: U.S. Department of Commerce, Economics and Statistics Administration.

5

A "Different Voice"?: Gender and Political Advertising

June Sager Speakman

Ad Title: "Arkansas Record"[*]
Produced by the 1992 Bush/Quayle Campaign

What you see: Black and white images of a rainy, windy day, a deserted road, desolate fields, and a large bird (looking vulture-like) sitting on a leafless tree.

The following phrases, referring to changes that occurred during Bill Clinton's tenure as governor of Arkansas, appear on the screen one after the other:

> *doubled state's debt*
> *doubled government spending*
> *largest tax increase in state's history*
> *45th worst to work [sic]*
> *45th worst for children*
> *worst environmental policy*
> *biggest increase in serious crime rate*
> *America can't take that risk*

What you hear: a woman's voice, soft but serious, with a hint of urgency:

In his 12 years as governor, Bill Clinton has doubled his state's debt, doubled government spending, and signed the largest tax increase in his state's history. Yet his state remains the 45th worst in which to work, the 45th worst for children. It has the worst environmental pol-

---

[*]Printed with permission of Sig Rogich, President, Rogich Communications, Las Vegas, NV.

*icy and the FBI says Arkansas had America's biggest increase in the rate of serious crime.
And now Bill Clinton wants to do for America what he's done for Arkansas. America
can't take that risk.*

This ad has many elements common to contemporary political advertising:
"simplicity of content, expert eye-ear appeal, and repetition of the message"
(Graber 1997: 244). And, as is increasingly the case with American political
advertisements, it is negative in tone, criticizing the opponent, rather than
touting the strengths of the candidate himself. Regarding the tone of the ad,
Sid Rogich, head of the Bush media campaign, said proudly, "*Arkansas Record*
was our most memorable ad. We drove Clinton to 41% negative . . . with more
time it might have made the difference" (Devlin 1993: 281).

Arkansas Record does have, however, one element that is not common to
political ads: the female voice-over. The voice that explains why Bill Clinton is a
bad choice for president is a *woman's* voice—a rare occurrence in the world of
political advertising. My analysis of more than seven hundred ads from elections at all levels, from the 1952 birth of television advertising to the 1996
election, reveals that male and female candidates alike, Republicans and
Democrats, winners and losers, use a female voice in *only 7 percent* of their advertisements. This number has been relatively stable over time despite increasing attention to the role of women in American politics. The so-called year of
the woman in American politics (1992), the emergence of a wide gender gap
and the 1996 emphasis on a cadre of "soccer moms," "waitress moms" and
other groups of women voters had little effect on the frequency of female
voices in political ads.

Table 5.1 contains a summary of several characteristics of the advertisements studied for this article: the number with female voice-overs overall, by
party, for male and female candidates, and with positive and negative messages.
The table shows that very few ads in the sample featured a female voice; that
male candidates are far more likely to use a female voice-over than are female
candidates; that Republicans are more likely to use a female voice than are
Democrats; and that female voice-overs are used in equal measure to deliver
positive and negative messages.

The world of political advertising remains a world in which the male voice
dominates. And this world matters. Televised political ads are now the dominant form of communication between candidates and potential voters. Since
1952, when the first televised political spot was aired, candidates and their
consultants have concentrated increasing amounts of time, money, and strategy on this aspect of the campaign so that by 1992, advertising costs—mostly
for television time—comprised about two-thirds of overall campaign spending
(West 1993: 7).

This investment has paid off as voters rely more on ads—and less on
news—for information about issues and candidates. In his analysis of 1996 ads
and news coverage, James Bennett concluded that "advertising seems to over-
whelm the generally perfunctory reports on the Presidential race on the local

Table 5.1
Content Analysis of Ads

Total ads in sample	722
Ads with female voice-overs	51
As a percentage of all ads	7%
Number of candidates using female voice-over	37*
Female candidates using female voice-overs	3
Male candidates using female voice-over	34
Republican candidates using female voice-over	26
Democratic candidates using female voice-over	11
Number of negative ads in sample	283
As a percentage of all ads	39%
Negative ads with female voice-over	25
As a percentage of all ads with female voice-over	49%
Ads for female candidates	108
As a percentage of all ads	15%

*Some candidates have more than one ad in the sample.

television news" (Bennett 1996: A1). Mayor Ed Rendell of Philadelphia, when asked by Bennett where voters were learning about the 1996 presidential race, replied, "It's the advertising; it's not on the news" (A1).

As news coverage has become more canned, less substantive, and more focused on the "horse race," voters have come to rely on it less, and on advertising more.[1] Consequently, both political scientists and experts in communications have begun to turn their scholarly attention to advertising as a source of voter information.[2] The increasing importance of ads has also led the political professionals who make them to become ever more skilled at their craft as they use tracking polls, focus group data, satellite tracking companies, and rapid response teams to tailor ads to narrow markets and produce technically sophisticated spots virtually overnight.[3]

The point of an ad is, of course, to "create and produce a message that will capture the attention, imagination and votes of its audience" (Witherspoon 1995: 347). Consultants understand—either through research or gut instinct—the verbal and nonverbal techniques that can be used to achieve these goals. Consultant Deno Seder, for example, describes the techniques used in the construction of one of his favorite ads—for the 1982 gubernatorial campaign of Edwin Edwards of Louisiana:

The spot opens with a medium/close-up shot of Edwards. The camera zooms back to reveal his wife and about a dozen supporters. The camera continues to zoom back and

begins to boom up, revealing several thousand supporters standing behind and around
Edwards. The camera continues to boom up to about forty feet, dramatically revealing
the Louisiana State Capitol in the background.

Reminiscent of scenes from the successful film Gandhi then in the theaters, the spot
was shot on 35 mm film and was a real "production number" in that it literally had a
"cast of thousands." (Seder 1995: 336)

As this example indicates, there are numerous elements, in addition to the
text, that make an ad persuasive, among them camera angles, film versus video-
tape, and crowd size. Kaid and Davidson point to others: kinesics (movement,
gestures), physical appearance, environments and objects, and paralanguage
(word emphasis and voice quality) (Kaid and Davidson 1986: 188).

One aspect of political advertisements that has, however, received very little
attention from either academics or political professionals is an element of paralanguage not mentioned by Kaid and Davidson: the gender of the voice-over
heard in political ads. In a collection of the 165 best articles from *Campaigns
and Elections* magazine, the self-proclaimed "magazine for political professionals," *not one* dealt with the gender of the voice-over artist (Faucheaux
1995). An extensive search of academic literature in political science and communications revealed only two analyses of political ads in which the gender of
the voice-over was considered to be a relevant variable (Biocca 1991: 103;
Johnston and White 1994: 321–29).

Does the gender of the voice-over matter? Clearly, those who make the ads
think it must. In 93 percent of the 722 ads analyzed for this study, the male
voice was chosen to deliver the message. This practice is not confined to political ads; it is mirrored in the world of product advertising as well. Here, too, the
female voice is heard far less frequently than the male voice. In their 1988
analysis of product ads, Ferrante, Haynes, and Kingsley found that a female
voice-over was heard in only 8 percent of product ads and concluded that
"women and men are not treated equally in television advertising" (1988:
236). Lovdal's 1989 review of the literature on gender bias in advertising cites
several studies from the 1970s in which between 87 and 93 percent of the
commercials sampled used male voice-overs. And in Lovdal's own sample of
353 ads, only 10 percent had a female voice-over. Further, "in virtually every
instance, women are speaking to something or someone in a subordinate position . . . cats, dogs, babies" (Lovdal 1989: 720). The Screen Actors Guild, in a
1989 study, found that women actors had 17 percent of all voice-over roles in
product commercials—a number higher than in other studies, but low enough
still to "keep the dream of making it as a commercial voice-over artist out of
reach for most actresses."[4]

For the creators of both product and campaign ads, the male voice is the
voice to use, the voice that—in the view of advertising professionals—projects
authority, evokes confidence, and persuades the consumer to buy a Mazda, or
a Budweiser, or to vote for Joan Smith for governor. As one political consultant

put it, "The voice of God is a male voice," and that is who you want speaking for your client.[5]

Despite the beliefs and practices of the producers of ads, there is little concrete evidence to support the claim that the male voice is more persuasive than a female voice. The Screen Actors Guild experimental study, conducted by McCollum/Spielman Research, concluded that, for product ads:

commercials were equally persuasive with either a female voice-over or a male voice-over. . . . The voice, which is but one of many executional elements in a television commercial, does not appear to be a factor that has significant influence on a commercial's motivational impact. . . . Viewers are not especially aware of the voice-over aspect of a commercial. Their ability to correctly identify the type of voice in these commercials was not very acute. . . . This would imply that the voice could as readily be female rather than the customary, almost automatic male voice. (McCollum/Spielman 1986: 5)

Perhaps political ads are different. Perhaps the male voice talking about politics *does* have "significant influence on a commercial's motivational impact." There is little research in this area. Biocca's analysis of the 1988 Bush-Quayle advertising campaign measures audience response to the gender of the speaker in *one* advertisement. In the ad, Barbara Bush speaks both on and off camera during the middle third of the ad. Thirty-five participants in Biocca's focus group watched the ad and registered their responses on a hand-held "computerized audience response system," dialing from one for "strongly dislike" to seven for "strongly like." When Barbara Bush's voice replaced the male voice-over, the response changed from positive to negative, especially among male viewers (Biocca 1991: 103). Thirty-five voters' laboratory responses to the voice of a well-known woman in a single ad can certainly not be taken as proof of the persuasiveness of the male voice.

Nonetheless, political consultants are convinced—even without scientific study—that using a male voice-over is a safe bet. Some consultants report that they occasionally run informal experiments of their own by taping both male and female voice-overs for a given spot and running each for a focus group and for the candidate him- or herself. According to one consultant, the male voice almost always "wins" with both audiences.

Other consultants reported their own reactions to male and female voices. One Democratic consultant said that he would like, on principle, to use more female voices but that the "quality of female voices is not that good." What is a "good" voice? The same consultant replied that he could not describe one, but he knew it when he heard it, and it was almost always male. A Republican consultant agreed, noting that both he and his clients expect his ads to have that "rich Reagan-era type of voice."

Consultants from both parties posited that most female voices have too high a tone to be appropriate for the serious business of politics. The female voice-over artists interviewed for this study had low serious voices and agreed that these qualities were the keys to their success in their profession. Nancy

Lewmans, who does voices for Democratic campaigns, said that "political people will not touch women with so-called 'vanilla voices'" (light and high) because they lack the weight needed to carry a political message. Scott Sanders,
described by the *New Yorker* as "one of the leading political voice-over artists
in the nation" and the voice behind approximately eight hundred ads in the
1994 campaign cycle, says that the key to his success is the "low pitch," "reso-
nance" and "carefully controlled energy of his voice" ("The Man Behind the
Voice" 1994: 49). Perhaps women just cannot provide these vocal qualities.

Whether these claims about the ineffectiveness of the female voice are true
cannot be assessed here. As noted Democratic consultant Robert Squier observes: "The very best people in this business [the production of campaign ad-
vertisements] probably understand only about five to seven percent of what it
is that they do that works. The rest is all out there in the unknown" (Diamond
and Bates 1992: 353). The relative persuasiveness of the male and female voice
is one of those unknowns. But, again, the consultants *believe* the male voice
works better, in most cases, than the female voice. And until there is proof that
the use of a female voice will lead to victory, consultants will continue to use
the male voice.

The stakes in their business are high. These are expensive ads, aired on expensive networks. These are ads that are frequently conceived, written, and
produced in a period of days, even hours. These are ads that may make or break
a candidacy. Under these conditions, the natural and understandable tendency
is to go with what has worked in the past. As one ad executive said, "Advertising tends to be not a reflection of the future. It tends to be a reflection of the
past. There's a reluctance from advertisers to talk right past the audience. You
need to touch base with points of familiarity. If you use devices or attitudes that
are ahead of people, you're likely to miss your target" (Kalish 1988: 31).

Political consultants—male and female alike—are notably risk-averse, and
thus unlikely to try something new, even when the striking imbalance between
male and female voices is pointed out to them. As one said, "We produce ads to
win races, not to win awards." And the practice in their business is: "You do
what you've done before and what you know works. . . . do the norm *unless
there's a reason to do otherwise*." The norm is the voice of a man.

But there are occasions when consultants wish to veer from the norm, and
then they will use a female. In other words, the male voice—because of its perceived greater authority—is the "default," the automatic choice, but the female voice has its place. If the consultant believes that his or her candidate is
perceived as being too harsh, a female voice can be used to smooth the hard
edges. If a consultant wishes to have a male candidate speak on a "female" issue, notably abortion, a female voice may be used to lend credibility.

NEGATIVE SPOTS

Of the 722 ads analyzed for this research, fifty-one had a female voice-over.
Of these fifty-one ads, twenty-five—just under one half—were negative ads, in

which the woman narrator delivered an attack on the candidate's opponent. (Of the total sample of 722, 39 percent were negative.)

All of the consultants interviewed for this study acknowledged that, in the rare cases where they do choose a female voice, it will often be with the explicit purpose of delivering an attack. There are two reasons for this. First, as one consultant said, she used this technique because "the female voice lends legitimacy to a negative spot." While the male voice is considered (by the consultants, and—in their view—by the voters) more weighty and authoritative, the female voice is seen (or heard) to be more credible and honest. In an attack ad, the words themselves have weight; the tone of the female voice makes those words more credible.

Second, there is considerable evidence that voters are often "turned off" by negative ads. Ansolabehere and Iyengar blame the "proliferation of negative political advertising" for "record lows in political participation, record highs in public cynicism and alienation, and record rates of disapproval" of elected politicians (1995: 3). Some consultants' concerns about this "bad taste" left by negative advertising have led them to use women's voices to soften the attack. A female voice-over artist observed that "when an ad is particularly vicious, a female voice will often be used to take the edge off the viciousness," and thus diminish the risk of offending the voter. One Republican consultant explained this practice as follows: "It's meant to take some of the meanness out of it. Sometimes an ominous male voice issuing a harsh attack can sound like an ad for a horror movie instead of a candidate you'd want to vote for" (Vaillancourt 1996: B1).

The anti-Clinton ad described at the beginning of this article is an example of this practice. Another illustration comes from the 1984 contest between Gordon Humphrey and Norm D'Amours for a New Hampshire Senate seat. In the ad—an attack by Humphrey on D'Amours—an elderly woman appears on camera sitting at a kitchen table with a steaming mug of tea before her. The viewer immediately likes this woman and wants to listen to her. The voices heard in the ad are hers and an off-camera female narrator. Together, they tell the viewer that D'Amours has been lying to the voters about Humphrey's record on social security. The viewer thinks, "How could anyone lie to the lovely woman, who reminds me so much of my sweet grandmother?" The last line, delivered by the tea drinker, is, "Shame on you, Mr. D'Amours." A male speaker could not deliver that line credibly, but the female voice has the desired impact.

ISSUE SPOTS

Negative ads are not the only ones for which female narrators are chosen. Consultants report that there are certain issues on which females can speak as credibly, or perhaps more credibly, than males. All of the fifty-one ads spoken by women concerned one of the following issue areas: abortion, children, family policies, health care, social security, the environment, and crime. Again, consultants acknowledge that these patterns are not the result of happenstance. The female voice is used because a purposive strategic decision has been made to use it. That decision is based on the assumption that certain issues are "women's issues."

With regard to abortion, the logic of this decision is clear. If a male candidate wishes to make either a pro- or an anti-abortion ad, he can increase the legitimacy of his position on this "women's issue" by using a female as the "voice of authority." A particularly pointed example of this practice is found in an ad from incumbent Republican Jesse Helms's 1990 campaign against Harvey Gantt for a South Carolina Senate seat. The ad is sharply negative in tone and is targeted at women voters in particular. It is difficult to imagine the ad's text being read by a man.

In the ad, a woman in a red sweater appears against a dark gray background. Her demeanor is serious, her voice low, with a slight southern accent. She says (Purdue University 1990):

It bothers me that a politician is running *ads that scare women* just to get votes. The truth is, Harvey Gantt is avoiding some important facts. Harvey Gantt is asking *you and me* to approve of some pretty awful things. Aborting a child in the final weeks of pregnancy, aborting a child *because it's a girl instead of a boy*. That's too liberal. Harvey Gantt is asking us to approve of some pretty extreme measures to vote for him (emphasis added).

A second—and equally effective—abortion ad with a woman narrator was produced by the Marshall Coleman campaign in his 1989 attempt to defeat Democrat Doug Wilder in the race for the governorship of Virginia. This spot was produced in response to Wilder's charge (also spoken by a woman) that Coleman had an extreme position on abortion. The ad shows three beautiful blond babies (Wilder, by the way, is African American; Coleman is white) clad only in diapers, playing together on the floor. A woman's voice—as always, soft, low, and serious— says (Purdue University 1990):

Do you think abortion should be allowed even in the late stages of pregnancy?
Doug Wilder does.
Do you think a father should be prohibited from having any rights whatsoever concerning the killing of his unborn child?
Doug Wilder does.
Do you think abortion should be allowed as a method of birth control?
Doug Wilder does.
Now, whose position sounds extreme? Yours? Or his?

As these two abortion ads show, the female voice can be used with powerful effect. Consultants understand that female voices can persuade voters, but (they believe) only in specific circumstances. So the consultants make careful and deliberate choices about when to employ a female narrator.

CONCLUSION

This may change. It may, in fact, have already changed. Most consultants interviewed for this study acknowledge that there have been dramatic changes in the role of women in American politics over the past two decades, both in terms of the numbers of women running for office and in the behavior of women as voters. After the 1996 election, 12 percent of the members of Congress were women, up from 4 percent in 1975; 25 percent of statewide elective offices were held by women, up from 10 percent in 1975; and 21 percent of state legislators were women, compared with 8 percent twenty years earlier (Conway et al. 1997: 107). More Americans than ever say that they are willing to vote for a qualified woman for president. Voter turnout has been higher among women than among men in every presidential election since 1984 (79). And despite Richard Nixon's claim that "the only difference between men and women voters is that women don't pull the lever as hard" (Mattei and Mattei 1998: 432), women have emerged as a distinct voting bloc. By 1996, some were referring to the so-called gender gap as the "gender chasm." In that presidential election, Bill Clinton received 54 percent of the women's vote and 43 percent of the men's vote, while Bob Dole received 38 percent of the women's vote and 44 percent of the men's vote. Women clearly made the difference in the reelection of President Clinton (Conway et al. 1997: 138). As Conway and her coauthors note, these trends reflect the fact that "cultural change has made politics less a 'man's thing'" (22).

Whether these changes will be reflected in the choice of voice-overs for political advertising remains to be seen. The architects of political advertising, as conservative and risk averse as they are, will not jump to adjust their campaign strategies to changing political and social realities. The male voice has, in the view of the consultants, helped to elect both male and female candidates. If they sense that this practice is no longer working, they will change. If however, the male voice still brings their candidates to victory, the consultants are bound to ignore the "different voice" and stay with the "voice of God."

A NOTE ON METHOD

The findings summarized in this chapter emerged from the analysis of 722 campaign ads. The ads came from a variety of sources: *Campaigns and Elections* magazine, the Purdue University Public Affairs Video Archive, the Devlin Archive at the University of Rhode Island, and directly from two dozen media consulting firms. The collection is broadly representative. The spots are from campaigns from 1952 through 1996, from candidates running for offices ranging from the mayor of New Orleans to president of the United States, from Republican and Democratic campaigns, and from winning and losing candidates. Each ad was viewed and coded by at least two, and usually three, coders. The following characteristics were recorded for each ad:

- Candidate's name and gender
- Gender of voice-over
- Office being sought
- Candidate's voice used?
- Political party
- Positive or negative in tone?
- State
- Issue
- Year
- Gender of people in the ad
- Consultant
- Funding source for the ad

NOTES

My thanks to the Roger Williams University Research Foundation for a Summer Faculty Development Grant and to Alyson Smith, my research assistant.

1. For recent analyses of these trends see "Point of View" website, http://www.pbs.org:80?pov/ad/ads/ad.facts.html; and Lichter and Noyes 1996.

2. See, for example, West 1993; Ansolabehere and Iyengar 1995; Kaid 1986; Patterson and McClure 1976; Biocca, ed. 1991.

3. See, for example, the anecdote in Rosenstiel 1993: 286–87.

4. "The Female. . ." 1990: 12; and Kalish 1988: 30.

5. All quotations from campaign consultants are taken from a series of phone interviews conducted in 1992, 1994, and 1997. Most of these interviews were done on a not-for-attribution basis.

REFERENCES

Ansolabehere, Stephen, and Shanto Iyengar. 1995. *Going Negative: How Political Advertisements Shrink and Polarize the Electorate*. New York: The Free Press.

Bennett, James. 1996. "With Political Ads, Little Goes a Long Way." *New York Times*, October 14, A1.

Biocca, Frank. 1991. "Models of a Successful and Unsuccessful Ad: An Exploratory Analysis." In Frank Biocca, ed., *Television and Political Advertising*. Hillsdale, NJ: Lawrence Erlbaum Associates.

Conway, M. Margaret, Gertrude A. Steuernagel, and David W. Ahern. 1997. *Women and Political Participation*. Washington, DC: Congressional Quarterly Press.

Devlin, L. Patrick. 1993. "Contrasts in Presidential Campaign Commercials of 1992." *American Behavioral Scientist* 37, 2 (November): 281.

Diamond, Edwin, and Stephen Bates. 1992. *The Spot: The Rise of Political Advertising on Television*. Cambridge: MIT Press.

Faucheux, Ron, ed. 1995. *The Road to Victory*. Washington, DC: Kendall Hunt.

"The Female in Focus: In Whose Image?" 1990. *Screen Actor* (fall): 12.

Ferrante, Carol L., Andrew M. Haynes, and Sarah M. Kingsley. 1988. "Image of Women in Television Advertising." *Journal of Broadcast and Electronic Media* 32, 2 (spring): 236.

Graber, Doris A. 1997. *Mass Media and American Politics*, 5th ed. Washington, DC: Congressional Quarterly Press.

Johnston, Anne, and Anne Barton White. 1994. "Communication Styles and Female Candidates: A Study of the Political Advertising during the 1986 Senate Elections." *Journalism Quarterly* 71, 2 (summer): 321–29.

Kaid, Linda Lee, and Dorothy K. Davidson. 1986. "Elements of Videostyle." In Linda Lee Kaid and Dorothy K. Davidson, eds., *New Perspectives on Political Advertising*. Carbondale: Southern Illinois Press: 188.

Kalish, David. 1988. "Which Sex Speaks Louder?" *Marketing and Media Decisions* (March): 30.

Lichter, S. Robert, and Richard Noyes. 1996. *Media Monitor*. Washington, DC: Center for Media and Public Affairs.

Lovdal, Lynn T. 1989. "Sex Role Messages in Television Commercials: An Update." *Sex Roles* 21, (Nov/Dec): 720.

"The Man Behind the Voice Behind the 1994 Elections." 1994. *The New Yorker* 70, 39 (November 28): 49.

Mattei, Laura R. Winsky, and Franco Mattei. 1998. "If Men Stayed Home. . . . The Gender Gap in Recent Congressional Elections." *Political Research Quarterly* 51, 2 (June): 411–26.

McCollum/Spielman Research. 1986. "Screen Actors Guild Voice-Over Study" (March): 5.

Patterson, Thomas, and Robert D. McClure. 1976. *The Unseeing Eye*. New York: Putnam.

"Point of View" website. Http://www.pbs.org:80?pov/ad/ads/ad.facts.html

Purdue University Public Affairs Video Archives. 1990. "1990 Congressional Campaign Commercials." Compiled Program.

Rogich, Sig, President, Rogich Communications, Las Vegas, NV. 1992. "Arkansas Record" (political advertisement).

Rosenstiel, Tom. 1993. *Strange Bedfellows*. New York: Hyperion.

Seder, Deno. 1995. "Film vs. Tape: Choosing a Format for Political Television Ads." In Ron Faucheux, ed., *The Road to Victory*. Washington, DC: Kendall Hunt: 336.

Vaillancourt, Meg. 1996. "Campaigns Try to Soften Image." *Boston Globe*, October 16, B1.

West, Darrell. 1993. *Air Wars*. Washington, DC: Congressional Quarterly Press.

Witherspoon, John. 1995. "Campaign Commercials." In Ron Faucheux, ed., *The Road to Victory*. Washington, DC: Kendall Hunt: 347.

6

Who Are "We" and What Do "We" Want? Representations of the Public in Election News

Stephanie Greco Larson

What the public wants is usually measured by public opinion polls and election outcomes. Although politicians look to both, they also use media coverage to ascertain the public's desires. Citizens, not in the business of reading polls, rely even more on this press coverage. Therefore, it is important to see what the media tells "us" about ourselves—who "we" are and what "we" want.

Answers to these questions are especially important when we consider the impact that media coverage has on public opinion. It can set the public's agenda by focusing attention on some issues rather than others (Iyengar and Kinder 1987: 33). It can influence how we judge politicians and candidates by "priming" the public to use certain issues in their evaluations (Iyengar 1991). It can lead to a minority silencing itself (Noelle-Neumann 1984). It can create "bandwagon effects," where people join the winning side, or "underdog effects," where they join the other side (Traugott 1992: 136–40).

One way that the media covers public opinion is by using polls. News organizations commission polls (Ladd and Benson 1992: 19–20) and use them extensively because precise, scientific, and seemingly impartial data are thought to capture a truth about public opinion (Salmon and Glasser 1995: 444). However, since polls only ask certain questions and reporters select among these to illustrate stories they are trying to tell, poll "truth" is at best a partial truth. During campaigns these stories are usually about the horse race

(Robinson and Sheehan 1983: 148; Patterson 1993: 72–73). The "game schema" that dominates reporting elections emphasizes strategies and outcomes (who's ahead and who's behind) (Patterson 1993: 60–68). Therefore, poll reporting often shifts the focus away from the public and toward the candidates (Kerbel 1994: 15–34).

Polling is not the only way that news can cover public opinion during an election. Reporters can also ask "people on the street" what they think and feel. Although little research has examined how members of the public are used in the news, Matthew Robert Kerbel (1994: 96) found that "voters or undifferentiated members of the mass public" were the subject or object of 18 percent of the 1992 presidential election coverage on ABC Evening News. Since who these members of the mass public are and what they say is still unknown, it is important to take a closer look at "people-on-the-street" coverage. This chapter will examine national television evening news' representations of the public in the 1992 and 1996 general election campaigns to answer this question: "According to ABC, CBS, and NBC, who are 'we' and what do 'we' want?" Specifically, how polls were used by the networks, what people were selected to interview, and what these people said about the candidates, issues, and campaign will be examined.

METHODS: MEASURING COVERAGE OF THE PUBLIC

Television coverage of the public in the 1992 presidential general election campaign (from Labor Day to Election Day) was analyzed by coding the Vanderbilt Television Archive Index. For the presidential general election campaign in 1996, the actual news stories that included polls and "people-on-the-street" interviews were coded.

Identifying Segments, 1992

Summaries of television news stories presented in the Vanderbilt Television Indexes from Labor Day until Election Day 1992 served as the data.[1] All news segments listed under "Presidential Election Campaign (1992)—Polls" were examined to see when and how polls were used in the reports. The general range of issues discussed in the campaign news was detected by using the "Presidential Election Campaign (1992)—Issues" index entry. Segments listed here were coded to see what issues were covered and whether polls were used in these issue stories. To find "people on the street," all descriptions of presidential election stories were examined for references to people and groups of people.

Coding Segments, 1992

Stories including polls were counted and categorized into the following groups: horse race, candidate evaluation, or issue. Those stories which covered issues were coded as to which issue was identified. Members of the general public (not politicians, academic experts, or spokespeople for interest groups) were considered "people on the street." These individuals were coded (when possible) for their sex, geographic location, and occupation.

Identifying Segments, 1996

From Labor Day to Election Day the three major networks' weekday evening news shows were taped and examined for relevant presidential election coverage. Election stories were selected for additional analysis if they contained public opinion polls or members of the general public talking.[2]

Coding Segments, 1996

Stories that mentioned public opinion polls were coded as to whether the poll focused on the horse race, candidate evaluations, issues, or "other" (which included evaluations of the status quo, the campaign, or politics). If the poll report was issue related, the type of issue and the position of the majority of respondents were noted. Stories that included members of the general public talking (referred to here as "people-on-the-street" interviews) were coded for their sex, race (based on appearance, name, and/or how the person was identified in the story), and age (as young, middle, old; using identification of age or relevant status—high school student, nursing home resident—or appearance).[3] If explicitly identified in the story, the person's occupation, geographic location, and vote choice were noted. The topics of their comments were also coded into these categories: candidate evaluations, issues, evaluations of the status quo, or evaluations of the government or campaign.[4] For qualitative interpretations, notes were taken on the individuals' comments and how the reporter framed these.

HORSE RACE POLLS AND "PEOPLE-ON-THE-STREET" REPORTING IN 1992

Polls

There were fifty-six segments of the national evening news during the general election of 1992 that used public opinion polls. These polls primarily focused on horse race standings and on the perceptions of the candidates' personal qualities. Only six of the stories dealt with the public's evaluations of issues (one of these stories talked about two issues). Therefore, 11 percent of the poll stories mentioned policy issues. The issues that were discussed in the poll coverage were: economic plans (three and a half stories), taxes (one half), health care (one), and family values (one).[5] These poll reports indicated that the public disapproved of Bush's handling of the economy, thought that Clinton would do a better job, supported Clinton's "economic plan," thought that the economy was the most important issue, and identified unemployment as the most important economic problem. The index descriptions were too vague to detect the public's positions on health care, family values (except that they were "turned off by the issue"), or taxes.

This paltry coverage of the public's issue positions using polls can be compared to the amount of issue coverage during the campaign overall by noting the 171 separate entries in the index under "Presidential Election Campaign (1992)—Issues." These included twenty-three different issue topics.[6] The most frequently discussed issues were (in order): economy, taxes, health care, and the budget. Although these issues were discussed, polls on how the public felt about the issues were infrequent, despite extensive polling during the campaign. Poll reporting instead told us who the public was likely to vote for—a message that would eventually be communicated on election day. It is interesting that the topics covered the most were ones that the president dealt with once he got into office (as would be expected by Fishel 1985: 50). Clinton attempted to reform the health care system, he helped lower the deficit and improve the economy, and he raised (some) taxes.

"People on the Street"

There were twice as many stories including "people on the street" as there were stories including polls. Four hundred and twenty-five "people-on-the-street" segments were included in 104 general election campaign stories.[7] The three networks did not differ substantially in their number of "people-on-the-street" stories (ABC, thirty-three; CBS, thirty-eight; NBC, thirty-three).[8]

Who represented the public in the "people-on-the-street" selections was difficult to detect from the abstracts. While there seemed to be more men (134) than women (ninety-seven), 194 people's sex was unidentifiable. Race was almost always impossible to code. Locations of the stories demonstrated that these "people on the street" were from sixty-nine different places. Occupation was identifiable for 190 of these individuals representing eighty-one different jobs.[9] Frequently the individuals were identified as unemployed (twelve people). This number fails to include others outside of the workforce such as welfare recipients, retirees, students, and housewives (forty-four people). The selection of these individuals reinforced the idea of economic vulnerability upon which Clinton campaigned (Just et al. 1996: 72).

These data indicate that poll coverage was not the dominant way that television news covered the public. Most poll coverage directed attention toward the candidates and the campaign, not toward the public. Despite the reliability of polls for measuring the public's positions, national television reporters were far more likely to use "people on the street" to assess the public's positions. Whether actually on the street, in network-created focus groups, on the job, or in their kitchens, an array of "everyday people" was asked to talk about the campaign. Most of what they were saying was impossible to detect from the index descriptions provided by the Vanderbilt Archive. Therefore, actual stories need to be looked at to get a clearer picture of who was talked to, what was said, and how this compares to polls.

MORE HORSE RACE COVERAGE FROM POLL REPORTS: FINDINGS FOR 1996

There were sixty-eight presidential general election news stories that included polls in 1996. This is slightly more than for 1992 despite less media coverage overall of the general election in 1996 (Just 1997: 97). Typically, when networks used polls, they defined "who" as all survey respondents (representing all Americans). They rarely broke the survey down to highlight the attitudes of subgroups (like blacks, southerners, or "angry white men"). ABC had more poll stories than the other two networks. Fifty percent of ABC's poll stories, compared to 11 percent of NBC's and none of CBS's, showed more than one poll to demonstrate how the relative positions of the three candidates had changed (or more often, not changed) over time.

Overall, poll coverage was dominated by horse race reporting with 89 percent of the poll stories including the relative levels of support for the candidates. Horse race coverage dominated all three network poll stories (see Table 6.1).

Issue coverage using polls was infrequent (8) and not always about the public's actual positions. Some dealt with issue saliency (using questions like

Table 6.1
Topics Mentioned in Poll Reporting, 1996

Network	All Polls	Horse Race	Candid. Eval.	Issue	Other
ABC	30	30 (100%)	3 (10%)	0	2 (7%)
CBS	20	15 (75%)	2 (11%)	6 (33%)	3 (17%)
NBC	18	14 (78%)	2 (11%)	2 (11%)	3 (17%)
TOTAL	68	59 (87%)	7 (10%)	8 (12%)	8 (12%)

Note: The top percentages indicate the percentage of times that these things appeared on that network's poll stories. For example, 10 percent of the 30 poll stories on ABC contained character discussion. These numbers do not add up to 100 percent because a poll story can include more than one of these topics. "Other" includes evaluations of the state of the nation or the campaign.

"How important are issues compared to character when you vote?" and "What's the most important problem facing the nation today?"). Sometimes questions were used that asked the respondents to predict rather than evaluate what candidates were doing or would do ("Do you think Dole will cut taxes?" "Which candidate dealt with the issues more during the debate?").[10] Therefore, much of the scanty issue coverage was actually about the campaign.

Among the eight poll stories coded as "issues," only four used polls to explicitly identify the public's policy positions. Two of these lacked any numbers or specificity. CBS reported on September 24, 1996, that Clinton's "private polls" indicated that he was "vulnerable on the tax issue," and a Republican pollster was shown on NBC saying that polls indicated that a majority of the public preferred Republican solutions until they were told that the positions were the Republicans' (October 14). Other issue positions reported were: disapproval of Medicare changes (CBS, October 2), opposition to the Republicans' role in the government shutdown (CBS, October 2), support for Clinton's military action in Iraq (CBS, September 19), and support for Clinton's handling of the economy (CBS, September 19).[11] Adding these four stories to those dealing with issue saliency and issue attributions produces a total of eight issue-related polling stories during the general election (12 percent of the total number of polling stories).

Other polls were used to discuss how the public evaluated Clinton and Dole. Seven stories dealt with the public's perceptions of the candidates' integrity, truthfulness, honesty, ethics, morality, trustworthiness, negativity, friendliness, likeability, or general character. Although the impact of character evaluations on voting was reported as being less influential than issues, polls measuring them were used just as often in the news.

Other stories demonstrated the public's cynicism and evaluations of the campaign itself. For example, NBC noted that 57 percent of the public thought that the election would have little or no impact on their lives (October 23), and Tom Brokaw stated (without providing any evidence) that "polls show that the campaign has been long and uninspiring" (November 5, NBC). Questions about how satisfied the public was with their choice of candidates were sometimes used to illustrate the public's dissatisfaction. For example, CBS reported that exit polls indicated that Colin Powell would have won the election had he run. ABC's October 14 report that a large percentage of Clinton's support was "with reservations" reinforced an impression of a disaffected electorate (critical of the quality of the candidates) and might have been inspired by reporters' desire for a close and exciting race (Robinson and Sheehan 1984: 107). On the other hand, ABC reported on September 30 that 71 percent of those who supported Clinton were satisfied with their choices. Other poll stories added information about the race: the finding that people said that Perot's running mate choice would make no difference in their voting choices (September 11, ABC) and that Clinton was thought to have won the debates.[12]

Overall, what did the networks' poll coverage in the 1996 campaign tell us about what the public wanted? It told us that more voters supported Clinton than Dole from the start to the finish of the general election campaign. They thought Dole was more honest and trustworthy than Clinton, but this did not bear heavily on their candidate preferences. It is hard to say from this coverage what policies the public wanted because of the infrequency and nature of the polls about issues. Basically, the news said that the public felt good about the state of the nation and the direction in which it was going. They credited Clinton for good management of the economy, protecting Medicare, choosing the appropriate action to take with Iraq, and they did not blame him for the drug problem or the government shutdown.

"PEOPLE ON THE STREET" IN 1996: A VARIETY OF VOCAL AMERICANS

Presence of "People on the Street"

In contrast to four years earlier, there were not as many stories in 1996 that included "people on the street" as there were stories including polls. Nevertheless, forty-two campaign news segments during the general election included members of the public talking; half of these were in news features—NBC's "Across America" (six), NBC's "Fixing America" (eleven), and CBS's "In Touch with America" (four).[13] In total, 145 different "people on the street" were talked to on the news.[14] More than half of the "people on the street" were on NBC (eighty-five). Even excluding the thirty-six people from the "Fixing America" feature, NBC had more "people" than the other networks. CBS talked to the fewest people (thirteen compared to ABC's forty-seven).

Characteristics of "People on the Street"

In 1996, 48 percent of the individuals talked to were women, which slightly underestimates the national demographics.[15] Fourteen stories explicitly discussed gender gaps. There were more white "people on the street" (83 percent) than nonwhite, which is similar to the nation's demographics. The age distribution included more middle-aged individuals (67 percent) than "old" (19 percent) or "young" (14 percent).[16]

"People on the street" were from thirty-one different geographic locations including twenty states. The largest numbers came from Pennsylvania (sixteen), Illinois (thirteen), and Ohio (eleven). Occupation was identified for eighty-four of these individuals representing fifty-one different jobs. The most frequent groups were teachers (seven) and students (six). Just as being unemployed seemed to help people get on the news in 1992, being identified with education seemed to help individuals get on the news in 1996.[17]

Statements by "People on the Street"

Table 6.2 illustrates the topical breakdown of comments made by the "people on the street." Clearly, issue coverage was the most prevalent (42 percent). Evaluations of the status quo got the least attention (8 percent). Candidate evaluations and evaluations of politics or the campaign fell in between (27 percent and 23 percent, respectively). Although NBC had the most comments and CBS had the least, for both, the largest percentage of comments were about issues (48 percent and 53 percent, respectively). Similar to the focus on the race found in ABC's poll reports, this network's "people-on-the-street" segments talked least about issues.

Only twenty-four "people on the street" declared their candidate preferences (fifteen people said they supported Clinton and nine supported Dole). In addition, much of what people talked about on the news was not explicitly related to their candidate choices. Often they talked about what they wanted for the future, how their situations compared to the past (usually economically), how they wanted the candidates to campaign, what they thought other people's opinions were, or how disillusioned they were.

There was much talk about hopes and dreams (especially on "Fixing America") that did not mention the election explicitly. "Across America" encour-

Table 6.2
Topics of Comments by "People on the Streets," 1996 by Network

	Candidate				Issue Specific Goals		Eval. of Status Quo	Eval. of Politics/ Campaign	Total
	BD+	BD-	BC+	BC-					
ABC	2	8	4	5	14	0	2	16	51
		(37%)			(28%)		(4%)	(31%)	(100%)
CBS	1	2	1	1	7	1	1	1	15
		(33%)			(53%)		(7%)	(7%)	(100%)
NBC	3	6	7	4	32	17	11	22	102
		(20%)			(48%)		(11%)	(21%)	(100%)
TOTAL	6	16	12	10	53	18	14	39	168
		(27%)			(42%)		(8%)	(23%)	(100%)

Note: The letters and +/- sign under candidates indicate the candidate and the direction of the comments made about them. For example, BD+ are comments about Bob Dole that were positive.

aged people to talk about their own economic situation as it related to the election and their lives. Comments like "If it's not broke, don't fix it" (NBC, September 19) and "Things are better" (NBC, September 26) reiterated positions that were reported in polls showing satisfaction with and optimism for the economy (Pomper 1997: 191). "People on the street" complained about Congress, specific policies, and the campaign (who the candidates were, what they were saying, what they failed to say, and how the media covered them). Cynicism about politics, the campaign, and nonvoting were themes when reporters talked to citizens in Vandalia, Illinois (NBC, September 26); Sante Fe, New Mexico (NBC, October 24); Cleveland (ABC, October 10); and Philadelphia (ABC, October 15). Despite the prevalent cynicism of the news, ABC's election night report (November 5) concluded with optimistic "people on the street" making system-supportive statements like, "People voting—that's what makes this country work."

Comments about the candidates included a greater proportion of positive statements about Clinton than Dole (see Table 6.2). Clinton was noted for caring about the disadvantaged, addressing the working class, improving the economy, cutting the deficit, and being in touch with the concerns of the people (especially young people). Favorable words were used to describe him: professional, a gentleman, presidential, and strong. His debate performances were also complimented (saying he had taken the "high road" and won).

Some "people on the street" criticized Clinton's debate performance saying that he talked down to the audience, did not say much, was too negative, and was too scripted. Some felt his ethics were a problem, that he was dishonest about the economy, and that he needed to show more leadership. One woman stated her opposition to the family leave bill as a reason she would not support him (ABC, October 9). The most negative statement made about the president was from a woman who yelled, "You're a draft-dodging, yellow-bellied liar" as he jogged on the beach (ABC, October 16). Overall, the "people on the street" seemed to illustrate what was later revealed in exit polls—that "the electorate preferred political to personal virtues" (Pomper 1997: 194), a preference that seems to have persisted long into Bill Clinton's second term of office.

Comments made about Dole were usually negative. He was described as appearing mean, desperate, out of touch, without a plan, and not a good communicator in the debates. Some people opposed his issue positions on abortion and Medicare. Others said he was out of touch (with reality, with the working class, with the middle class, and with them). Still others claimed he was "too old" or "too Republican." These assessments are also consistent with those expressed in exit polls (Pomper 1997: 193). Dole's Republicanism was criticized because it included Newt Gingrich and was thought to have moved too far right, caused the government shutdown, had a bad history on racial issues, and an undesirable position on immigration. Many "people on the street" were skeptical about Dole's proposed tax cut and some dismissed his

("Just Don't Do It") antidrug rhetoric ("You need more than a slogan to change the world," one person noted on CBS, September 18). This response seems to clash with the exit poll showing that Dole did slightly better among those who said the drug issue influenced their voting (197).

Positive statements about Dole were that he did well in the debate (was natural, won, and seemed sincere). One person at a rally communicated support without specifics saying, "Can I vote for you twice?" (NBC, September 13). But even a woman who said that she was supporting Dole (ABC, September 23) lamented that "it would have been nice to have a different (Republican) candidate." Overall, the voices on the news were more favorable to Clinton than Dole, which is consistent with exit polls (Pomper 1997: 193).[18]

CONCLUSIONS

Poll coverage in both 1992 and 1996 focused little on what the public wanted besides Clinton as president. Despite the potential for poll coverage to tell us what the public wanted of their government and its leaders, polls were not used in this fashion by the networks. However, "people-on-the-street" interviews were. A variety of people—women, men, blacks, whites, young, old, middle aged from across the country and different jobs—expressed their points of view on television news during the general election. This picture of the public contrasts greatly with the undifferentiated "public" of public opinion poll reporting.

An interesting finding is how different 1992 and 1996 were in terms of the news' issue emphasis. Despite the fact that the economy was the number one issue that people said they used to decide whom to vote for in both elections (Pomper 1997: 197; Ceaser and Busch 1993: 167), it only dominated the coverage in 1992. This emphasis was reflected in the news in the issue coverage (which did not always include the public), the issue poll coverage, and the choice to use unemployed "people on the street." It might also have been reflected in the substance of the "people-on-the-street" interviews that were not examined here. This focus reflected (or perhaps facilitated) Clinton's dominant campaign strategy—"It's the economy stupid" (Ceaser and Busch 1993: 19).

The economy did not dominate 1996 public opinion coverage. Another issue important to the public, education, did. This issue was emphasized in "people-on-the-street" coverage through framing of the stories (reporters said that people they talked to were interested in education without providing illustrative sound bites), the use of schools as locations to find people to talk to (done on NBC, September 3; NBC, October 14; ABC, October 7; and ABC, September 18), and the occupational dominance of people in the education field. Education was the issue deemed "the most important" by a CBS poll reported on October 21 and the second "most important" in an ABC poll reported on September 20. However, people claimed to be more influenced by the economy/jobs and Medicare (and equally influenced by the deficit) when they voted (Pomper 1997: 197). Therefore, it seems that the reporters and editors used discretion in deciding which issue to focus on. To some extent they followed the public's lead (because education was important to them), but there were many other issues important to the public (jobs, health care) and emphasized by the candidates (drug use) that reporters rejected in favor of this education emphasis. One possibility for the network's focus on education is that it gave them a "handle" on the gender gap. By focusing on education, the media was able to talk about "soccer moms"—the "electoral interpretation establishment['s]" 1996 "darling" (DiIulio 1997: 169)—by oversimplifying their concerns.

The ability of the media to choose education over other popular issues and emphasize it through the questions they asked, the places they went, and the people they chose to talk to could affect voting. In this case, "priming effects"—voters using the issues discussed on the news to evaluate the candidates (Iyengar and Kinder 1987: 197)—would have worked to Clinton's advantage since exit polls indicated that 78 percent of those who said that the issue of education influenced their votes voted for him (Pomper 1997: 197).[19]

The potential for reporter selectivity to distort the "public's voice" is perhaps greater for "people-on-the-street" reports than for polls. Poll questions that deal with substance might be cast aside in search of horse race polls, but their results are harder to misrepresent than "people-on-the-street" interviews are. The interviews that reporters choose among are more varied and the messages within them easier to edit and frame. Examples of how a reporter used "people-on-the-street" comments to tell a different story than the one intended by the people interviewed were observed on NBC's "Across America" feature. During the November 24 segment, the reporter asked members of the Toastmasters Club in Sante Fe, "Why don't people vote?" Despite the fact that their answers were about "other people," he concluded that their comments revealed why *they* were disaffected. In fact, when one speaker said, "They're not interested because we're in good shape" the camera showed a close-up of a red light. This light was used by the club to indicate when a speaker's time had expired, but it conveyed a different message when used by the reporter. In another "Across America" segment (September 26), the same reporter introduced a story that contained many optimistic comments about the town and its economic recovery by saying "Legend has it that people here don't trust politicians" and concluded it by warning that the townspeople are keeping "an eye down the road for trouble."

Despite these problems, in most ways "people on the street" represented the majority of the electorate: they were more positive about Clinton than Dole and had little interest in Perot (Keeter 1997: 192–97). They thought Clinton was unethical, but it did not matter much to them (Keeter 1997: 122; Pomper 1997: 193–94). They thought that the economy was doing well (and the incumbent should be rewarded for it), but government and politics had flaws that were not the fault of one party or candidate (Keeter 1997: 120). The "people-on-the-street" interviews also conveyed more than the polls did by providing opinions on a wider range of issues than typically found on poll questionnaires. Therefore, television news' answer to "Who are 'we' and what do 'we' want?" is: *Both* an undifferentiated mass (public) who wanted Clinton to be president (though the reasons are widely varied or unclear) *and* a diverse array of individuals (of different sexes, colors, ages, occupations, hometowns) with a range of opinions about the candidates, the issues, politics, and the nation.

NOTES

1. Missing data for 1992 would include all of the dates that Vanderbilt excluded from their indexes.

2. For the eight shows that were missing, the Vanderbilt News Index was examined instead. Three of these shows included material that needed to be coded. All were on CBS (September 5, October 16, and October 30). They included two poll references and five "people-on-the-street" references that could not be coded for some variables like content of message.

3. For 1996, interest group spokespeople, experts, and campaign workers/volunteers were not included.

4. Each person's comments could be coded into more than one category. For example, if the person said he/she thought Clinton was weak and he/she wanted a president who could stop the import of drugs into our country, that would be coded as a negative comment about Clinton and an issue position. However, if the person said we need to stop the import of drugs, reduce crime, and end pollution, it was only counted once in the issue category.

5. The "one-half" indicates that the story included this issue and another issue.

6. The twenty-three were: abortion, AIDS, budget, cable television regulations, crime, drugs, education, economy, government size, environment, family leave, family values, foreign policy, gun control, health care, lawsuits, NAFTA, the S&L bailout, social security, taxes, unemployment, welfare, and women's issues.

7. There were also four "groups" that were interviewed whose size was unreported. If any of the same people were used in more than one story (and it seems likely that this occurred since some "quasi-panel groups" were used), they were still counted as "different" people. This was done for practical reasons (it was impossible to tell who was used more than once) and has face validity (since viewers should not be assumed to be viewing the news with the knowledge or memory of which everyday people might have been on the news before).

8. These people were not campaign workers, spokespeople, or labeled as "supporters" of a candidate—they were simply people asked to talk about what they thought. These numbers could be lower than the actual number of everyday people because individuals identified in the descriptions as "Perot supporters" were not coded because they were assumed to be working for the campaign rather than "people on the street." If the label was based on their comments rather than on their role in the campaign, they would fit the "people-on-the-street" definition and should have been included.

9. Again, some people might have been counted twice if they were talked to on more than one show and their occupations were identified both times. None of the "people on the street" in 1996 were included in more than one show.

10. Not coded as issue reporting were evaluations of the current economic situation, whether or not respondents thought that they were better off than they had been four years ago and whether the nation was moving in the "right direction." These were coded as "other" since they did not indicate what fiscal policies the public preferred.

11. Not counted was ABC's report on September 16 which noted that crime was the public's most important issue according to "all measures we have." Since this statement is vague as to whether or not a poll was used, and it is suspect given the documented findings from the "most important problem" question reported on NBC ("jobs," September 20) and CBS ("education," October 21), this was not included in the poll analysis.

12. One could argue that some of these could be coded as horse race coverage since they dealt with the relative placement of the candidates. I chose instead to use a "pure" operational definition of horse race—simply the reporting of who was ahead and by how much. I did not include those stories that might have implications for who would be ahead. This decision did not influence the results because questions like "Does Perot's selection of Choate as his running mate influence your decision?" were typically used in conjunction with the traditional type of horse race poll.

13. "Fixing America" started on October 17 and was introduced as a campaign feature that asked famous "non government" people and everyday people to tell politicians what they wanted.

14. Recall how this variable was operationalized. These are not people who work or volunteer for the campaigns or are commenting on the campaigns in their capacity as experts or interest groups. They are not necessarily interviewed "on the street," nor are they excluded for being famous.

15. While it might appear that the 1996 numbers of men and women contrast dramatically with those in 1992, it is unclear whether this is due to a change in coverage or validity problems with coding this variable from the 1992 indexes. It is quite possible that a higher percentage of "unable to code" individuals from 1992 were women than those in the "codeable" group.

16. This might result, in part, from the coding scheme that required clear indicators of age or youth to warrant being placed in a group other than "middle group." The fact that Clinton had a strong advantage in both of these groups might also have muted attention to them.

17. There was also a "school activist," college professor, historian/author/professor, and guidance counselor.

18. The only person to talk about Perot (NBC, September 17) said that he "still has fire and energy." However, when asked if he would vote for Perot, he said coyly, "maybe, maybe, maybe."

19. This level of support for one candidate based on an issue was larger than either candidate's advantage on the six most popular voting issues.

REFERENCES

Ceaser, James, and Andrew Busch. 1993. *Upside Down and Inside Out: The 1992 Elections and American Politics.* Lanham, MD: Rowman & Littlefield Publishers, Inc.

DiIulio, John J. Jr., 1997. "Conclusion: Valence Voters, Valence Victors." In M. Nelson, ed., *The Election of 1996*. Washington, DC: Congressional Quarterly Press: 167–74.

Fishel, Jeff. 1985. *Presidents & Promises: From Campaign Pledge to Presidential Performance*. Washington, DC: Congressional Quarterly Press.

Iyengar, Shanto. 1991. *Is Anyone Responsible? How Television Frames Political Issues*. Chicago: University of Chicago Press.

Iyengar, Shanto, and Donald R. Kinder. 1987. *News that Matters: TV and American Opinion*. Chicago: University of Chicago Press.

Just, Marion R. 1997. "Candidate Strategies and the Media Campaign." In Gerald M. Pomper, ed., *The Election of 1996*. Chatham, NJ: Chatham House Publishers, Inc.: 77–106.

Just, Marion R., Ann N. Crigler, Dean E. Alger, Timothy E. Cook, Montague Kern, and Darrell M. West. 1996. *Crosstalk: Citizens, Candidates, and the Media in a Presidential Campaign*. Chicago: University of Chicago Press.

Keeter, Scott. 1997. "Public Opinion and the Election." In Gerald M. Pomper, ed., *The Election of 1996*. Chatham, NJ: Chatham House Publishers, Inc.: 107–34.

Kerbel, Matthew Robert. 1994. *Edited for Television: CNN, ABC, and the 1992 Presidential Campaign*. Boulder, CO: Westview Press.

Ladd, Everett Carll, and John Benson. 1992. "The Growth of News Polls in American Politics." In Thomas E. Mann and Gary R. Orren, eds., *Media Polls in American Politics*. Washington, DC: The Brookings Institution.

Noelle-Neumann, Elisabeth. 1984. *The Spiral of Silence: Public Opinion—Our Social Skin*. Chicago: University of Chicago Press.

Patterson, Thomas E. 1993. *Out of Order*. New York: Knopf.

Pomper, Gerald M. 1997. "The Presidential Election." In Gerald M. Pomper, ed., *The Election of 1996*. Chatham, NJ: Chatham House Publishers, Inc.: 173–204.

Robinson, Michael, and Margaret Sheehan. 1984. *Over the Wires and on TV*. New York: Russell Sage Publications.

Salmon, Charles T., and Theodore L. Glasser. 1995. "The Politics of Polling and the Limits of Consent." In Theodore L. Glasser and Charles T. Salmon, eds., *Public Opinion and the Communication of Consent*. New York: The Guilford Press.

Traugott, Michael W. 1992. "The Impact of Media Polls on the Public." In Thomas E. Mann and Gary R. Orren, eds., *Media Polls in American Politics*. Washington, DC: The Brookings Institution.

C. CAMPAIGN FINANCE: IS THE SYSTEM "BROKE"?

7

Public Funding and Political Campaigns in New York City: The Limits of Reform

Jeffrey Kraus

INTRODUCTION

Since 1989 municipal elections in New York City have been contested on what might be termed a "graded" (although not necessarily a "level") playing field. The New York City Campaign Finance Act, adopted in 1988, provided for partial public financing of campaigns for local office (Local Law No. 8 of 1988). By enacting this local law, New York joined twenty-two states and a handful of localities that had established similar programs in the years since Watergate (Alexander 1991: 1). As the program has been operational for a short period, only Brecher et al. (1993: 113–39) has provided an independent analysis. Examining the 1989 election, they concluded that the reforms had partially met their goals but that some changes in the law mandating debates, assuring access to broadcast and cable television, and limiting the gathering of contributions by intermediaries should be considered. Here we will briefly review the background that led to the law's passage, outline its key provisions and objectives, and make some observations as to the statute's impact. Finally, we will take notice of some weaknesses and limitations that have come to light.

THE PATH TO PUBLIC FINANCING OF CAMPAIGNS
IN NEW YORK

New York's program came about in response to growing concern about the influence of money in local politics and the series of political scandals that buffeted Mayor Edward I. Koch's third term.[1] Leichter (1985) found that sixteen of the twenty-five largest campaign contributors had some matter pending before the city government between 1981 and 1985. Leichter also asserted that there were at least ten instances where donors significantly increased their financial support when they had matters pending before the Board of Estimate.[2]

Another cause for anxiety was the escalating cost of campaigns. In 1985, Mayor Koch spent nearly $6.3 million, Council President Andrew Stein $3 million, and Comptroller Harrison J. Goldin $1.3 million (Brecher et al. 1993: 126). Only Stein had serious opposition. Spending had become an issue in down-ballot elections (contests located lower on the ballot), where incumbent borough presidents outspent and overwhelmed their opponents. In Brooklyn, Howard Golden spent $1.3 million, while his two Democratic primary opponents' combined expenditures were $500,000 (NYPIRG 1987). In the Bronx, the incumbent outspent his opponent by nearly four-to-one (126).

This excess was made possible by large monetary contributions. Leichter (1986) found that the five largest donors between 1981 and 1986 had given more than $1.5 million to members of the Board of Estimate and the five Democratic county committees.[3] He asserted that "the line between a bribe and a contribution is almost invisible" (Barbanel 1985). Mayor Koch countered that there was nothing "immoral" (Barbanel 1985).

In September 1987, campaign finance reform legislation was introduced in the City Council. After considerable debate, the Council passed and Mayor Koch signed a local law intended to reduce campaign spending, limit the size of contributions, provide optional public funds, increase participation by candidates and the electorate, and require the disclosure of financial information.[4] A five-member board was established to oversee the program.[5]

THE NEW YORK CITY CAMPAIGN FINANCE ACT: KEY
PROVISIONS AND OBJECTIVES

In enacting the statute, the council had declared that it sought to "ensure that citizens, regardless of their personal wealth, access to large contributors or other financial connections are enabled and encouraged to compete effectively for public office" (New York City Campaign Finance Board 1990).

Contribution Limits

Contribution limits speak to the studies and journalistic accounts alleging that large contributions made by PACs (political action committees) influence the votes of legislators on matters of concern to those PACs (Adamany 1986;

Frendreis and Waterman 1985; Wilhite and Theilman 1987). Donors and recipients respond that PACs do not "buy" votes. Rather, PACs give to those already supporting their position. Lobbyists also downplay the intent of the contributors, arguing that donors are merely seeking "access" rather than influence. This view is supported by a number of studies that conclude there is little or no proof that PACs are able to "buy" votes (Chappell 1982; Welch 1982; Alexander 1984; Sorauf 1988; Wright 1985; Grenzke 1989; Sabato 1989). However, the perception that PACs "buy" influence persists. Chartock observed that "while most lobbyists claim their PACs have little clout, their proliferation suggests otherwise" (Sabato 1989: 240).

The Campaign Finance Act placed a ceiling on donations to candidates. While such limits already exist under state law, the local law imposed a much lower ceiling on donors. State law allows individuals to give up to $50,000 per election (primary, runoff, and general) to candidates for mayor, public advocate (known as City Council president prior to 1993), and comptroller. In 1989, candidates for citywide office participating in the public finance program were limited to contributions that did not exceed $3,000 per election (New York City Campaign Finance Board [NYC/CFB] 1990). Candidates for City Council were allowed to accept no more than $2,000 per election. The limits also apply to political parties, corporations, labor unions, partnerships, and PACs. Another distinction between state law and the city program is the treatment of contributions made by corporate subsidiaries. State law treats subsidiaries, or affiliated entities, as separate entities. Therefore, each can make donations, up to the limit, to a candidate. Under the local program, these subsidiaries are considered to be a single donor, regardless of the number of entities through which funds are channeled.

Expenditure Limits

The act set spending limits for primary, runoff, and general elections, as well as for the year preceding the election (see Table 7.1). The limits cover all expenditures made to advance a candidate's campaign or in furtherance of his or her opponent's defeat. Expenses covered by the limit include the costs of campaign literature, media advertising, campaign offices, campaign workers' salaries, and political consultants' fees (CFB 1990: 15).

Certain expenses were exempt from the limits. These included costs associated with compliance with the Campaign Finance Act or the state election law. Of particular weight was the exemption of costs related to challenging or defending designating petitions. Since ballot access litigation is costly, exempting it (especially challenging an opponent's petition) was significant.[6]

These limits were based on the perception that campaign spending was out of control (Alexander 1991: 2). In addition, the ability of some candidates (particularly incumbents) to raise and spend large sums of money made it difficult for their opponents to make competitive races.

Table 7.1
Expenditure Limits Under the Campaign Finance Act, 1989–2001
(per election)

Office	1989	1991	1993	1997	2001
Mayor	$3,000,000	n/a	$4,000,000	$4,732,000	$5,231,000
Comptroller and Public Advocate	$1,750,000	n/a	$2,500,000	$2,958,000	$3,270,000
Borough President	$625,000	n/a	$900,000	$1,065,000	$1,177,000
City Council	$60,000	$105,000	$105,000	$124,000	$137,000

Source: NYC/CFB 1990, 15; 1993, 33; 1998, 58.

Increased Competition

Another objective of the legislation was to encourage greater competition
for local office. This was to be achieved through the aforementioned contribution and spending caps, as well as partial public financing of campaigns. As explained in the New York City CFB (hereafter referred to as the CFB) first
report:

To restrict the influence of money on electoral campaigns, the Campaign Finance Program sets limits on contributions and expenditures and also imposes strict requirements for disclosure of campaign finances. By providing matching public funds to
candidates who agree to observe these limits and requirements and who reach certain
threshold levels in fundraising, the Program also intends to "level the playing field" for
all candidates, whether or not they have access to substantial wealth. In this way, wider
participation in the electoral process by both candidates and voters can be encouraged.
(NYC/CFB: 1990, ix)

Pursuant to the U.S. Supreme Court's decision in *Buckley v. Valeo*, 424 U.
S. 1 (1976), the program is voluntary. Candidates must "opt in" to the program.[7] Participating candidates must meet financial "threshold requirements" before they receive funds. The requirements vary, depending upon
the office, but are based on the premise that candidates must demonstrate
"public support," defined by the number of contributions from eligible donors (ironic, considering the program is intended to reduce the influence of
money in politics).
Candidates meeting the threshold are eligible for a dollar-for-dollar match
of contributions.[8] However, if the participating candidate is in a contest with a

nonparticipant, he or she can receive two dollars in public funds for each dollar raised. This proviso serves two purposes. First, it attempts to "level the playing field" for candidates running against nonparticipants by enhancing their fund-raising capability. Second, the "two-to-one" bonus serves as an inducement to join the program or for launching a candidacy. The prospect of giving your opponent the chance for two dollars of public funds for every dollar you raise might lead some candidates to join the program, lest their opponents obtain the bonus. The bonus might also encourage an underfunded candidate to stand against a well-funded non-participant, knowing that their efforts will receive significant financial support from the program.

The law limits the use of public funds. "Qualified campaign expenditures" are those made to educate the public about candidates and issues in the election. Public funds cannot be used for payments to a candidate or the candidate's family or business, cash payments, petition challenges or defense, entertainment, or the salaries of campaign workers (although consultants' fees can be paid). Surplus funds remaining after the election are to be returned to the city.

Political Education

The political education objectives of the reform were to be attained through two means: disclosure requirements and the *Voter's Guide.*

Participants in the program are required to submit financial disclosure reports. While such documentation has been required by state law since 1974 (all candidates for municipal office are required to file periodic reports with the Board of Elections), the local law, modeled on the federal disclosure rules, requires a more detailed divulgence of campaign finances.

The second feature designed to improve voter education was the publication of a *Voter's Guide.* The guide was mandated by a 1988 amendment to the City Charter, and includes voter information and candidate-supplied profiles (New York City Charter, Chapter 46 Section 1053). A copy of the guide is mailed to every household having at least one registered voter.

Taken together, the New York City Campaign Finance Act and the subsequent charter revision is probably one of the more ambitious and comprehensive electoral reform measures ever enacted in the United States. Initially, even its proponents were unsure of the prospects for its success. The Reverend Joseph A. O'Hare, first chair of the CFB, acknowledged that the program faced "the genuine problem of starting something from scratch when you don't have experience. . . . People can become discouraged, cynical and critical of a program before it is given a chance" (quoted in Lynn 1989a).

THE PUBLIC FINANCE PROGRAM AFTER FOUR ELECTION CYCLES

While the law has had some impact on elections, loopholes have been found and exploited. At the time of its enactment, a major loophole was evident: the program was voluntary. Other flaws, not obvious at the outset, have emerged. In other instances, the law, while laudatory, has not had the desired impact due to other factors.

Contribution Limits

One of the program's goals was to eliminate large contributions so as to end the perception that big donors had a disproportionate degree of influence in the political process. For example, in the 1985 election cycle, $3.3 million (47 percent) of the funds raised by Mayor Koch's campaign came from 453 benefactors who gave at least $5,000 (State of New York, Commission on Government Integrity 1988). Comptroller Goldin (64 percent) and City Council President Stein (66 percent) raised even greater proportions of their campaign treasuries from donors who gave at least $5,000 (State of New York, Commission on Government Integrity 1988). The public finance program's lower contribution limits have had some impact on large contributors.

The 1989 election cycle provides an interesting contrast between pre- and post-reform fund-raising. The campaign finance law took effect February 29, 1988, and different patterns were evident. Koch and Goldin had both relied on major donors. According to the CFB (NYC/CFB 1990: 53), between July 12, 1983, and February 28, 1989, 20.4 percent of Koch's contributions were in excess of $6,000 (the limits for both a primary and general election). For the same period, 28.6 percent of Goldin's receipts were in the form of gifts greater than $6,000. After February 29, 1988, Koch's receipt of donations in the $3,000-and-under range increased from 55 to 86 percent of the total collected. For Goldin, the increase was from 28 percent to 96 percent of his contributions. In 1989 the law appeared to have an impact on the amount of money raised: the victorious Democratic candidates for mayor and comptroller spent less than their counterparts had four years earlier (Brecher 1993: 130–31). Therefore, the measure did control costs initially.

Perhaps the most significant development related to contribution limits has been the creation of new fund-raising sources, strategies, and techniques. Candidates could no longer rely on real estate developers, lawyers, lobbyists, bankers, and business people to directly capitalize their campaigns.

Candidates for citywide office have made extensive use of bundling. In both the 1989 and 1993 mayoral elections, intermediaries played a significant role. In 1989, 19 percent of the funds raised by the participating mayoral candidates came through 391 intermediaries. In contrast, intermediaries accounted for 0.6 and 1.8 percent of the funds raised, respectively, by candidates for borough president and city council in 1989. Republican Rudolph Giuliani's campaign raised almost 45 percent of its funds through 252 intermediaries, more than any other candidate in that cycle (NYC/CFB 1990: 73).[9]

In the 1993 mayoral election, intermediaries again were important. The New York Public Interest Research Group (1993: 5), analyzing CFB data, determined that intermediaries who delivered more than $10,000 played major roles in both mayoral campaigns. Through October 25, 1993, the Dinkins campaign had raised 20 percent of its $9.2 million war chest through 58 intermediaries; Giuliani, one-third of his $7.8 million campaign fund through thirty-two bundlers. As Lawrence A. Mandelker observed, "by virtue of bundling, special interests still have the same influence" (Lynn 1989b).

Another loophole in the legislation is that the state law's more generous contribution ceilings apply to nonparticipating candidates. Wealthy individuals, or those with access to money, still have an advantage. In 1989, Ronald Lauder, the cosmetics heir seeking the Republican mayoral nomination, spent almost $12.3 million, most of it his own (Brecher 1993: 132). By not taking public funds, he was able to spend his own money without restraint, since donations by candidates, or their spouses, are exempt from even the loose limits of the state law (New York State Board of Elections 1988: 11).

In both 1989 and 1993, Andrew Stein declined public financing, declaring that it was "almost unconscionable . . . that while people are dying in city hospitals for lack of care, this money should be used to pay for TV commercials and shopping bags" (Lynn 1989c).

Affluent candidates have also run for the council. The most expensive race for City Council in New York's history was a 1993 special election held to fill the seat vacated by the election of Carolyn Maloney to Congress. Andrew S. Eristoff, a descendant of the industrialist Henry Phipps, spent $343,711 ($256,000 of which was in the form of a personal loan he made to his campaign) to defeat Jane Crotty by fifty-seven votes (McKinley 1993a). Eristoff outspent Crotty by almost $100,000 and conceded he would not have won without his loan, since it paid for television and radio advertising (rare in city council races) and for ten mass mailings. This included a decisive posting of sixteen thousand absentee ballot applications to Republicans (Eristoff was the only Republican in a seven-candidate field). Eristoff defended his outlay, saying that he didn't "owe anything to any union or to any leadership person in the Council" (McKinley 1993a). Chris Meyer of NYPIRG viewed it differently, suggesting that Eristoff's victory meant "that if you are rich enough in this town you can win an election with your own money" (McKinley 1993a). Eristoff repeated the feat eight months later, spending almost $600,000 in winning a full term.

In the 1993 mayoral election, large contributions resurfaced. While contributions to participating candidates are limited, donations of up to $62,500 can be made under state law by individuals to party organizations, which can then use the funds for so-called independent campaign efforts. Independent spending has been upheld by the courts on First Amendment grounds.[10] While some concern was raised about such efforts in 1989, the magnitude of these efforts attracted greater attention four years later.

In 1993, the CFB for the first time had to adjudicate claims that "independent" expenditures were, in fact, coordinated with candidate committees and should be charged against their spending limit. Under pressure from the CFB, the Dinkins campaign voluntarily reimbursed the State Democratic Committee $226,000 for mail that the Giuliani campaign alleged was an attempt to circumvent the spending cap (McKinley 1993d). A Dinkins campaign claim that a Republican State Committee-financed $750,000 election day operation should be charged to the Giuliani campaign was dismissed by the CFB.

Therefore, while large contributions to individual campaigns have been limited, bundling, the inability to regulate contributions to nonparticipating candidates, and the funneling of large contributions to independent campaigns remain problems.

Limiting Campaign Expenditures

A second objective of the statute was to contain expenditures by imposing campaign spending limits. Once again, the program has achieved partial success. In 1985, the last mayoral campaign before regulation, Mayor Koch's campaign spent $7.1 million against insignificant opposition (NYC/CFB 1990: 84).

In subsequent mayoral elections, spending did level off among program participants. Despite the intense competition in 1993, no participant exceeded Koch's 1985 spending.[11] In 1993, both campaigns increased their outlays, with Dinkins spending $10.9 million (primary and general election) and Giuliani $8.7 million (general election) (McKinley 1993b). In 1997, Giuliani spent $11.8 million and Ruth Messinger, his Democratic opponent in the general election, $6.1 million (NYC/CFB 1998: 1). In both cases the spending was within the CFB's limits. The program's accomplishments in slowing the growth of campaign expenditure can be ascribed to its willingness to sanction those exceeding the limit.[12]

In City Council races, public financing seems to have limited spending (Table 7.2). In 1985, eight candidates spent in excess of $100,000 in the Democratic primary.[13] The 1991 primaries, which featured an unusually high level of competition, offer some data on this point. In the thirty-two contests where participating and nonparticipating candidates competed, the candidates receiving public financing were the leading fund-raisers in nineteen primaries.[14] Thus, it can be argued that public funds actually subsidized candidates who already had access to financial support.

One criticism of public financing after the 1989 election was that the spending limits for City Council candidates were too low, making it difficult for nonincumbents, who must mount credible campaigns against well-known officeholders, to take part in the program.[15] The expenditure limit was increased 75 percent ($60,000 to $105,000) for the 1991 and 1993 Council elections.

In some cases, the public finance program has encouraged spending. In all four election cycles there were a number of cases where candidates facing to-

Table 7.2
City Council Expenditures—Participating Candidates

Year	Primary	Average	General	Average	Total	Average
1989 (31)	$1,567,007	$54,035	$544,836	$27,246	$2,111,943	$65,998
1991 (136)	$4,132,347	$36,569	$2,770,286	$40,169	$6,902,633	$50,755
1993 (87)	$1,760,753	$53,396	$2,455,458	$43,078	$4,216,211	$48,462
1997 (121)	$3,602,116	$54,577	$3,693,927	$47,263	$7,241,413	$59,846

Number in parentheses is the number of participating candidates in that cycle.

Source: NYC/CFB data (1989, 1991, 1998) and disclosure statements filed with the Board of Elections in the City of New York (1993).

ken opposition expended public funds. In 1989, Ruth Messinger, a candidate for Manhattan borough president, spent $1.6 million (including $600,714 in public funds) although she had no serious opposition (NYC/CFB 1990: J-1).[16] Messinger testified at the CFB's 1989 public hearing that she spent the funds because they were "an entitlement to a candidate, not a revocable gift" (Lynn 1989d).

Four years later, Messinger, Fernando Ferrer (the Bronx borough president) and Charles Millard (a Manhattan councilman) all made large expenditures in the general election despite token opposition.[17] In the 1997 election, Council Speaker Peter Vallone spent over $231,000 even though his only opponent was a minor party candidate who polled 761 votes out of almost 13,000 cast (NYC/CFB 1998). Such campaigning can serve one of two purposes. First, by increasing turnout, it may help other candidates (and amounts to an "independent expenditure" on their behalf). It may also help the candidate spending the money by raising his or her name recognition for a subsequent election.[18] Without public financing, candidates facing token opposition might have been unwilling to make such large disbursements.

Increased Competition

Another aim of public financing is to increase the level of competition for public office. The New York program has not had the desired effect. As Table 7.3 indicates, there were fewer citywide candidates in the 1997 Democratic primary than in 1985. Data for the City Council shows that the law has not led to an increase in the number of office seekers. In 1989, the program's first year, there were fewer candidates in both the Democratic primary and the general election than in 1985. While the number of candidates increased fivefold in the

Table 7.3

Number of Candidates for Citywide Offices, Borough President, and City Council in Democratic Primaries, 1981–1997

Year	Mayor	Comptroller	Pubic Advocates	Borough President	City Council
1981	3	2	2	2	n/a
1982	n/a	n/a	n/a	n/a	47
1985	3	3	6	8	59
1989	4	5	2	2	30
1991	n/a	n/a	n/a	n/a	162
1993	3	3	6	2	49
1997	5	0	2	6	70

Source: The New York Times, 23 September 1981, B4; 25 September 1982, 33; 11 September 1985, B4; 14 September 1989, B2; 15 September 1993, B11; 1991 data from NYC/CFB 1992, 108–135. 1997 data from the Board of Elections in the City of New York,1998.

1991 Democratic primary, there were ten fewer candidates in 1993 than in 1985. In 1997, the number of Council hopefuls increased by 30 percent.

The 1991 increase can be attributed to the creation of sixteen "open seats" by the expansion of the Council from thirty-five to fifty-one. Of the 162 Democratic primary candidates, 100 (61.7 percent) were in districts with no Democratic incumbent. The remaining 62 (38.3 percent) competed for the nineteen seats in which a Democrat was seeking reelection. There were twelve districts where no Democratic primary was held (in eleven there were Democratic incumbents, while the remaining seat was held by a Republican). In the twenty "open" seats there was an average of 5.0 candidates; in the thirty-one seats contested by incumbents, the average number of candidates was 2.38. In 1997, there were primaries in eight seats where no Democratic incumbent was seeking reelection (compared to two seats four years earlier). The average number of candidates in the "open seat" primaries was 3.75. In the fifteen primaries where Democratic incumbents sought renomination the average was 2.66. It appears that facing an incumbent, as well as the higher costs faced by insurgents, are impediments to candidates. In 1991 and 1997, the unusually large number of open seats attracted many candidates. In 1993, with only two open seats, the number of candidates declined precipitously.[19] In 2001, when the vast majority of incumbents are "term limited," there is likely to be an increase in the number of candidates.[20]

While public financing may mitigate the cost factor, it does not address incumbency. As Table 7.4 illustrates, fund-raising is one of the advantages of incumbency.[21]

Another dimension is the degree of competition in an election. Has campaign finance reform in New York resulted in more competitive elections?

It appears that campaign finance reform has had little bearing on the "competitiveness" of elections (see Table 7.5). City Council Democratic primaries
offer the best opportunity for evaluating the competitive level of electoral contests. For purposes of this study, "competitive" elections are defined as those
where the margin between the winning and second-place candidates is 10 percent or less.

In 1985, the last cycle prior to public financing, six of the twenty races were
"competitive." Only 1991, a reapportionment year where the City Council's
size was expanded from 35 to 51, yielded a higher proportion of competitive
races (41.5 percent). In 1989 and 1993, two cycles featuring few open seats,
there was actually a smaller proportion of contested races than in 1985. In
1997, despite more open seats (eight), there were fewer competitive races than
in 1993. As for the general election, the availability of public funds has not
ended the Democratic party's hegemony. There has not been more than one
competitive council race in each of the last five general elections. The increase
in the Republican party's presence on the Council has been due to the creation
of Republican-oriented districts in the 1991 reapportionment rather than any
change in the competitive balance due to an infusion of public funds.[22]

Table 7.4
Average Total Contributions to City Council Candidates, 1989–1997

Year	Incumbents	Challengers*
1989	$100,532 (19)	$43,921 (13)
1991	$57,557 (34)	$15,084 (84)
1993	$62,239 (49)	$29,334 (46)
1997	$99,548 (43)	$23,654 (52)

*Challengers in contests against incumbents. Does not include candidates in "open" seats.
Number in parentheses is number of candidates

Source: NYC/CFB data (1989, 1991, 1998) and disclosure statements filed with the Board of
   Elections in the City of New York (1993).

Table 7.5
"Competitive" City Council Contests, Democratic Primaries and General
Elections, 1985–1997

Primary	Contested Seats	Competitive Seats
1985	21	6 (30%)
1989	12	2 (16.7%)
1991	36	15 (41.5%)
1993	19	5 (26.3%)
1997	23	4 (17.4%)
General Election		
1985	35	1 (2.8%)
1989	35	0
1991	51	1 (1.9%)
1993	51	1 (1.9%)
1997	51	1 (1.9%)

Sources: The New York Times, 11 September 1985, B4; 7 November 1985, B6; 14 September
1989, B2; 9 November 1989, B6; 15 September 1993, B11; 3 November 1993, B5. 1991
data from NYC/CFB 1992, 108–135. 1997 data from the Board of Elections in the City of
New York, 1998.

The program's compliance process may actually discourage participation.
Candidates must maintain extensive records documenting the receipt and disposition of all campaign funds. As Brecher (1993: 135) noted, many incumbents chose not to participate in the program during its early years, deciding
that the program was too complicated and required additional staff. In 1997,
fifteen of the forty-three incumbents seeking reelection did not join. According to one lawyer familiar with the process, compliance costs (for Council campaigns) may approach the amount of funds received by the typical campaign.[23]

In the 1993 election cycle, a new loophole was exploited. As noted earlier, a
key provision of the statute mandates that participants receive two dollars of
public funds for every dollar they raise when a nonparticipant triggers the "bonus" by reaching specified thresholds. In addition, participants are then exempt from spending limits.

The "two-for-one" rule was put to the test in a Brooklyn council district
when a non-participating candidate evaded the penalty by failing to file state-
required financial reports. While it was obvious that the candidate had spent

far more than the threshold amount, the participating candidate was denied the bonus since there was no proof his opponent had triggered the bonus. State law provides for less stringent reporting requirements and higher spending and contribution limits, and the penalties for noncompliance are trivial.[24] As a result, the CFB changed its policy. In lieu of state reports they now "rely on other information to determine whether the double matching rate has been triggered" (NYC/CFB 1997: 27).

Public Education

The program's primary vehicle for political education is the *Voter's Guide*. Editions are published for the primary and general election. While the Guide has been recognized nationally for offering voters a nonpartisan source of information on the elections, there is no empirical evidence that it has affected voter turnout.

While increased public awareness may lead to higher turnout, competition is a more critical variable.[25] Turnout in the 1989 and 1993 general elections was high because of competitive mayoral races. In contrast, turnout in 1997 was lower because of a lackluster mayoral election.[26]

One form of voter education that was not addressed by the original legislation was debates. In its 1992 report, the CFB noted that a number of those who testified at public hearings in 1989 and 1991 had expressed support for mandating participation in debates by recipients of public funds. However, the CFB expressed concern "that its involvement in the administration and enforcement of the debate requirement might interfere with its ability to appear nonpartisan and objective" (1992: 93).

In 1993, there were no debates between the major mayoral candidates during the general election campaign. The law was then amended to require candidates for citywide office to debate as a condition for receiving public funds (NYC/CFB 1997: 4).

CONCLUSION

The New York City Campaign Finance Act, regarded as a landmark in election law reform, is an ambitious and comprehensive statute. The law limits contributions and expenditures, requires greater financial disclosure, and encourages participation. As with most ambitious reforms, there have been mixed results and some unintended outcomes.

Campaign finance reform has slowed the growth of expenditure in citywide races and forced candidates to broaden their fund-raising efforts. The days when citywide candidates could rely on a small coterie of lawyers, lobbyists, and real estate developers to directly finance their campaigns are over. However, "bundling" of campaign contributions by intermediaries and "independent expenditures" by state party organizations proves that "big money" is still part of the process. The statute's disclosure requirements, more detailed than those of the state law, do offer great insight into the financing of political campaigns.

The program has flaws. The voluntary nature of the program offers an escape for well-off candidates or those willing to raise large sums of money. A public finance act cannot stop candidates from spending their personal fortunes. While the *New York Times* has used its editorial columns to urge participation, calling the program a "commitment to cleaner politics," not all are attracted by the siren song of political reform (1993).

Nonparticipating candidates, "bundlers," and the donors to independent campaigns have all found ways around the act. In some cases, candidates without significant opposition actually spend more since they are using public funds. These expenditures may allow them to help other candidates or generate higher levels of name recognition for future campaigns. The framers of the legislation surely did not have this in mind when they crafted the bill.

It would be difficult to assert that the program has increased competition. There were actually fewer City Council candidates and a smaller proportion of "competitive" Council seats in 1993 than in 1985. The law cannot control for the advantage of incumbency. Indeed, it is difficult to ascertain, as far as City Council elections are concerned, whether the problems the program addresses are real. Few candidates (including incumbents) spend anywhere near the amounts allowed. Candidates who can, usually choose not to participate in the program. While their opponent might receive "bonus" funding, they still must raise funds in conformance with the statute. They must also spend money to comply with the more rigorous local law. Public financing may make some candidates viable, but it does not neutralize incumbency or the candidate who wishes to "buy" a council seat. Given the barriers to broad candidate participation (incumbency, dominance of the Democratic party in council elections, ballot access requirements, the complications of an urban setting), it seems unlikely that public funds alone will smash the roadblocks to political participation.

The *Voter's Guide* and enhanced financial disclosure do provide the electorate with more information about the candidates. However, there is no empirical evidence that these endeavors have actually stimulated voter turnout or provided for a more aware electorate. Levels of competition and the efforts of the candidates seem to be the more important variables that influence voter turnout.

As for the CFB, it is threatened with entanglement in what is often the contact sport of New York City politics. Mayor Giuliani's effort to appoint one of his supporters to the CFB on the morning when the body was considering sanctioning the mayor's campaign is an example of how the board can be politicized.[27] Council member Kenneth Fisher, in testimony before the CFB, warned, "there's no guarantee . . . that every decision for all time is going to be made on the merits" (NYC/CFB 1991b: 117).

Political candidates now see the CFB as another arena in which to challenge their opponents. Complaints for violations of the Campaign Finance Act are becoming routine. Even when complaints are groundless, they serve as a diversion, as staff and resources are expended to respond to the complaint, and to delay the receipt of public funds (since the CFB will not disburse funds until complaints are adjudicated). Here, participants are at a disadvantage; nonparticipants, while not required to adhere to the act, can initiate actions against candidates who are in the program. Public financing, while "leveling" the playing field in some areas, has created new hazards in the political landscape.

The city's program demonstrates the limits of campaign finance reform. The rough and tumble political environment of New York City, where candidates, consultants, and operatives seek every edge, is still an obstacle to reform. Some reform objectives will remain unattainable simply because finances, while important, may be only one of a number of factors affecting the outcome. Even where finances are decisive, until meaningful reform takes place at the state level, the dual system of campaign finance in New York City reduces participation in public finance to a strategic political decision based more on a candidate's ability to raise money than on his or her commitment to cleaner politics. Participants will attempt to stretch the limits of the program, seeing how far they can go in circumventing the act. After four cycles, New York's experiment in campaign finance reform is a cautionary tale for those who believe that reducing the influence of money will transform the political process.

NOTES

1. For more on these events, see Newfield and Barrett 1988.

2. New York's real estate boom of the mid-1980s had an impact on contributions to members of the City's Board of Estimate (the mayor, City Council president, comptroller, and the borough presidents), which had final authority on land use matters. The donors cited in Leichter's report had leased real property to the city, received zoning variances for various projects, purchased property from the city on favorable terms, or were involved in city-sponsored redevelopment projects.

3. The five were Donald Trump, $350,000; Gerald Guterman, $349,000; Robert Brennan, $310,000; Seymour Cohn, $297,000; and Bear, Stearns and Company, $268,000 (Leichter 1986).

4. A brief history of the law can be found in NYC/CFB 1990: 9–12.

5. Two members are mayoral appointees and must not be members of the same political party.

6. The City Council speaker appoints two members, who cannot belong to the same party. The mayor, in consultation with the speaker, selects the chairperson. Members serve staggered five-year terms and can be removed only for cause. CFB members must be registered voters in the City of New York and cannot take part in any campaign under the panel's jurisdiction. For a discussion of New York's ballot access laws, considered the most byzantine in the United States, see Scarrow 1983.

7. Candidates must sign up no later than the thirtieth day before the first day to submit designation petitions, or, if petitions are not filed, within seven days after nomination.

8. Contributions are matched to a maximum of $1,000 per donor.

9. The proportion of funds raised by intermediaries may actually be underreported. A bundler can encourage those solicited to make their contributions directly to the campaign, instead of giving their check to the intermediary. This practice would not constitute, by the CFB's definition, bundling.

10. The U.S. Supreme Court, in *Buckley v. Valeo*, ruled that restrictions on "independent expenditures" were unconstitutional as long as there is no coordination between a candidate and the independent effort.

11. In 1989, Dinkins won a four-way primary with 51 percent, and then narrowly defeated Giuliani. Giuliani faced competition for the Republican nomination from Lauder, a nonparticipant (Brecher 1993: 133).

12. In 1991 the CFB fined Mayor Koch's campaign committee $35,000 for violating limits on contributions and expenditures in the 1989 campaign. The agency's auditors found that Koch's campaign spent $84,785 more than permitted (Strom 1991). In 1993, the Dinkins campaign was fined $320,000 for overspending during the 1993 primary (McKinley 1993e).

13. The leading spender was David Rothenberg, who spent $258,368 (Source: campaign disclosure filed with the Board of Elections in the City of New York).

14. Of the sixty-nine nonparticipating candidates in the 1991 primaries, four candidates' expenditures exceeded the cap of $105,000. Their average expenditure was $22,655. In the 1991 general election, no candidate exceeded the limit. The average expenditure by a nonparticipant in the general election was $7,400. From data found in NYC/CFB (1992: 108–20).

15. Thomas Duane, a candidate who spent $163,000, testified that he decided not to participate in the program because the spending limit was "not a realistic amount of money"(NYC/CFB 1991a: 6).

16. Messinger polled 84.4 percent in the primary and 83.1 percent in the general election. Source: Board of Elections in the City of New York.

17. According to disclosure statements furnished by their committees for the 1993 election cycle, Messinger spent $732,159; Ferrer, $1,319,932; and Millard, $229,389.

18. In 1993, Messinger sent out mail urging Mayor Dinkins's reelection and Millard distributed literature featuring Mr. Giuliani.

19. Vallone became a candidate for governor in 1998. Millard was an unsuccessful congressional candidate in 1996. Ferrer and Messinger would run for mayor in 1997 (Ferrer withdrew before the primary to run for reelection as Bronx borough president).

20. In 1993 only two incumbents, Susan Alter and Sam Horowitz, chose not to run for reelection. Alter gave up her seat to run as Giuliani's "fusion" running mate for public advocate. After losing the Democratic primary, she ran as the Republican-Liberal candidate. She was defeated in the general election by Mark Green, the Democrat. Horowitz, who had served for two decades, retired.

21. In 1993, the voters revised the City Charter by voting to limit all municipal officials to two terms in office. *New York City Charter*, chapter 50.

22. For a discussion of the electoral advantages of incumbency, see Mayhew 1974.

23. Few Republican council candidates have qualified for public funds. In 1989, a single candidate received funds. Two years later, the number increased to twelve. In 1993, seven candidates participated in the program. In 1997, nine Republicans received funds.

24. The high costs were not limited to personnel. Kenneth Fisher, Brooklyn Borough President Howard Golden's election lawyer, said that he had set up a campaign finance computer system that cost $25,000 for hardware and software (Lynn 1989a).

25. Section 14-126 (1) of the State Election Law provides that the maximum penalty for failing to file a financial statement is $100 (State of New York, Board of Elections 1988: 27).

26. In 1993, 57.5 percent of the registered voters cast ballots. Four years later, 40.83 percent of the registered voters turned out for the general election (New York City Board of Elections 1998: 36). For more on voter turnout, see Piven and Cloward 1988; Wolfinger and Rosenstone 1980; Phillips and Blackman 1975.

27. The mayor attempted to appoint Joseph Erazo to the CFB as the body was considering sanctioning the Giuliani campaign for accepting illegal contributions. Mr. Erazo was not permitted to sit since the Department of Investigation had not completed its background investigation.

REFERENCES

Adamany, David. 1986. "The New Faces of American Politics." In Lloyd N. Cutler, Louis R. Cohen, and Roger M. Witten, eds., *Regulating Campaign Finance*, Annals of the American Academy of Political and Social Sciences. Beverly Hills, CA: Sage Publications: 12–23.

Alexander, Herbert E. 1991. *Reform and Reality; The Financing of State and Local Campaigns*. New York: The Twentieth Century Press.

————. 1984. *Financing Politics*. Washington, DC: Congressional Quarterly Press.

Barbanel, Josh. 1985. "Leichter Says Builders Gave Most To Members of Board of Estimate." *New York Times*, November 27, B4.

Brecher, Charles, Raymond D. Horton, with Robert A. Cropf and Dean Michael Mead. 1993. *Power Failure: New York City Politics and Policy Since 1960*. New York and Oxford: Oxford University Press.

Chappell, Henry W., Jr. 1982. "Campaign Contributions and Congressional Voting: A Simultaneous Probit-Tobit Model." *Review of Economics and Statistics* 64 (February): 77–83.

Frendreis, John P., and Richard W. Waterman. 1985. "PAC Contributions and Legislative Behavior: Senate Voting on Trucking Deregulation." *Social Science Quarterly* 66 (June): 401–12.

Grenzke, Janet M. 1989. "PACs and the Congressional Supermarket: The Currency Is Complex." *American Journal of Political Science* 33 (February): 1–24.

Leichter, Franz S. 1986. "Campaign Contributions to Members of the Board of Estimate and the Democratic County Committees, 1981–1986, A Report by State Senator Franz Leichter, 28th Senate District, Manhattan."

————. 1985. "Study of Campaign Contributions by State Senator Franz Leichter."

Lynn, Frank. 1989a. "Campaign Fund Rules Befuddling Candidates." *New York Times*, April 13, B2.
———. 1989b. "Finance Law Called a Partial Success." *New York Times*, November 12, 42.
———. 1989c. "Stein Attacked on Campaign Finance Refusal." *New York Times*, January 25, B3.
———. 1989d. "Candidates Ask for More Public Campaign Money." *New York Times*, December 14, B2.
Mayhew, David R. 1974. *Congress: The Electoral Connection*. New Haven: Yale University Press.
McKinley, Jr., James C. 1993a. "A Costly Council Victory ($70 a Vote to Be Precise)." *New York Times*, March 27, 24.
———. 1993b. "Steering Around the New York City Campaign Finance Law." *New York Times*, December 26, 33.
———. 1993c. "Giuliani Favors Linking Debates And Public Campaign Financing." *New York Times*, December 9, B3.
———. 1993d. "Dinkins Campaign to Pay Party Panel for Some Ads." *New York Times*, October 20, B2.
———. 1993e. "Campaign Finance Board Fines Dinkins Over Spending." *New York Times*, October 21, 1.
Newfield, Jack, and Wayne Barrett. 1988. *City for Sale: Ed Koch and the Betrayal of New York*. New York: Harper and Row.
New York City Board of Elections. 1998. "Annual Report." (January).
New York City Campaign Finance Board. 1998. "2001 Disclosure Guide." (March).
———. 1997. "Campaign Finance Handbook." (January).
———. 1994. "Types of Contributors." Data as of April 5, 1993 (draft).
———. 1993. "New York City Campaign Finance Board Holds Public Hearings Today and Tomorrow Following the 1993 Elections." Press release (December 8).
———. 1992. "Windows of Opportunity: Campaign Finance Reform and the New City Council." (July).
———. 1991a. "1991 Post-Election Public Hearings." Transcript (December 11). Carol Mele and Catherine M. Donohue, reporters.
———. 1991b. "1991 Post-Election Public Hearings." Transcript (December 12). Carol Mele and Catherine M. Donohue, reporters.
———. 1990. "Dollars and Disclosure: Campaign Finance Reform in New York City," September.
New York Public Interest Research Group, Inc. (NYPIRG). 1993. "Testimony of Neal Rosenstein and Gene Russianoff, Government Reform Coordinator and Senior Attorney, New York Public Interest Research Group, Inc., before the New York City Campaign Finance Board hearing on Impact of Campaign Finance Program and Voter Guide on 1993 City Elections," December 8.
———. 1987. "Wanted: A Government That Money Can't Buy."
New York Times editorial. 1993. "Deadline for Cleaner Politics," April 13, A30.
Phillips, Kevin, and Paul Blackman. 1975. *Electoral Reform and Voter Participation*. Stanford: American Enterprise System.

Piven, Frances Fox, and Richard Cloward. 1988. *Why Americans Don't Vote*. New York: Pantheon.

Sabato, Larry J. 1989. *Paying for Elections*. New York: Priority Press Publishers.

Scarrow, Howard A. 1983. *Parties, Elections, and Representation in the State of New York*. New York and London: New York University Press.

Sorauf, Frank J. 1988. *Money in American Elections*. Glenview, IL: Scott, Foresman and Company.

State of New York, Board of Elections. 1988. "Guide To Campaign Financial Disclosure." June.

State of New York, Commission on Government Integrity. 1988. "Unfinished Business." September 28.

Strom, Stephanie. 1991. "Koch's Campaign Panel Fined $35,000 for '89 Race." *New York Times*, May 22, B3.

Welch, William P. 1982. "Campaign Contributions and Legislative Voting: Milk Money and Dairy Price Supports." *Western Political Quarterly* 35 (December): 478–95.

Wilhite, Allen, and John Theilmann. 1987. "Labor PAC Contributions and Labor Legislation: A Simultaneous Logit Approach." *Public Choice* 53: 267–76.

Wolfinger, Raymond, and Steven Rosenstone. 1980. *Who Votes?* New Haven: Yale University Press.

Wright, John R. 1985. "PACs, Contributions, and Roll Calls: An Organizational Perspective." *American Political Science Review* 79 (June): 400–14.

8

Money, Elections, and Public Policy in New York Politics

Jeffrey M. Stonecash

There is little positive to say about money and politics (Alexander 1991). That applies across the nation and in New York. The list of evils associated with money is lengthy and infamous. Incumbents raise more than challengers, who have little ability to fund a campaign that can question the record of incumbents (Abramowitz 1989; 1991). Well-financed incumbents rely on consultants and pollsters, who manipulate images and themes and reduce the importance of reasoned discourse in campaigns (Dworkin 1996). Participation of the public through party organizations is reduced as the well financed turn more and more to consultants and direct mail to get their message out. Money determines outcomes as those with fewer resources are overwhelmed by campaign ads and targeted mailings (Breaux and Gierzynski 1991; Giles and Pritchard 1985; Gierzynski and Breaux 1991; Jacobson 1978, 1990; Shan and Stonecash 1994). Finally, money determines public policy. PACs give large amounts of money to politicians to make them sensitive to the concerns of special interests. Politicians worry about pleasing the PACs and are more responsive to those who give than to those who don't. That shapes policy decisions. It is a miracle that the public has any role in the process.

To paraphrase Twain, however, the stories of the death of democracy are greatly exaggerated. While all of the above conventional wisdoms have some truth, the set of statements has become a simplistic and very limiting view of how the political process works. That view excludes several crucial matters about New York politics that make the role of money much murkier than critics acknowledge. This essay is to propose a fuller view of the role of money and to argue that constituencies shape public policy debates.

CAMPAIGN FINANCE IN NEW YORK LEGISLATIVE ELECTIONS

Money is important. No one should ever dispute that. It buys advertising and mailings. It is also true that incumbents have more money than challengers and that incumbents now raise considerably more than challengers. Figure 8.1 presents the average expenditure for incumbents and challengers in New York state legislative elections for the years 1984–1996. Since 1984 there has been a consistent increase in the amount that incumbents spend, while challengers' funds have not increased nearly as much.

It is also the case that almost all incumbents win when they run for reelection (Stonecash 1993). The percentage of incumbents who have won in recent elections is around 95 percent.

Figure 8.1
Incumbent and Challenger Average Expenditure, by Year, 1984–1996, New York Assembly

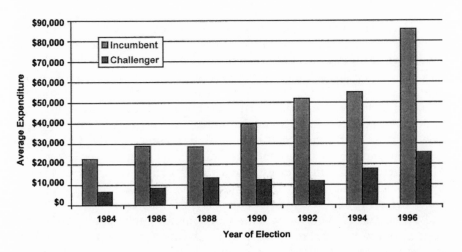

These data were taken from the files of the New York State Board of Elections. The data were recorded as they are presented in the files. It is clear that there are some errors in the files, and that the board is not always capable of getting candidates to file a corrected report. While there are some errors, it does appear that the large percentage of the reports are internally consistent. Whether reports systematically under or overreport expenditure is not known, however. The presumption is that the reports are substantially accurate.

The data suggest there is considerable validity to the perception that incumbents have a significant advantage in campaign fund-raising. The imbalance in money may, however, not be as severe as it appears. The argument of this paper is that in the situations in which money really matters—the races in which both parties have some chance of winning—the imbalance in money is much less. Further, in close races, it is very unclear as to whether money determines electoral outcomes. The imbalance in access to campaign funds is greatest where it does not matter and much less where it does matter.

To explain this argument, it is first necessary to review the political geography of the state and to explain how this is related to campaign finance. A perspective about what does drive public policy will then be offered.

THE POLITICAL GEOGRAPHY OF NEW YORK ELECTIONS

New York is a state divided by regional loyalties (Stonecash 1985, 1994, 1998). New York City is heavily Democratic and has been for decades. The upstate rural and small town areas are heavily Republican and have been for decades. In each of these areas the parties win overwhelmingly, and there is little political competition. Long Island is heavily Republican, and Democrats have difficulties winning in many districts there. In the remainder of the state, partisan loyalties are more evenly balanced, and each party has some chance of winning. Figure 8.2 shows the extent of competition for the different areas of the state. It indicates the percentage of seats won by the majority party by areas of the state. New York City is dominated by Democrats, while upstate rural areas are dominated by Republicans. Only in the suburbs around New York City and in some upstate urban areas is there a reasonably even division of seats between Democrats and Republicans.

These strong regional loyalties mean that there are not many close elections within the state. A close election is often regarded as one in which the winner receives less than 55 percent of the vote. Figure 8.3 presents the distribution of seats in the Assembly by the percent of the vote won by Republicans and Democrats in 1996. Only a few races fall into the category of being a close race. Many of them are won by very large margins. In the 1996 elections, the average margin of victory in Assembly elections was over 50 percent. Even if the definition of a close race is increased to winning with 60 percent of the vote or less, the percentage of close races does not change much. Close elections are not a feature of New York legislative elections, and they have not been for several decades.

ELECTORAL CLOSENESS AND RAISING CAMPAIGN FUNDS

A primary concern in elections is whether challengers are able to raise as much money as incumbents. In New York that is largely a function of the likely

Figure 8.2
Race and Income Bases of New York State Parties: Percent of Seats Won by Race and Income of District, Senate Republicans and Assembly Democrats, 1996

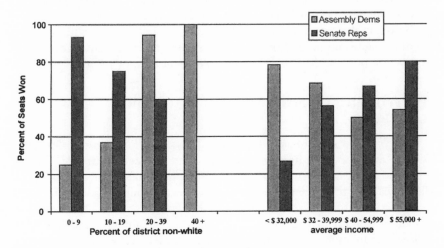

The groupings are based on classifications by the author.

Figure 8.3
Distribution of New York State Assembly Districts by Vote Proportions, 1996 Elections

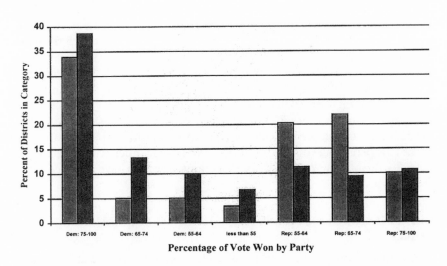

closeness of the election (Stonecash 1988, 1990; Shan and Stonecash 1994; Stonecash and Keith 1996). The closer the election, the greater the ability of challengers to raise money. Contributors do not donate money to candidates likely to lose. Figure 8.4 presents the average amounts of money raised by incumbents and challengers in the 1996 Assembly elections. The pattern shown, which also exists in the Senate, has prevailed for a number of years. Incumbents consistently raise more than challengers, but challengers in close races are able to raise much more than other challengers in lopsided races. There is, of course, some dynamic between being a strong candidate, raising more money, and being a marginal district (one that fairly regularly has close elections). The important matter is that challengers are able to raise more money when there is a reasonable prospect of beating an incumbent. When money could have an impact, challengers do fairly well in matching the resources of incumbents.

For various reasons (the district has balanced party enrollment, an incumbent has neglected the district, or a well-known challenger has decided to enter the race) challengers are seen as viable in some races and not in others. Legislative campaign committees, which have become more important over time (Jones and Borris 1985; Dwyre and Stonecash 1992; Gierzynski 1992), spend considerable resources on polling to monitor campaigns to determine the races in which their incumbents face a strong challenger, in which their challenger has a chance to defeat an incumbent, or in which the seat is open (no incumbent) and their candidate has a reasonable chance to win. When a

Figure 8.4
Average Expenditure for Incumbents and Challengers by Proportion of the Vote Won, 1996 New York State Assembly Elections

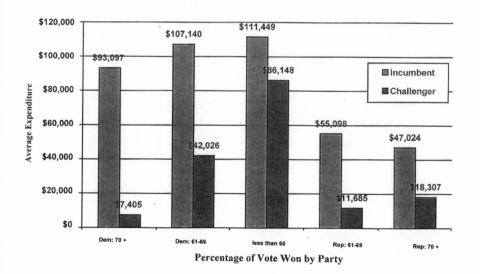

candidate has a chance to win, the legislative campaign committees then spend money helping the candidate (Stonecash 1988, 1990; Dwyre and Stonecash 1992; Stonecash and Keith 1996). These expenditures involve polling, research, and campaign mailings, and are called on-behalf-of (OBO) expenditures. To calculate the total recorded expenditure on a race, it is necessary to add the two sources of expenditure together. This is done, with races again grouped by closeness, in Figure 8.5. The parties direct their resources to close elections, with most of their funds going to challengers (Stonecash and Keith 1996: 319). Again, challengers do fairly well compared to incumbents in close races, but not otherwise.

ASSESSMENT

The reality of campaign finance in New York politics is that incumbents generally win by large margins, and most party members run in districts that have lopsided party loyalties. Incumbents raise much more than challengers, but this occurs in districts where large sums of challenger funds would be unlikely to produce challenger wins because of the distribution of party enrollment. The enormous advantage that incumbents have in campaign fund-raising is largely in districts where their advantage in fundraising is not necessary and unlikely to be the source of their margins of victory. In the marginal districts, those that tend to be close, challengers do much better match-

Figure 8.5
Average Expenditure for Incumbents and Challengers, with Party OBO Money Added, by Proportion of the Vote Won, 1994, New York State Assembly Elections

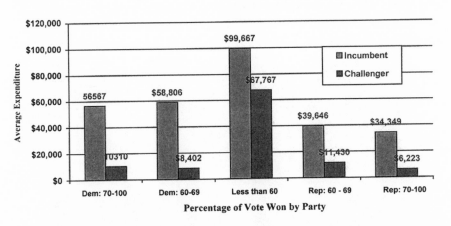

The groupings in the left of the table are based on classifications by the author. Those on the right are based on the classifications presented in Michael Barone, William Lilley III, Laurence J. Defranco, and William M. Diefendefer III. 1988. *State Legislative Elections.* Washington, DC: Congressional Quarterly Press.

ing the funds of incumbents. Incumbents do much better than challengers in situations where they probably do not need to do so much better. When it matters, challengers are able to come close to incumbents.

If there has been a significant change in the last decade in campaign finance, it is the tendency of incumbents without serious challenges to raise more and more money. They probably do so in part because the money is there for the asking, and because it is better to be safe than sorry in a political world of more volatile voters. It is also possible that with more legislators who come from a background in politics (Stonecash and Lo 1995) are staying longer (Stonecash 1994) and are more concerned with staying in office, they may raise money to discourage challengers. But the fact that Republicans win regularly by large margins in upstate rural areas and Democrats win regularly by large margins in New York City is not due to money (Sorauf 1992). It is due to party enrollment advantages. Money is not going to elect a Democrat in rural upstate areas. Conservative policy positions will help that. Money is not going to elect a Republican in the Bronx or Manhattan. Liberal policy positions will help that.

ELECTIONS AND PUBLIC POLICY POSITIONS

It is often argued that money drives campaigns and public calculations. The argument here is that it is difficult to attribute outcomes to money, so it is difficult to conclude that the ability of relatively safe incumbents to raise large sums of money from PACs, affluent contributors, and interest groups determines their policy positions.

What, then, shapes policy discussions? The factors that shape party margins of victory—regional differences—shape the parties and their positions on issues. The parties have very different constituency bases that shape many of the positions they develop and advocate. Figure 8.6 indicates how well Democrats do in legislative elections in each house by the income of the district and the percent of minorities in the district.

The higher the median family income of a district, the higher the percentage of seats Republicans win (Stonecash 1998: 68–69). In the Assembly the tendency is less pronounced because Democrats in the Assembly draw Assembly district boundaries, and they have been able to create more affluent districts in which Democrats have a reasonable chance of victory. Another indicator of the differences in party bases is how the parties fare by the percentage of nonwhites in the district. When the percent of nonwhites is relatively high, Republicans have little chance of victory, while it is very high when the district has few nonwhites.

These patterns create significant differences in the electoral bases of the two legislative parties. Democrats are much more likely to have seats in low to moderate income districts, while Republicans are more likely to have seats in affluent districts. Democrats are more likely to have seats in districts with

Figure 8.6
Race and Income Bases of New York State Parties: Percent of Seats Won by
Race and Income of District, Senate Republicans and Assembly Democrats
1996

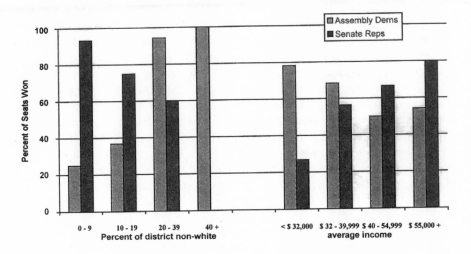

higher proportions of nonwhites, while Republicans are more likely to have seats in districts with a very low proportion of nonwhites.

These electoral bases drive the policy positions taken by the parties. The impact of these party differences can be seen in two fundamental policy choices made in the last decade. In 1987 and 1995 the governor and legislature revised the state income tax system. This issue entails some of the most fundamental policy questions in state politics. It involves the overall level of taxes and the amount of revenue the state will have for programs such as school aid and Medicaid. Tax decisions also determine who will pay what taxes, which involves questions of equity and fairness.

When taxes became an issue in these two years, the two parties made very different proposals as to what should be done about taxes. The tax revisions proposed by the parties in those years are shown in Figures 8.7 and 8.8. In 1987, Assembly Democrats, with a substantial proportion of their electoral base derived from low-income districts, proposed cuts that gave much smaller reductions to the affluent. Senate Republicans proposed larger reductions for the affluent. In 1995 the differences became even more pronounced. Republican Governor George Pataki, who won only about 26 percent of the vote in liberal New York City, proposed a tax cut that would have given substantial cuts to the affluent. He also proposed eliminating many low-income individuals from the rolls, but the actual reductions in taxes paid was very small for these individuals since they already paid little in taxes. Senate Republicans en-

Figure 8.7
Contrasting Tax Proposals: Senate, Assembly, and Cuomo Proposed Tax Cuts in 1987

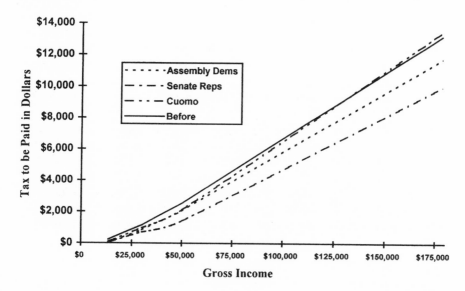

Figure 8.8
Contrasting Tax Proposals: Pataki and Assembly Proposed Tax Cuts for 1995 and 1996

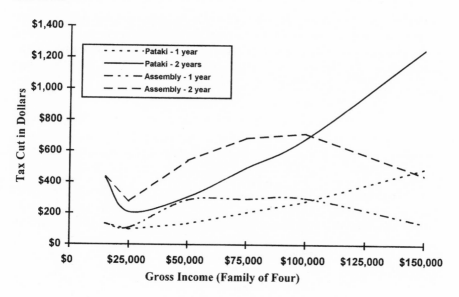

dorsed his proposals. The Assembly Democrats again proposed cuts that would be distributed very differently than those proposed by the Republicans.

Money is presumed to dominate campaigns and to then dominate the decision process after the election. Democrats are particularly interesting in this process because they are generally expected to represent liberal interests, the less affluent, and minorities. Democrats take large sums from PACs and regularly hold fund-raisers in which the affluent are asked and expected to contribute. If money shapes the positions candidates and parties adopt, then we should not see Democrats focusing their advocacy on low-income groups. Yet, the positions adopted by Democrats on the major issue of levels of taxation and the distribution of tax burdens over the last decade indicate that their prime focus has been on lower- and middle-income constituents, the very groups that are not the major contributors to campaigns. The reason is that the *constituency base* of Democrats is primarily low- and middle-income groups.

Incumbents may raise large sums of money, but they generally do not need it because they run in districts that already heavily favor one party over another. It is the constituency base of politicians and parties that shapes their policy concerns and drives their behavior.

REFERENCES

Abramowitz, Alan I. 1989. "Campaign Spending in U.S. Senate Elections." *Legislative Studies Quarterly* 14, 4 (November): 487–507.

———. 1991. "Incumbency, Campaign Spending, and the Decline of Competition in U.S. House Elections." *Journal of Politics* 53, 1 (February): 34–36.

Alexander, Herbert E. 1991. *Reform and Reality: The Financing of State and Local Campaigns.* New York: The Twentieth Century Fund Press.

Breaux, David A., and Anthony Gierzynski. 1991. "'It's Money that Matters': Campaign Expenditures and State Legislative Primaries." *Legislative Studies Quarterly* 16, 3 (August): 429–44.

Dworkin, Ronald. 1996. "The Curse of American Politics." *The New York Review of Books* (October 17): 19–24.

Dwyre, Diana, and Jeffrey M. Stonecash. 1992. "Where's the Party: Changing State Party Organizations." *American Politics Quarterly* 20, 4 (July): 326–44.

Gierzynski, Anthony. 1992. *Legislative Party Campaign Committees in the States.* Lexington: University of Kentucky Press.

Gierzynski, Anthony, and David Breaux. 1991. "Money and Votes in State Legislative Elections." *Legislative Studies Quarterly* 16, 10 (May): 203–18.

Giles, Michael W., and Anita Pritchard. 1985. "Campaign Expenditures and Legislative Elections in Florida." *Legislative Studies Quarterly* 10, 1 (February): 71–88.

Jacobson, Gary C. 1978. "The Effects of Campaign Spending in Congressional Elections." *American Political Science Review* 72: 469–91.

———. 1990. "The Effects of Campaign Spending in House Elections: New Evidence for Old Argument." *American Journal of Political Science* 34: 334–62.

Jones, Ruth S., and Thomas J. Borris. 1985. "Strategic Contributing in Legislative Campaigns: The Case of Minnesota," *Legislative Studies Quarterly* 10, 1 (February): 89–105.

Shan, Chao-Chi, and Jeffrey M. Stonecash. 1994. "Legislative Resources and Electoral Margins: The New York State Senate, 1950–1990." *Legislative Studies Quarterly* 19, 1 (February): 79–93.

Sorauf, Frank J. 1992. *Inside Campaign Finance: Myths and Realities.* New Haven: Yale University Press.

Stonecash, Jeffrey M. 1985. "State-Local Relations: The City and Upstate." In Peter W. Colby, ed., *New York State Today.* Albany: State University of New York Press: 41–50.

———. 1988. "Working at the Margins: Campaign Finance and Party Strategy in New York Assembly Elections." *Legislative Studies Quarterly* 13, 4 (November): 477–93.

———. 1990. "Campaign Finance in New York Senate Elections." *Legislative Studies Quarterly* 15, 2 (May): 247–62.

———. 1991a. "The Significance of House Control for Campaign Finance: New York, 1986–1988." *Comparative State Politics* 12, 2 (April): 6–14.

———. 1991b. "Observations from New York: The Limits of 50-State Studies and the Case for Case Studies." *Comparative State Politics* 12, 4 (August): 1–9.

———. 1993. "The Pursuit and Retention of Legislative Office in New York, 1870–1990: Reconsidering Sources of Change." *Polity* 26, 2 (Winter): 301–15.

———. 1994. "Political Parties and Partisan Conflict." In Jeffrey M. Stonecash, John K. White, and Peter Colby, eds., *Governing New York State.* Albany: State University of New York Press: 83–101.

———. 1998. "Political Parties and Conflict." In Sarah F. Liebschutz, ed., *New York Politics and Government.* Lincoln: University of Nebraska Press: 63–79.

Stonecash, Jeffrey M., and Rebecca Lo. 1995. "The Decline of Private Sector Experience Among New York Senators, 1890–1990." *Comparative State Politics* 16, 4 (August): 14–24.

Stonecash, Jeffrey M., and Sara E. Keith. 1996. "Maintaining a Party: Providing and Withdrawing Campaign Finance Funds." *Party Politics* 2, 3: 313–28.

9

Best Chance Since Watergate: Campaign Finance Reform in the 105th Congress

Monica Bauer

INTRODUCTION: WHY NO REFORM?

As campaign costs have soared for both congressional and presidential elections, and money provided by large soft money donations to parties has grown, people within the campaign finance reform community have been hard-pressed to understand why reform does not come. The results of an ABC News/*Washington Post* poll in July of 1997 confirmed past polling results: 63 percent of the public "opposes the way Presidential and Congressional campaigns are financed." Yet, in the same poll, 67 percent "said they had little hope that Mr. Clinton or the Congress would substantively change things" (Berke 1997c:1).

Reform proponents describe the Watergate scandals as the impetus for the only comprehensive campaign finance reform legislation ever signed into law, the 1974 revisions of the 1971 Federal Elections Campaign Act (FECA). The 1974 reforms, coming as a direct result of the Watergate scandal, gave us a model of the possibilities of future reforms. It takes a scandal to raise a campaign finance reform bill, or so the wisdom went. This was frustrating to the reform community, but it made sense. The next sweeping campaign finance reform would come only after another scandal.

In 1996, a new campaign finance scandal appeared in the form of donations to the Democratic party and the Clinton campaign from individuals with ties to foreign governments. This produced optimism among reform activists and journalists that at last something would be done to reform the influence of big money on politics. This has not happened, and this article will explain why, by analyzing the major reform activity in the legislative and executive branches of the federal government from 1996 to 1998.

In this highly charged setting of scandal and investigation, campaign finance reform was thought to have its best chance of passage since Watergate. The most senior campaign finance reform group, Common Cause, editorialized in February 1997, coinciding with the introduction of S-25, the new McCain-Feingold bill:

At no time since Watergate has public discontent with government been higher. And at no time since that scandal has the public's ire been so clearly identified with a specific problem—the campaign finance abuses that have dominated political news during and since the last election.

Just as the Watergate scandal led to the passage of sweeping political reform in the mid-1970's, the scandals of 1996 can lead to fundamental campaign finance reform in this Congress, reformers note. (Common Cause 1997b)

This was still the feeling among press and pundits months later, even as the McCain-Feingold bill managed to pick up only one additional Republican co-sponsor, Senator Fred Thompson (R-Tenn.), who, not coincidentally, tried to seem as fair and bipartisan as possible while gearing up to chair hearings into the alleged money scandals of 1996. Although the bill went nowhere from the moment it was introduced in the 105th Congress, the hope was expressed over and over that the hearings would galvanize both voters and their representatives, enabling the bill to pass. Even the usually reliable *Congressional Quarterly* predicted in April 1997: "Looking ahead, the temperature seems sure to rise. Weeks of congressional hearings highlighting the failings of the campaign finance system are likely to create or intensify demand for change. Members of Congress, especially those facing the voters in 1998, will ignore this demand at their own peril" (Cassata 1997).

So, by early 1997, conditions looked ripe for reform. Yet, as this book goes to press, no real reform has taken place. This author has concluded that the campaign finance reform community was wrong in its assumptions. Much of the enthusiasm for campaign finance reform's chances after the 1996 elections rested on an analogy between scandals and reforms. Since the 1973 scandals had led to 1974 reforms, so would the 1996 scandals lead to reform by 1997 or at the latest before the 1998 elections. However, this analysis ignores the real reason for the 1974 reforms.

THE REAL STORY BEHIND THE 1974 REFORMS:
OVERWHELMING PARTISAN ADVANTAGE

Let's pose another way of looking at the 1974 reforms. Richard Nixon, a Republican president, had been governing with a Democratic majority in both houses of Congress. During 1974, there was a unique dynamic where the president, dodging impeachment, with the lowest recorded favorability score in the history of polling, was faced with trying to govern through a hostile and newly energized Democratic Congress. This Congress had the power to rewrite the campaign finance laws any way it wished, with no need to compromise with a weakened president or a defensive minority. Any Republican opposing campaign reform in 1974 would be painted as a defender of the most corrupt practices of the first president likely to be convicted of impeachment. No Republican senator would risk a filibuster under such conditions. Should Nixon veto the reform, Congress could easily override it. They demonstrated their ability to override a veto with the War Powers Act in the same period.

Under those unique historical circumstances, the Congress, responding partly to the impetus of scandal, the suggestions of the national media, but mostly the needs of its incumbent Democratic majority, wrote campaign finance laws that would favor Democrats and punish Republicans. They could pass such a law without having to come to any sort of compromise with the opposition. The 1974 reforms were intended to cement the Democratic advantage in labor union money into law, while decimating what had been the base of the Republican party, corporate and individual big givers. Using the language of moral outrage, and using the supposed outrage of their constituents like a blunt instrument, Democrats crafted a bill to suit themselves that also qualified as genuine reform.

One part of the Watergate analogy left to be discussed is the myth that an outraged public demanded these reforms. If that were true, one could reasonably expect that another scandal would produce another suitably outraged public, demanding reform. This is such accepted wisdom that it is scarcely challenged. Yet, a little digging uncovers the sad fact that, even during Watergate, voters were hardly mobilized behind campaign finance reform. Unfortunately, "political reform has historically never topped the public's agenda, even during the Watergate crisis. In a June 1974 Gallup poll, completed two months before Nixon resigned, only 36 percent of adults polled named dissatisfaction with government, political corruption, *or* Watergate as the nation's top problem. Forty-eight percent said the biggest problem was the high cost of living" (America Online 1997b). It is important to note that the 36 percent figure combined those who said yes to one or more of three polling questions, and this at a time when the national debate was fixated over daily revelations of big money political corruption linked to Watergate.

When one looks more carefully at public opinion polling, one sees very little evidence of a mobilized mass of angry voters demanding reform, either in 1974 or 1997. This fits with the picture of American voters assembled by political scientists: the vast majority are nonideological, practical people most concerned with issues of importance to their personal lives. The great masses of American voters can be moved by "high salience" issues such as war or peace, depression or recovery, but they pay far less attention to politics as the game is played in Washington than they do to how well their local sports team is doing.

Journalists and reformers read polling information and believe they see evidence of outrage, and look to Congress to respond. For example, this *New York Times* editorial is typical: "Many in Congress wish that the whole issue [of reform] would go away. They need to understand that the public has put a high priority on reform. If they need any reminders on this score, they might spend some time listening to their constituents while they are home for the holidays" ("Some Hope" 1997).

The *New York Times* editors decide that the people place a "high priority on reform" by reading polls. However, like most who read polls, they don't understand what polls measure, or fail to measure. Polls are a mirror of what people say when asked off the top of their heads for their opinions. Rarely can an opinion poll measure the intensity of an opinion. Thus, it can be said that there might be agreement on supporting reform by a large number of respondents (support appears to be "a mile wide"), but these opinions are not strongly held, nor do they result in action on the part of voters (support is "an inch deep").

While polls would lead a person to believe campaign finance was a high priority, other evidence about the strength of the opinion can lie buried deeper in the poll results. For example, in a *New York Times*/CBS News poll, it was reported, "Almost nine out of ten people surveyed see a need for changes in fundraising procedures, or even a total overhaul. But only three in ten believe that the President really wants to change it, despite his announced commitment to it. The resolve of Congress is subject to even greater doubt, with only 23% of the public convinced that the lawmakers . . . actually want to change current laws" (Clines 1997:A1). This page one material implies that the public will be upset with the president and Congress if they don't provide changes, or even a total overhaul, of campaign finance. But buried in the story comes more data. A surprised Francis Clines writes:

[F]or all the heat that the issue is generating in Washington, the public is far from rating campaign law overhaul a compelling priority in comparison with crime, schools, and the economy. In fact, only 2 respondents, out of 1,347 polled, cited campaign fundraising when asked to name the nation's most important problem. . . . Further, only 12 percent of respondents said they had been following news of the issue "very closely," and 43 percent complained that the news media had been spending too much time on it. (1997:A8)

At nearly the same time as the *New York Times*/CBS News poll just cited, Princeton Survey Research Associates conducted a similar poll for the Center for Responsive Politics. The similarities are striking. In the Princeton poll, a clear majority, over 60 percent, said that "campaign finance reform should at least be a high priority this year," but "only 15 percent ranked it as the top priority for Washington." They "overwhelmingly believed other issues—improving education, reducing crime, reforming Medicare and Social Security—deserve higher priority" (America Online 1997b).

Members of Congress and their staffs generally know how to read polls. Dick Gephardt, the House minority leader, has not made campaign finance reform a priority, not because he arrogantly dismisses public demand for reform, but because he understands that the public is much more interested in other things of higher salience to their personal lives. Laura Nichols, spokesperson for Gephardt, recently said about campaign finance reform, "It's at the bottom of concerns of almost all constituents, which is why you get such a slow reaction" (Skorneck 1997).

In reality, campaign finance reform will only come about when the real conditions under which the 1974 FECA reforms were passed are repeated. Those conditions have less to do with public opinion or demand for reform, and more to do with the partisan makeup of our lawmaking bodies, the House and Senate. As long as three conditions exist, namely (1) the status quo in campaign financing remains advantageous to incumbents of both parties, (2) the partisan balance remains such that no single party can use campaign finance reform as a blunt instrument to hurt the other side, and (3) public opinion favoring campaign finance reform is a mile wide and an inch deep, there will be no campaign finance reform.

IN CONTRAST TO 1974, IN THE 1990s, SOFT MONEY HELPS BOTH PARTIES

By the 1990s, the status quo was advantageous to incumbents in both parties. The biggest boon had been the creation of "soft money." Just as PAC (political action committee) restrictions on federal candidates began to make fund-raising harder, the soft money gravy train began to roll. No sooner had the reform community celebrated a new era of campaign finance than the ground shifted in a way that would provide a new source of unregulated money to both presidential and congressional nominees. By 1979, the Congress had amended the FECA to allow soft money donations to political parties.

What is soft money, and why has it become the lightning rod for a new generation of reformers? Soft money is the unregulated, unlimited amounts of money that may be given to political parties by both individuals and corporations. Whereas the 1974 reforms outlawed all corporate contributions and placed limits on the amounts that individuals and PACs could give to campaigns, the 1979 revision created a new way to support candidates and get around the intent of the 1974 law. The difference between soft money and "hard" (regulated and limited) money was this lawyerly distinction:

Soft money, given to parties, is supposed to support nonfederal activities, or to fund state and local portions of political activities carried out in a particular state in so-called "mixed activities" (where both local and federal candidates will receive a benefit, such as voter registration drives). Hard money is supposed to pay for the "federal" portion of mixed activities. . . . But soft money CAN end up financing portions of a political activity attributable to federal races. . . . the ambiguities in its regulation create a system ripe for abuse. (Bauer 1994)

Soft money has become more necessary as costs increase, while the allowable hard money donations remain at the same dollar level as the 1974 legislation, now eroded by inflation to less than one-third of what it would have bought in 1974. In 1974, the total amount spent on all House elections was a little over $53 million, and the Senate races cost an aggregate of over $34 million. By 1994, the House races totaled $405.7 million, and Senate races cost $318.4 million (Beck 1997). During this same twenty-year period, the limits on hard money remained fixed, at $1,000 per person (in both primary and general elections), and $5,000 per PAC (also potentially doubled by giving $5,000 in both primary and general elections). It is simple math. How are federal candidates going to make up the difference between what they want to spend and what the law says they may raise from individual donors? By 1996, soft money raised by both parties totaled $263.5 million. This was a 200 percent increase over soft money totals in 1992 ("Soft Money"). Although earlier there might have been a partisan advantage for one group to wipe out soft money, now both parties are so dependent on soft money that it is hard to believe either one wants to give it up. When Democrats surpassed Republicans at soft money fund-raising in the 1988 elections, a top Republican fund-raiser proposed a cap of $50,000 on soft money donors; this was rejected by top Democratic fund-raiser Bob Farmer, who had breathed new life into the party by tapping big contributors (Bauer 1994: 243). Although by 1998 the Republicans were raising twice as much soft money as the Democrats, both sides would lose under any attempt to ban soft money.

By the 1996 elections, soft money was being used to fund so-called "independent expenditure campaigns," which allowed parties and groups to spend unlimited amounts of money to persuade voters as long as these monies were not used in coordination with a candidate's campaign committee or didn't directly mention the candidate they supported. So if you wanted to give a million dollars to Jayne Q. Candidate, you could give indirectly to ads that promoted her issues or agenda or even trashed her opponent. As long as the ads didn't say "Vote for Jayne," they were legal. Such campaigns were waged on behalf of both Democrats and Republicans and became another useful tool for evading the 1974 contribution limits.

A consensus had been growing in the campaign finance reform community that soft money was flooding into politics, allowing for the return of the $100,000 donor and the implication that large donations are thinly veiled bribes. Responding to this perception, members of the House and Senate introduced a number of reform bills throughout the 1980s and early 1990s. Most appeared either deliberately drawn as veto bait (allowing politicians to claim they had at least tried to reform politics), or blatantly unconstitutional and hence unlikely to pass.

In the 1992 presidential election, reform groups such as Common Cause threw their enthusiastic support to Bill Clinton, who had campaigned on a campaign-finance reform platform. Although Clinton talked a great game, he only sent to the Hill a single campaign finance reform bill, in 1993. That bill, which would have hurt incumbents of both parties by further cutting PAC funds, died a quick death, even though the bill didn't touch the biggest issue in reform, soft money. The next attempt at reform, developed in the Senate but supposedly championed by the White House, was even less realistic: a frontal assault on a system that both parties had come to understand, manipulate, and use for their own benefit.

THE DRAMA BEGINS: THE LONG SLOW DEATH OF THE McCAIN-FEINGOLD BILL

At first, senators wrote off the McCain-Feingold bill as originally introduced in 1996 as another of those doomed pieces of legislation that quixotic reformers periodically throw into the legislative hopper. But McCain and Feingold would not take their first rejection as definitive. They insisted the time was ripe for a major campaign finance overhaul and were convinced that the time was even more opportune after the 1996 elections, with revelations of new campaign finance scandals. This tenacity has made McCain and Feingold the central figures in the drama of campaign finance reform in the late 1990s.

The centerpiece of efforts to reform campaign finance in 1997 was a bill that had been barely noticed in the previous Congress. Its authors were the powerful Republican Commerce Committee chair, Senator John McCain of Arizona, and the least senior member of the minority party, Senator Russell Feingold of Wisconsin. What McCain saw in Feingold was a reformer's zeal that matched his own. Feingold had won a Senate campaign where he had been the underdog, outspent and outgunned. But in reform-minded Wisconsin, Feingold's pledge to clean up politics struck a chord that had been resonating since the days of "Fighting Bob" LaFollette's Progressive Party bid for president in 1924. Feingold blasted the effects of big money on American politics, and was well known for his defense of federally funded elections where not a dime of special interest money could flow.

McCain was dedicated to destroying politics as usual, a fact that had not endeared him to his own leadership. For example, McCain kept a person on staff whose major function was to identify pork-barrel spending in legislation and alert the press as to the offending member. This staffer became known as "the Ferret," and was a potent symbol of McCain's intention to shake up the system (Lewis 1997:34). Although McCain didn't agree with Feingold on federal funding of elections, he admired the junior senator's outspoken reform agenda. Also, reform in the past had been a vehicle for partisan wrangling; McCain's strategy was to reach out to a Democrat and attempt to avoid the partisan nature of previous bills. If campaign finance reform were to succeed, a bipartisan effort might be the best route. The team of McCain and Feingold just might have a chance.

The centerpiece of the second McCain-Feingold bill, introduced after the 1996 elections, is a ban on all soft money. Since banning soft money hurts both parties but hurts the majority party more, it was never likely to pass, no matter how many reformers continued to use the faulty logic of the Watergate reform analogy. Since the party in control of both houses of Congress raised nearly twice as much soft money as the Democrats, it was particularly unlikely to pass (Superville 1998b). But there is little reason to believe its fate would have been different if the Democrats had been in control.

Outwardly, from the first introduction of S-25 in February 1997, Democrats from the president on down claimed to support it. But these claims proved to be very thin indeed, as the months from February to June wore on, with no effort by the Democrats to bring the bill up for a vote. So the question remains, what did Democratic party leaders mean when they purported to support the McCain-Feingold bill? Here is a clue: "All Democrats, including Daschle [Senate Minority Leader Tom Daschle, D-S.D.], claim publicly to support McCain-Feingold. Their enthusiasm derives from their certainty that Republicans will find a way to kill it" (Lewis 1997:34).

As originally introduced, S-25 included other provisions guaranteed to anger large groups of senators from both parties. Writing in May 1997, journalist Michael Lewis catalogued the sins of McCain-Feingold:

Senators tight with well-financed causes (pro-life, pro-trial lawyers, pro-women in Congress) want to ditch the McCain-Feingold ban on political action committees. . . . Senators beholden to broadcasters object to the provision of free television ads for candidates who accept voluntary spending limits. Senators from small states decry the provision that requires politicians to raise 60% of their funds from people eligible to vote for them—that would cut into their advantage raising money from the causes and the corporations.(34)

In short, McCain-Feingold, which originally would have banned all soft money, ended all PACs, and required a raft of new regulations to keep special interest money to a minimum in politics, had something for just about every incumbent to hate.

THE COMPROMISING BEGINS

Senator McCain soon let his colleagues know that he was open to compromise and was willing to talk to any potential cosponsor on the Republican side (the Democrats, on paper at least, were supporting it already). McCain let it be known that "as far as he was concerned, a McCain-Feingold bill needed only to pass two simple tests: 1) it must limit the influence of private money in public life; 2) it must reduce the financial advantage incumbents enjoy over challengers, and thus make it easier for outsiders to get in and for insiders to be tossed out ... but everything else was negotiable" (Lewis 1997:34). Was Senator McCain unaware that the two "nonnegotiable" items were the largest benefits available to incumbents of both parties? Making "everything else ... negotiable" didn't leave much important to negotiate.

Three months after the bill was introduced, on May 25, McCain-Feingold finally added a third Republican cosponsor, Senator Susan Collins (R-Me.). In order to get Senator Collins's support, the authors agreed to drop the ban on PACs, opting instead to reduce their influence by cutting the maximum PAC donation in half, to $2,500 per election. The newly revised bill also added a "bright-line test" to show the difference between political ads (which are considered campaign contributions in hard money) and so-called "issue ads," which had popped up all over the 1996 elections as thinly disguised campaign ads skirting campaign finance limits on contributions.

Also to please Senator Collins, language was added to limit the amount of money a candidate could spend from his or her own personal funds, phrased as a voluntary limit to be rewarded with free television time and other perks for those who complied. Collins said the experience of running against three millionaires in two years helped her decide to work for campaign finance reform. "'I am a living example of how difficult it is for a person who is not wealthy to pursue elected office' she said. 'Thus, I am especially gratified that the substitute proposal will more effectively sever the link between personal wealth and public office'" (Clymer 1997:1).

Was this revision likely to move the bill forward? The fact that by April 1997, there were fifty-seven different campaign finance bills in the House and Senate signaled that few were pinning their reform hopes on McCain-Feingold (Clymer 1997:1). As long as the bill retained its centerpiece, the ban on soft money, senators and representatives would not coalesce behind McCain and Feingold in the Senate, or the authors of the House version, Representatives Christopher Shays (R-Conn.) and Martin Meehan (D-Mass.). Instead of building momentum toward passage, McCain-Feingold and Shays-Meehan were merely the opening shots in a volley of proposals, some obviously designed to fail, some with intriguing origins and possibilities.

PARTISANSHIP AND POSITION TAKING;
COUNTER-PROPOSALS ON REFORM IN 1997

The front-page headline on the *New York Times* of April 6, 1997, seemed to say it all: "Many Proposals, Few Supporters, On Campaign Law: 57 Measures Languish; Each New Idea for Regulations on Finance Succeeds Only in Stiffening Resistance" (Clymer 1997:1). Just two months after the new McCain-Feingold bill was introduced, with the president demanding that Congress pass it and send it to his desk for approval by July 4, two powerful congressional forces were hard at work: partisanship and symbolic politics.

Partisanship remains the one constant in congressional life. It doesn't seem to matter whether a bill has the slightest chance of passing (even Common Cause's chief lobbyist on reform considered McCain-Feingold largely dead or dying by April), members of Congress have a gut instinct to press partisan buttons. Senator Mitch McConnell (R-Ky.), the leader of the antireform forces, made statements that indicated he might vote for McCain-Feingold if it were only a little less partisan, a little less biased toward the Democrats: "A sticking point will be requiring organized labor to operate only with voluntarily contributed money [a swipe at the powerful labor PACs funded partially by union dues]. I hope that won't be a killer provision for Democrats. It's only elementary fairness" (Clymer 1997:1). As McConnell uttered these words, virtually everyone in Washington understood that McConnell had every intention of tacking on killer amendments, and these would not be seen by any Democrat as "elementary fairness."

A month before Senator McConnell's statement indicating he might support reform if it were more evenhanded, McConnell had organized a press conference where he stood with groups on the left and on the right, all united on one thing: the centerpiece of McCain-Feingold, the soft-money ban, drove a stake through the heart of political free speech and was an unconscionable millstone around the neck of the body politic. At the highly publicized March 14 press conference on Capitol Hill, McConnell stood with representatives from groups otherwise ideologically opposed, such as the National Education Association and the National Rifle Association, to proclaim that the McCain-Feingold bill ought to be dead and buried. McConnell's coalition partners had contributed jointly over $243 million in political contributions in the previous ten years, tripling their soft money contributions in 1996 (Common Cause 1997a).

A combination of partisanship and position taking could be seen in the fifty-seven different campaign finance proposals that had been introduced in Congress by early April. Some would have punished Democrats by singling out unions for regulation, others Republicans by cracking down on independent campaigns by supposedly nonpartisan groups such as the Christian Coalition. Why so many plans? It appeared that most of the bills were designed not for passage but for their ability to allow their authors and cosponsors to make symbolic statements like, "Yes, I am also concerned about campaign finance reform." These classic position-taking maneuvers tend to be noticed by media in the home district, giving the politician a chance to look good in the newspapers and the nightly news, thus enhancing visibility and chances for reelection, according to David Mayhew in his 1974 book, *Congress: The Electoral Connection.*

Civics textbooks describe Congress as a lawmaking body, but that is only a small slice of what Congress actually does. Members of Congress, whose first goal is reelection, need to show their constituents that they are doing something, even when Congress is so lacking in consensus that nothing much gets done. Symbolic actions, such as introducing bills without any real hope of passing, fulfill the function of "position taking." Clearly, if the members who authored and cosponsored these fifty-seven different measures were truly interested in reform, they could coalesce around one or two of the most likely bills and work to amend them. Introducing fifty-seven substitutions for McCain-Feingold (and Shays-Meehan in the House) is an indication that we have left the land of serious reform and entered the land of symbolic action.

By April, there was no pure Democratic position on campaign finance reform. The leadership was supposedly promoting McCain-Feingold (and its counterpart in the House, Shays-Meehan), but in fact did not put muscle behind either bill. Senate Majority Leader Daschle, publicly in favor, "has told fellow Senators that as written, McCain-Feingold won't fly" (Lewis 1997: 34). Senators Paul Wellstone (D-Minn.) and John Kerry (D-Mass.), introduced the "left-most" bill first proposed by Ellen Miller, once head of the Center for Responsive Politics, who announced in April that she was starting a new group, Public Campaign, dedicated to 100 percent public financing of campaigns. This "Clean Money and Campaign Reform Act" would give public funds to candidates who stayed within spending limits and took no PAC money, and would ban soft money. As it obviously hurt incumbents by helping challengers, it gained even less support than McCain-Feingold.

The purest Republican proposal was offered by Representative John Doolittle (R-Calif.), whose idea of campaign finance reform included ending all limits on donations. The only check on the power of money in politics under the Doolittle bill would be full disclosure, as soon as technically practical, of every dollar raised and spent. "He argues that soft money and independent spending play a big role only because individual contributions have been held down, and says he is tired of 'the constant leftward push for campaign reform. . . . Freedom works,' Mr. Doolittle said. 'The promoters of the left-wing bills basically don't think freedom works'" (Clymer 1997: 24).

The position that "freedom works" was reiterated by the Republican National Committee (RNC), meeting in July, two weeks after Clinton's July 4 1997, deadline for McCain-Feingold had come and gone without much notice, while the number of campaign finance proposals in Congress increased from fifty-seven to seventy. RNC Chair Jim Nicholson argued that the problem was not in the campaign finance system, but in how the Democrats sought to evade the rules. In trying to bolster his case, Nicholson unveiled the conclusions of a Republican party working group, which suggested that the best way to improve the system was not to limit spending, but to do a better job of disclosing contributions to the public. The group turned aside the calls of reform advocates that the campaign system be overhauled and concluded that, if anything, candidates should spend more money on campaigns. (Berke 1997a)

THE ACADEMIC ALTERNATIVE

Some of the most interesting new ideas in the debate came out of a group of four academics and a journalist: Norman J. Ornstein of the American Enterprise Institute, Thomas E. Mann of the Brookings Institute, Michael J. Malbin of the State University of New York at Albany, Anthony Corrado of Colby College, and former journalist and campaign finance reform activist Paul Taylor. This group of five had no need to attack or defend partisan positions and no need to engage in symbolic actions of "position taking" to show constituents symbolic concern for reform. These hard-nosed realists set out to design a plan that could be passed by this Congress, giving something to both sides of the reform debate.

The Ornstein and Company plan, favored by the League of Women Voters, would set no voluntary spending limits; raise the limit on hard money donations by individuals, leaving present PAC limits as they are; prohibit soft money at all levels, while allowing individuals to give up to $25,000 a year to parties; and allow parties to spend unlimited money to help their candidates. The only public financing would be free broadcast time offered as a reward to candidates who raise money from small, instate contributions (Clymer 1997: 24).

This plan offers Republicans higher contribution limits and Democrats an end to soft money and some very limited public financing of some campaigns, that is, something for both parties. It was designed as a consensus reform bill. However well designed, it still would end soft money, and it is unclear how willing either party would be to abandon its only way to raise large amounts of cash. When this plan was announced, in 1997, the Republican party remained $4 million in debt from the 1996 campaign, while the Democrats, forced to give back questionable donations in the "Indo-gate" scandal, were at least $14 million in debt (Berke 1997a). With a margin of just ten seats separating the Democrats from regaining a majority in the House, it was difficult to imagine the Democratic National Committee (DNC) raising the millions needed for 1998 without recourse to soft money. The academic alternative might have worked if both parties had been highly motivated toward reform. But it also appeared dead in the water.

By June 1997, senators were still looking for an alternative to McCain-Feingold that would allow some type of campaign finance reform, in response to editorials from major papers such as the *New York Times* and the *Washington*

Post and polling data that suggested the public was disgusted with the amount of special interest money in politics. Rather than focus their efforts on a revision of McCain-Feingold (Senator McCain was still saying to no avail that he was willing to compromise even further to get support) a group of senators proposed a bipartisan commission on campaign finance reform. Never mind that this had been tried earlier in the 1990s, with a Senate-appointed panel that consisted of experts such as Herbert Alexander of the Citizen's Research Foundation, and that that panel's recommendations had been quickly swept under the rug. Proposing a commission at least allowed the senators to hold another press conference.

So on June 11, 1997, these senators proposed their blue-ribbon campaign finance reform panel, ignoring the fact that the bipartisan Ornstein group had already presented senators with a model reform plan. This would be different, they said, because their bill would create a nine-person panel whose recommendations would come to the Senate for an up or down vote. In other words, the plan couldn't be amended, eviscerated, or left to languish in committee with no recorded vote.

In their press conference, this new group of reformers reported that 321 previous campaign finance proposals had already been debated and/or disposed of in Congress in the previous ten years. This staggering number, along with the seventy current proposals to replace McCain-Feingold, led one of the group's leaders, Senator Robert Torricelli (D-N.J.) to remark, "The institution of Congress may not be capable of writing campaign finance legislation on its own" (America Online 1997a).

Some saw this move as an effort to deflate McCain-Feingold by substituting a bill to appoint a commission for a bill that would actually reform campaign finance. An unhappy Ann McBride, chair of Common Cause (the chief lobbying group pushing for McCain-Feingold) told reporters that the commission approach was just another delaying tactic. "The issue has been studied to death. We know the problems," McBride said. "What we need is not a commission, but some action" (America Online 1997a.) But the only action was the eventual killing of the House version of the commission bill, by a vote of 201–156 on June 17, 1998, with two of its cosponsors voting against it (All-Politics 1998).

CLINTON GIVES UP ON McCAIN-FEINGOLD EARLY IN THE GAME

In January 1996, President Clinton promised his full support to Senators McCain and Feingold. In February 1997, they introduced their second attempt at the bill. What happened to the president's full support of McCain-Feingold? After highlighting the McCain-Feingold bill in his State of the Union speech in February 1997, where he literally demanded that Congress send him this bill by the Fourth of July, President Clinton spoke hardly a word about campaign finance reform until June. Then the president publicly abandoned the McCain-Feingold approach. On June 6, 1997, President Clinton announced he would ask the Federal Election Commission (FEC) to change its rules and ban soft money, assuming that the FEC had the power to make such a change (Bennet 1997).

Clinton's announcement had been preceded by an earlier request to the FEC from a group of House members to ban soft money. Thus, the commission had already begun the tedious bureaucratic effort needed to look into such a change, setting a hearing for the following week. The process consisted of hearings, a time for citizen comments and input, and deliberation that could take "at least months, and possibly years" to decide (Bennet 1997).

McCain was angered by the President's action, describing it as partisan and a move that would "hurt our efforts." "Because soft money disproportionately benefits Republicans, Mr. McCain said, it would be unfair to ban it without also restricting practices of greater benefit to Democrats like advertising campaigns by unions. His proposed legislation would do both" (Bennet 1997).

Clinton's actions divided the reformers. Representatives Christopher Shays, cosponsor of the Shays-Meehan bill, heartily approved of the president's actions, saying, "Soft money is the primary culprit in corrupting the political process, with no close second" (Bennet 1997). In an op-ed piece, Shays acknowledged his break with McCain: "Some Republicans who want reform, including Sen. John McCain of Arizona, say the President's action will undermine our efforts to enact more comprehensive measures. I disagree. . . . Some Republicans also argue that banning soft money alone would punish our party unfairly. . . . All the calculations of who gains and who loses in various reform proposals miss the fact that soft money contributions are so large they corrupt the entire process itself" (Shays 1997).

It was apparent that Clinton had not been in contact with McCain, despite his pledges to ensure the bill's passage in his State of the Union address and in a private meeting with McCain and Feingold in January. Since that day, McCain reported, "We haven't been back" to speak with Clinton about reform. And in the months after his State of the Union speech, as the McCain-Feingold bill became buried under numerous substitutions, Clinton was silent. When asked about this silence, Clinton aides "said other tasks like the budget negotiations had intervened" (Bennet 1997).

By shifting the issue to the FEC, Clinton was aware that he had taken steam out of other proposals. Members of House and Senate were now free to explain to their constituents that campaign finance reform is in the hands of a government commission. However, no one is certain that the FEC has the legal authority to ban soft money outright. It is possible that after months or years of debate, should the FEC decide to ban soft money, their actions could be overturned by the Courts, putting campaign finance reform all the way back to square one. It is also possible, given the partisan makeup of the FEC (six members, three appointed from each party), that they could deadlock at three to three, with all of the Republican commissioners voting in favor of soft money. Meanwhile, the illusion of having done something about reform would exist, although both parties continued to raise and spend millions in soft money for the 1998 elections.

It could be argued that Clinton's move was the right choice, given the slim possibility of passage of McCain-Feingold. However, Clinton must shoulder some blame for the way McCain-Feingold was treated in the Senate and House by members of his own party. It was not the case that Clinton led a united Democratic party filled with zeal over campaign finance reform, blocked only by partisan concerns of the GOP. The fact that Clinton was unable (or perhaps, unwilling) to convince his Senate minority leader to wholeheartedly support McCain-Feingold says something about either Clinton's leadership ability or his sincerity.

Presidents with low approval ratings can be excused for not placing their meager political capital behind a controversial position; but Bill Clinton in 1997 was at the height of his presidential popularity, with a public approval score of 64 percent (Berke 1997b). Despite "Indo-Gate," despite other investigations such as Whitewater, the American people were happy in early 1997, enjoying an economic boom with low unemployment and little inflation. Clinton was pursuing moderate social policies such as welfare reform and basking in his role as a world leader in European conferences. Bill Clinton had no excuse not to spend more time and effort on campaign finance reform and yet he abandoned it, at the apex of his popularity. In 1998, with the explosion of the Monica Lewinsky affair and all the distractions that came with it, an argument could be made that the president was too busy to push reform; but that does not explain his behavior in 1997. One can speculate as to motives, but it will remain for historians to explain why the president first promoted, then dropped, the McCain-Feingold bill.

So the campaign finance reform community, aware that the president would lead no great crusade, pinned their hopes in 1997 on the committee to investigate the president's fund-raising scandals. However, the pundits generally agreed: the Thompson hearings were a bust. Journalists scrambled to analyze why the hearings weren't riveting, with some blaming the press for refusing to cover proceedings unless they were dripping with dramatic revelations. Richard L. Berke, who has covered campaign finance stories for at least a decade for the *New York Times*, said of the Senate hearings:

The telltale sign came only three hours after the much-touted hearings on campaign finance finally opened this week in the Senate; several spectators got up and left, leaving a noticeable swath of empty seats in the public gallery. These people did not go home to watch the proceedings on television, because even cable channels like C-Span and MSNBC devoted scant time to on-air coverage. . . . The lack of evident public outrage over the campaign finance practices described at the hearings is further evidence that there is not an angry, galvanizing constituency on the issue of money and politics. (Berke 1997b)

THE DEATH OF McCAIN-FEINGOLD AND SHAYS-MEEHAN

The "best chance since Watergate" was officially dead in the Senate on February 26, 1998, when a vote to end a filibuster by reform enemy Senator Mitch McConnell (R-Ky.) fell nine votes short of the number necessary for cloture (Clymer 1997: 24). Reformers turned all their energy to the House, where Speaker Newt Gingrich (R-Ga.) had promised the reformers a chance for a full and open debate on campaign finance reform. Since the House lacks the mechanism of the filibuster, the Republican leadership was faced with a challenge: find some way to kill Shays-Meehan without recorded votes that could be used against antireform members in the 1998 elections. This would be especially tricky as Speaker Gingrich had gone on record in favor of allowing debate.

As the House was gearing up to debate Shays-Meehan, Gingrich took it off the agenda on March 27, 1998, after "a frantic but fruitless effort by his aides to round up the votes to block genuine reform on the House floor" ("The Ebb and Flow" 1998). Speaker Gingrich wanted to move the vote onto a special calendar, one usually reserved for bills with no opposition, which would have required a two-thirds vote for passage. This provoked widespread outrage to which the Speaker was forced to respond a few days later in the most comic moment of the campaign finance reform debacle.

Late in the evening of March 31, the House finally debated campaign finance reform, although the Shays-Meehan bill was never on the floor. Instead, a so-called reform bill sponsored by Representative Bill Thomas (R-Calif.) was brought to the floor for debate. It was hard even for the Republican leadership to champion the Thomas bill, which called for tripling the amount of money that could be contributed to candidates; contained a "poison pill" to require unions to get written permission from members before spending their money on political purposes (sure to infuriate Democrats); and, in another measure aimed to reduce Democratic votes, would have set up citizenship tests for voters. Thomas threw in a ban on soft money, knowing full well that the bill in its current form would fail. In this way, the Republican leadership hoped to have a recorded vote on reform and then blame Democrats for the defeat. The bill was so blatant a fraud that it got only seventy-four votes on the floor (Berke 1997a).

The Gingrich move backfired, and on April 1 reform supporters announced they had collected 190 of the 218 signatures needed on a discharge petition to force a vote on Shays-Meehan, using a parliamentary maneuver to end-run the Speaker. More signatures were in the offing, since the 190 names included only six Republicans, while fourteen had cosponsored Shays-Meehan (America Online 1997a). It would have been an enormous embarrassment to

Speaker Gingrich if a revolt against his authority of this magnitude had succeeded. With that in mind, Gingrich caved in and promised a vote on Shays-
Meehan in return for having all Republicans remove their names from the discharge petition.

But Gingrich was not finished trying to outfox the reformers. Late in the
evening of May 21, the House began to debate reform, but Gingrich had
enough votes to debate reform his way. There would be a number of measures,
at least eleven, debated during the same period as Shays-Meehan. Each bill
would have unlimited amendments. In the end, the bill that received the highest number of votes would be the winner (America Online 1997a). This would
allow members both to vote for Shays-Meehan and to claim the banner of reform, while also voting for other bills more likely to pass with the highest vote
total.

Gingrich had another trick up his sleeve to kill campaign reform. On June
19, the House voted along partisan lines, 221–189, to allow Shays-Meehan to
be debated virtually all summer long, with 258 amendments to the bill to be
considered in that time. Minority Whip David Bonior (D-Mich.) said of the
flood of amendments that a lot of them "don't even have anything to do with
campaign finance reform. . . . They're poison pills. They're booby traps. And
each of these amendments, if adopted, could open the floodgates to even more
amendments" (Bennet 1997).

The heavy-handed way that the Speaker had acted began to attract Republican mavericks, eager to show the Speaker that his power was less than he imag-
ined, to Shays-Meehan. All the substitutes went down to defeat, including
what became known as the "freshman bill," cosponsored by House rookies
Representatives Asa Hutchison (R-Ark.) and Tom Allen (D-Me.). Their bill,
which would have banned soft money at the national party level but allowed
state parties to accept it, was derided as no reform at all by Common Cause and
other reform groups. Arguing before the vote on the freshman bill, Hutchison
said, "Let's pass something . . . that will get through the Senate" (Superville
1998a), alluding to the slim chances of McCain-Feingold.

Yet, perhaps partly because it was doomed in the Senate and therefore a
"free vote," the Shays-Meehan bill passed on a late-night vote of 252 to 179. It
gained strength during the long battle the Republican leadership waged
against it, and eventually got sixty-one Republican votes (while 15 Democrats
voted against it) (Mitchell 1998). Now the pressure was supposedly on the
Senate to act.

Shays-Meehan passed just before the August recess. When the senators returned, McCain-Feingold died a second death on September 10, with the
same supporters and opponents. It was as if all the effort that had been put
forward in the House of Representatives carried no weight at all (Broder
1998: 9b).

CONCLUSION

The McCain-Feingold and Shays-Meehan bills were doomed from the start, and the optimism at the beginning of the 105th Congress proved to be groundless. This optimism was based on a faulty understanding of when and why Congress engages in sweeping, fundamental reforms that affect incumbent chances of reelection. The faulty model assumed public pressure for change produced reforms, as it had in 1974. The evidence is that there has never been strong public pressure for change in campaign finance, then or in 1998. What allowed the 1974 reforms was an overwhelming partisan advantage on the part of Democrats and a beaten Republican party unable to fight back. The conditions of 1974 did not exist in 1998.

President Clinton and other politicians engaged in position taking on this issue but backed away as soon as they realized this difficult reform was not truly part of the public consensus about important government action. Some might argue that the Clinton-Lewinsky scandal, which took most of the press attention in 1998, prevented the president from taking a stronger stand in favor of campaign finance reform. But he had already backed away from the issue well before the storm broke. During the endgame, for one brief, dramatic moment, it seemed as if the victory of Shays-Meehan would create momentum toward passage in the Senate. Or, in another interpretation, cynical House politicians took advantage of a "free vote," knowing that the Senate could be relied on to kill reform one more time. In other words, self-interested politicians realized they could maintain their popularity without seriously engaging in campaign finance reform.

Voters may get what they *most want* from government but that can't be deduced simply by looking at polls. Voters want campaign finance reform, but they don't want it enough to base their votes on it. And members of Congress are quite aware of that fact. While reformers were trying to ban it, both parties raised $115.8 million in soft money between January 1997 and June 1998 (Superville 1998a). No public outcry was heard.

REFERENCES

AllPolitics Online. 1998. "House Considers Campaign Finance Legislation" (June 18).
America Online News. 1997a. "New Campaign Funding Panel Sought" (June 11).
———. 1997b. "Americans Want Campaign Reform" (June 6).
———. 1997c. "Revised Campaign Finance Bill Proposed" (May 22).
Bauer, Monica. 1994. "Money and Politics: In Pursuit of an Ideal." In Arthur H. Miller and Bruce E. Gronbeck, eds., *Presidential Campaigns and American Self-Images*. Boulder: Westview Press.
Beck, Paul A. 1997. *Party Politics in America*. New York: Longman.
Bennet, James S. 1997. "Clinton Supports Plan to Ban Soft Money in Campaigns." *New York Times* on the World Wide Web, June 6.

Berke, Richard L. 1997a. "GOP Panel Sees No Major Flaw in Fund-Raising Rules." *New York Times* on the World Wide Web, July 19.

———. 1997b. "A Scandal Falls Victim to its Own Irrelevance." *New York Times* on the World Wide Web, July 13.

———. 1997c. "Hard of Hearing." *New York Times*, July 13, Week in Review 1.

Broder, David. 1998. "Lessons of Campaign Finance Reform." *The Denver Post*, September 29, B 9.

Cassata, Donna. 1997. "Overhaul Remains Unpopular, But Hearings Raise the Heat." AllPolitics Online, April 9.

Clines, Francis X. 1997. "Most Doubt Resolve to Change Campaign Financing, Poll Finds." *New York Times*, April 8, A 1.

Clymer, Adam. 1997. "Many Proposals, Few Supporters on Campaign Law." *New York Times*, April 6, A 1.

Common Cause Press Release. 1997a. "Senator McConnell's Coalition of Campaign Finance Opponents Gave $243 Million in Political Contributions During Decade," April 9.

Common Cause Press Release. 1997b. "McCain-Feingold Offers Bipartisan Opportunity for Comprehensive Campaign Finance Reform in 1997," released February.

"The Ebb and Flow of Reform; Mr. Gingrich Retreats." 1998. *New York Times* on the World Wide Web, editorial, March 27.

Lewis, Michael. 1997. "The Subversive." *New York Times Magazine*, May 25, 34.

Mitchell, Alison. 1998. "House Approves Shays-Meehan Bill on Campaign Finance Reform." *New York Times* on the World Wide Web, August 7.

Shays, Representative Christopher. 1997. "The GOP Cops Out." *New York Times* on the World Wide Web, June 6.

Skorneck, Carolyn. 1997. "Campaign Reform on Shaky Ground." America Online News, May 25.

"Soft Money in the News." Center for Responsive Politics website.

"Some Hope for Campaign Reforms." 1997. *New York Times*, May 25, Editorial 10E.

Superville, Darlene. 1998a. "House Passes Campaign Finance Bill." America Online News, August 6.

———. 1998b. "House Debates Campaign Finance." America Online News, May 22.

D. THE ROLE OF PARTIES IN ELECTIONS

10

The Values of Political Party Activists: Ideology, Elections, and Governing

Richard P. Barberio

INTRODUCTION

Parties and their candidates are often assumed to succeed or fail (in both elections and governing) depending on their ability to unify the party by means of an overarching set of values, beliefs, and goals—something that is often called an ideology (e.g., Lane 1962; Converse 1964). This is incorrect for many reasons, but in the main, the lack of distinct ideological positions in the United States, coupled with a fluid system of elections and government based more on coalition building than central command, make ideology in American politics more window dressing than guiding force (e.g., Hartz 1955; Campbell et al. 1960; Epstein 1986; Ginsberg and Shefter 1990; Beck 1997).

This study examines the ideological orientations—as expressed by a measurement of values—of a sample of New York state delegates to the 1996 Democratic and Republican National Conventions in order to come to some conclusions about the importance of ideology between and within the two major parties. The findings point to the way ideology may affect both elections and governing.

The use of values as the main point of analysis makes this study uncommon in that social scientists tend to avoid values as being too normative (Barry 1970: 87–97) and that other factors, such as attitudes, are frequently used to stand for values. The research design of this study is intended to show how values can be used to create a broad picture of the aggregate ideology of a party as well as a more closely cropped view of the dominant ideological configurations within a party.

The analysis of these two views of ideology—an aggregate interlevel and an intralevel view—point to three major findings, all of which have an impact on elections and governing. First, the ideological differences between the parties are slighter than convention would hold them to be. A few specific issues are more likely to divide candidate from candidate and party from party than are well-developed sets of shared values forming an ideology. Second, segments of each party are visible over much of the set of values tested in this study. In other words, party wings or segments are identifiable not only by their orientation toward issue positions and feelings toward the parties but also by their values. Third, neither party seems to be the captive of any issue-based or unflinchingly party-loyalist wing—at least for the time and sample studied. This finding would seem to place in doubt the notion that party politics in the United States is mostly at the mercy of shifts in the ideological winds generated by extremist party elements.

IDEOLOGY AND AMERICAN POLITICS

Ideology—usually expressed as a shared view of what is desirable in the social arena—has long been a means of explaining the success or failure of individual political actors, parties, governments, and even nations. Central to such theories is the belief that unity in ideological orientation gives collectives—such as interest groups and political parties—the centripetal force that holds them together (e.g., Paehlke 1994; Loomis 1998). This bonding holds the ranks solid and can win political battles when the opposition is not as strong. A few examples from the recent past are illustrative of this line of thinking.

The conventional wisdom goes that, in the 1980s, Democratic party strategists must have secretly wished for the party cohesiveness of their Republican counterparts. After all, the GOP held a lock on the presidency for the decade. The U.S. Senate was in their control for the majority of that time. Much of the initial Reagan agenda was passed into law. The electorate was becoming more Republican. The House still eluded the Republicans, but Democrats had to envy the solidarity of the Reagan and Bush years, a unifying conservative ideology based on bedrock values and beliefs and a generally placid intra-party world. At least this is the way things seemed on the surface.

Flash forward to 1996: The Democratic party seemed to shake the ghosts of its past. There was little of the rancor of past party conventions, certainly not of the magnitude of 1964 or 1968. The Republicans faced a more turbulent electoral season, even though this one came on the heels of a seismic change in the control of Congress via the 1994 midterm elections. Pat Buchanan's primary challenge and an abortion rights faction within the party made the preconvention phase a rocky one. Some began to wonder if the Republicans were becoming the Democrats of the late 1960s through the 1980s, a party struggling to keep itself from dying a death of a thousand factions.

What happened to the much vaunted cohesiveness of the GOP? Were the Democrats finally in possession of the magic formula of unity? Of course incumbency, the openness of the presidential selection process, and other systemic factors do much to explain these occurrences. Questions still remain: Which party is the more ideologically cohesive of the two? What does the ideology of each party look like? Does an ideologically driven faction(s) steer the candidate selection and policy preferences of a party? Trying to answer these questions will help lead to some conclusions about the importance of ideology in both elections and governing. If one party is more cohesive than the other, then the conventional wisdom may be correct—a coherent ideology is the tide that lifts a party's boat. If this is not the case, then the impact of ideology may be much more limited, indicating that a reevaluation of what helps to win elections and influence governance is in order.

Parties are divisible into wings—part liberal, part conservative—with a centrist spine. Elite party members, those who are directly involved with the parties in government or the parties as formal electoral organizations (clearly more consistently partisan than the average voter) can also be painted with this brush, but they may also be distinguished by another set of traits. Some elite party members are said to be loyalists, others activists—also commonly termed professionals and amateurs (e.g., Wilson 1962; Wildavsky 1965; Soule and Clarke 1970; Sullivan et al. 1974; Soule and McGrath 1975; Kirkpatrick 1976; Roback 1980; Reiter 1985; McCann 1995). Loyalists are party men and women above all. Their devotion to the party is not wholly or even mostly derived from a stance on one or a few issues. Rather, the loyalist is one who sees the party in a larger, perhaps even historical, scale. Activists are said to be involved in party politics because they support or oppose one or a few issues they feel are critical for the party's overall well-being. Loyalists would rather keep internal battles small or stamp them out for the good of the party; activists see such battles as good for the soul of the party. Certainly, if values are as important as they are assumed to be, then the hardest test of their importance as a marker of political distinctions would be to see if the values of activists and loyalists are discrete from one another.

What the study presented here establishes, then, is a two-tier test for the impact of values on political identification and behavior at the party level. The main test is the comparison between Democrats and Republicans. The second, harder set of tests involves the activists and loyalists in each party. With the results of these two tests in hand, preliminary conclusions about the impact of values on the connections between values and ideology as well as those between electoral politics and governing can be drawn.

SUBJECTS, THEORY, AND METHOD

According to researchers who use values to explain or predict political behavior, a value is a conception of what is sought after in life or a desirable way of
conducting one's life (Rokeach 1973; Inglehart 1971). The former can be
called a terminal value and the latter an instrumental one (Rokeach 1973:
7–9). In this scheme, there are no negative values, only positive goals and ways
of living.[1]

Values can be thought of as a special type of belief, not of what is true or false
but of what is desirable or undesirable. Values may sit at the center of a person's
mind, working to allow or preclude ideas and actions from taking place, or if
two values conflict with one another, they may cause distress as well as the ensuing actions to relieve that dissonance. As such, values can be conceptualized
as encompassing attitudes and opinions. Because of the unique qualities that
values are thought to possess—their centrality in decision making, their sub-
suming of attitudes and opinions—a person's values may be the most telling
dispositions when it comes to understanding political thought and behavior.

Building on the theories of Rokeach and his disciples, this study's value
measurement tool is unlike attitudinal survey instruments. The word or phrase
used to prompt a response is far less suggestive of what cognitive psychologists
would term an attitude object than is the standard style of attitude survey.[2]
More important is Rokeach's argument that because of the nature of values as
positive goals or ways of living, the respondent is more likely to use his or her
values as the basis for judgment when presented with a value word. Attitudes
are narrowly confined to many specific objects needing context, whereas values are available regardless of context. Their existence as general indicators of
what is good makes them approachable without context, therefore measurable
as long as the method does not rely too heavily on attitude objects.

The main instrument of the study is a value survey based on the well-known
Rokeach Value Survey (RVS), a form designed to rank order a person's values.
Having used the RVS in other research applications and found it to be lacking
(Barberio 1995) the author constructed a new survey for this study.[3]

Ten interviews were also conducted with delegates from across New York
state.[4] The subjects, five Republicans and five Democrats, were interviewed to
test an underlying question pertaining to the measurement of values. Namely,
does relying on surveys alone to measure values miss the multidimensional
characteristics of values since the meaning of each value may differ for each
person? Other studies point to this possibility concerning measurement (e.g.,
Gibbins and Walker 1993; Braithwaite and Law 1985). If there is great variation in the meaning of the values, as may be unearthed in the interviews but
not in the surveys, then the survey results require a more intensive analysis.
Not only would a difference of meaning influence the interpretation of the
surveys, such variation may point to a questioning of the entire assumption
about the shared values of a politically based group. For this reason, interviews
with a subset of the subjects sampled were undertaken. Interviews are able to

get at the meanings of values in a more facile way than are surveys while help-ing to test the validity of the survey instrument.

Freedom and *equality* were claimed by Rokeach to be the two values that, when used in conjunction, gave a full rendering of a person's political ideology. His "two-value model" proffered to show how high or low rankings of these values indicated congruence with four major ideological orientations: capital-ist (high on freedom, low on equality); socialist (high on both freedom and equality); communist (high on equality, low on freedom); and fascist (low on both freedom and equality) (Rokeach 1973: chapters 6–7). The two-value model is of interest to this study, but it begs the question as to whether there are other political values. In essence, the approach taken by Rokeach needed to be modernized and made more useful to the analysis of the specific population sampled for this study.

In order to facilitate these goals, a content analysis of Democratic and Re-publican policy statements and goals was undertaken. The sources of the con-tent were the Democratic and Republican party platforms for 1996. Each platform was analyzed by a standard content analysis program (Conc) using a specific set of criteria.[5] The result of this content analysis was a set of thirteen words or phrases—*community, equality, family, fair, freedom, hard working, honest, national security, opportunity, peace, prosperity, religious,* and *respect. Freedom* and *equality* are included as a test of the two-value model advocated by Rokeach. The other eleven words are those that are distinct from *freedom* and *equality* (i.e., liberty is not included), fit with the study's definition of a value as a goal or way of living, and are mentioned with some frequency by one or both party platforms.[6] *Equality* did not meet this standard, but is included in order to interact with its mate in the two-value model. Of the handful of val-ues stated by both parties as being descriptors of their particular party, only *hard working, religious,* and *honest* were mentioned enough times to merit their inclusion.[7]

In order to make the outcome of the tests of aggregate party samples and intraparty comparisons of activists and loyalists as clear as possible, it was nec-essary to sample respondents from the two parties who were the most likely to have well-defined political beliefs. As previously noted, elite party members fit this criterion more than the average party voter. Additionally, sampling re-spondents from New York—a state with competitive, strong parties—increases the likelihood of obtaining individuals with clearly articulated value systems.

Using national convention delegates also facilitates the second test con-cerning activists and loyalists. By using a mix of the questions common to both the Party Elite and the Active Minority studies suggested by McCann (1995), a scale was produced that was used to separate each party's sampled delegates into three broad categories: party loyalist, party activist, and middle-of-the-road party membership. The questions used to build the scale concerned the willingness of the individual to sacrifice electoral fortunes of the party in favor of the consistency of their party's ideology or stands on specific issues. People who indicated that they were willing to put ideology and issues ahead of a victory in the general election were classified as party activists. Their opposites were tagged as party loyalists. A mixed response was labeled as middle party, or "mid party."

In order to increase the probability that any existing ideological differences between the parties could be made evident, the subjects sampled for this study came from New York state, a competitive two-party state with robust party organizations (Keefe 1994: 57–59). In terms of election dynamics and ideological commitment, New York can be thought of as a "strong party state," making it a likely source of partisans with well-developed value systems. The original data that was gathered for this study is the result of survey instruments sent to all of the New York state delegates and alternates to both the Democratic and Republican conventions who were not holders of elected office. In all, 196 Democratic and 116 Republican party members were mailed a packet containing four separate survey instruments. Each survey was designed to obtain data on points of interest ranging from the demographic background of the respondents to their values.[8] Thirty-one Republicans and seventy-two Democrats returned completed questionnaires for a respective response rate of 27 percent and 37 percent (total response rate was 33 percent).

FINDINGS: A DIME'S WORTH OF DIFFERENCE?

Much is made over the assumed differences between the beliefs and goals of the two main parties, just as there is a widely expressed notion that the parties themselves are rent with fissures adding up to wings or other ideological cleavages. However, there is the competing axiom, perhaps most trenchantly encapsulated by George Wallace, which states that there is not a "dime's worth of difference" between the two main parties. In other words, Democrats and Republicans—at least when broadly compared to one another as whole entities—have stronger commonalities than differences. Certainly, the values of the parties would be a point of comparison for testing the differences or similarities of the two parties writ large. After all, the definition of values used in this study as desirable goals or end states of existence, or ways of living, fits well with the doctrinaire and programmatic elements that are evidenced in the analysis of the party platforms just described.

In the next section of the paper, the results of the two tests employed in the study are discussed. Recall that the first type of test seeks to answer if the parties are more alike than different from one another. The second is aimed at the variation within each party. Does the boilerplate division of the parties into right, center, and left wings hold true—at least as evidenced by an associated pattern of value holding? This second type of test is also concerned with the source of aggregate strength for each value: Is one party wing the main wellspring for the importance of a value?

The First Test—Comparison of Democratic and Republican Party Samples

The nature of the value survey instrument used in this study makes it possible to take two approaches to the analysis of the data. Respondents were asked to use a five-point scale to express their evaluation of each value item. The fourth and fifth points on the scale indicated a favorable judgment of a value.

If the percentages of the fourth and fifth positions of the scale are combined and then compared between all Democratic and Republican respondents, sizable differences do exist. The values of *community*, *hard working*, *national security*, and *religious* were all ten or more percentage points apart, with Republicans favoring the last three values more than Democrats. Does this mean that the Republicans are the party of the hard working, national security-conscious, faithful (in the religious sense) and that the Democrats are not? Figure 10.1 contains a graph illustrating each of these values.

The graphs for both *community* and *hard working* depict a ten-point gap between the combined measure for Democrats and Republicans and a twenty-point gap for the fifth position measure. Even more notable are the seventeen- and thirty-one-point distances over the value *national security*. The value *religious* also demonstrates the power to separate partisans with fifteen- and twenty-two-point variances for the two measures. At first blush, what these graphs show is that there may be more than a "dime's worth of difference" between the two parties, at least among the sample obtained for this study.[9]

Overall, then, a few values work to highlight distinctions within the two party samples. *National security* and *religious* are the most easily recognizable points of cleavage between the values of the two groups of individuals. If these are the ingredients of the ideological division between the two major parties, then the results are not terribly dramatic. The differences between the parties that are so fervently trumpeted in the words of the party platforms do not have a strong connection to the values of the party members themselves. In most ways, the two samples fail to differ greatly from one another except on two, or perhaps a few more values. This may indicate that issues associated with national defense and religion are the motivating factors that attract and keep individuals within the workings of the parties. In terms of religion, this may be the case, since a question concerning the prohibition of abortion—an issue associated with more conservative Catholics and Protestants—was included in the study. Democrats were more willing than Republicans to disapprove of the banning of abortions by a difference of 34 percent. If abortion is the religious and political issue that it is reputed to be, the Republican party would seem to be the home to people who define their religious values by the metric of the abortion issue. Similarly with defense spending (what might be considered an issue area related to *national security*) Republicans were more than twice as likely to support cuts in domestic spending to maintain this outlay.

Figure 10.1
Graphs of Selected Values

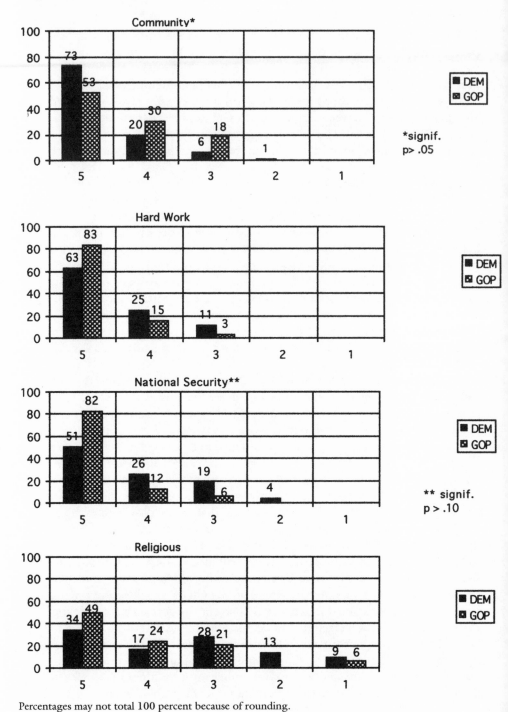

Percentages may not total 100 percent because of rounding.

That Republicans favor defense spending and Democrats oppose the banning of abortions are not unexpected findings. What is interesting is that the values of individual party members sampled seem to reflect this tried and true issue division.

A more critical finding about the ideological orientations of the parties concerns the values of *freedom* and *equality*. Rhetoric from the parties themselves and common perceptions about the parties would foster a view of Democrats and Republicans being sharply divided over these key political values. However, the values of *freedom* and *equality* evidenced only modest differences between the samples. Figure 10.2 contains the graphs of these two values.

If great ideological differences were to divide the two parties, then these two values with their forceful connection to views of governmental power and policy direction would seem to be useful yardsticks. Namely, it could be expected that Republicans would represent the more conservative of the two main parties by resembling what Rokeach deemed to be the "capitalists" ideal value type, that is, one who holds *freedom* to be highly important but sees *equality* as having little, if any, importance. The conservatism of the Republican party as espoused by William Bennett and other GOP luminaries may well fit with this individualist, "pull yourself up by your own bootstraps," configu-

Figure 10.2
Equality and Freedom

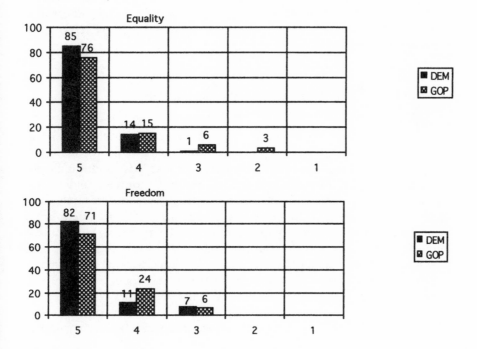

ration of the "capitalist." Democrats, with their legacy of the New Deal, Great Society, and other redistributive programs seem to fit more with what Rokeach envisioned as the "socialist" ideological type, one who gives great personal weight to both *freedom* and *equality*.[10]

Note from Figure 10.2 that there seems to be slight evidence to justify this application of the two-value model to the two party samples present in this study. *Equality* is a less important value for Republicans in that they have less of a percentage of maximum ranking for this value than do the Democrats. Also note that, unlike the Republican sample, no Democrats give *equality* a nega- tive rating (i.e., no responses for choices one or two). Overall, the Republicans sampled offered 9 percent of their responses as ambivalent or negative toward this value, whereas the Democrats had only a 1 percent response of ambiva- lence. The value *freedom* indicates that, while not inclined to negatively evalu- ate this value, Republicans are less willing than Democrats to give it the maximum ranking. This does not seem to indicate a "fascist" ideological type (negative on both *freedom* and *equality*). Rather, the findings surrounding *freedom* simply indicate a weaker level of importance for Republicans concern- ing this value.

Clearly, there are differences in the rankings of both *freedom* and *equality* for both Democrats and Republicans. As would be expected in a political sys- tem that is less ideologically stratified than many others, the differences be- tween the party samples are not stunningly large nor do the observed differences make exact fits with the ideal types suggested by Rokeach. For the most part, the differences between *freedom* and *equality* (as well as with many of the other values tested) are matters of degree. It is not readily discernible from the data if the variation between the two possible positive responses is substantively significant.

Second Test: Part One—Intra-party Ideological Cohesiveness

It is widely held that the Republican party is more ideologically unified than the Democratic party. It has also been a favorite theme of press coverage of American politics that various wings of each major party have undue influence on the parties' selection of candidates and the policy platforms of candidates as well as of officeholders. Both of these assumptions speak to the strength of ideological orientation of the members of each party. The argument being made here is that sustained, complex participation with a party (such as that found with delegates and alternates) is connected with both affective alle- giance to the party and more issue-driven goal seeking. In other words, it may be that individuals become involved with party politics for at least three rea- sons: They have an emotional attachment to the party; they wish to see the party champion or discontinue the support of an issue or set of issues; they share a mixture of both of these motivational elements. If a party is highly ideologically constrained, it could be expected that only mild value variations would exist across the three kinds of party members (party loyalists, party activists, and middle-party types). This is arguably the case, since values are thought to be of such behavioral importance that political participation contrary to one's values is not easily managed by the individual (Rokeach 1973).

The tests offered in this section endeavor to first show if there is greater cohesiveness of value holding across the party member types—indicating a more "ideological" party. Second, the level of variation within each party sample can be analyzed to discern the strength of a party wing on a specific value. That is to say, if the Democrats or Republicans sampled have a marked aggregate difference on a given value, is this difference driven by any one segment of the party? Knowing this will also expand the ideological frame of reference for each party.

A basic way of evaluating the strength of cohesiveness of the ideological orientation within each party sample is to compare the amount of variation among the three party member types for each value. This task is made easier when it is recalled that the majority of the responses given by the respondents from both parties to each value item came from the highest value choice, number five on the survey form. By looking at only the variation in this one choice, most of the variation of all choices can be adequately explained. This is done here by taking the median value percentage from each party's three member types and noting the difference between the other two percentages. For example, Figure 10.3 offers a graph for the value *freedom*.

Figure 10.3
Freedom

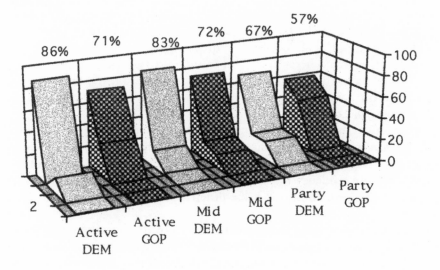

The numbers to the left side of the floor of the three-dimensional graph indicate the responses, one through five, possible for each value. The back and side wall of the graph show the percentage of response given to each of the five possible choices for the value *freedom*. The labels running across the front of the graph denote each of the three types of party member for each of the two parties. In this example, the median Democratic response (83 percent) is that of the Mid DEMs—those Democrats who gave responses to survey questions about party loyalty and ideological conviction that scaled them as neither party loyalist nor as activist types. The Active DEMs are a close match with their 86 percent placement of this value at the maximum ranking. The Party DEMs weigh in at 67 percent. Using a similar heuristic used in the discussion of the differences between the two parties as aggregates, a 10 percent margin is also employed in this section. In the present example, the Party DEMs vary from the median by well over 10 percent, whereas the Active DEMs do not. In other words, there is evidence in this case of the Party DEMs holding a different view of the importance of *freedom*. This indicates that the Democrats are somewhat less than totally cohesive on this value. The Republicans share nearly the same result on this value, with the exception that the median is held by the Active GOPs.

Several outcomes are possible from this type of analysis. First, as demonstrated in the example, a third of the party can show itself to hold different value intensity from that of the other two-thirds. If the same third consistently differs from the others, then this lends some credence to the idea that an identifiable ideological wing is functioning in the sample. It is also possible that the same two-thirds consistently vary from the median. In general, it would be assumed that the party loyalists and the activists would fork out from the more centrist value leanings of the moderate middle-of-the-road party members. The three party types may seem to randomly occupy the median and wing positions depending on the value in question. This indicates a diversity of value holding that is out of place with even the relatively weak level of ideological consistency expected here. Finally, all of the thirds of the membership of a party sample could be within the ten-point margin, demonstrating a homogeneous take on that particular value. This is the outcome that would be assumed of ideologically constrained parties.

After undertaking this type of analysis for each value, a few general patterns emerge. On the whole, Republicans tend to be only slightly more obviously homogeneous than Democrats.[11] Looking more intently, the Republicans exhibit a definite tendency for one-third of their members—the Party GOPs (loyalists)—to have consistent value differences from the remainder of the sample.[12]

Like their Republican counterparts, Party DEMs also established themselves as distinct from their fellow partisans by giving less importance to a few specific values.[13] Unlike the GOP sample, however, the Democrats also had the activist third of their members maintaining a distance from the Mid DEMs and Party DEMs on specific values.[14]

What such findings seem to say about the level of ideological consistency within each sample is this: both the Republicans and Democrats have about an equal number of values that are indicative of a high level of value congruence. Interestingly enough, only *honest* is held in the same manner by both groups of partisans. At a more detailed level, the Republicans have a pronounced party-loyalist wing that is easily contrasted with the other segments of the party. However, the Democrats are in possession of two segments that substantially differ over the holding of values. The Active DEMs are as distinct as the Party DEMs when it comes to differences in value holding. If values are one of the main sources of the motivation for political behavior, then these differences evidenced within the parties, especially the Democratic party, indicate value differences as a probable source of friction within the workings of the parties.

Second Test: Part II—Analysis of Party Segment Strength and Overall Value Importance

The analysis offered here illustrates which party segment has the most impact on the overall importance of each value. The comparisons of the two major party samples offered in the first test gave some insight into the differences and similarities of the parties as aggregates. In this test, a basic comparison is presented that shows which party segment has the most sway on these aggregate rankings. This process helps to answer one of the main questions laid out at the start of this section of the paper: Are segments—or wings—of a party more responsible than others for the ideological stance of the party as a whole? The proposition derived from this question speaks to the electoral and policy preferences of the party elites sampled for this study.

What is immediately evident in looking at the "Always Important" response category for the three party segments for both party samples is that the middle partisans (Mid DEM and Mid GOP) dominate the other two party segments on every value. The average percentage for Mid DEMs and Mid GOPs is thirty-eight and thirty-nine, respectively. In only a few cases do other segments of each party rival the middle for prominence. For example, the value *prosperity* finds the activist Republicans within three percentage points of the Mid GOPs, and the loyalist GOP subjects within seven points, a demonstration of the widely dispersed holding of this value more than a powerful wing exerting an unusual weight of beliefs. This story is played out for both parties on all values where the middle partisans seem to lose some of their grasp on the determination of the overall value score for their party. What may be more telling is that the three segments of each party look remarkably similar to their partisan counterpart. The graph of the value *fair* typifies this resemblance, as shown in Figure 10.4.

Figure 10.4
Fair

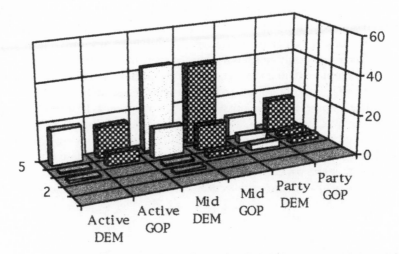

Notice that the Mid DEMs and Mid GOPs tower over the other party segments and that Active and Party GOPs and DEMs fall off in a fairly uniform
fashion. This general pattern is only broken on what must be some of the more
ideologically contentious values found in the survey, such as *national security*
and *peace*, but the variation in the pattern has more to do with the ratio of the
relationship than the relative strength of each segment.

The conclusion drawn from this is that the main source of the ideology of
each party—as expressed as a general value system—comes from the centrist
elements of each party. But, variations do exist. For example, activist Democrats pull down a bit more of the value strength than do party-loyalist Democrats, and party-loyalist Republicans have more of an impact on the value
scores than activist Republicans. However, the variations do not challenge the
dominance of the middle-stratum partisans over the tenor of the aggregate
value system of each party sample. If it can be argued that the behavior of the
elite partisans sampled for this study is correlated with their value systems, then
the answer to the question concerning the impact of partisan blocks or wings
on functioning of the parties themselves would likely be that centrist partisans
are in control. While this can only be inferred from the construction of this
study, such a finding adds weight to the idea that party politics in America is the
politics of centrism and not of even a mild form of extremism.

A Final Take on the Role of Values in Ideology and Partisan
Behavior—The Meaning of Values

One more aspect of values needs to be addressed as it concerns the main
roots of this study or any study that takes on the task of using values to investi-

gate ideology and behavior. The very real possibility exists that a value may have different meanings to separate individuals. For instance, the value *equality* may indicate the opportunity for equal treatment and advancement. Another person may believe this value to mean equal outcome for all, not just the opportunity to produce favorable results (see Stone 1997 for an excellent treatment of these ideas). For example, in this study 85 percent of all Democrats gave *equality* the highest possible ranking and 76 percent of Republicans did likewise. However, such figures do not let on about the meaning of this value. Furthermore, it is problematic to directly ask a respondent to provide this information on a written questionnaire.

It is far more appropriate and useful to use interviewing to get at the meaning of a subject's values. Interviews are appropriate for a number of reasons. First, they remove the need to construct cumbersome surveys that contain multiple responses, a problem with surveys that can be a source of confusion to respondents. Second, interviews are especially useful for uncovering the meaning of values in that they are less prone to prime the respondent into giving a response. Asking a person what they think a word or phrase means to them is more likely to get past the layer of attitudes and penetrate the individual's values; the person is not directed to evaluate the word or phrase as being good or bad (much as attitudinal surveys often do). The nature of values as conceptualizations of what is good or desirable makes it possible to interview a person for his or her definition of a set of values and be more assured of getting a genuine response. This is so since asking for meaning does not necessarily connote the direction or intensity of feeling about a value. Interviews are also useful in that they offer a check on the validity of the survey instrument used in this study. Ten subjects, five Democrats and five Republicans, were interviewed by phone on a wide range of matters that included the meaning of both *freedom* and *equality*. These two values were singled out for their theoretical connection with ideology. This snapshot of the meaning of values to the two groups of partisans was designed to be a supplement to the survey work, not as a study unto itself.

If patterns emerged on the meaning of these values it would be useful to discuss these patterns with those seen in the aggregate comparisons of the two parties' samples. In other words, if most of the Democrats interviewed held *equality* to have a meaning pertaining to outcomes and most Republicans saw this value as opportunity, then it is possible that such a distinction is related to the survey rankings supplied for this value by both parties.

The aggregate survey data indicates that Republicans are out in front of Democrats in their favoring of the value *opportunity* (79 percent to 68 percent at the fifth position). This allows a clear inference that Republicans are more inclined to see *equality* as the opportunity variant rather than outcome. In the phone survey, three Democrats thought that the value was linked with outcome, while the other two expressed notions that indicated that this value was more connected with opportunity. Three Republicans from this phone sample also viewed this value as the equality of *opportunity*, while the other two gave responses that were a mixture of opportunity and outcome. The best that can be said of this result is that it is a wash—roughly the same pattern exists for each phone survey group.

Political thinkers from John Stuart Mill to Tocqueville described *freedom* as having two faces—one positive, the other negative. In terms of politics, negative *freedom* has generally been considered to mean *freedom* from government intrusion. This is the classic formulation of Mill. Tocqueville is more associated with positive *freedom*, the ability to do what one wishes. In the realm of politics, positive *freedom* is often used in conjunction with government intervention in society. Largely construed, these basic uses of negative and positive *freedom* fit well with the general views of the Democratic and Republican parties; the Democrats are the party of more government (positive freedom) and the Republicans are the party of less government (negative freedom). From the interviews this simplistic axiom seems to hold water. Four of the five Republicans interviewed saw *freedom* in a negative light. The fifth Republican had a response that mixed both positive and negative views. This pattern was reversed in the Democratic sample, with four giving positive responses and one offering a mixed response. This finding does not indicate that *freedom* is less important to one party than another. In fact, all eight of the subjects who expressed purely positive or negative views gave *freedom* the highest rating. Those who gave it mixed responses gave lesser rankings.

These findings concerning the meaning of values indicate that the overall lower rankings of the values by Republicans are connected with their more mixed view of values in general. This may be similar to what Tetlock (1993) has referred to as "cognitive complexity," or "value pluralism." People with expanded meanings for their values tend to be less extreme in other ideological measures. From this point of view, the Republicans sampled are ideologically more moderate than are the Democrats. However, this is scant evidence upon which to make such a sweeping claim. It may very well be that the Democratic delegates in this study have a high degree of cognitive complexity and that, by this measure, they are more moderate than dogmatic. These possibilities warrant further study.

SUMMARY AND CONCLUSION

The major findings of this study indicate that the values of Democrats and Republicans are markedly different on only a few values—namely *community*, *hard working*, *national security*, and *religious*—and that these values are clearly tied to "hot button issues" that may have a limited shelf life. A war, an economic depression, or even a more minor event could easily make any of the issues tied to these values rise or fall in importance to a party and its members. At least in terms of value rankings, ideological differences between the parties exist, but they are not as dramatic as some would claim.

Ideological wings or segments are identifiable and stable for each party over the range of values tested in this study. Both parties support large activist and loyalist wings that are dominated by the middle factions within the parties. The two more extreme thirds of the parties do not dominate the shared value system for either of the parties. The middle stratum is always the source of the largest amount of value preference in the party samples. In other words, neither party's ideology is dominated by an extremist faction.

A more mixed set of meanings for the key value *freedom* may indicate that the Republicans sampled are slightly more moderate than are the Democrats. Interviews of a small sample of both Democrats and Republicans illustrate that values are multidimensional because of their variety of meanings.

There does not seem to be a pattern in which one party dominates the other in the importance of the values tested. Since the values used here were mostly drawn from the platforms of both of the parties, it is reasonable to conclude that it is incorrect for either party to attempt to lay claim to being the sole home of "family," "traditional," "American," or another subset of values. Both parties have, in large part, a shared conception of what is desirable in life; they have very similar ideologies. This should come as no surprise. The weakness of strong ideological positions in American culture would make a finding to the contrary very astonishing.

Finally, the findings of this study provide reasons to counsel caution for the parties in the electorate, the parties as organizations, and even the parties in government when it comes to the connections between elections and governing; none of these players may get what they bargain for in both electoral results and policy outcomes if they predicate their goals on the use of values as rhetorical tools of partisan division. Particularly at the aggregate level of analysis that formed the main portion of this study, the rankings of values by the two main party samples mirror more than oppose one another.

This is certainly not the stuff of a responsible party model in which clear ideological differences exist between two contending political organizations. However, at the individual level, the interviews with a subset of subjects indicate that the key to understanding party ideologies may hinge more on the meaning of values rather than the rankings of these variables. Future work on the connections between elections and governing needs to consider the importance of the meaning of values. This aspect of the parties may harbor both the centripetal force that keeps each party together as well as the root distinctions that drive them against one another in both the electoral and policy-making arenas.

NOTES

1. See Braithwaite and Law (1985: 251) for a concise history of the major value-based theories and approaches.

2. Instruments now exist and have been used in numerous studies to measure the *attitudes* of party-activists (especially important in this regard are the Party Elite study

and the Active Minority study). However, measuring *values* is not at all like measuring attitudes. Values differ from attitudes (as well as from opinions) in that attitudes need to be triggered by way of what cognitive psychologists term an attitude object (see Fiske and Taylor 1991).

3. Taking a cue from Braithwaite and Law (1985) the instrument uses a five-point scale to assess the strength of the values held by each individual.

4. This is not a scientific sample of interviews, nor is it intended to be. Clearly, a sample taken from such a geographically limited area adds all manner of possible effects, chief among them, the ever-present distinctions of upstate and downstate factors in New York state politics. The sample is included as a means to test the validity of the surveys and the general theory.

5. First, all words over three letters in length were compiled in an index for each platform. The three-letter cutoff was needed to keep the index down to a readable size. Next, a search for the basic Rokeach values was undertaken. This included synonyms that were derived from a standard thesaurus function of a word processing program. Key words, such as *God* and *value(s)*, were put in for a separate search. Finally, the platforms were each read to find the stated values of each party (e.g., "The values of our party are X, Y, and Z").

6. The cutoff for inclusion was for a value word to be used by one or both of the parties in at least .090 percent of the words of the platform. Since each platform was quite long (Democrats = 19,382 words, Republicans = 29,094 words), this cutoff works out to approximately twenty uses of the word, its variant, or synonym.

7. The most mentioned value word by either party was *family*. The Democrats used this word sixty-four times (0.33 percent of their total) and the Republicans eighty-one times (0.27 percent of their total). The word *values* was mentioned the most by the Democrats (28 times or 0.14 percent of total) with the Republicans using the word slightly less (18 times or 0.06 percent of total). Both Democrats and Republicans cited *family values* twice and *American values* once. Only the Republican platform specifically mentioned *God* and this occurred four times.

8. Because of the nature of the information that was requested in the survey packet and the particular effect it could have on someone holding office, it was decided that elected officials would be less likely to return completed surveys and to be less open in their responses. Searing (1979) notes similar concerns.

9. It should be noted that the graphs indicate that the parties' samples are generally favorable toward all the values that have been selected for discussion. Additionally, none of the other values received negative evaluations by a majority or even a plurality of either sample.

10. Reichley (1995) has a similar theoretical take on ideology with very different aggregate findings as the basis of his argument.

11. On the values *fair* and *hardworking*, the Republicans were solidly within the 10-point margin and *honest* and *opportunity* are only a percentage point outside of this circle. Democrats scored solid unity on *equality* and *peace*, missing by 1 percent on *honest*. On the values of *community*, *peace*, *religious*, and *prosperity* the Republicans spread out, forming three distinct blocks. With the exception of *prosperity*, the Mid-GOPs maintained the median place, the Active GOPs holding higher value percentages and the Party GOPs having lower numbers. In the case of *prosperity*, the Party and Mid-GOPs are reversed.

12. The Party GOPs gave substantially lower overall value rankings to four values: *equality, family, freedom,* and *respect.*

13. The values are *freedom, hardworking, prosperity,* and *respect.*

14. The Active DEMS had substantial value differences on *community, family, national security,* and *opportunity.* Also, the values *fair* and *religious* produced a stratification of the Active, Party and Mid-DEMs into distinct thirds, with the Mid-DEMs holding the median position and the Active and Party DEMs possessing the high and low value rankings, respectively.

REFERENCES

Barberio, Richard P. 1995. "The Role of Values in Environmental Group Participation." Presented at the Northeastern Political Science Association, November 9–11, Newark, New Jersey.

Barry, Brian. 1970. *Sociologists, Economists and Democracy.* Chicago: University of Chicago Press.

Beck, Paul Allen. 1997. *Party Politics in America.* 8th ed. New York: Addison-Wesley.

Braithwaite, V. A., and H. G. Law. 1985. "Structure of Human Values: Testing the Adequacy of the Rokeach Value Survey." *Journal of Personality and Social Psychology* 49 (1): 250–63.

Campbell, Angus Philip E., Warren E. Miller, and Donald E. Stokes. 1960. *The American Voter.* New York: Wiley.

Converse, Philip E. 1964. "The Nature of Belief Systems in Mass Publics." In David Apter, ed., *Ideology and Discontent.* New York: Free Press: 206–61.

Epstein, Leon D. 1986. *Political Parties in the American Mold.* Madison: University of Wisconsin Press.

Fiske, Susan T., and Shelley Taylor. 1991. *Social Cognition.* 2d ed. New York: McGraw-Hill.

Gibbins, Keith, and Iain Walker. 1993. "Multiple Interpretations of the Rokeach Value Survey." *Journal of Social Psychology* 133 (6): 797–805.

Ginsberg, Benjamin, and Martin Shefter. 1990. *Politics by Other Means: The Declining Importance of Elections in America.* New York: Basic Books.

Hartz, Louis. 1955. *The Liberal Tradition in America.* New York: Harcourt Brace.

Inglehart, Ronald. 1971. "The Silent Revolution in Europe: Intergenerational Change in Post-Industrial Societies." *American Political Science Review* 65: 991–1017.

Keefe, William J. 1994. *Parties, Politics, and Public Policy.* 7th ed. Washington: Congressional Quarterly Press.

Kirkpatrick, Jeane. 1976. *The New Presidential Elite.* New York: Russell Sage Foundation and Twentieth Century Fund.

Lane, Robert E. 1962. *Political Ideology: Why the American Common Man Believes What He Does.* New York: The Free Press.

Loomis, Burdett A. 1998. *The Contemporary Congress.* 2d ed. New York: St. Martin's Press.

McCann, James A. 1995. "Presidential Nomination Activists and Political Representation: A View from the 'Active Minority' Studies." In William G. Mayer, ed., *In Pursuit of the White House: How We Choose Our Presidential Nominees.* Chatham, N.J.: Chatham House Publishers: 77–104.

Paehlke, Robert C. 1994. "Environmental Values and Public Policy." In Norman J. Vig and Michael E. Kraft, eds., *Environmental Policy in the 1990s.* Washington, DC: Congressional Quarterly Press: 349–68.

Reichley, A. James. 1995. "Republican Ideology and the American Future." In John K. White and John C. Green, eds. *The Politics of Ideas: Intellectual Challenges to the Party after 1992.* Lanham, MD: Rowman & Littlefield Publishers, Inc: 70–99.

Reiter, Howard L. 1985. *Selecting the President.* Philadelphia: University of Pennsylvania Press.

Roback, Thomas H. 1980. "Motivations for Activism Among Republican National Convention Delegates." *Journal of Politics* 42: 181–201.

Rokeach, Milton. 1973. *The Nature of Human Values.* New York: The Free Press.

Searing, Donald D. 1979. "A Study of Values in the British House of Commons." In Milton Rokeach, ed., *Understanding Human Values.* New York: Free Press: 154–78.

Soule, John W., and James W. Clarke. 1970. "Amateurs and Professionals: A Study of Delegates to the 1968 Democratic National Convention." *American Political Science Review* 64: 888–98.

Soule, John W., and William E. McGrath. 1975. "A Comparative Study of Presidential Nomination Conventions: The Democrats 1968 and 1972." *American Journal of Political Science* 19: 501–17.

Stone, Deborah. 1997. *Policy Paradox: The Art of Political Decision Making.* New York: W.W. Norton & Company.

Sullivan, Dennis G., Jeffrey L. Pressman, Benjamin I. Page, and John J. Lyons. 1974. *The Politics of Representation: The Democratic Convention of 1972.* New York: St. Martin's Press.

Tetlock, Philip E. 1993. "Cognitive Structural Analysis of Political Rhetoric: Methodological and Theoretical Issues." In Shanto Iyengar and William J. McGuire, eds., *Explorations in Political Psychology.* Durham, NC: Duke University Press: 380–406.

Wildavsky, Aaron. 1965. "The Goldwater Phenomenon: Purists, Politicians, and the Two Party System." *Review of Politics* 17: 386–413.

Wilson, James Q. 1962. *The Amateur Democrat.* Chicago: University of Chicago Press.

11

National Party Committees and Presidential Campaigns: Performance and Promise

Samuel B. Hoff

INTRODUCTION

The national party committees form an integral part of the history of presidential campaigns in the United States. As comprehensive organizations, their impact on the election process has been relatively ignored; recent studies have focused on how state and local party organizations affect elections at each level (Dwyre and Stonecash 1992; Hill and Leighley 1992; Margolis 1992). Even less literature exists on the link between a party committee's efforts on behalf of a winning presidential candidate and ensuing relations among them.

This essay seeks to illustrate the manner by which various presidential campaign activities are inextricably meshed throughout national party committee structure and functions. First, the founding and evolution of national party committees is reviewed. Second, the party reforms advocated by national committees are analyzed. Third, the role of the national party committees in financing campaigns and assisting in the formation of party platforms is evaluated. Fourth, the manner by which the Democratic and Republican National committees dealt with delegate selection rules, financing, and platforms in the 1996 presidential campaign is covered. Finally, potential future contributions of national party committees are advocated. Given the perceived candidate-centered era of American elections as well as the continuing degeneration in cooperation within and between parties, the results of the research have important ramifications for both institutions and individuals in the American political system.

DAWN AND DEVELOPMENT OF PARTY COMMITTEES

According to Herrnson, the creation of national party organizations represented "the outgrowth of forces impinging on the parties from the broader political environment and of pressures emanating from within the parties themselves" (1990: 4). Bibby (1992: 83) believes that party committees "were created in the mid-1800's to serve as interim agents of the party conventions." Goldman (1990: 556) cites several reasons for the establishment of national committees, including "the need of party leaders from different regions to consult and contest presidential candidacies, public policies, and election campaign strategies." The Democratic National Committee (DNC) was founded in 1848, whereas the Republican National Committee (RNC) was created by resolution at the party's first national convention in 1856 (Bone 1971; Henderson 1976; Feigert and Conway 1976; Scott and Hrebenar 1984).

The national committees developed slowly and were initially subservient to state party leaders. By the beginning of the twentieth century, the party committee chair emerged as "a position of public visibility and political strength" (Bass 1984: 61). Bone (1971) postulates that the ratification of the Nineteenth Amendment increased the membership of both major parties' committees. Bibby (1992: 83) points out that not until the 1920s did either national committee establish a permanent headquarters with a full-time paid staff. He elaborates on the growth of these organizations: "Gradually, the national committees became more institutionalized with expanded full time staff, elaborate division of labor, heightened professionalism, and larger budgets. Thus since 1950, the size of the DNC staff had never dipped below forty persons, and the RNC has exceeded eighty."

Goldman (1990: 566) states that "the basic organizational functions and duties of the Democratic and Republican national committees, chairmen, and headquarters were fairly well defined and stabilized" by the 1960s; Herrnson and Menefee-Libey (1990: 25) add that national party entities "have been transformed from poor, transitory, 'powerless' committees to financially secure, stable, and highly influential political organizations" over the last few decades. Cotter et al. (1989: 155) contend that national party organizations "have experienced continuous development since the 1920's, despite electoral vicissitudes, in spite or because of long-term changes in the attitudes and behavior of the voting age population, and in the face of substantial enlargement of the regulatory and support roles of government in relation to parties and campaigns."

The contemporary duties of the national party committees are diverse yet dependent on those who serve on them. Henderson (1976: 118) holds that "[t]he functions of the national committee are largely what the members decide they will be." Feigert and Conway delineate those factors that provide direction to these organizations:

The functions of a party's national committee are determined by the interest of the individuals serving on the committee, the tasks preferred to be performed by its staff members, and the interests and desires of its chairperson. These in turn are influenced by the presidential candidate, or the competing candidates for the nomination, the incumbent president for the party's national committee, and others of substantial influence in the party, such as its leading spokesmen, public officeholders, and fund-raisers. (1976: 141)

Sorauf and Beck (1988), Gelb and Palley (1975), and Bone (1971) share the view that running the presidential nominating convention is the most important function of the national party committees. Huckshorn (1984) examines a number of specific roles of the national party committees, including research, public relations, training programs for candidate and campaign staff, auxiliary group activities, fund-raising, and managing the national convention. Bibby (1992: 89) observes that while official titles vary somewhat, both the RNC and DNC "have staff specialists for fund-raising, political operations (assistance to candidates and party organizations), public relations, voter mobilization, liaison with voter groups, convention and meeting arrangements, and administration."

Party Committees and the Presidential Nomination

The presidential selection process has changed dramatically since the early 1800s when "members of Congress who identified with particular parties were meeting in caucuses to nominate their party's presidential and vice-presidential candidates" (Goldstein 1991: 2). Indeed, national nominating conventions had all been employed for several elections preceding the founding of party committees and continued with little change until 1912. In that year, a direct way for some voters to select delegates to the national convention was added through presidential primaries. Edwards and Wayne report that the percentage of convention delegates chosen through primaries increased from 33 to 67 percent in the Democratic party and from 42 to 77 percent in the Republican party between 1912 and 1988.

Epstein (1986: 208) argues that "[w]hat happened to national party organizations in the 1970's and early 1980's is not entirely separable from the post-1968 transformation of the presidential nomination process." Goldstein (1991: 4) notes that "some observers say post 1968 changes in the convention system have resulted in an entirely new presidential selection system." Edwards and Wayne (1990: 23–24) explain the reasons for and goals of the procedural changes in the presidential nomination sequence:

Largely as a result of the tumultuous Democratic convention of 1968 whose nominee, Hubert Humphrey, had not competed in the primaries, demands for a larger voice for the party's rank and file increased. In response to these demands, the party appointed a series of commissions to examine its rules for delegate selection and to propose changes. The commissions had two basic goals: to encourage participation in party activities and to make the convention more representative of typical Democratic voters.

Some of the changes included choosing delegates in the calendar year of the convention, lowering or abolishing fees for entering primaries, selecting delegates at the congressional district level, public announcements of caucus meetings where convention delegates would be chosen, allocating delegates in a closer proportion to the popular vote candidates received in the state, and encouraging more equal representation of various demographic groups in state delegations (Edwards and Wayne 1990: 23–24).

There appears to be no agreement on the effect of changes in the delegate selection process. Pika et al. (1992) postulate that whereas the influence of party leaders in the nomination declined, better representation of disadvantaged groups was a positive outcome. Wayne (1988:107) contends that delegate selection changes have caused activists "who have less of a tie to the party and more of a tie to a candidate and his or her issue positions, to get involved" and that the reforms have heightened "differences between the ideological and demographic characteristics of convention delegates and those of the electorate as a whole." Hershey (1984: 137) holds that although the Democratic reforms provided the national organization with augmented authority over state parties, they likewise "made it easier for issue-oriented enthusiasts and candidate loyalists, rather than party regulars and public officials, to control the party's nominating machinery." Thomas et al. (1993: 49) suggest that the changes have enhanced the importance of another institution—the media.

Although the national Republican organization has never adopted delegate selection rules that are binding on state parties, in part because of the more homogeneous composition of the party, Democratic changes have nonetheless impacted on Republican procedures, according to Goldstein. He points out that "Democratic-controlled state legislatures often have required Republicans as well as Democrats to conform to their changes in delegate selection procedures" and that the Republican party has sought to broaden the groups represented at its conventions (1991: 6).

Party Committees and Campaign Financing

A plethora of researchers have probed the impact of the Federal Election Campaign Act on presidential campaigns; most of their findings have direct relevance for national party committees. Pomper (1977) proposes that financial regulations have increased competition during the nomination stage and augmented the proportion of state primaries. Orren (1983) asserts that expenditure limits imposed on those presidential contenders accepting federal matching funds during the nomination sequence require candidates to select states in which they want to compete and also lead to their concentrating resources in early primaries. He further finds that spending caps reduce disbursements for vital activities, enhance the impact of independent expenditures, and heighten centralization of primary campaigns. DiClerico and Uslaner (1984: 101) identify three effects of presidential campaign-finance reforms: "First, they have substantially curbed the ability of fat cats to use money as a means of obligating Presidential candidates. Second, they have narrowed the disparities in financial resources among competing candidates, particularly at the general election stage. Third, through a system of full and timely disclosure, the public may ascertain where candidates get their money and how they spend it."

Davis (1987) determines that nomination finances have increased the overall cost of presidential primaries, necessitated active campaigning in most states, and lengthened the duration of nomination campaigns. Wilcox (1988) and DiClerico (1990) each cite the tendency of candidates in nomination contests to seek ways to circumvent state and national spending limits.

Edwards and Wayne (1990) review several consequences of campaign finance reform in presidential nomination contests, including reducing unaccounted contributions and lessening dependence on large donors. Conversely, Alexander and Bauer (1991: 47) find that "[t]he limits also have spurred the creation of several alternative means of avoidance, including presidential PACs [political action committees], delegate committees, soft money, and independent expenditures." Without question, the amount spent by all primary election candidates in both parties has increased: the total went from $66.9 million in 1976 to $234 million in the 1996 presidential nomination period (Corrado 1997).

The national party committees appear to be exploiting opportunities available through campaign finance laws, although not to the same degree. Atherton (1982) states that before 1980, Republicans scored most financial successes. Herrnson (1990: 49) furnishes evidence that the RNC raised more money than their Democratic counterpart in each of four presidential elections between 1976 and 1988, although "following the 1980 election, the Democrats began to narrow the gap in fund-raising." He credits the GOP financial advantage to three factors: an earlier start in direct mail solicitation programs; the greater wealth of their supporters; and the use of negative appeals because of the Republicans' minority status. Bibby (1992: 92) likewise attributes the RNC's financial position to its direct mail and large contributor activities. However, he asserts that both national party organizations have "achieved substantial autonomy as well as enhanced leverage over their state party organizations because of their superior financial and technical resources."

Party Committees and Party Platforms

Since the national party committees are directly responsible for the quad-rennial nominating conventions and their respective platforms are finalized at these gatherings, it can be assumed that the party committees contribute to these guideposts for the subsequent general election campaign. Pomper (1967: 319) postulates that a "party's policy commitments are found in its platform. Adopted by its only meaningful organ, the nominating convention, and presented to the voters as the Presidential election approaches, it most fully represents the party's intentions." Smith (1992: 533) claims that plat-form writing has three functions at presidential nominating conventions: "(1) to identify the combatants (the characters in the story); (2) to establish party values; (3) to generate the story lines or plots that provide motives for partisan action."

EVALUATING PARTY COMMITTEES IN THE 1996 CAMPAIGN

The 1996 presidential campaign may be utilized to determine how the na-tional party committees performed in the areas of delegate selection, fund-raising and spending, and platform writing.

Delegate Selection

The national parties continued to maintain influence over the nomination function of presidential campaigns in 1996. Goldstein (1995: 25) labels 1996 delegate selection rules by Democrats as the product of DNC actions in 1990 and 1994. He notes that the "Republicans' rules for the selection and alloca-tion of delegates to their national convention have also changed, but they re-flect much more continuity than the ever-changing Democratic rules."

The delegate count remained at a nearly two-to-one ratio favoring the Democrats, at 4,295 to 1,984 (Cook 1995). However, the Republicans re-versed a 1992 trend by holding more primaries than the Democrats—forty-three to thirty-six (Edwards and Wayne 1997). Other differences are summa-rized:

- Republicans scheduled 19 primaries with a winner-take-all allocation procedure; the Democrats, eschewing the latter form, selected 71 percent of delegates by propor-tional representation;

- Democrats adopted a 15 percent vote standard threshold in primaries and caucuses in order to earn either district or statewide delegates; Republicans employed diverse threshold levels across states;

- Democrats mandated that all state delegations be equally divided between men and women; Republicans established no quotas for gender or race;

- Democrats required most delegates to be bound to a candidate, though reserved 18 percent of the convention slots to unpledged "superdelegates"; Republicans allowed state parties to set rules on binding delegates;

- Democrats set a much more strict time frame for running primaries and caucuses than Republicans (Goldstein 1995).

Overall, Bob Dole won forty of forty-three primaries and garnered 59.1 percent of the primary vote on his way to the 1996 Republican nomination (*Guide to the 1996 Republican National Convention* 1996). According to Abramson et al. (1998: 25), "the ingredients that went into making Dole the initial front-runner were the ingredients that enabled him to withstand challenges and survive in a highly truncated primary season." President Bill Clinton, facing token opposition, won all thirty-eight Democratic primaries and accumulated 88.5 percent of the vote in those contests in 1996, the best showing by any candidate in either party since Ronald Reagan's successful renomination in 1984 (*Guide to the 1996 Democratic National Convention* 1996).

Still, as much as national party committees seek to control the nomination process, the "fact that there are more than fifty separate contests in each campaign creates numerous layers of complexity" as well as competition (Abrahamson et al. 1998: 16). The decision by Delaware Republicans to hold their maiden presidential primary on February 24, 1996, provides a stark example of the limits of national party committees' reach. Because it would be held four days after the New Hampshire primary rather than seven, New Hampshire Republicans demanded that Delaware relent. The Republican National Committee promised to reduce Delaware's convention delegation if it didn't comply, and New Hampshire officials threatened political retribution against GOP presidential hopefuls who campaigned in Delaware. Nonetheless, the primary went on as scheduled, from which Steve Forbes, one of two candidates to visit Delaware, gained an important victory. The RNC failed to penalize Delaware at its convention (Hoff 1997).

Campaign Finance

The monetary resources employed in the 1996 presidential nomination season may be analyzed from individual candidate and party committee perspectives.

Running as an incumbent president seeking reelection, Bill Clinton earned $13.4 million in federal matching funds, second to Republican candidate Bob Dole with $13.5 million. President Clinton, who spent a total of $38.1 million to earn renomination, was outspent by two Republican contenders during that period, Bob Dole ($42.1 million) and Steve Forbes ($41.7 million). Forbes, who rejected federal matching funds, financed $37.5 million of the latter sum through a personal loan to his campaign (Corrado 1997).

A study by Hoff (1996) examined efficiency in use of monetary resources by 1996 candidates for president. He found that Democratic nominee Clinton finished 25–0 in state primaries where his campaign spent the least amount per vote among all candidates, while Republican nominee Bob Dole went 22–0 under such conditions. Further, Clinton won in all nineteen primaries where he spent the most among Democratic contenders, whereas Dole won twenty-two of twenty-four primaries when spending most. Using performance in all primaries as a gauge, President Clinton spent just $.36 per vote in 1996, which is by far the most efficient use of funds by any candidate in any party over the last three presidential election cycles. On the other hand, though Bob Dole had the lowest cost per vote among 1996 Republican presidential candidates, his $3.76 amount per vote was higher than any successful party nominee over the 1988–1996 time frame.

From a party perspective, the 1995–1996 election cycle witnessed the following trends ("FEC Certifies Public Funds for the Dole-Kemp Ticket" 1996; "FEC Reports Major Increase in Party Activity for 1995–96" 1997; "PAC Activity Increases in the 1995–96 Election Cycle" 1997; Keen and Daly 1997):

- The Democratic National Committee collected $108.4 million, 48.9 percent of the total $221.6 million received by all Democratic party committees. The DNC spent $105.6 million, 49.2 percent of the $214.3 million expended by all Democratic committees in 1995–96. The Republican National Committee collected $193.0 million, 46.3 percent of the total $416.5 million received by all Republican party committees. The RNC spent $192.4 million, 47.1 percent of the $408.5 million expended by all Republican party committees in 1995–96;

- Overall, Republican fundraising by all party committees increased 57 percent over the 1991–92 presidential election cycle, while spending by national, state, and local Republican party committees increased 62 percent over the previous period. Democratic party committee fundraising and spending at all levels both rose by 36 percent compared to the 1991–92 election cycle;

- The RNC outpaced the DNC in soft money donations in 1995–96, $141.2 million to $122.3 million. These donations, which fall outside federal election law donation limits and the ban on corporate contributions, are supposed to be used for party-building activities only, not in connection with federal campaigns;

- The RNC led the DNC in soft money contributions in seven of ten source categories during the 1995–96 presidential election cycle, with two other sources tied in their donations to the respective national party committees;

- Although PAC contributions accounted for only about two percent of total receipts by presidential candidates in 1995–96, Republican contenders for all federal offices received $118.2 million from political action committees, while Democrats were given $98.9 million;

- Both national party committees received $12.3 million from the Federal Election Commission for their 1996 presidential nominating conventions.

The expanding money race during presidential campaigns affected national party committees in several ways during the most recent election cycle. Keen and Daly (1997: 1) contend that the "national parties exploit soft money loopholes in campaign finance laws, and they did so in record fashion" in 1996. Corrado (1997: 147) says the DNC spent $34 million on issue advocacy advertising on behalf of the Clinton reelection campaign between June 1995 and June 1996. "The DNC's spending and Clinton's financial advantage entering the final months of the campaign encouraged the RNC to adopt a similar strategy as soon as its presidential nominee was determined," according to Corrado. The RNC proceeded to spend $14 million in just three months.

One consequence of the $150 million spent by the party nominees during the general election phase of the 1996 presidential campaigns is that both national party committees ended the 1995–1996 election cycle in debt: $5.0 million by the RNC and $6.2 million by the DNC ("FEC Reports Major Increases in Party Activity for 1995–96" 1997). Further, as a result of soft money and foreign contributions to national parties, there continue to be attempts to change the current finance laws. Yet, Congress turned back eighteen major attempts at reform between 1980 and 1997 ("Eighteen Years of Stalemate" 1997). Finally, the unprecedented use of patronage to solicit wealthy donors undertaken by the Clinton reelection team has spawned a plethora of congressional investigations and heightened cynicism with the political process.

Platform Formulation

The process by which the party platforms were finalized by the presidential nominating conventions in 1996 obviously included input by national party committees. Kalb (1996: 33) notes the distinction between platform preparation by the Democrats in 1992 and 1996: "As recently as 1992, the Democratic platform deliberations necessitated lengthy debates over such issues as welfare, the death penalty, term limits, and campaign finance laws. All this has seemed a distant memory for the Democrats in 1996. The platform deliberations were as placid as the primaries. With President Clinton the only contender for the presidential nomination, there was harmony almost from the beginning in composing the choir music to accompany him." Page (1996: 8A) believes that the "contrast with Republicans was deliberate. While the GOP platform committee began several days of divisive debate in San Diego, the Democrats provided a portrait of family unity."

Indeed, the Republicans were hobbled in their platform writing by the debate over abortion, so much so that it "often sidetracked the campaign of presumed GOP nominee Bob Dole in the weeks and months leading up to the convention" (Greenblatt 1996: 13). Hall (1996: 8A) explains that a last-minute, preconvention compromise offered by Dole on the abortion controversy probably made matters worse. Still, the final draft of the abortion plank was accepted and pro-choice supporters refrained from waging an even more divisive floor fight at the convention.

While the 1996 Democratic platform had many similarities with its 1992 predecessor, the Republican platform excluded some of the 1992 ideas that became part of the 1994 Contract with America, most notably the term limits plank.

The 1996 Presidential Election in Retrospect

Amid President Clinton's successful reelection in 1996 are some basic facts that should concern national party committees and the American public as a whole. First, while Clinton defeated Dole by a 31–19 state vote, he failed to garner a majority of votes cast, earning 49.2 percent of the popular vote to 40.7 percent for Dole. (Clinton's Electoral College margin over Dole was 379 to 159.) Second, the 1996 presidential election witnessed the lowest turnout among eligible voters—48.8 percent—in seventy-two years. Third, voters once again opted for divided government by returning Bill Clinton to the presidency and a Republican majority to Congress (Edwards and Wayne 1997).

CONCLUSION

There is general agreement among most scholars that national party committees have made recent progress in reestablishing their preeminent place in presidential politics. Herrnson (1990: 64) holds that "the 1980s witnessed the re-emergence of national party organizations as important players in party politics and elections." Reiter (1993: 97) observes that "[i]t seems fairly clear that national and state party organizations are more active than they were a few years ago."

Some proposals to improve party committees, such as developing constant lines of communication with party regulars and the public (Saloma and Sontag 1973) or increasing party control over the financing of presidential campaigns (Atherton 1982) are noteworthy and should be implemented. However, other ideas such as a national primary or simultaneous election of the president and all members of Congress, are too extreme and inimical to the realities of modern electoral politics. In any case, national party committees, like political parties themselves, should always strive to become "instruments of effective democratic governance in a large scale polity" through linking elections with public policy (Shannon 1991: 265).

REFERENCES

Abramson, Paul A., John H. Aldrich, and David W. Rohde. 1998. *Continuity and Change in the 1996 Elections.* Washington, DC: Congressional Quarterly Press.

Alexander, Herbert E., and Monica Bauer. 1991. *Financing the 1988 Election*. Boulder: Westview Press.

Atherton, F. Christopher. 1982. "Political Money and Party Strength." In Joel Fleishman, ed., *The Future of American Political Parties*. Englewood Cliffs: Prentice Hall.

Bass, Harold F. 1984. "The President and the National Party Organization." In Robert Harmel, ed., *Presidents and Their Parties*. New York: Praeger Publishers.

Bibby, John F. 1992. *Politics, Parties, and Elections in America*. Chicago: Nelson-Hall Publishers.

Bone, Hugh A. 1971. *American Politics and the Party System*. New York. McGraw-Hill.

Cammarano, Joseph, and Jim Josefson. 1995. "Putting it in Writing: An Evaluation of Presidential Candidate Platforms in the 1992 Election." *Southeastern Political Review* 23:2: 187–204.

Cook, Rhodes. 1995. "DNC Under Wilhelm Seeking a New Role." *Congressional Quarterly Weekly Report* (March 13): 634.

Corrado, Anthony. 1997. "Financing the 1996 Elections." In Gerald M. Pomper, ed., *The Elections of 1996*. Chatham: Chatham House Publishers.

Cotter, Cornelius, James L. Gibson, John F. Bibby, and Robert J. Huckshorn. 1989. *Party Organization in American Politics*. Pittsburgh: University of Pittsburgh Press.

Davis, James W. 1987. *The American President: A New Perspective*. New York: Harper and Row.

DiClerico, Robert E. 1990. *The American President*. Englewood Cliffs: Prentice Hall.

DiClerico, Robert E., and Eric M. Uslaner. 1984. *Few Are Chosen: Problems in Presidential Selection*. New York: McGraw-Hill.

Dwyre, Diane, and Jeffrey M. Stonecash. 1992. "Where's the Party: Changing State Party Organizations." *American Politics Quarterly* 20: 326–344.

Edwards George C., and Stephen J. Wayne. 1990. *Presidential Leadership: Politics and Policy Making*. New York: St. Martin's Press.

Edwards. George C., and Stephen J. Wayne. 1997. *Presidential Leadership: Politics and Policy Making*. New York: St. Martin's Press.

"Eighteen Years of Stalemate." 1997. *Congressional Quarterly Weekly Report* (October 11): 2450.

Epstein, Leon. 1986. *Political Parties in the American Mold*. Madison: University of Wisconsin Press.

"FEC Certifies Public Funds for the Dole-Kemp Ticket." 1996. Washington, DC: Federal Election Commission (August 15).

"FEC Reports Major Increase in Party Activity for 1995–96." 1997. Washington, DC: Federal Election Commission (March 19).

Feigert, Frank B., and Margaret Conway. 1976. *Parties and Politics in America*. Boston: Allyn and Bacon, Inc.

Fine, Terri Sue. 1995. "Economic Interests and the Framing of the 1988 and 1992 Democratic and Republican Party Platforms." *The American Review of Politics* 16 (spring): 79–93.

Fishel, Jeff. 1985. *Presidents and Promises*. Washington, DC: Congressional Quarterly Press.

Gelb, Joyce, and Marian Lief Palley. 1975. *Tradition and Change in American Politics*. New York: Thomas Y. Crowell Company.

Goldman, Ralph M. 1990. *The National Party Chairman and Committees: Factionalism at the Top*. Armonk: M. E. Sharpe.

Goldstein, Michael L. 1991. *Guide to the 1992 Presidential Election*. Washington, DC: Congressional Quarterly Press.

———. 1995. *Guide to the 1996 Presidential Election*. Washington, DC: Congressional Quarterly Press.

Gosnell, Harold F., and Richard G. Smolka. 1976. *American Parties and Elections*. Columbus: Charles E. Merrill Publishing Company.

Greenblatt, Alan. 1996. "The Platform Dance." *Congressional Quarterly Weekly Report* (August 3): 13–16.

Guide to the 1996 Democratic National Convention. 1996. Washington, DC: Congressional Quarterly Press (August 17 Supplement).

Guide to the 1996 Republican National Convention. 1996. Washington, DC: Congressional Quarterly Press (August 3 Supplement).

Hall, Mimi. 1996. "GOP: Dole's Effort to Please Both Sides on Abortion Fails." *USA Today* (August 6): 8A.

Henderson, Gordon G. 1976. *An Introduction to Political Parties*. New York: Harper and Row.

Herrnson, Paul S. 1990. "Reemerging National Party Organizations." In L. Sandy Maisel, ed., *The Parties Respond: Changes in the Party System*. Boulder: Westview Press.

Herrnson, Paul S., and David Menefee-Libey. 1990. "The Dynamics of Party Organizational Development." *Midsouth Political Science Journal* 11: 1–30.

Hershey, Marjorie Randon. 1984. *Running for Office: The Political Education of Campaigners*. Chatham: Chatham House Publishers.

Hill, Kim Quaile, and Jan E. Leighley. 1992. "Party Ideology, Organization, and Competitiveness as Mobilizing Forces in U.S. Elections." Paper presented at the Annual Meeting of the American Political Science Association, Chicago, September 3–6.

Hoff, Samuel B. 1997. "Delaware." In Andrew W. Appleton and Daniel S. Ward, eds., *State Party Profiles: A 50-State Guide to Development, Organization, and Resources*. Washington, DC: Congressional Quarterly Press: 52–57.

———. 1996. "Money and Votes: Tracing Spending and Performance in Presidential Primaries." Paper presented at the National Social Science Association Conference, New Orleans, November 13–15.

Huckshorn, Robert J. 1984. *Political Parties in America*. Monterey: Brooks/Cole Publishing Company.

Kalb, Deborah. 1996. "Building With Broad Planks." *Congressional Quarterly Weekly Report* (August 17): 33–35.

Keen, Jennifer, and John Daly. 1997. *Beyond the Limits: Soft Money in the 1996 Elections*. Washington: Center for Responsive Politics.

Maisel, L. Sandy. 1993. "The Platform Writing Process: Candidate Centered Platforms in 1992." *Political Science Quarterly* 108:4: 671–78.

Margolis, Michael. 1992. "Studying the Role of Local Party Organization in Democratic Governance." Paper presented at the Annual Meeting of the American Political Science Association, Chicago, September 3–6.

Orren, Gary R. 1983. "Presidential Campaign Finance: Its Impact and Future." In James Lengle and Byron Shafer, eds., *Presidential Politics: Readings on Nominations and Elections*. New York: St. Martin's Press.

"PAC Activity Increases in 1995–96 Election Cycle." 1997. Washington, DC: Federal Election Commission (April 27).

Page, Susan. 1996. "Democrats: In a Show of Unity, a Quick Approval." *USA Today* (August 6): 8A.

Pika, Joseph, Zelma Mosley, and Richard A. Watson. 1992. *The Presidential Contest*. Washington, DC: Congressional Quarterly Press.

Pomper, Gerald. 1967. "If Elected, I Promise: American Party Platforms." *Midwest Journal of Political Science* 11: 318–52.

———. 1977. "The Nominating Contests and Conventions." In Gerald Pomper, ed., *The Elections of 1976: Reports and Interpretations*. New York: David McKay Company.

Reiter, Howard. 1993. *Parties and Elections in Corporate America*. New York: Longman Publishers.

Saloma, John S., and Frederick H. Sontag. 1973. *Parties: The Real Opportunity for Effective Citizen Politics*. New York: Random House.

Scott, Ruth K., and Ronald J. Hrebenar. 1984. *Parties in Crisis: Party Politics in America*. New York: John Wiley and Sons.

Shannon, W. Wayne. 1991. "Yes—Political Parties Should Govern the Presidential Selection Process." In Gary Rose, ed. *Controversies in Presidential Selection*. Albany: State University of New York Press.

Smith, Larry David. 1992. "The Party Platforms as Institutional Discourse: The Democrats and Republicans of 1988." *Presidential Studies Quarterly* 12: 531–43.

Sorauf, Frank J., and Paul Allen Beck. 1988. *Party Politics in America*. Glenview: Scott, Foresman, and Company.

Thomas, Norman C., Joseph A. Pika, and Richard A. Watson. 1993. *The Politics of the Presidency*. Washington, DC: Congressional Quarterly Press.

Wayne, Stephen J. 1988. *The Road to the White House*. New York: St. Martin's Press.

Wilcox, Clyde. 1988. "Financing the 1988 Prenomination Campaigns." Paper presented at the Annual Meeting of the Northeastern Political Science Association, Providence, RI, November 10–12.

PART TWO

THE IMPACT OF ELECTIONS ON SPECIFIC POLICIES

On the basis of the extensive consideration of election mechanics in Part One, we can now turn to the effect of elections on specific policies. We do this first through Jo Freeman's "Sex, Race, Religion and Partisan Realignment," which traces the impact of major aspects of American culture on our parties and elections, and conversely their effect on our culture. This is followed by Erika Pilver's answer to "What Do Women Get For Their Vote?" a specific consideration of the effect of elections on gender and gender politics.

Next, Jean Wahl Harris and Rodd Freitag provide two views of the impact of elections on social welfare policies. Harris examines the early results of the 1993 "Motor-Voter" act and its potential effect on the monumental 1996 welfare reform act. Freitag provides a history of the major welfare reform efforts of the U.S. national government over the past thirty years and the reasons for their failures, *until* passage of the 1996 reform. Both are dramatic illustrations of the "voters-elections-policies" connection, or the lack thereof.

Mark Kemper closes this section of the book by studying the electoral connection (which the uninitiated observer would doubt exists) with decisions of the U.S. Supreme Court.

By the end of Part Two, the reader will have found powerful instances of linkage between elections and public policy, but also that that linkage is highly sporadic and unpredictable, frequently broken by interest group intervention and the independence of government officials, often frustrating millions of voters (and mystifying even the experts). The stage will then be set for an extensive examination of proposals for electoral reform in Part Three.

12

Sex, Race, Religion, and Partisan Realignment

Jo Freeman

Sex, race, and religion are primary sources of partisan conflict in American politics. Race and religion are themes of long standing. Their guise and their proponents change from era to era, they coincide and collude with sectional and economic cleavages, they emerge and recede as dominant topics of public debate; but whatever form they take, race and religion have been crucial components of our political conflicts since the country's founding. Sex, more specifically the role of women and how it affects relationships between the sexes, is a theme that emerges only sporadically and manifests itself less directly than the other two. Since the rise of the contemporary feminist movement in the late 1960s, the importance of sex has increased until in many ways it is a dominant, albeit understated, theme in current partisan contests. This conflict has largely been one of feminism versus antifeminism, seen most explicitly in the polarization of the two major political parties around issues raised by the feminist movement. However, sex as act as well as gender is also important as evidenced by the acrimonious debates over abortion and homosexuality. Since attitudes toward feminism strongly coincide with attitudes toward these issues, and in many ways provide the ideological basis for the pro-choice and pro-gay rights position, sex and feminism can be treated as a single theme.

Sex, race, and religion are fundamental to politics for two reasons. First, they define the communities in which people live. For race, and to a lesser extent religion, these communities are homogeneous; those in them constantly have their values and attitudes reinforced by others like themselves. Common communities are conducive to political consistency. Since women usually live with men, this is clearly not true of sex, though it is more true of homosexuals. Sex is only a sporadic theme, emerging only when structures or institutions are created which bring women together on a regular basis. The emergence in the last twenty years of a gay and lesbian community that is also politically conscious and willing to organize to elect sympathetic public officials may give sex the permanence of race and religion.

Second, ideas about race, sex, and religion embody fundamental values and consequently are a source of conflicts over values even among members of the same race, sex, or religion. These values go to the heart of what we mean by culture. When they are threatened or attacked or even challenged the response is far more ferocious and obstinate than in the "normal" politics of who gets what, when, and how. As a "nation of immigrants," founded by religious dissidents and political malcontents who brought many different cultures to our shores, our politics has often required us to channel and contain cultural conflict, to "civilize" it. Indeed some of our most exalted principles, such as the separation of church and state, or "that government is best which governs least," are the result of trying to keep cultural conflict out of politics. But for most of our history cultural conflict has been an underlying theme, whether it stays within the boundaries of electoral politics or spills over into direct community conflict.

The meaning of "race" has varied throughout our history. In today's popular parlance race is used almost exclusively for "blacks" and "whites," and sometimes "Hispanics." "Racial" issues are those of particular concern to African Americans, or reactions to African-Americans, though occasionally other groups identified as minorities, such as Native Americans and Asian Americans, are included as well. Whites, like blacks, are referred to as a single race, but this is of recent vintage. Previously, groups we now call ethnics—Irish, Italians, Jews, etc.—were viewed as distinct races. Here, race will mean what it meant in the historical period referred to. Politically, the common element in the attribution of race is community. Identifiable races live in common communities where they share institutions, values, information, and viewpoints. Members of these communities often practice the same religion and the same politics. Over time, most "races" have integrated into the larger American polity as their members dispersed geographically and economically. The more they disperse, the looser the community ties, the less important race is as a determinant of identity or political views. Thus most of the "races" of the 19th century are merely ethnic groups today.

The cultural and political impact of our three major religious traditions — Protestant, Catholic and Jewish—has not been equal or even. Each religious group brought different values that were initially resisted, then gradually layered on top of that which came before. Our cultural foundation is Protestant, the lasting legacy of the initial immigrants (Herberg 1955: 94). The Irish immigration of the 1840s and 1850s brought a fervent Catholicism, whose building blocks did not sit well on the Protestant base. The Jewish wave was last and smallest, adding decorative touches more than basic cultural themes, except for New York City where the cultural influence is considerable. Jews were met with intolerance as Catholics had been before them, but as they have assimilated, a subtle shift of belief has ensued from one that ours is a Christian culture to one that it is Judeo-Christian. The impact of other religions has not yet been widely felt.

Religion has always been a major source of community and identity for most Americans, with important differences in religious practices, socioeconomic status, and attitudes. Catholics were urban, voted Democratic, and joined labor unions. Nineteenth-century Jews were merchants and voted Republican; those who came or were born in the twentieth century shifted to the Democratic column. Protestants were predominantly rural, and outside the South voted largely Republican (Herberg 1955).

As important as the three traditions have been as creators of values, the smaller units were the crucibles of community. Protestantism in particular has always been deeply divided by denomination, so much so that "religion" will be used here to mean differences in denomination as well as tradition. Indeed the black Protestant church is really a fourth tradition; the formation of separate black churches, and then denominations, began after the Revolutionary War and accelerated after the Civil War (Niebuhr 1929: 253–59). The black and white Protestant churches have diverged so widely that black Baptists have more in common with black Methodists than with white Baptists.

In the post World War II era there has been a striking increase in secularism—that portion of the population that doesn't identify with any major religious tradition, even when raised in one. There is no "secular" community, and secularism by itself is not an equivalent identity to a religious one, but "seculars" do share values as do members of religious bodies. The rise of secularism has had major consequences for both religion and politics.

In the nineteenth century men and women lived in separate worlds, even while sharing their homes. As prosperity created a middle class, the number of women grew who had sufficient leisure and education to work together in many movements. By the end of the century women had created a vast network of women's clubs concerned with individual and community improvement. The community of women formed by these groups, and the attitudes and values many shared, eventually made the movement for woman suffrage more than a radical idea pursued only by a few. For much of the nineteenth century, the separate spheres of men and women created separate political subcultures, in which men engaged in electoral politics and women in moral reform (Baker 1984). However, in the 1880s, and particularly in the 1890s, women began to move into political parties, aiding men in the election of candidates. Their organizations were separate from men's, but not their politics.

After the Nineteenth Amendment was ratified in 1920, women's groups went in different directions and were often bitter opponents. For many reasons, feminism slid from the public agenda. It was revived in the late 1960s and 1970s, when a new feminist movement emerged and painstakingly created new organizations and communities of women (and some men) to alter women's role and enlarge their opportunities.

PARTY SYSTEMS AND ELECTORAL REALIGNMENTS

In the nation's two-hundred-year history many different political parties have been active in one or more of the United States. But, with occasional exceptions, there has always been a national two-party system. Contenders for public office have organized themselves into two competing ideological traditions. "Each of the two ideological traditions has given rise to a series of major parties in American national politics; [one] to the Federalists, National Republicans, Whigs, and modern Republicans, and the [other] to the Antifederalists, Democratic-Republicans and modern Democrats." Political scientist Jim Reichley calls the first the party of order because it prioritizes "public order and economic growth" while the latter is termed the party of equality because it favors "economic and social equality" (Reichley 1992: 4–6).

Although concerns with order and access (equality) have been constants in party history, concerns about the role of government have not been. Until the Civil War, the party of equality was dominant nationally though not in every region; between the Civil War and the New Deal, the Republican party prevailed as the vehicle through which economic growth and public order was sought; since then, the Democratic party has mostly governed. In each of these three eras the dominant party favored stronger national government. Whichever party, or tradition, is in power is the one that favors the institutions through which it exercises power.

The two ideological traditions have always incorporated many communities, interests, and associations within them, some as active participants in the parties and some only as voters. They have not always been the same ones. Different interests or blocks of voters sharing similar characteristics and views emerge, grow, and decline. The size of the effective electorate changes as the eligible population increases and voting rates rise or fall. Sometimes a voting community moves from one party to the other. These shifts, when permanent, alter a party's base—the coalition of interests on which it depends and which write its fundamental policies. Alterations in voting patterns may lead to an electoral *realignment*—that is, a shift in which party wins elections, or some elections, in different locales (Sundquist 1983: chapter 1). Sometimes the electorate realigns gradually and sometimes quickly; some realignments have been durable and some only temporary (Campbell 1966; Burnham 1970;

Sundquist 1983). These realignments may cause a redistribution of power between the parties, reinforce and solidify an existing distribution, and/or give rise to new parties, but they do so within one of the two main traditions.

Realignments occur when new *cleavages* in the electorate attain political saliency, or when changes in the size and composition of the electorate alter the impact of existing cleavages. Our pluralistic polity always has cleavages, but not all are important to everyone, and not everyone votes. Realignments reflect changes in major cleavage patterns. Generally new cleavages are superimposed on old ones, with some otherwise identical voters voting the new and some the old lines of partisanship. Many decades later, old cleavages fade from importance.

A durable distribution of partisan power is called a party system or electoral system. Political scientists generally agree that there have been at least five such systems in our national history, but disagree about further ones (Burnham 1970: 135). The breaking points between these five party systems were roughly: 1828–1832, 1856–1860, 1892–1896, and 1928–1936. The transition between national party systems has usually been sudden, taking place over one or two "critical elections," though there is some disagreement on exactly how many elections are necessary to complete a transition (Key 1955: 3–4; Kleppner 1987: 18; Burnham 1970). Because no critical election marked the end of the fifth party system, while the others ended abruptly, no consensus exists on whether or when it ended. There was also no critical election between the first and second party systems, though there is agreement that a seismic shift occurred.

A BRIEF HISTORY OF THE FIRST FIVE PARTY SYSTEMS

The first party system was more one of factions among the founding elites than a true party system. Nonetheless, the "revolution of 1800," as Jefferson called it, marked the emergence of parties in American politics (Sisson 1974: 11). Initially parties were driven by issues and events, rising and falling with electoral crises and displaying little institutional continuity. While meetings and caucuses selected candidates, participation was limited to "respectable" men and organization was from the top down. The "spirit of party" radiated a suspicion of corruption. This period also saw the decline of the Federalists as a national party, leaving the Democratic Republicans as the dominant—sometimes the sole—party outside of New England (Formisano 1981).

Serious competition reappeared in the 1820s, initially within the one major party. By the 1830s the extension of suffrage through the abolition of property qualifications and the addition of several new states led to the formation of mass parties with complex and continuing organizations. The public attitude toward parties softened. During the second party system, lasting from roughly 1828 until the eve of the Civil War, partisan competition became the accepted way to elect public officials, and party conventions, local and national, became the primary means of selecting party candidates. Although several parties ran candidates in the 1830s, by the 1840s the traditional division had reasserted itself; groups allied in two major coalitions (Whigs and Democrats) contested elections in all states but one. Nationally there was a two-party system; organizationally, parties remained state and local affairs. Even after the Democrats elected the first national party chairman in 1844 and the first national committee in 1848, their primary task was to elect the party's ticket; the national officers did not run the party between elections (McCormick 1966; Formisano 1971, 1981: 67; Shade 1981).

In the first party system, region, religion, and to a lesser extent race, were the major sources of party loyalty. Region often coincided with economic interests, but those interests were particular to the region rather than a reflection of the relative wealth of those within a region. Most voters followed their racial and religious peers in deciding their party allegiance, though these allegiances were affected by local politics and might differ from state to state. Congregationalists and Episcopalians were Federalist, as were Quakers except in New England; Methodists, Baptists, and Presbyterians were not. Older immigrants, for example, the English, generally favored the Federalists while the newer ones, for example, Germans and Scots Irish, did not (Formisano 1981: 60–66; Shade 1981: 102; Reichley 1985: 177–82).

The second party system was shaped by the new immigrants. "[M]ost, being social and economic outsiders, were attracted, at least at first, to the party of equality. The great majority of Irish Catholics, as well as other Catholics and most Germans, Lutherans, and Reformeds became Jacksonian Democrats." Competition for jobs fanned an existing anti-Catholic prejudice, which, fed by "Protestant intellectuals and divines," frequently erupted in nativist violence. This persuaded some Protestant religious groups to shift to the party of order (Reichley 1985: 183–88; Shade 1981: 102).

The second party system collapsed into Civil War; the third party system was built upon its ruins. Slavery split both major parties in the 1850s, but the Whigs did not survive. "The Whigs' underlying problem was that their alignment with the moral program of northern Protestantism, a principal source of the political dynamism they briefly enjoyed in the 1840s, brought them into collision with the institution of slavery, thereby antagonizing and alienating their own southern wing," while the Democrats managed to unite all of the outsiders—cultural, religious, and sectional (Reichley 1992: 107). This opportunistic alliance allowed the Democrats to survive, but shifted the balance of power to the party of order. The new Republican party, founded in 1854, elected its first president in 1860 and dominated national and northern politics for the next seventy years.

The Civil War fractured traditional alliances. Many Protestants who had supported the Democratic party's egalitarian emphasis left because it would not take a stand against the evil of slavery. The new party they helped form combined support for economic growth with a strong stand for moral order and saw government as a means to attain both of these ends. The third party system created some strange alliances. The party of equality ruled in the South, where it was the defender of white supremacy, while the Republican party brought under its banner both the champions of industrial capitalism and those of social justice. Partisanship was still a function of region, religion, and race, but these had shifted. The sectional cleavage dominated. In the South, the freed slaves were gradually disenfranchised and with them the Republican party. The rest of the country had a slight Republican majority but it was not evenly spread throughout. In three New England and four Midwest states the Republican party dominated; in the rest statewide elections were closely contested with wide variations within each state. The primary cleavage outside the South was religion; Catholics were Democrats, most Protestants were Republicans (Kleppner 1981: 124). Partisanship was strong and many state and national races were very competitive; outside the South 75 percent of those eligible to vote did so—more than in any era before or since.

The third party system was not static; it was molded by Reconstruction and then retrenchment in the South and by immigration, externally and internally, elsewhere. The Puritans who had been Federalists in New England took their values with them as they pushed the frontier further west and brought more states into the Union. Where they settled the Republican party flourished. As the Puritans moved west, European immigrants replaced them in the major cities of the East and Midwest (Kleppner 1979: 198). They could become citizens after five years but could often vote before that; many states wishing to increase their population allowed the foreign born to vote upon filing a declaration of intent to become a citizen (U.S. Bureau of the Census 1975: 1068). "Immigrants from each European nation generally joined the party advocated by earlier immigrants of their nationality, the Germans, Scandinavians and Italians usually allying themselves with the Republican party, and the Irish, Greeks and other southeastern nationals with the Democratic party" (Catt and Shuler 1923, 1926: 161; Kleppner 1981: 132).

During this period the country was undergoing vast economic changes, industrializing and pushing the frontier of development further West each year. While the major parties fought at the national level over free trade versus the protective tariff, the most bitter political battles were local ones over the schools, use of English, the control of liquor, Sunday blue laws, and other cultural issues. Minor parties flourished in the third party system because the major parties, whether in one or two party states, did not articulate many of the interests the conflicts of the day generated. Indeed it was the inability of the third party system to channel conflicts between economic groups, by providing clear programs and choices, that led to the populist revolt and the critical elections of the 1890s (Kleppner 1981: 127; Burnham 1981: 152).

The third party system ended with a crash—literally. The Democrats had the misfortune to be in control of the White House and both Houses of Congress when the economy collapsed in the spring of 1893. Northern voters punished the party as the "party of hard times" (Kleppner 1987: 97–107; Burnham 1981: 160; Sundquist 1983: 149). Even before the Crash of '93, distressed farmers of the West and South had organized a new People's party (populist) to articulate their demands. It recruited from the Democrats in the South and the Republicans in the West to protest the exploitation of agricultural producers by the industrial capitalist barons of the Northeast. When William Jennings Bryan was nominated by the 1896 Democratic convention, and then by the Populists the next week, the Democratic party's Eastern wing bolted. Bryan's agrarian radicalism and "free silver" campaign drove the urban Democratic voters into the arms of the Republican party. Although Bryan tried to draw a new fault line between the "monied interests" and the "common people," industrial workers did not identify their economic needs with those of agricultural producers. Even New York City voted Republican for the first time (Goldschmidt 1972: 520–32). The votes the Democrats gained in the sparsely populated West were more than offset by the losses in the urban East and Midwest (Kleppner 1987: chapter 4). Furthermore, the gains were temporary, the losses were permanent.

The fourth party system saw growing one-party dominance everywhere and Republican party dominance nationally. Sectionalism flourished, involving "the virtual destruction of the Republicans as an organized political force in the ex-Confederate states and a parallel and almost as complete a destruction of the Democrats throughout large areas of the North and West" (Burnham 1981: 164; Schattschneider 1942: 113, 115). Democratic national elites disintegrated, leaving power in the hands of state organizations and urban machines. While the national parties continued to debate the tariff, changes in the role of women, control of alcohol use, and the use of law to regulate working conditions and political parties were fought out on the state level.

As the cities grew, the conflict between the urbanizing East and the rural West and South that precipitated the fourth party system became an urban/rural conflict that was intra- as well as interstate. Increasingly populated by immigrants from southern and eastern Europe, the cities were perceived as an alien presence in need of control. This polarization had religious overtones. The frontier churches of the previous centuries—Methodists, Baptists, Disciples of Christ—were now the religious homes of the rural population. The churches of the earlier elites—Episcopal, Congregationalist, Presbyterian, Lutheran, and Unitarian—had urban congregations. The immigrants, coming from eastern and southern Europe, were mostly Catholic (and Jewish in New York City), but most of them did not vote. Nor were they represented in the state legislatures. It was 1964 before the Supreme Court required that legislative districts represent "one person, one vote." As the cities grew, members of the state legislatures increasingly represented acreage rather than people. Thus while there were many battles between urban and rural interests, especially over the use of tax dollars, they were not necessarily partisan ones.

The fourth party system ended as it began—with a crash. The 1929 drop of the stock market, and the resulting Great Depression, caused voters to turn on the ruling Republican party in 1932 as they had turned on the Democrats almost forty years before. But these voters were not the same voters who had voted Republican in previous decades. The depression and the Roosevelt candidacy mobilized new voters who had been ineligible or uninterested in voting during most of the fourth party system. The first decade of the century had seen the largest wave of immigration ever known; by 1930 most had become citizens and their children had reached voting age. When foreign immigration was restricted after World War I blacks and poor whites continued to migrate from rural, especially southern, areas to more urban manufacturing centers, though not to the same ones (Andersen 1979; Henri 1975: 50–59, 68–69). Southern blacks went north, and southern whites went west. These states didn't have the high barriers to voting common to the southern states. The consequence of high foreign immigration and high birth rates before World War I and rapid internal immigration afterwards was that the American population shifted from one living on farms to one living in small towns and large cities. Most of the new voters in 1932 lived in cities (Lubell 1956: 31–42).

The dominant cleavage of the fifth party system was class. Class had not been absent from previous party systems. By and large, the Democratic party had spoken for the working man while the Republican party articulated the ideals of the growing middle class. But the depression elevated class consciousness over other divisions. "Put crudely, the hatred of bankers among the native American workers had become greater than their hatred of the Pope or even of the Negro." The major policy clashes were over the use of federal law to regulate business practices, the protection of labor unions and the right to organize, and the creation of and payment for various welfare programs. With Roosevelt's encouragement, labor unions increased their influence every decade and class consciousness "suppressed racial and religious antagonisms" (Lubell 1956: 49). Even blacks saw their loyalty to the party of Lincoln fade in favor of the party that addressed their economic concerns.

During the fifth party system the Democratic party became even more a coalition of cultural, ethnic and economic minorities, especially those living in cities. Catholics remained Democratic, Jews became more so, while additional Protestants shifted to the Democratic column, especially unionized industrial workers in the cities outside the South (Burnham 1970: 59; Sundquist 1983: 214–24). Outside the South the Republican electoral base remained in the small towns and rural counties, particularly among Protestants, the better educated, and the wealthy. The shift of working-class white Protestants into the Democratic fold was not uniform throughout the nation. White Protestants in the Northeast were more likely to stay Republican than elsewhere. At the same time Catholics moving into the middle class and the suburbs began to vote Republican. Nonetheless, the great partisan divide between Catholics and Protestants continued until at least the 1960s though the regional and class cleavages left the Republican party with only a minority of the regular voters in most states (Ladd and Hadley 1978: 54–57).

The politics of class created the fifth political system and the politics of race ended it. This transformation was not as sudden as prior ones. Political scientists didn't even notice when the fifth party system ended, steeping themselves in debate over why there was no critical election, and whether this lack meant a realignment had or had not occurred. Only with hindsight did the changes that happened between 1964 and 1972 become evident, and it was among political elites more than among the electorate that a partisan realignment occurred (Wilson 1985).

ELITE REALIGNMENT

Electoral realignments are not the only kind. Elite realignments occur when political elites, particularly elected officials, change their votes, or their positions on issues, so that the partisan distribution of issue positions changes as well. "Elites" refers to those persons occupying influential roles or offices in our political system. A change in voting patterns does not necessarily mean that specific individuals changed their votes or their views, though it may. It may also mean that new people are elected to important positions who hold different views, or at least vote differently. It may also mean that individual officeholders changed their parties rather than their views. Whatever the cause, elite realignments result when the partisan distribution of votes, or positions, on clusters of cognate issues changes significantly among political elites.

Elite realignments are much more frequent than electoral realignments. Elites (at least the ones who vote in the legislatures and write the party platforms) make many decisions on discrete issues and make them directly. Voters make few decisions—only about which people will occupy which positions in the political elites—and their impact on policy is indirect. Many factors go into a voter's decision on whom to support for each office, but it is unusual for any single issue, or even a cluster of issues, to be definitive. Mass realignments require issues that are very simple, highly salient, and sharply polarized by party. This is rare.

Elite realignments can have major effects on public policy. Like electoral realignments, significant changes in partisan voting patterns by those entrusted with the power to make policy shape the policies that result. Even when the major parties do not have strong disagreements over the general direction of a proposed policy, which party takes the lead affects the outcome because the Democratic and Republican parties have distinct political cultures. Each party culture is partially derived from its separate tradition and the priority it gives to order or equality. And it is partially dependent on the groups in its coalitional base, which shift over time and may change with new party systems (Freeman 1986). These cultures shape activity within each party as well as the policies each propounds. Thus which party supports what issues and how it does so is significant for the development of public policy in any given policy arena.

Elite realignments have received little attention because the conventional wisdom among both political practitioners and political scientists in the middle of the twentieth century was that differences between the Republican and Democratic parties were no more than tweedledum and tweedledee. Each party sought to appeal to the center because that was how to get elected; public office was viewed as an end in itself, not a means to effect policy changes (Schattschneider 1942: 86). This search for the center was reflected in the national platforms that, while they differed occasionally, generally followed each other's lead in supporting issues that seemed successful in a previous election (Polsby and Wildavsky 1984: 258–59). While competition for the center was disparaged by some as depriving voters of a *real* choice, others realized that it reflected the centrist position of most voters themselves. Indeed studies regularly showed that party activists held positions "further out" than party voters (McClosky et al. 1960: 406–27). Elected officials, on the other hand, were assumed to vote the way their districts wanted them to vote, most of the time.

When one looks at the votes of those elected officials since World War II, however, party competition for the center, at least on issues of race and sex, is revealed as illusory. In fact, the parties were switching sides. Throughout the third, fourth, and most of the fifth party systems, the Republican Party was the party of racial progress. For all five party systems it was also the party of women's rights—much more receptive than the Democrats to women enhancing their role in society. In part, Democratic votes were weighed down by the South, which was always more conservative on issues of "sex" as well as race. And in part they were determined by its class and religious components, which were also more conservative on these issues than those of the Republican party. But the social bases of both parties were changing. After World War II the children of the working class went to college, acquiring more liberal attitudes on issues of race and sex, while orthodox members of all religious traditions began to look to the Republican party for leadership. In the 1960s party votes in Congress converged on race and in the early 1970s they converged on sex; then they diverged in the opposite direction.

The most documented case of elite realignment was done by Carmines and Stimson who analyzed party platforms and congressional votes on racial issues over a forty-year period. During World War II black civil rights was put on the national agenda. In response to organized pressure, antidiscrimination clauses and fair employment practices provisions began to see legislative light in bills and executive orders. Because of Southern Democratic opposition, Republicans collectively were more likely to vote for these provisions than were Democrats. Sometime in the late 1950s partisanship began to decline; the votes taken during the early sixties did not appear to follow a party line. However, by the late 1960s party once again becomes a predictor of how an MC will vote on racial issues, but this time it is Republicans who are more likely to be racial conservatives (Carmines and Stimson 1989).

Why and how this switch occurred is too complex to discuss here; the Republicans did not become segregationists as the Southern Democrats had been and all of Congress voted more liberally on racial issues (Carmines and Stimson 1989: 117). But the fact that the issues had changed, as well as many of the MCs who voted on them, does not obscure the fact that on this highly salient issue, the political elites had realigned. The Democratic party, including the Southern bloc, became the home of racial liberals.

A similar switch happened with sex, but it is harder to chart because there were fewer relevant roll-call votes and they were taken over a longer period of time. However, the Equal Rights Amendment (ERA) is one of those few. There were three clusters of recorded congressional votes on the ERA. The first cluster occurred in the Senate in 1946, 1950, and 1953. The 1946 vote, shown in Table 12.1, was a simple yes or no, and the record shows more Republicans in favor than Democrats.

In 1950 the simplicity of the issue was clouded by opposition maneuvering which added a rider that gutted the Amendment. In 1953 the same rider was added. As seen in Table 12.2, members of both parties voted for the ERA, knowing that it would be recommitted to committee. Nonetheless, even with the rider, many Democrats still voted against the ERA; indeed all but one "no" vote on the ERA was by a Democrat.

The ERA stayed in committee for almost twenty years. When it was voted on again in 1970 some of the Democrats who had fought it in the 1950s continued to vote and speak against it. They were few in number, but because they had so much seniority they could speak loudly and carry big sticks. Again crippling amendments were added and the ERA allowed to die, but it was revived the following year and passed in the next Congress. More important, the votes in all three years—1970, 1971, and 1972—did not show a partisan pattern. The final votes are seen in Table 12.3.

The third set of ERA votes occurred in 1978, and is shown in Table 12.4. After only thirty-five of the thirty-eight states necessary to ratify it had done so

Table 12.1
1946 ERA Vote, U.S. Senate

	Yes	No
Republican	23	10
Democrat	15	24

(*Congressional Quarterly* 1946: 568)

Table 12.2
1950 and 1953 ERA Votes with Hayden Rider, U.S. Senate

	1950		1953	
	Yes	*No*	*Yes*	*No*
Republican	30	0	42	1
Democrat	33	19	31	10

(*C Q Almanac* 1950: 539; *CQ Almanac* 1953: 386)

Table 12.3
1971 and 1972 ERA Votes, U.S. House and Senate

	1971 Final House ERA Vote		1972 Final Senate ERA Vote	
	Yes	*No*	*Yes*	*No*
Republican	137	12	37	6
Democrat	217	12	47	2

(*C Q Almanac* 1971: 68–69 H; *CQ Almanac* 1972: 17–18 S)

Table 12.4
1978 ERA Votes, U.S. House and Senate

	1978 Final House ERA Vote		1978 Final Senate ERA Vote	
	Yes	*No*	*Yes*	*No*
Republican	41	103	16	21
Democrat	186	85	44	15

(*C Q Almanac* 1978: 64–65 S, 176 H)

within the seven-year limit, Congress voted to extend the deadline. There were several votes in both houses on amendments and cognate issues. All showed a partisan pattern, but it was clearest in the final vote that passed the extension.

The party platforms show a similar convergence, crossover, and polarization on issues relating to sex. Until 1972, the Democratic and Republican party platforms manifested similar attitudes toward women, but the Republican party tended to lead in adopting a feminist position on new issues. For example, the ERA was endorsed by the Republicans in 1940, but the Democrats delayed doing so until 1944. The ERA was removed from the Democratic party platform in 1960, deliberately by its foes, but inadvertently, due to lack of attention, from the Republican party platform in 1964. In 1968 the GOP gave "sex" an honorable mention in a plank expressing concern for the disadvantaged; the Democrats left women out altogether. Women reappeared in both party platforms in 1972, with similar statements, including support for the ERA. By 1976 the parties diverged again when the Republicans opposed a woman's choice (to have an abortion). By 1980 the divide widened as the ERA was removed from the Republican party platform. Since then the parties have polarized sharply on all issues touching on women, sex, and the family. Instead of seeking the center, the national parties are staking out distinct ideological territories.

Endorsements by party leaders also switched sides. The first major party presidential candidate to support the ERA was Thomas Dewey in 1944. The first three sitting presidents to endorse it were Eisenhower, Nixon, and Ford. In the presidential primary races of 1968 every major party candidate except Robert Kennedy supported the ERA, though none campaigned for it. Carter was the first Democratic president to publicly declare his support; by 1976 it was impossible to seriously run for the Democratic nomination if opposed to the ERA. By 1988 no serious Republican candidate could support it.

Elite realignment also manifests itself in changes in party affiliation by party leaders and elected officials. Some very prominent Southern Democrats became Republicans, including Strom Thurmond, John Connally, and Phil Gramm—as did Ronald Reagan, but before he ran for office. Abortion had an even stronger realigning effect on politicians' positions than race or the ERA. George Bush once supported Planned Parenthood; Jesse Jackson and Bill Clinton were pro-life until they got the presidential bug. They changed their positions to court voters in their parties. Politicians who were no longer running for office were less likely to change positions. For example, Barry Goldwater remained pro-choice; abortion was not on the public agenda when he ran for president in 1964.

On racial issues, the crossover point in congressional voting was 1964, the year a milestone Civil Rights Act became law. Republicans and Democrats worked together to pass this law, but the Republican party candidate for President, Barry Goldwater, opposed it. He was not a segregationist; he believed in less government regulation, especially federal government regulation. African American voters never forgave him, voting heavily for Lyndon Johnson in 1964, and more heavily for subsequent Democrats.

On sexual issues, the crossover point was between 1970 and 1972. There were no roll call votes in Congress on women's issues between 1953 and 1970, so an earlier change would be harder to identify, though there may have been illuminating votes in state legislatures. The addition of "sex" to Title VII of the 1964 Civil Rights Act was done by a teller vote of the House in a Committee of the Whole. However, Representative Martha Griffiths (D-Mich.) told an interviewer many years later that the "yes" votes came from Southerners and Republicans—the latter apparently saw it as a surrogate for the ERA (Brauer 1983: 51; Freeman 1991). There were many votes on bills to improve the status of women after 1970. Without going into the details, the initial votes lacked obvious partisan leanings, but they diverged radically by party over time.

One of the most divisive issues of the last twenty-five years has been abortion. Republic commentator William Kristol wrote in 1997: "Abortion is today the bloody crossroads of American politics. It is where judicial liberation (from the Constitution), sexual liberation (from traditional mores) and women's liberation (from natural distinctions) come together" (Kristol 1997: 32).

Party polarization on abortion can be charted through congressional votes. Adams' examination of 176 House and Senate roll calls from 1973 through 1994 shows that in the Senate Democrats became more pro-choice over time while Republicans became more pro-life. Unlike the Senate, Democrats in the House were already more pro-choice than Republicans in 1973; they became more so over time. One cannot see the crossover in partisan voting patterns because there were no congressional votes on abortion prior to the crossover years for issues of "Sex" (1970–1972). However, an examination of state legislative votes in the 1960s, when states were debating liberalization of abortion, might well show a greater Republican affiliation with the pro-choice position (Adams 1997).

The answer to why party elites change positions before the voters that elect them is to be found in the internal dynamics of each party. Between elites and masses is an important strata of party activists, who donate time and money to elect their candidates and are particularly active in the primaries and caucuses that select each party's candidate. This cadre is often interested in issues and involved in interest groups and social movements. They push politicians to support their causes and push into becoming politicians those who share their views. Surveys of delegates to party nominating conventions have shown that their views diverge from the center more strongly than party elites or voters. It is this internal cadre that has provoked elite realignment (McClosky 1960; Wilson 1985; Freeman 1993, 1998).

THE SIXTH PARTY SYSTEM

During the time that elites were realigning, the voters were also changing but not as dramatically as they had in 1928–1932. Political scientists noted that fewer and fewer were identifying with either major party; they tended to vote for persons rather than party, particularly at the top of the ballot. Thus a search for the expected electoral realignment resulted in questioning of the entire theory of realignment, at least as something that reoccurred periodically, and an attempt to understand why the voters were *de*aligning (Shafer 1991).

My own interpretation of this is that there was in fact a change in party systems in the 1960s and 1970s. The fifth party system, in which class was the major line of cleavage, gave way to the sixth, in which race, or more specifically views on racial issues, was the dominant division. Like previous cleavages, it didn't replace class but was superimposed on top of it. Political elites were in the vanguard of this change, signaling to their followers as much as following their direction. The result was a rolling realignment, which started at the top, and in some sections of the country, slowly worked its way down through the electorate (White 1985).

Even though this realignment was not like the big three, one can still describe the characteristics of the sixth party system. Its chief attribute was ticket splitting, in which voters tended to vote Republican at the top but continued their habitual votes for Democrats at the bottom. However, this habit was waning. More and more voters declared themselves to be independent, and many began to vote differently than their parents did. While traditional ties to party loosened everywhere, this was particularly evident in the South. The 1968 presidential candidacy of George Wallace served as a transition for Democratic voters to the Republican party. With time, more and more conservative Democrats voted Republican further and further down the ballot. At the same time, more educated voters were switching to the Democratic party; since education correlates with income, this confounded the tendency of the more wealthy to vote Republican. A gender gap appeared in which women, particularly unmarried women, voted Democrat, while white men leaned to the Republicans. African American voters continued to vote Democratic, women even more so than men. Since the Civil Rights Movement and the Voting Rights Act brought them back into the Southern electorate from which they had been largely excluded during the twentieth century, they swelled the ranks of the Democratic party, replacing Southern white elites who were moving into the Republican party. The movement of Southern whites into the Republican party made their voting patterns more like those of Northern whites; as the sixth party system matured, the Civil War cleavage was closing.

SEEDS OF THE SEVENTH

In the meantime other lines of cleavage were opening up: sex—or more specifically attitudes toward sex, gender, and family—was emerging as a major source of partisanship. So was religion. However, the new line of religious cleavage was not between Protestants and Catholics but between traditionals and progressives with the latter significantly augmented by seculars who don't practice any religion. To a great extent groups holding similar views on issues of sex and religion coincide. Traditionals on one are also traditionals on the other, as are progressives. While this is not surprising, what was new was the politicization of sex, the repoliticization of religion, and the polarization of the parties along these lines.

Partisan polarization is following the "realignment of American public culture" described by Hunter in *Culture Wars* (1991). As a sociologist who studies religion, Hunter documented the development of the "pragmatic alliances" being formed between the orthodox wings of Protestantism, Catholicism, and Judaism on the one hand and the progressive wings of these "faith traditions" on the other in their effort to influence public culture. The "orthodox and progressive factions of the various faiths do not speak out as isolated voices but increasingly as a common chorus. In this, the political relevance of the historical divisions between Protestant and Catholic and Christian and Jew has largely become defunct." The progressive wing of organized religion has been joined, and often led, by a growing group of secularists, who, while often raised in a particular faith, as adults adhere to none. "[They] are disproportionately well educated and professional and are found most commonly in the larger cities of the Northeast and West." Their growth was fed largely by the enormous expansion of higher education after World War II. By 1982, they were 8 percent of the population (Hunter 1991: 47, 75, 105).

The roots of this cultural realignment can be traced back many decades but until the 1960s it was confined to intellectual elites. The social movements and events of the 1960s radicalized the generation then attending or just out of college. Their experiences taught them to "question authority"—a popular slogan of the sixties—and this questioning in turn made them receptive to progressive and secular ideas. By the 1970s a backlash was gathering steam, stimulated by policies it found reprehensible, such as busing and abortion, and behavior, such as opposition to the Vietnam War, it deemed subversive and un-American. Those who adhered to traditional practices, values, and morals slowly allied in opposition to those who would change them.

According to Hunter,

The central dynamic of the cultural realignment is not merely that different public philosophies create diverse public opinions. These alliances, rather, reflect the *institutionalization and politicization of two fundamentally different cultural systems.* Each side operates from within its own constellation of values, interests, and assumptions. At the center of each are two distinct conceptions of moral authority—two different ways of apprehending reality, of ordering experience, of making moral judgments. Each side of the cultural divide, then, speaks with a different moral vocabulary. (1991: 128. Italics his)

During the 1980s the cultural divide became a partisan divide, at least on the national level. Feminism was not the cause of the cultural divide though it contributed a great deal to its growth. However, it was the driving engine of partisan polarization. While race was the lead mare of the progressive team, sex was the wicked witch that spurred the opposition. Abortion in particular was a realigning issue because it merged concerns about changing sex roles and the consequences of sex acts and gave them a political basis. The 1973 Supreme Court decision legalizing most abortions shifted the weight of governmental authority away from what religious conservatives felt to be the morally correct position (Sullivan 1998: 49–50). By 1980 feminism had put on the public agenda issues that in 1960 had not been considered political, and it had compelled the major political parties to take (opposing) stands on issues that in 1970 had not been considered partisan. It did this by redefining the scope of the political. As Thompson, Ellis, and Wildavsky pointed out in their book on *Cultural Theory*: "The type of behavior or institution that is deemed political, or whether a boundary is even drawn at all, is itself a product of political culture. . . . the study of *political* culture . . . should pay special attention to the ways in which the boundary between political and non political is socially negotiated (Thompson, Ellis, and Wildavsky 1990: 215).

Contemporary feminism declared that "the personal is political." This became a frame of reference that redefined the boundary of politics. Its value was soon recognized by women who were part of the highly educated, progressive culture, and they persuaded the men in that culture. Once the personal was acknowledged as political, feminism could expand beyond ending legal and economic discrimination into enhancing women's autonomy and addressing how women were treated inside the family. In effect, this expansion of the political legitimated as proper concerns of public policy practices that had traditionally been considered nonpolitical or relegated to the jurisdiction of the family. The growth and partisanship of the right wing was a response to this threat.

Four events have been identified as triggering the political organization of social conservatives and Christian evangelicals, two of which were explicitly feminist issues, and another of which involved sex (Zwier 1982: 23–27). The first was the January 22, 1973, decision by the Supreme Court that legalized most abortions. Some pro-life groups had existed prior to *Roe v. Wade* in states with liberalized abortion laws, but the Supreme Court's stamp of approval on a woman's right to privacy on the grounds that a fetus was not a person under the Constitution was so repulsive to a particular stratum of American citizens that it crystallized opposition all over the country.

The organization of the religious right capitalized on the framework created by the right-to-life movement but not until after its leaders were themselves convinced that political action was necessary. Ironically, it was the successful candidacy of a Democrat, Jimmy Carter, himself a born-again Christian, that accomplished this by legitimating political activity for Protestant evangelicals who had traditionally thought of politics as corrupt. When Carter subsequently supported efforts by the Internal Revenue Service to remove the tax-exempt status of private religiously oriented schools unless they were racially integrated it created a storm of protest. This furor persuaded Congress to deny the IRS funds for implementing its order and convinced evangelical ministers such as Jerry Falwell of the efficacy of organized protest.

A third triggering event was the growth of the gay rights movement in the 1970s. One organization in California, Christian Voice, was created to oppose a 1978 ballot proposal to protect homosexuals against discrimination. Because the IRS threatened the tax-exempt status of their churches if they engaged in political activity, several ministers formed a separate political organization.

The fourth triggering event was the Equal Rights Amendment, the opposition to which also provided an organizing framework on which the New Right could capitalize. Phyllis Schlafly is often given credit for single-handedly stopping the ratification of the ERA, thought a "sure thing" when it emerged from Congress in 1972. However, Schlafly could not have so rapidly mobilized an opposition had not an infrastructure of sympathizers already existed. The language of the ERA is quite tame—"Equality of rights under the law shall not be denied or abridged . . . on account of sex"—but its implications were not. Social conservatives read into the ERA everything they feared about the emerging women's liberation movement, and what they feared most was women's autonomy from the traditional patriarchal family, which they held to be the basic institution of society.

These triggering events persuaded practitioners of evangelical denominations that they could not ignore politics. One result was the formation of the Moral Majority in 1979, the largest and best known of the New Right religious organizations, at the urging of secular conservatives such as Richard Viguerie, Paul Weyrich, Howard Phillips, and Terry Dolan. They convinced Jerry Falwell to form a political organization to mobilize Christian evangelicals for Ronald Reagan through the use of mass mailings and the electronic church (Zwier 1982: 9–10, 27–32; Viguerie 1982: chapter XI).

While Jerry Falwell abandoned the Moral Majority in 1987, it was soon replaced by the Christian Coalition (CC), built by televangelist Pat Robertson from the supporters of his losing 1988 presidential bid. Aided by a $64,000 grant in 1990 from the National Republican Senatorial Committee, by 1994 the CC claimed 450,000 members in a thousand chapters in all fifty states. Using what former executive director Ralph Reed, Jr., described as "stealth" tactics to avoid the stigma attached to religious activism, by 1994 it had taken over the state Republican party in eighteen states and exercised substantial influence in another dozen (Persinos 1994: 22–24).

The strength of the Christian Coalition in the Republican party was based on growing support from evangelical Protestants and conservative Catholics for the Republican party. Throughout the sixth party system many voters in both groups were switching their votes from Democrats to Republicans. In 1960 most had been Democrats—especially those living in the South or in the lower SES (socioeconomic status) ranks. By 1992 a majority were Republicans, and a super majority of those regularly attending church. Catholics, who at one time were virtually all Democrats, were also switching. Barely a majority were Democratic identifiers in 1992, less among those regularly attending church. On the other hand, mainline Protestants still identified with the Re-

publican party but by 1992 were more likely to vote Democratic. Those pro-
fessing no religious allegiance (seculars) were also moving into the Democratic
fold. As Kellstedt, et al., said in 1993, "These trends suggest that a new kind of
party alignment may be in the making: a division between religious and non-
religious people rather than disputes between religious traditions" (Kellstedt
1993: 2, citing Green and Guth 1991: 207).

These changes can particularly be seen in the shift in party identity by attitudes toward abortion, as revealed in the annual General Social Survey from
1972 to 1994. Adams found that the Republican masses had more liberal attitudes than Democrats toward abortion prior to 1988 and less so afterward
(Adams 1997). The move of pro-lifers to the Republican party followed that of
elites by several years, consistent with White's concept of a rolling Republican
realignment, and with the active efforts of Christian evangelicals to mobilize
their followers into the Republican party (Green 1999).

The congressional elections of 1994 reflected a culmination of many of
these trends. Overall, the gender gap was 8 percent; more women voted
Democratic and more men voted Republican. This was augmented by marital
status; the gap was 4 percent between married women and men, and 14 percent between the unmarried. Blacks and Hispanics strongly favored Democratic candidates, women more so than men; whites less strongly favored
Republicans. As expected, the Democratic party commanded a majority of
votes among the less educated and those with lower family incomes, but also
among the most highly educated. This combination reflects both the class
cleavage of the fifth party system and Democrats' newer gains among the most
educated voters. The gender gap was sharpest at the extremes; women were
more likely than equivalent men to favor the Democrats at the lowest and
highest educational levels. Those identifying as born-again Christians voted
Republican by 76 to 24 percent. A majority of Catholics still voted Democratic, but at 52 percent it was the lowest Democratic vote in over a decade
("Portrait of the Electorate" 1994: 24).

By 1996, the outlines of a seventh party system were taking shape. The
Democrats kept the presidency and the Republicans kept the Congress, with
many voters unwilling to commit to either party wholeheartedly. The gender
gap widened to 11 percent; men and women essentially chose different presidents. Even among blacks, who are still the most Democratic of voting groups,
there was a decided gender gap. The gap was biggest among independent voters, and between unmarried men and women, but present as well in Democratic and Republican party identifiers, and married couples. Sex differences in
voting patterns spread to other elected offices ("Portrait of the Electorate"
1996: 28). Although the Democrats staged a slight comeback in 1998—unusual in a non-presidential year—these outlines did not change. The overall
gender gap in House races was seven points, it was larger among blacks than
whites, and nonexistent among Hispanics. Class, as seen in family income, is
still a partisan divide, but it is mitigated by education and enhanced by union

membership. White Protestants (but not black) lean Republican while Catholics lean Democratic and Jews are second only to blacks in their Democratic loyalties. The gender gap remained large among the young and the unmarried but narrowed somewhat between independents ("A Look Voting Patterns" 1998: A20). After several elections it has become evident that sex, like race, has become an established electoral cleavage. But it is not only the fact of sex and race, but attitudes toward sexual and racial issues, that constitute the real divide.

While it is not clear which, if either, party will be dominant in the seventh party system, the coalitions are solidifying and the issues over which major battles will be fought are crystallizing. With the demise of the cold war foreign policy issues are less partisan. Economic concerns are still important, but social issues are the most divisive (Sullivan 1998: 48). The sharpest conflicts are those that combine economic and social issues. While the extent of government regulation motivates some political elites, it is *who* is regulated for what purpose that motivates ordinary voters. Fights over welfare policy and affirmative action have some economic characteristics, but they are really about race and sex.

The composition of the two major parties has changed, but not drastically; each has retained its basic flavor. However, the changes that did occur have accentuated differences that were submerged in the fifth party system when class concerns were dominant. The Democratic party is still the party of minorities and marginal groups, but it is particularly the party of racial minorities and of those who espouse feminist views on women, the family, and the regulation of sexual activity. It is no longer the party of Catholics, though it is still of Jews. The Republican party is still the party of order, and still overwhelmingly Protestant, despite the presence of more Catholics. But it has completely forsaken its Progressive tradition. Instead it has become the party of traditional "family values" as expressed by the practitioners of evangelical denominations. While these practitioners are still a minority of the national party, they are strong enough to veto who can be on the presidential ticket, and thus what views Republican nominees espouse. In each party groups reflecting sharply polarized views on "feminism" and "family values" are strong enough to veto party policy (Freeman 1993, 1998).

After two decades of party polarization, the "culture wars" have become "party wars." Consequently, the seventh party system promises to be very acrimonious. Partisan competition is being transformed from a mere fight for office into a surrogate civil war. Both parties, and their candidates, are carriers of a conflicting cluster of values in which the winner gets to decide the role of government, or each of the many governments in our federal system, in promulgating those values. The partisan politics of the twenty-first century will be more like the nineteenth than the twentieth. Culture, not class or economics, will define the great debates (Shafer 1985).

188   The Impact of Elections

REFERENCES

"A Look at Voting Patterns." 1998. *New York Times*, November 9, A20.

Adams, Greg D. 1997. "Abortion: Evidence of an Issue Evolution." *American Journal of Political Science* 41:3 (July): 718–37.

Andersen, Kristi. 1979. *The Creation of A Democratic Majority: 1928–1936*. Chicago: University of Chicago Press.

Baker, Paula. 1984. "The Domestication of Politics: Women and American Political Society, 1780–1920." *American Historical Review* 89 (June): 620–47.

Brauer, Carl M. 1983. "Women Activists, Southern Conservatives, and the Prohibition of Sex Discrimination in Title VII of the 1964 Civil Rights Act." *Journal of Southern History* 49 (February).

Burnham, Walter Dean. 1970. *Critical Elections and the Mainsprings of American Politics*. New York: Norton.

———. 1981. "The System of 1896: An Analysis." In Kleppner, et al., eds., *The Evolution of American Electoral Systems*. Westport, CT: Greenwood Press: 147–202.

Campbell, Angus et al. 1966. *Elections and the Political Order*. New York: Wiley.

Carmines, Edward G., and James A. Stimson. 1989. *Issue Evolution: Race and the Transformation of American Politics*. Princeton: Princeton University Press.

Catt, Carrie Chapman, and Nettie Rogers Shuler. 1923. *Woman Suffrage and Politics: The Inner Story of the Suffrage Movement*. New York: Charles Scribner's Sons.

Congressional Quarterly 2. 1946 (July-September): 568.

Congressional Quarterly Almanac 34. 1978.

———. 28. 1972.

———. 27. 1971.

———. 9. 1953.

———. 6. 1950.

Formisano, Ronald P. 1971. *The Birth of Mass Political Parties: Michigan, 1827–1861*. Princeton: Princeton University Press.

———. 1981. "Federalists and Republicans: Parties, Yes—System, No." In Kleppner et al., eds., *The Evolution of American Electoral Systems*. Westport, CT: Greenwood Press: 33–76.

Freeman, Jo. 1986. "The Political Culture of the Democratic and Republican Parties." *Political Science Quarterly* 101:3 (fall): 327–56.

———. 1991. "How 'Sex' Got Into Title VII: Persistent Opportunism as a Maker of Public Policy." *Law and Inequality: A Journal of Theory and Practice* 9:2 (March): 163–84.

———. 1993. "Feminism vs. Family Values: Women at the 1992 Democratic and Republican Conventions." *off our backs* 23:1 (January): 2–3, 10–17. Abridged 1995 in Marianne Githens, Pippa Norris and Joni Lovenduski, eds., *Different Roles, Different Voices: Women and Politics in the United States and Europe*. New York: HarperCollins: 70–83.

———. 1998. "Change and Continuity for Women at the Republican and Democratic Conventions." *American Review of Politics* 18 (fall): 353–67.

Fuchs, Lawrence H. 1956. *The Political Behavior of American Jews*. New York: Free Press.

Goldschmidt, Eli. 1972. "Labor and Populism: New York City, 1891–1897." *Labor History* 8: 520–32.
Green, John. 1999. "The Spirit Willing: Collective Identity and the Development of the Christian Right." In Jo Freeman and Victoria Johnson, eds., *Waves of Protest: Social Movements Since the Sixties.* Lanham, Md.: Rowman and Littlefield.
Green, John, and James L. Guth. 1991. "The Bible and the Ballot Box: The Shape of Things to Come." In James L. Guth and John C. Green, eds., *The Bible and the Ballot Box: Religion and Politics in the 1988 Election.* Boulder, CO: Westview Press: 207–26.
Henri, Florette. 1975. *Black Migration.* Garden City, NY: Anchor Books.
Herberg, Will. 1955. *Protestant, Catholic, Jew.* Garden City, NY: Anchor Books.
Hunter, James Davison. 1991. *Culture Wars: The Struggle to Define America.* New York: Basic Books.
Kellstedt, Lyman A., John C. Green, James L. Guth, and Corwin E. Smidt. 1993. "Religious Voting Blocs in the 1992 Election: The Year of the Evangelical?" Paper given at the 1993 American Political Science Association convention, September 2–5, Washington, D.C.
Key, V.O., Jr. 1955. "A Theory of Critical Elections." *Journal of Politics* 17 (February): 3–18.
Kleppner, Paul. 1979. *The Third Electoral System, 1853–1892.* Chapel Hill: University of North Carolina Press.
———. 1981. "Partisanship and Ethnoreligious Conflict: The Third Electoral System, 1853–1892." In Paul Kleppner et al., eds., *The Evolution of American Electoral Systems.* Westport, CT: Greenwood Press: 113–46.
———. 1987. *Continuity and Change in Electoral Politics, 1893–1928.* New York: Greenwood Press.
Kristol, William. 1997. "On the Future of Conservatism." *Commentary* 103:32–33.
Ladd, Everett Carll, with Charles D. Hadley. 1978. *Transformations of the American Party System,* 2d ed. New York: Norton.
Lubell, Samuel. 1956. *The Future of American Politics.* Garden City, NY: Doubleday Anchor.
McClosky, Herbert, Paul J. Hoffman, and Rosemary O'Hara. 1960. "Issue Conflict and Consensus Among Party Leaders and Followers." *American Political Science Review* 54: 406–27.
McCormick, Richard. 1966. *The Second American Party System: Party Formation in the Jacksonian Era.* Chapel Hill: University of North Carolina Press.
National Party Conventions: 1831–19—. Washington, DC: Congressional Quarterly Press (updated every four years.)
Niebuhr, H. Richard. 1929. *Social Sources of Denominationalism.* New York: Henry Holt.
Persinos, John F. 1994. "Has the Christian Right Taken Over the Republican Party?" *Campaigns & Elections* (September).
Polsby, Nelson W., and Aaron Wildavsky. 1984. *Presidential Elections: Strategies of American Electoral Politics,* 6th ed. New York: Charles Scribner's Sons.
"Portrait of the Electorate: Who Voted for Whom in the House." 1984. *New York Times,* November 13, 24.
"Portrait of the Electorate." 1996. *New York Times,* November 10, 28.

Reichley, A. James. 1985. *Religion in American Public Life*. Washington, DC: The Brookings Institution.

———. 1992. *The Life of the Parties: A History of American Political Parties*. New York: The Free Press.

Schattschneider, E. E. 1942. *Party Government*. New York: Reinhart & Co.

Shade, William G. 1981. "Political Pluralism and Party Development: The Creation of a Modern Party System: 1815–1852." In Paul Kleppner et al., eds., *The Evolution of American Electoral Systems*. Westport, CT: Greenwood Press.

Shafer, Byron E. 1985. "The New Cultural Politics." *PS* (spring): 221–31.

———, ed. 1991. *The End of Realignment?* Madison: University of Wisconsin Press.

Sisson, Daniel. 1974. *The American Revolution of 1800*. New York: Knopf.

Sullivan, Andrew. 1998. "Going Down Screaming." *New York Times Magazine* (October 11): 46–51, and 88–91.

Sundquist, James. 1983. *Dynamics of the Party System: Alignment and Realignment of Political Parties in the United States*. Washington, DC: The Brookings Institution.

Thompson, Michael, Richard Ellis, Aaron Wildavsky. 1990. *Cultural Theory*. Boulder, CO: Westview Press.

U.S. Bureau of the Census. 1975. *Historical Statistics of the United States: Colonial Times to 1970*. Washington, DC: Government Printing Office.

Viguerie, Richard A. 1982. *The New Right: We're Ready to Lead*. Falls Church, VA: The Viguerie Company.

White, John Kenneth. 1985. "The Rolling Republican Realignment." Paper delivered at the 1985 convention of the American Political Science Association, August 29–September 1.

Wilson, James Q. 1985. "Realignment at the Top, Dealignment at the Bottom." In Austin Ranney, ed., *The American Elections of 1984*. Durham, NC: Duke University Press: 297–310.

Zwier, Robert. 1982. *Born-Again Politics: The New Christian Right in America*. Downer's Grove, IL: Inter-Varsity Press.

13

What Do Women Get for Their Vote?

Erika E. Pilver

Who are "we"? What do we want? What are we getting?

Well, "we"—women—are 51 percent of the population and, in recent national elections, 51 to 54 percent of those voting. Women are 21 percent of state legislators, 11 percent of the Congress, an unprecedented 22 percent of the Supreme Court, 1 percent of the governors, 26 percent of those who hold statewide elective office, 17 percent of large-city mayors and 22 percent of municipal council seats (Center for the American Woman and Politics). No woman has ever been president nor even nominated for that position by a major political party; only one woman has ever run for vice president. We have come a long way from 1872, when Elizabeth Cady Stanton was arrested for voting in the national election or from 1917 when Jeannette Rankin of Montana was the first woman elected to Congress. Recent statistics are far better than they were twenty or even ten years ago, but they are far from parity.

Do the numbers of women in public office make a difference for women? What are women's issues? What do women want? Women, like men, are not monolithic in what they want from government, but increasingly sophisticated studies show that women's life experiences are different from men's, and this shows up in how women vote and, once they reach something approaching a critical mass in office, what they do. Since exit polls originated in the late 1970s, a gender gap has opened between men and women voters—a gap even greater for issues than for candidates. In fact, what women want from and, once elected, do in government are more the result of their life experiences than whether they are Republican or Democrat. The issues feminists raised in the 1970s are the major policy issues of the 1990s. Moreover, these issues echo the issues that were pushed by Jeannette Rankin eighty years ago!

Rankin, who was seated three years before the suffrage amendment became law, campaigned on suffrage, but she also campaigned for an eight-hour day for women, improved health care for mothers and children, and prohibition. She began her term just in time to vote against America's involvement in World War I, was redistricted out of her district in 1918 and therefore ran for the Senate instead, losing in the primary. She spent the next twenty years lobbying for federal wage-and-hour laws, a child-labor amendment, and a maternity and infancy bill. In 1940 she was elected again to the House of Representatives, beginning this term just in time to vote against America's involvement in World War II. Rankin, then, had an agenda that was antiwar and was concerned with health and working conditions for women and children (Tobias 1997: 32–33, 172).

Conversely, in 1920 anti-suffragette Alice M. Robertson (R-Okla.) was the second woman elected to Congress. She railed against exchanging women's privileges for a man's rights (suffrage) and "sob-stuff" (women's and children's issues); she voted against the Sheppard-Towner Bill for mothers and newborn infants, the creation of a federal Department of Education, and, alas for her, the payment of a bonus to World War I veterans—the issue on which she was defeated (Foerstel and Foerstel 1996: 2–6).

These examples foreshadow the continued history of women in Congress: attention to matters of economic interest to women, short tenure in office, and a backlash in which women are complicit.

In 1992 the Center for Policy Alternatives in Washington, D.C., and the Ms. Foundation co-sponsored a national poll of one thousand and four hundred women and two hundred men. They found that women are concerned about money (but in a way different from men: women are worried about making ends meet) and time (to meet the requirements of their lives). The poll found that women's concerns also include universal health care, equal pay (if you work full time, you should get paid a wage on which you can support your family), flexible work arrangements, and family and medical leave (Foerstel and Foerstel 1996: 6).

These issues have been characterized as of a "female coloration rather than a male coloration" (Kevin Phillips quoted by Linda Williams of the Congressional Black Caucus Foundation). Williams feels that the issues of the 1980s were of a "male coloration," concerned with regaining respect for Americans abroad, gunboat diplomacy, Darwinian economics, whipping inflation, being tough on crime. The 1990s issues have a "female coloration," stressing national and household budgets, health care, education, pressures on families, repairing the safety net, enforcement of child support laws, and legislation on spousal abuse, sexual harassment, and gender discrimination (Ford Foundation 1994).

These may well have percolated up from the women serving in state legislatures in the 1980s and from the increased presence of women in Congress in the 1990s. The Center for the American Woman and Politics (CAWP) at Rutgers in the late 1970s did a survey on state legislatures (because that's where the highest proportion of women in office was found). The center found that about twelve states had developed women's legislative caucuses, which at the time had little or no contact with each other, but which had very similar agendas: pension reform, employment equity, divorce reform, domestic violence, credit for women, the Equal Rights Amendment (ERA), rape shield laws, abortion rights, child care, licensing of midwives, family and medical leave, child support, and women's health. Ruth Mandel, director of the CAWP, saw three periods in the recent political experience of women:

1. The early 1970s: women in state legislatures had no gender consciousness as we understand it today. It was not part of the way they saw themselves in office, in spite of the issues they were raising.

2. The mid 1970s to 1980s: a kind of gender defensiveness: women shouldn't focus on traditional women's concerns, but on the so-called hard, serious, real power issues (as defined by men). A woman had to back away from women's concerns and embrace the power issues if she were to be viewed as a real political player.

3. The 1990s: gender friendliness; no more artificial division ("I'm not a woman, I'm a candidate"). Women are almost falling all over themselves to run as women, to assert that women bring something different to office. At a minimum, women are willing to press the point that they bring a presence to office; at a maximum, they are willing to talk about challenging old values and priorities and calling for a reassessment of what those hard issues should be. "Today's power issues sound an awful lot like yesterday's soft women's issues," Mandel concludes ("Rutgers Report" 1995).

Various studies seem to indicate that Democratic women of the 1990s, especially in Congress, seem to be more whole—that is, more willing to see themselves as people interested in women's issues—than Republicans, who seem more likely to continue with the 1970s attitude that women representatives are just like men.

That women are not monolithic in their opinions and in the issues they support is shown in an intricate study by Cal and Janet Clark (1996). Even so, the authors conclude, women officials seem to produce cumulatively a set of overlapping concerns. For example, women of color and women in blue- and pink-collar occupations share common interests about and support for economic policies and welfare issues, which are also supported by feminists. More surprisingly (the authors' words) the perspectives of homemakers and even fundamentalist women differ in degree, rather than representing strong conservative opposition. Feminists find more agreement in regard to cultural issues from younger and more highly educated women, whether feminist or not.

The authors conclude that given this complex set of interests and groups among women, the splintering of women into warring camps over issues is certainly not foreordained, and that, rather, it may well provide coalescence on issues of all categories.

Additionally, some observers feel that the 1990s election results have underscored voters' desire for representatives who were more in touch with them—the desire to vote for someone who had a genuine understanding of the everyday issues faced by American voters, for someone who would fight for their interests, and for someone who would make their lives more secure. This is especially true not only of women voters but also of minority voters of both sexes (Ford Foundation 1994).

Linda Wertheimer of National Public Radio, who has been covering politics and elections since 1972, has a number of interesting observations.

- What fuels the gender gap is women's increased sense of their own marginality and that of their children;

- Women don't generally vote as a bloc, but they do make a difference on the margin, especially in close races.

- People are so interested in the idea of change that a vote for a woman is a vote for change.

- More women are running for office than we've previously seen because more women are ready. Women who ran for local offices are percolating up through the system; women are more plausible candidates in their own eyes and in the eyes of those around them.

- Once these women are elected, they do not necessarily expect to vote as a bloc. They promise to represent their constituents and to deal with each issue as it comes up. But something very interesting generally happens to women once they get into the House or the Senate. They find that if they don't act on the issues that concern women, nobody else does very much. If women don't take care of business that affects women, they can wait a long time for anyone else to pick up those cudgels. (Ford Foundation 1994: 7)

Wertheimer's conclusions are reinforced by comments of women in Congress, particularly Republican women. Typical is a quotation from Representative Marge Roukema (R-N.J.):

I didn't really want to be stereotyped as the woman legislator. . . . I wanted to deal with things like banking and finance. But I learned very quickly that if the women like me in Congress were not going to attend to some of these family concerns, whether it was jobs or children, pension equity or whatever, then they weren't going to be attended to. So I quickly shed those biases that I had and said, Well, nobody else is going to do it; I'm going to do it. (Rutgers Report on Women in the 103rd Congress 1995: 9)

Still, women in Congress are far from united on most issues. They cover the political spectrum from liberal to conservative; even when the family leave bill came up for a vote, half the Republican women in the House voted against it. In fact, the new Republican women elected in 1994 showed a greater loyalty to their party ideology than to their female colleagues, voting unanimously to abolish the Women's Caucus and joining in presentation of a "Rush was Right" plaque to Rush Limbaugh (Foerstel and Foerstel 1996: 140).

From another angle, women in Congress do not support and work on only "women's issues." They were active in support of the ban on assault weapons in the Omnibus Crime Bill and helped pass President Clinton's budgets. They work on environmental, labor, military, foreign relations and trade, veterans affairs, consumer protection, and general civil rights matters. Also, women are not alone in their fight. The Foerstels point out that the original ERA bill in 1923 was introduced by a man and in 1993 of the 357 bills introduced on women's issues, 230 were introduced by men (seventy were introduced by members of the Women's Caucus) (Foerstel and Foerstel: 104–8, 134).

With this cooperation, passage of measures of importance to women has occurred more often. The Foerstels show that in the congresses of 1985 through 1991, an average of just four bills dealing with women's issues was passed in each. That number has been multiplied many times since. The Family and Medical Leave Act; more funding for breast cancer research; language ensuring the inclusion of women and minorities in National Institutes of Health clinical research studies; and increased openings for women serving in the military are part of what women have accomplished. Women have also been increasing their numbers in Congress and in state legislatures and are slightly more prominent in the national and state cabinets and other appointive offices, including heading a number of the campaigns for major male candidates in the 1992 and 1996 national elections. The increase of women running and winning in state and congressional campaigns is not due to happenstance or even so much the result of individual efforts as it is to the proliferation of state and national women's PACs (political action committees), which not only are raising amounts of money equal to that raised by men, but are also seeking out and encouraging women to run (concentrating on districts where they have a chance of winning), training them to win, network, and take positions of leadership, and making sure male candidates know when women's votes helped get them elected. In short, the national PACs particularly have a coordinated, long-range strategy to increase and maintain the numbers of women holding public office.

These groups are well aware of the traditional causes of the small percentage of woman office-holders, particularly at the state and national level, and are encouraging women to recognize and find ways to rise above them. One author lists three such major causes:

1. Women's traditional primary care responsibility. Unlike men, women tend to defer political careers until children are in school and take local positions while their children are young. Distance from the statehouse is related to the proportion of women elected as state representatives, and a woman running for Congress who has

school-age children will have that brought up by her opponent in a campaign. As a result, women in higher office are, on average, older than their male counterparts, are therefore likely to stay for shorter periods, and are thereby disadvantaged in the seniority system when it determines leadership.

2. Incumbency is the single most important factor in winning. This is true for both men and women, but there are far fewer women now in office. Additionally, women do just as well as, and lately often better than, men in contests for open seats. The women's PACs are well aware of this; in fact, they have tracked and publicized the phenomenon and therefore focus on open seats. However, until there are open seats, women will be represented only marginally—which leads to the third major cause.

3. This is the electoral system itself. Term limits, adopted for state officials in twenty-two states, some of which will take effect this year, will benefit women by creating more open seats. However, the Supreme Court has struck down the state laws on term limits for Congress, and despite election promises in 1994, Congress has taken no action on limiting its own terms. Women's PACs and caucuses have also not acted on other procedural changes that would enhance women's chances of winning: multi-member districts, and party rules governing the recruitment and nomination of candidates. (Darcy et al. 1994)

However, as indicated above, women's PACs know that if women don't run they can't win. Harriet Woods, head of the National Women's Political Caucus (a major woman's PAC), notes that 1992 was not so much "the year of the woman in politics" as "the year of political opportunity that women seized." Groups supporting women targeted the open seats created by redistricting, women's PACs had been putting women into the political pipeline, and consequently there were very powerful women who were role models (Ford Foundation 1994: 12).

This paper has concentrated on women in state and national legislatures, mainly because that is where the published information is concentrated. As noted earlier, the Center for Policy Alternatives and the Ms. Foundation studied state legislatures because that was the highest level at which women appeared in any significant numbers in the late 1970s. Although the book by Sue Thomas on state legislatures is based on information gleaned from a twenty-year-old study, the conclusions she draws are current and look to the future. Like other authors, commentators, and participants, she sees women politicians, their conduct, success, and issues as multilayered. Women have not only gained acceptance as candidates and officeholders, she says, they are seen as legitimate alternatives to "business as usual" politicians when reform is sought. She also has concluded that women have not only been successful in getting individual bills passed, they have also substantially altered the agenda of public discourse and expectation. And, she notes, women have not only mastered the traditional procedures of governing, they are introducing less hierarchical, more inclusive ways of proceeding (the Ford Foundation report, among others, has reached this conclusion also) (Thomas 1994: chapter 7).

However, Thomas is not entirely sanguine about women's achievements and the future of changes in government. She notes that women are constantly "adopting a lengthened time frame" (a conclusion supported by the ongoing actions and constantly revised goals of active women's PACs), and expresses doubt that any of the accomplished changes are by themselves lasting. Indeed, she predicts a backlash, as men who believed they could hold on to central positions of power despite the continued influx of women react to the challenge (Thomas 1994: 12).

The Foerstels likewise are not encouraging about the future; indeed, they are more pessimistic than Thomas. They conclude that "the reality is that women have gained such a negligible slice of power that any optimism would be inappropriate" (Foerstel and Foerstel 1996: 190).

Some women in office share pessimism about women's influence. When Representative Barbara Kennelly (D-Conn.) was asked in 1992 to name the most powerful women in Congress, she responded with surprise, "Why, none of us" (190).

CONCLUSION

Women are not seen as one-half the population. They are classed by many as a "special interest group" and as such are condemned to perpetual effort not only to forge ahead but simply to avoid losing the gains that have been made. It is not hard to identify the reason for this. Our culture is replete with the persistent vision of separate spheres: men in the public and women in the private (home). Consequently women battle dual responsibilities if they leave the home. Every backlash movement includes reinforcement of the belief that the home is where women belong and are most happy and fulfilled.

Indeed, the idea of women in public office is a relatively new one. It was not part of the political tradition of the West (no political theorists except Plato and John Stuart Mill envisioned political life in which women participate); it was explicitly denied as a possibility by the Founders of our republic (in contrast to the preconstitutional period when there were no consistent or universal barriers to the participation of women in political life, even though few women participated); and it was not the goal of the suffrage movement (which saw the ballot as giving women the ability to more effectively lobby male legislators and to use the initiative and referendum, in both cases to bring about needed reform) (Darcy et al. 1994: introduction and chapter 1).

John Adams, one of the major authors of the U.S. Constitution, wrote that a representative assembly "should be an exact portrait, in miniature, of the people at large, as it should think, feel, reason and act like them." However, Adams, like the other philosophers before him and like his founding peers, was not talking about non-white, non-male, nor even non-property-owning "people." Indeed, his wife, Abigail, wrote to him in Philadelphia, "In the new Code of Laws which I suppose it will be necessary for you to make I desire you would

Remember the Ladies, and be more generous and favourable to them than your ancestors. . . . Remember all Men would be tyrants if they could." His reply to her shows some humor: "As to your extraordinary Code of Laws, I cannot but laugh. . . ." He then mentions turbulence in schools and among Indians and Negroes and adds, "but your Letter was the first intimation that another Tribe more numerous and powerfull than all the rest were grown discontented. . . . Depend upon it, We know better than to repeal our Masculine systems. . . . [W]e are obliged to go fair, and softly. . ." (Hymowitz and Weissman 1978: 36). The reply to Abigail may have been humorous, but the new code of laws did not in fact include "negroes" or women.

It took seventy-five years of active struggle for women to pass the suffrage amendment; after fifty years of active struggle the national equal rights amendment was defeated; federal legislation giving women more rights of choice, such as in jobs, pay, and the use of their bodies is under constant attack and in peril of being overturned; and even at a somewhat accelerated rate of increase, women will reach parity in elected office only in the upcoming new century, in not less than three hundred years, or never, depending on the level or degree of pessimism of the forecaster.

Are we—women—getting more than we used to get? Yes. Are we getting what we pay for? Absolutely not. Our "Tribe," as John Adams characterized us, is still numerous but not powerful. And we are still discontented.

REFERENCES

Many books and articles bear on this topic, but the sources I have found most useful are:

Center for the American Woman and Politics, Eagleton Institute of Politics, Rutgers University, New Brunswick, NJ 08901. This organization tracks local, state, and federal elections and appointments through the years.

Clark, Janet et al. 1984. "Women as Legislative Candidates in Six States." In Austin Ranney, ed., *Political Women: Current Roles in State and Local Government*, 141–55, Beverly Hills, CA: Sage.

Clark, Janet and Cal Clark. 1996. "The Gender Gap: A Manifestation of Women's Dissatisfaction with the American Polity?" In Steven C. Craig, ed., *Broken Contract? Changing Relationships between Citizens and their Government in the United States*, Boulder, CO: Westview Press: 167–82,.

Conway, M. Margaret, David W. Ahern, and Gertrude A. Steuernagel. 1995. *Women and Public Policy: A Revolution in Progress*. Washington, DC: Congressional Quarterly Press. Also has chapters by Earlean McCarrick and Robert H. Jerry II and provides in-depth information about legislation in a number of specific areas including education, health care, equal employment, economic equity, insurance, family law, child care, and the criminal justice system—all as it pertains to women.

Darcy, R., Susan Welch, and Janet Clark. 1994. *Women, Elections, and Representation*. Lincoln: University of Nebraska Press. A historical and theoretical framework is provided in chapter 1, followed by election information on

women candidates at local, state, and national levels, discussion of structural
barriers and a conclusion about the tasks ahead.

Duke, Lois Lovelace. 1996. *Women in Politics: Outsiders or Insiders?* 2d ed. Upper
Saddle River, NJ: Prentice Hall. This is a reader that provides theory, views,
statistics, policy, and government. The editor provides short but comprehensive introductions to each section. Special emphasis in this paper is given
to "Wither the Gender Gap: Converging and Conflicting Attitudes Among
Women" by Cal and Janet Clark.

Foerstel, Karen, and Herbert N. Foerstel. 1996. *Climbing the Hill: Gender Conflict in
Congress.* Westport, CT: Praeger. A well-organized and incredibly detailed
but riveting history of women in Congress, starting with Elizabeth Cady
Stanton's attempt in 1866 and ending in 1996. Much insider information
and many compelling quotes. Ends with a rather negative prognosis.

Ford Foundation. 1994. *Women in American Politics: A Symposium of the Women's
Program Forum.* New York: Ford Foundation (September). A slim booklet
containing summaries of talks by seven leaders in women's rights.

Hymowitz, Carol, and Michaele Weissman. 1978. *A History of Women in America.*
New York: Bantam Books and the Anti-Defamation League of B'nai B'rith.
Although old, this book is still in print and is one of the best overviews of
the history of women in America, at least through its publication date.

National Women's Political Caucus, 1211 Connecticut Avenue, N.W., #425, Washington, DC, 20036. Another source of valuable statistics and analysis of
women and elections.

"Rutgers Report on Women in the 103d Congress." 1995. Center for the American
Woman and Politics, Eagleton Institute of Politics, Rutgers University, New
Brunswick, NJ 08901.

Siegel, Roberta S. 1996. *Ambition and Accommodation: How Women View Gender
Relations.* Chicago: University of Chicago Press.

Thomas, Sue. 1994. *How Women Legislate.* New York: Oxford University Press. Although published recently, the book is based on research done on women in
state legislatures in the 1970s. A very detailed and well-organized survey.
The book provides valuable historical information, and is updated by a
well-reasoned and prescient conclusion.

Tobias, Sheila. 1997. *Faces of Feminism: An Activist's Reflections on the Women's
Movement.* Boulder, CO: Westview Press.

14

No Race to the Bottom: The 1993 National Voter Registration Act and the 1996 Personal Responsibility and Work Opportunity Reconciliation Act

Jean Wahl Harris

One of the many concerns raised by opponents of the most recent national welfare reform, The Personal Responsibility and Work Opportunity Reconciliation Act of 1996, is that there will be a race to the bottom among the states. Some predict that the states will utilize their new authority over social welfare programs to cut back their assistance to the poor; devolution will lead to the elimination of the safety net for the poor. Another possibility is that the combined impact of the Personal Responsibility and Work Opportunity Reconciliation Act and the 1993 National Voter Registration Act (NVRA) will lead to the mobilization of citizens with lower socioeconomic status (SES). If lower SES citizens are mobilized to register, and therefore become much more apt to vote, there will be no race to the bottom for the greater the representation of lower SES citizens in the state electorate, the higher the state level of welfare spending.

ELECTIONS, REPRESENTATION, AND SOCIAL WELFARE POLICY

In a representative democracy it is assumed that elected officials represent their voting constituents. More specifically, the public policy decisions of elected officials are expected to be influenced by the voters in the officials' districts. While we might hope that the public policy decisions of elected officials are influenced by the majority of *residents* in the official's district, realistically it is only the opinions and interests of the majority of *voters* that appear to be represented. Political interest groups and political action committees are perceived as threatening the representation of voters, yet "[p]oliticians get re-elected by looking after the voters who elected them the time before" (Clymer 1996). Politicians interested in remaining in government over successive elections must continually represent the majority of their voting constituents (at least on highly visible, voter relevant issues).

Today, elected state officials are apt to be career politicians looking to be reelected numerous times. Since the 1960s, the federal government has devolved more and more domestic policy to state governments. To competently deal with their expanding policy responsibilities, state governments have moved from institutions with part-time staff and legislators, serving in short working sessions for low pay, to institutions comprised of full-time staff and legislators, serving in almost year-round sessions for decent pay. As a result of this professionalism, state elected officials more often run for reelection. They tend to run campaigns that are independent of the party and therefore do not rely on party loyalty for votes (Salmore and Salmore 1996: 58–60). State politicians who are concerned with their political survival are "more likely to choose the safest course and are less likely to confront difficult choices" (Van Horn 1996: 240). To stay in office then, state elected officials must represent the voters and they must continue to represent the voters who voted for them last time. Therefore, we would expect state policy to be in line with voter appeals.

The welfare reform movement that started in the states in the 1980s "was an appeal to the voters" (Lurie 1996: 223). Voters were calling for cutbacks in welfare entitlement spending and increases in the personal responsibility of welfare recipients. State governments found it more expedient to meet these voter appeals through new programs than to fully implement existing federal welfare mandates (Lurie 1996). By 1995 more than thirty states had been approved for waivers from federal welfare mandates so that they could "experiment" with welfare within their borders. The welfare reform bill signed into law by President Clinton in 1996 (the Personal Responsibility and Work Opportunity Reconciliation Act) continued devolving welfare policy to the states. By collapsing numerous social welfare programs into one block grant (Temporary Assistance for Needy Families [TANF]) with a cap on spending (thereby eliminating entitlements for the poor), the federal government was appealing to the preferences of voters.

The amount of financial support a state provides for social welfare programs appears to be impacted by several factors, including the preferences of voters. Past research has identified state economic resources (personal income per capita), socioeconomic diversity, and public support for liberal policies as explanatory variables of the level of state welfare spending (Hill and Leighley

1992: 356–58; Peterson and Rom 1989: 725). Research has also shown that in states with strong party competition, both political parties formulate social welfare policies, since the poor are potential voters (Peterson and Rom 1989: 718).

In more recent research, Hill and Leighley found that in addition to the explanatory variables noted, "one of the most prominent, independent explanations of variations in welfare spending" across states was the representation of lower SES persons in the electorate (1992: 358). The greater the representation of lower SES persons in the electorate, the more responsive government policy is to the interests of the lower class (Hicks and Swank 1992; Hill and Leighley 1992; Hill, Leighley, and Hinton-Andersson 1995; Hill and Hinton-Andersson 1995; Peterson and Rom 1989). Hill and Leighley's finding that redistributive policy preferences are "inversely related to social class" (1992: 353) helps to explain this positive correlation between SES representation in the electorate and social welfare spending.

While state spending on social welfare is correlated with the representation of low SES citizens among the electorate, citizens of low SES are less apt to register to vote, and even when registered are less apt to vote (Jackson 1996: 342–43). In addition, Bennett and Resnick found that the public welfare policy preferences of nonvoters differ from those of voters. While voters are not necessarily strongly opposed to greater federal spending on domestic programs, nonvoters are more strongly in favor of increased federal spending on domestic programs such as social security, food stamps, assistance for the unemployed, programs that assist blacks, child care, public schools, care for the elderly, and care for the homeless (Bennett and Resnick 1990: 793).

Hill and Leighley conclude that electoral participation of the poor is critical to the formulation of social welfare policies that address the needs of the poor. They also note that the "prospects for increased participation of the poor" are limited due to legal-institutional voter registration barriers as well as the "absence of any true working class party" to mobilize citizens to register and to vote (1992: 363).

REMOVAL OF LEGAL/INSTITUTIONAL
REGISTRATION BARRIERS

When comparing the demographic characteristics of registered voters to those of nonregistered citizens, there are significant differences. Those who are more apt to vote are citizens of higher socioeconomic status (Clymer 1996; Nie, Verba, and Petrocik 1976; Piven and Cloward 1988; Rosenstone and Hansen 1993; Rosenstone and Wolfinger 1984; Teixeira 1992). Citizens who are better integrated into their community and into work and political organizations are also more apt to vote (Highton 1997: 573); these citizens tend to be of higher SES (Rosenstone and Hansen 1993). Registered voters are better educated, are employed in better paying, more prestigious jobs, have greater residential stability, and have stronger partisan identities than nonregistered citizens (Jackson 1996: 342).

Research suggests that registration procedures unique to the United States make it more difficult for U.S. citizens with lower SES status to register (Avey 1989; Piven and Cloward 1988; Powell 1984; Rosenstone and Wolfinger 1984). That is, if U.S. registration procedures were less onerous, then more citizens with lower SES status would register. Other industrialized democracies where the registration process is the responsibility of the state and not the individual citizen do not have the registration gap between lower and higher SES persons that is found in the United States (Avey 1989; Powell 1984).

To better understand the relationship between registration procedures and voter turnout in the United States, Highton compared the turnout of eligible voters living in North Dakota (which does not require voter registration) and Maine, Minnesota, and Wisconsin (states that allow registration on Election Day) with turnout of eligible voters in the country, and with turnout of registered citizens in all other states. He concludes that "policies like the National Voter Registration Act of 1993 (NVRA) will modestly increase overall turnout and diminish socioeconomic differences among voters" (Highton 1997: 573).

Certainly the partisan battle over the passage of the NVRA suggests that the Democratic and Republican parties understand the negative impact of legal-institutional registration barriers on lower SES persons. In general, Democrats have supported voter registration bills that eliminate registration barriers. Their support is based on the assumption that the Democratic electoral base would grow as the percent of lower SES persons registered to vote increases due to the elimination of registration barriers. Republicans have opposed such laws based on the same assumption. After the NVRA was signed into law, several Republican governors refused to implement it (Earle 1996; Piven and Cloward 1996). To the surprise of both Democrats and Republicans, the impact of the NVRA has been a greater increase in the number of registered Republicans than the increase in registered Democrats (Harwood 1996).

Signed into law by President Clinton on May 20, 1993, the National Voter Registration Act "mandates, for all states currently without election-day voter registration, the establishment of mail-in and agency-based registration programs, and eliminates the purging of registrants solely for nonvoting" (Knack 1995: 796). The NVRA, and subsequent state voter registration laws, require an active effort by government employees to offer voter registration assistance to driver's license applicants and public assistance applicants (that is, those applying for Aid to Families with Dependent Children[now TANF], Food Stamps; Medicaid; the Women, Infants and Children Program; and disability services programs). In practice, an active effort means that government employees working with such applicants must tell the applicants of their right to register to vote and must offer assistance in the completion and mailing of the voter registration form.

From January 1995 to June 1996, "Some 20 million people either registered to vote for the first time, reregistered or updated their registrations using the law. . . . 44.4 percent, registered at a department of motor vehicles. . . . 24 percent registered through the mail. Voters also registered at other government agencies like unemployment offices, libraries or military recruiting offices" ("20 Million Motor Voters" 1996). By January 1, 1997, twenty-eight million people had taken "advantage of the law's provisions to register to vote or update their voter registration" (Duskin 1997: 6). "While most states were able to implement the DMV portion of the NVRA without any trouble," as evidenced by the fact that "the majority of registrations come through the DMV" (8–9), registering voters through public assistance agencies appears to be less successful. Earle (1995) found that as of August 1995 only 8 percent of new voter registrations came from public assistance agencies. In Florida, where most people offered the opportunity to register at the motor vehicle offices take advantage of the opportunity, it is "a far different picture down the road at the state office that administers the welfare, food stamp and Medicaid programs" where the offer to assist in the voter registration process usually receives a negative response (Harwood 1996).

Evaluating the success of state motor-voter laws implemented between 1976 and 1992, Knack found that mail-in programs that did not require notarization or witnessing (which the NVRA also does not require), and active effort motor voter programs (such as those required by the NVRA) were effective in increasing registration and voter turnout in presidential elections (1995: 805). Prior to 1988 there were no active effort public assistance agency-based registration programs, and only a few existed as of the 1992 election; therefore, Knack was unable to evaluate the success of active effort public assistance agency-based programs. Yet, based on recent data collection, there does not appear to be a significant increase in voter registration via public assistance agencies. It is not yet known whether this lack of success is due to the negative response of public assistance applicants or due to less than active implementation of the voter registration laws. While the Florida case suggests the former explanation, a study by the League of Women Voters suggests the latter explanation. The League notes that several states are being sued over their implementation of the NVRA in public assistance agencies. In addition, it appears to be common practice to not bother to offer individuals currently in programs the opportunity to register, while new applicants may be offered the opportunity (Duskin 1997: 10).

Even if implementation of the NVRA were improved in public assistance agencies, that is, if all program participants—new and continuing—were offered the opportunity to register to vote, would the Florida case scenario still occur? Would nonregistered voters who were offered the opportunity to register in public assistance agencies choose not to register? A review of the factors that have been used to explain voter turnout may be helpful in understanding the decision to register to vote.

Avey (1989: 16) offers a summary of the factors that have been considered in explanations of voter turnout. The citizen who has a sense of duty and a strong political party identification has the "sociopsychological status" that leads to voting. Interest in political issues in general increases the likelihood of voting. The citizen who perceives the election as a close race between candidates with identifiable positions on issues relevant to her will make a "rational choice" to participate due to self-interest. Social movements and partisan mobilization help to identify the relevance of politics and candidate platforms, creating rational choice voters. Yet, a rational choice to vote assumes that the voter is registered and has a sense of political efficacy, that is, a sense that she understands politics and the issues and that her vote can impact policy in the direction she prefers.

Higher SES is associated with a greater sense of political efficacy, citizen duty, and voter registration. These individual factors, coupled with party voter mobilization efforts that focus on past supportive voters (Rosenstone and Hansen 1993) and on high SES citizens (Avey 1989: 22) help to explain who votes and who does not. Even among registered voters, those with higher SES are more apt to vote.

Zipp's (1985) research found that indifference (no clear distinction between candidates) and alienation (no candidate with the same policy preferences) were positively correlated with the choice to not vote. Kevin Chen (1992) reports that those who are less apt to vote have a distrust of the political system—a sense that they cannot influence politics because they are not competent to participate effectively. And they are indifferent to politics: they just do not care about politics.

If the factors summarized by Avey (1989) and presented by Zipp (1985) and Chen (1992) to explain who votes also explain who registers to vote, then even the proper implementation of the NVRA will not be successful in increasing the proportion of lower SES citizens registered to vote. As Highton notes, while the "poor and uneducated will benefit most from the NVRA, their turnout will continue to fall short of the turnout of those with higher socioeconomic status" (1997: 573–74) for "registration barriers do not come close to completely accounting for turnout disparities between the most and the least educated" (571), or the low and high SES. Highton reminds us that removing registration barriers will not impact the turnout of citizens who "are not particularly interested in voting" (566). Hill and Leighley (1992) note that the lack of a group interested in mobilizing low SES citizens to register and to vote will limit the political participation (registering and voting) of low SES citizens.

Before the elimination of legal-institutional registration barriers will ameliorate the SES bias in registration and voting, lower SES citizens must be mobilized. Their sense of political efficacy and their sense that the government is interested in them must both be enhanced. Some entity must work to mobilize them. Once citizens are mobilized to register, campaign factors (the stimulus of a presidential election, amount spent in senatorial and gubernatorial campaigns, competitiveness of elections, and mobilization efforts) become more important in determining who will vote, and individual demographic factors become less important. "Campaigns do mobilize potential voters [registered citizens], and campaign influences are quite important to the explanation of turnout" (Jackson 1996: 344).

Timpone found that while the Voting Rights Act of 1965, which eliminated institutional barriers to voter registration, had a positive impact on the registration of Southern black citizens, the real increase in the registration of Southern black citizens "occurred primarily through the efforts of the Civil Rights movement and the impetus from the 1964 election. These results, along with the observed success of the mobilization drives in the 1984 election campaign, show the great impact that mass mobilization and motivation have in expanding the franchise" (1995: 435). According to Timpone, the combination of door-to-door canvassing for mobilization (as opposed to general advertising), competitive election campaigns, and the elimination of registration barriers is key to expanding voter registration and voting.

MOBILIZATION OF LOWER SES CITIZENS

The NVRA has made registration easier. What would encourage political parties, individual organizations, or coalitions to mobilize citizens, especially low SES citizens, to register and to vote?

Cameron puts forth the argument that public policy decisions are important precursors of political mobilization. He states that "mobilizations arise out of particular policy contexts involving the decisions of national elites" (1974: 159) and that "the success of mobilization depends upon the creation of an infrastructure of political organizations at the local level" (150). Timpone (1995) finds that grassroots mobilization, door-to-door or face-to-face mobilization, is more successful than general mass media attempts to mobilize citizens.

The National Voter Registration Act may indeed be a public policy decision that leads to the mobilization of more voters. While the Republicans feared that the NVRA would lead to an increased number of registered Democrats, it appears to be having the opposite effect, with more of the newly registered voters registering as Republicans and most frequently doing so at motor vehicle departments (Harwood 1996). Since research suggests that the greatest barrier to voting is registering (Erikson 1981), the Democrats may find the need to counterbalance these Republican registrants by mobilizing other eligible registrants, such as those applying for public assistance, who to date do not appear to be taking advantage of the registration opportunity in public assistance agencies (when it is offered).

The League of Women Voters actively engaged in Get-Out-the-Vote (GOTV) campaigns in the 1996 general election. Taking advantage of the

NVRA, and with a focus on "getting racial and ethnic minorities and other un-derrepresented populations to the voting booth," a number of local Leagues formed coalitions with community groups and used grassroots efforts to mo-bilize eligible voters. The League claims that these local, grassroots efforts were successful in increasing turnout in GOTV campaign communities during the 1996 general election (an election for which there was a national all-time low voter turnout rate) (Duskin 1998).

The Personal Responsibility and Work Opportunity Reconciliation Act of 1996 coupled with the 1993 National Voter Registration Act may collectively be public policy decisions that lead to the mobilization of more voters in gen-eral and grassroots mobilization of low SES persons specifically. The devolu-tion of social welfare policy may assist in the creation of political coalitions at the local level of government as county welfare workers attempt to implement new welfare programs that include finding jobs for welfare clients within two years of their first application for assistance.

The American Public Welfare Association, an organization of state and local officials and policy experts, is in the process of training welfare agency employ-ees throughout the country so that implementation of new welfare programs will be successful. "The new law is forcing state officials to change the culture of welfare agencies around the country, shifting the focus from the determina-tion of eligibility and the issuance of checks to employment and jobs. . . . State employees must now collaborate with welfare recipients and help them find jobs, a goal that may be thwarted if case workers are too paternalistic" (Pear 1996).

Under the new laws, caseworkers will no longer be able to treat all clients the same. They will have to treat them as individual adults as they attempt to help them find work and to become "well-functioning, high performing adults" (Pear 1996). Such a change in the culture of welfare agencies might foster the development of an advocacy role for welfare employees—that is, it may foster the mobilization of low SES citizens.

Due to the lack of available well-paying jobs, lack of child care, lack of trans-portation, and the lack of training and educational programs, welfare workers in some communities may find it difficult to move clients off of welfare in two years (as mandated). If welfare workers are unable to do their job successfully, they may see the need to mobilize themselves and their clients to put pressure on state governments to change welfare policy. Welfare workers may assist in the development of a sense of political efficacy and an interest in politics among their clients as they see the need for welfare recipients to lobby for po-litical policies and government programs that will assist them in getting good jobs, or in changing the latest welfare programs. The need to help clients de-velop into self-sufficient adults may also foster a sense of "community" where there are expectations to participate in elections. "The greater the sense of community, the greater the level of political participation" (Rosenstone and Hansen 1993: 86; Highton 1997: 573). Such grassroots mobilization efforts of social welfare workers might help low SES citizens develop an interest in politics, a sense of politcal efficacy, and a sense of duty.

Grassroots mobilization of low SES citizens, brought on by the Personal Responsibility and Work Opportunity Reconciliation Act and fostered by the National Voter Registration Act should lead to a greater representation of low SES citizens in the electorate. State career politicians who must appeal to the preferences of such an electorate—that is, an electorate with a greater proportion of lower SES citizens—should not be interested in a race to the bottom in terms of state social welfare spending. As Hill and Leighley (1992) found, states with greater proportions of low SES registered voters are more supportive of social welfare policies.

CONCLUSION

States with competitive elections, greater personal income per capita (economic resources), socioeconomic diversity, and public support for liberal policies are more supportive of social welfare policies. More important to the thesis of this paper, states with greater proportions of low SES registered voters are also more supportive of social welfare policies (Hill and Leighley 1992). Theoretically then, the combined effects of the 1993 National Voter Registration Act and the 1996 Personal Responsibility and Work Opportunity Reconciliation Act could lead to the mobilization of citizens in general, and specifically the mobilization of low SES citizens to register and to vote. Such a mobilization of low SES citizens, in our representative democracy where elected officials must appeal to voters, should prevent a race to the bottom. It might even result in enhanced social welfare policy in states with liberal political cultures, high personal income per capita, socioeconomic diversity, and competitive elections.

REFERENCES

Avey, Michael J. 1989. *The Demobilization of American Voters.* Westport, CT: Greenwood Press, Inc.

Bennett, Stephen Earl, and David Resnick. 1990. "The Implications of Nonvoting for Democracy in the United States." *American Journal of Political Science* 34, 3: 771–802.

Cameron, David R. 1974. "Toward a Theory of Political Mobilization." *Journal of Politics* 36, 1: 138–71.

Chen, Kevin. 1992. *Political Alienation and Voting Turnout in the United States, 1960–1988.* San Francisco: Mellen Research University Press.

Clymer, Adam. 1996. "Class Warfare? The Rich Win by Default." *New York Times,* August 11, IV, 14.

Duskin, Meg S. 1998. "Motor Voter's First Road Test." *The National Voter* 46, 4: 6–12.

———. 1998. "Getting Out the Vote: Lessons from 1996." *The National Voter* 47, 4: 12–13.

Earle, Geoff. 1996. "Motor Trouble for the Democrats." In Thad L. Beyle, ed., *State Government: CQ's Guide to Current Issues and Activities 1996–97.* Washington, DC: Congressional Quarterly Press: 8–11.

Erikson, Robert S. 1981. "Why do People Vote? Because They Are Registered." *American Politics Quarterly* 9: 259–76.

Harwood, John. 1996. "In a Surprise for Everyone, Motor-Voter Law Is Providing a Boost for GOP, Not Democrats." *Wall Street Journal,* June 11, A16.

Hicks, Alexander M., and Duane H. Swank. 1992. "Politics, Institutions, and Welfare Spending." *American Political Science Review* 86, 3: 658–74.

Highton, Benjamin. 1997. "Easy Registration and Voter Turnout." *The Journal of Politics* 59, 2: 565–75.

Hill, Kim Quaile, and Angela Hinton-Andersson. 1995. "Pathways of Representation: A Causal Analysis of Public Opinion-Policy Linkages." *American Journal of Political Science* 39, 4: 924–35.

Hill, Kim Quaile, and Jan E. Leighley. 1992. "The Policy Consequences of Class Bias in State Electorates." *American Journal of Political Science* 36, 2: 351–65.

Hill, Kim Quaile, Jan E. Leighley, and Angela Hinton-Andersson. 1995. "Lower-Class Mobilization and Policy Linkage in the U.S. States." *American Journal of Political Science* 39, 1: 75–86.

Jackson, Robert. 1996. "A Reassessment of Voter Mobilization." *Political Research Quarterly* 49, 2: 331–49.

Knack, Stephen. 1995. "Does 'Motor Voter' Work? Evidence from State-Level Data." *The Journal of Politics* 57, 3 (August): 796–811.

Lurie, Irene. 1996. "State Welfare Policy." In Carl E. Van Horn, ed., *The State of the States.* Washington, DC: Congressional Quarterly Press.

Nie, Norman H., Sidney Verba, and John R. Petrocik.: 1976. *The Changing American Voter.* Cambridge: Harvard University Press.

Pear, Robert. 1996. "State Welfare Workers Inherit Burden of Explaining Changes." *New York Times,* October 22, A1, D26.

Peterson, Paul, and Mark Rom. 1989. "American Federalism, Welfare Policy, and Residential Choices." *American Political Science Review* 83, 3: 711–28.

Piven, Frances Fox, and Richard A. Cloward. 1988. *Why Americans Don't Vote.* New York: Pantheon Books.

———. 1996. "Northern Bourbons: A Preliminary Report on the National Voter Registration Act." *PS: Political Science and Politics* 29, 1: 39–42.

Powell, G. Bingham. 1984. "Voting Turnout in Thirty Democracies." In Richard G. Niemi and Herbet F. Weisberg, eds., *Controversies in Voting Behavior,* 2nd edition. Washington DC: Congressional Quarterly Press.

Rosenstone, Steven J., and John Mark Hansen. 1993. *Mobilization, Participation, and Democracy in America.* New York: Macmillan Publishing Company.

Rosenstone, Steven J., and Raymond E. Wolfinger. 1984. "The Effect of Registration Laws on Voter Turnout." In Niemi and Weisberg, eds., *Controversies in Voting,* 2nd edition. Washington, DC: Congressional Quarterly Press: 54–86.

Salmore, Stephen, and Barbara Salmore. 1996. "The Transformation of State Electoral Politics." In Carl E. Van Horn, ed., *The State of the States.* Washington, DC: Congressional Quarterly Press: 51–76.

Teixeira, Ruy A. 1992. *The Disappearing American Voter.* Washington, DC: The Brookings Institution.

Timpone, Richard J. 1995. "Mass Mobilization or Government Intervention? The Growth of Black Registration in the South." *The Journal of Politics* 57, 2: 425–42.

"20 Million 'Motor Voters.'" 1996. *The New York Times,* October 16, A15.

Van Horn, Carl E. 1996. "Power to the States." In Carl E. Van Horn, ed., *The State of the States.* Washington, DC: Congressional Quarterly Press: 231–42.

Zipp, John F. 1985. "Perceived Representativeness and Voting: An Assessment of the Impact of 'Choices' vs. 'Echoes.'" *American Political Science Review* 79, 1 (March): 50–61.

15

The Never Ending Story of Welfare Reform

Rodd Freitag

The contest for office is the machinery used by Americans to change policy.[1]

Democracy requires that citizens influence public policy. While the power of the people over government action need not be immediate and unmitigated, the potential for citizen influence over policy should always be present, especially with respect to policies of particular importance to the public. That is, the principles underlying the notion of democracy dictate "that the citizenry have the ability to convert its views on the issues of the day—certainly the pressing, salient issues—into public policy" (Maisel 1993: 8).

In a representative democracy frequent elections translate the public's desires into policy. Herbert B. Asher, a leading scholar on presidential elections, asserts that "elections occupy a central role in democratic theory, especially as they provide a linkage between the preferences of citizens and the actions of government" (1992: 33). Elections link citizen preferences with government action by first moving issues onto the policy agenda.

Welfare reform is a perfect example of such an issue. Presidential elections have moved welfare reform, an issue of high salience, to the top of the policy agenda for most of the past thirty years. From Richard Nixon to Bill Clinton, candidates for president have severely criticized the most prominent cash public assistance program, Aid to Families with Dependent Children (AFDC), describing it as a "colossal failure" (Richard Nixon), a "disgrace to the human race" (Jimmy Carter), or a "narcotic, a subtle destroyer of the human spirit" (Ronald Reagan). Bill Clinton was only the latest to pledge to "end welfare as we know it" if elected.

Moving issues onto the policy agenda through elections, however, is only the first step in translating citizen preferences into government action. Once issues are on the policy agenda, they must proceed through a complex and politically charged process of policy formulation and adoption. The American political structure of separate institutions sharing powers was designed to make the creation of public policy difficult. Moreover, vested interests and partisan division today make changing existing policy even more arduous. Thus, elections will most likely fail to translate public desires into policy during these later stages of the policy process.

Once again, the welfare reform efforts of the past thirty years illustrate the limited impact elections can have on policy. Until recently, despite the repeated election year calls for sweeping welfare reform by victorious presidential candidates, comprehensive proposals to overhaul AFDC have not been translated into policy. While the Work Incentive (WIN) program of 1967 and the Family Support Act of 1988 made some important changes to AFDC programs in the states, these reforms left the existing structure of the welfare program intact. Nixon's welfare reform, the Family Assistance Plan (FAP), and Carter's Program for Better Jobs and Income (PBJI), on the other hand, would have truly ended welfare as we know it by completely restructuring the provision of cash assistance to the needy. But dramatic reform repeatedly stalled in Congress.

Stalled, that is, until 1996 when a major restructuring of welfare did pass. In August of that year, President Clinton signed the Personal Responsibility and Work Opportunity Reconciliation Act that created the Temporary Assistance for Needy Families (TANF) Block Grant to replace AFDC in the states.

For the student of American politics and policy, the passage of comprehensive welfare reform raises an interesting question. Why did the more recent campaign promise to end welfare as we know it become policy while the earlier attempts did not? This chapter addresses this question by examining each of the three comprehensive welfare reform efforts and analyzing those factors that help explain the failure of the FAP and PBJI proposals and the successful passage of the TANF Block Grant.

This article is divided into three parts. First, the AFDC program is described with a focus on the objections that have driven the calls for reform. Next, the provisions and legislative history of the three comprehensive welfare reform efforts are outlined. Finally, explanations for the failure of FAP and PBJI are reviewed and analyzed for their relevance to our understanding of the passage of welfare reform in 1996.

AFDC: WELFARE AS WE KNOW IT

Biting critiques of welfare and bold calls for reform were popular presidential candidate applause lines for years. But what was this evil welfare? The program most commonly understood as welfare was AFDC, cash assistance for low-income families with children. A small part of the 1935 Social Security Act, AFDC (then known as ADC, Aid to Dependent Children) nationalized state mothers' or widows' pension programs by requiring that all states provide cash payments to help support the children of single, usually widowed, mothers.[2] AFDC was a shared responsibility with national guidelines and funding (54 percent funding on average according to a matching formula) and significant state discretion over eligibility and payments.[3]

Early on, AFDC was small and politically appealing. By the 1960s, however, the program was no longer so small; the AFDC rolls doubled each decade between 1947 and 1967 and again between 1967 and 1972 (Levitan 1990: 49). Along the way, AFDC had lost much of its popularity. Three objections were particularly prominent: the perception that the recipients of AFDC were undeserving of assistance, the belief that AFDC discouraged work and encouraged dependency, and dissatisfaction with the considerable variation in AFDC payments across the states.

AFDC as originally conceived and defended was targeted to a select population—blameless widows deserving of government assistance. As Teles (1996: 24–26) demonstrates, the recipient population of AFDC had changed by the late 1960s and early 1970s. The participation rate had increased dramatically, causing an explosion in the number of recipients (Levitan 1990: 49). Moreover, the nature of AFDC recipients changed. Widows were increasingly covered by Survivor's Insurance (created in 1939), leaving AFDC benefits for women who were divorced or unmarried mothers. The racial composition of the AFDC rolls also changed dramatically throughout the 1940s and 1950s as the percentage of blacks receiving AFDC rose to match roughly the level of whites. These changes led to a population of recipients perceived as much less deserving of government assistance than widows.

The dependency objection to AFDC received greater prominence as working moms became the norm (by the mid-1980s more than half of American mothers were employed). AFDC was attacked for discouraging work by taking away benefits from recipients who earned an outside income, thereby offering an attractive income to those choosing not to work (Gilder 1981). Under these conditions, work was no longer considered an option and poor families eventually found themselves permanently dependent upon the government for support (Mead 1992).

As a federal-state program, AFDC provided widely differing benefits across the states, and this led to considerable dissatisfaction with the program's effectiveness. The maximum monthly AFDC grant for a family of three in January 1992 varied from a high of $680 in Connecticut to a low of $120 in Mississippi, resulting in an average maximum payment of $392.34, a mere 42.1 percent of the federal poverty line.

COMPREHENSIVE REFORM PLANS: ENDING WELFARE AS WE KNOW IT

These objections to AFDC generated numerous reform ideas. Only FAP, PBJI, and the TANF Block Grant, however, proposed the elimination of the AFDC program.[4] Each comprehensive reform plan addressed the objections outlined above, but in different ways and to varying degrees.

The original FAP proposed in 1969 drew on the idea of a guaranteed annual income by calling for a *national* minimum benefit (with allowance for continued state supplements) for *all* low-income families with children, the working poor included.[5] The proposed benefit level was $1600 for a family of four (42.7 percent of the federal poverty level) with no other income: $500 for each of the first two family members and $300 for each additional member. To encourage work, there was an annual $720 earnings exemption. For family earnings above $720, the benefit received would be reduced fifty cents for each dollar earned until the benefits reached zero. So, a family of four with a working household head could receive federal benefits until its total annual income (earned income plus benefits) reached $3,920. Work was further encouraged through work registration requirements for certain recipients and federal child care provisions.

Carter's PBJI also called for a national minimum benefit structure (and an allowance for state supplements), but with two tiers: an upper tier for recipients not expected to work and a lower tier for those expected to work.[6] Those not expected to work included aged, blind, and disabled persons, as well as single-parent families with children under age seven. The benefits for these recipients differed according to status, with the aged, blind, and disabled eligible for somewhat higher benefits. The minimum guaranteed benefit for a single parent with three kids and no other income was $4200 (67.8 percent of the federal poverty line): $2400 for the adult and $600 for each additional child. Those expected to work included two-parent households, single parents with no children under fourteen, single parents with children ages seven to thirteen (expected only to work part time), single individuals, and childless couples. The benefit levels for those expected to work were lower: a four-person family would receive $2300 (37.2 percent of the federal poverty level) on the lower tier, an unrelated single person would receive $1100, and a couple without children would receive $2200. The latter two groups were eligible for benefits only if jobs were not available. For the four-person family on the lower tier, the higher benefits would apply if a job were not found or offered by the government (1.4 million new public sector jobs were proposed) in eight weeks. As under FAP, there were proposed earnings exemptions of $3800 for families with an adult expected to work, $1800 for single-parent families with one child, and $3600 for single-parent families with two or more children. Additional earnings would result in a 50 percent marginal tax on benefits, until total earned income plus benefits reached $8400 at its most generous.

The third comprehensive welfare reform plan was proposed by congressional Republicans in 1995. While Nixon's FAP and Carter's PBJI addressed all three objections to AFDC—undeserving recipients, dependency, and inequity—the congressional Republican plan purposely ignored inequitable state payments. The centerpiece of the plan was the creation of the TANF Block Grant to replace AFDC.[7] Under this new approach, states would have nearly complete control over eligibility, benefits, and other rules, with the exception of a handful of federal requirements, including: a limit on the overall amount of time adults could receive federal welfare funds (no more than five years), a restriction requiring adults receiving welfare benefits to begin working within two years of receiving aid, and a minimum on the percentage of the welfare caseload getting jobs (half by the year 2002) under penalty of reduced block grant funds. Further, financial incentives would be provided to states moving the most recipients off welfare into work and reducing illegitimate births.

The legislative fate of these proposals is already known: FAP and PBJI failed to pass, while the TANF Block Grant was signed into law. FAP did, however, come very close to passing Congress. The plan was introduced in 1969, passed by the House in 1970, but killed by a close 10–6 vote in the Senate Finance Committee. The House passed a revised version of the plan the next year and the Senate approved the bill in yet another altered form in 1972, but FAP was ultimately killed for good on the floor later that same year. PBJI, on the other hand, did not come so close to successful passage. Carter's plan was introduced in 1977, ignored by Congress in 1978, reintroduced in a slightly scaled-down form and passed by the House in 1979, but killed by Senate inaction in 1980.

The most recent version of welfare reform was a story of high drama until the very end. The House Republicans passed their version of welfare reform—giving states almost complete control over a host of programs for the needy, including AFDC, Medicaid, foster care, adoption programs, school meals, and nutritional assistance for pregnant women and young children—early during the 104th Congress. The Senate delayed its consideration, finally passing its more moderate plan in September 1995. Eventually, many of the welfare provisions were rolled into the deficit-reducing budget-reconciliation bill vetoed by President Clinton in late 1995. Clinton again vetoed a separate welfare bill in January of 1996, claiming that the provisions were harmful to children. After intervention by the National Governors' Association, which encouraged even greater state flexibility in the bill and more federal child care assistance, the Republicans once again moved on welfare reform. In July, the Republican leadership dropped the link between Medicaid and welfare reform, opening the way for eventual bipartisan congressional approval later that month. Clinton soon succumbed and signed the Personal Responsibility and Work Opportunity Reconciliation Act in August.

EXPLAINING THE FATE OF COMPREHENSIVE WELFARE REFORM

Why did welfare reform stall for Nixon and Carter but pass in 1996? While many factors influence the policy process, there are four common explanations for a proposal's success or failure: opinion, ideology, interests, and institutions. Both mass and elite opinion set the parameters for the policy proposal and debate. The ideological preferences of elected officials can similarly influence policy outcomes. Organized interests can play an important independent role in swaying the actions of elected officials. Finally, various institutional considerations, including executive and legislative leadership and comity, can affect legislative outcomes.

The failure of the Nixon and Carter welfare reform proposals has been examined in previous studies. Public opinion, however, has not been identified as a significant factor. Public opinion, in fact, has been quite favorable toward comprehensive welfare reform. Heclo (1986) identifies four relevant characteristics of public attitudes toward poverty policy through recent decades. First, Americans want government to help the poor. Second, the public supports aid based on need. Third, these needs are clearly differentiated according to desert—those unable to work should be provided for, while those able to work should only be supported through education and training. Finally, the American public strongly dislikes AFDC. The result is that the public favors comprehensive change that provides assistance but emphasizes work for the able-bodied. Thus, the work provisions in the plans overrode public misgivings about the guaranteed income so that the proposals received 65 percent and 70 percent public support shortly after their introduction.[8]

The failure of the FAP is most often attributed to liberal opposition to the plan, particularly among interest groups and a few key senators (Bowler 1974; Burke and Burke 1974; Moynihan 1973; Salamon 1978; Teles 1996). Conservative displeasure with the plan, despite a Republican president's emphasis on the work provisions, was to be expected given the basically liberal nature of a guaranteed income. In addition, the regional interests of southern and western members of Congress favoring a low-wage labor base and limited welfare payments combined with ideology to cement their opposition (Marmor and Rein 1973: 25; Bowler 1974: 124–26; Moynihan 1973: 455–56). The northern, liberal position on FAP, thus, was key. The liberal interest group opposition was led most adamantly by the National Welfare Rights Organization (NWRO), which opposed FAP because the low benefit floor and strong work requirement threatened the status of current northern recipients of welfare. Eventually, other liberal groups who either opposed or significantly tempered their support for the Nixon plan, including Americans for Democratic Action, the Urban League, and the National Association for Advancement of Colored People joined the NWRO. Ultimately, FAP failed in the Senate Finance Committee when three Democratic liberals—Eugene McCarthy (Minn.), Fred Harris (Okla.), and Albert Gore, Sr. (Tenn.)—voted along with the conservative majority against the plan. Most scholars and participants agree that those three votes, influenced by prominent liberal groups, were all that stood in the way of FAP becoming law.

A related interpretation was that moderates were unable to hold the center in the debate, leaving the extreme right and left to coalesce against the reform proposal (Bowler 1974: 147; Teles 1996: 89–94). Salamon (1978: 96) points out that the revised FAP came very close to passing again in the Senate in October of 1972, falling only eight votes short. These eight votes could have easily come from moderates who voted only 40 percent in favor of the revised bill.

Institutional leadership played a part in weakening the center, especially in the Senate. In the House of Representatives, the two conservative leaders of the Ways and Means Committee, Wilbur Mills (D-Ark.) and John Byrnes (R-Wis.), overcame their own ideological views and supported FAP, whereas the party leaders of the Senate Finance Committee, Russell Long (D-La.) and John Williams (R-Del.), did not. Thus, there was little effort from the committee leadership to convince the moderates in the Senate and on the Finance Committee to pass FAP. Moreover, President Nixon and Senate Majority Leader Mike Mansfield (D-Me.) have been criticized for not being effective leaders at crucial moments in the legislative life of FAP (Bowler 1974: 152–56; Salamon 1978: 96). In fact, Nixon's support for his own proposal dwindled considerably as the legislative debate dragged on in Congress.

The Carter plan, despite the complicated two-tiered distinction between those able and those not able to work, fell as a result of the determined conservative and eventual moderate opposition from Democrats and Republicans. PBJI included two provisions, beyond the national guaranteed income, that offended free market conservatives: the creation of 1.4 million public sector jobs and the relaxed income eligibility standards (Anderson 1978). These two provisions made the Carter plan very expensive. At a time when voters in California had just approved Proposition 13 limiting property taxes, many members of Congress, not just free market ideologues, were unwilling to vote additional funds for welfare even if it might improve the system (Weil 1978: 104–5; Coughlin 1980: 128; Lynn and Whitman 1981: 232–43).

Liberals were more unified in their support this time around, but liberalism was a weakening force by the late 1970s—certainly not strong enough to overcome unified conservative and moderate opposition. Ferguson and Rogers (1986: 78–113) demonstrate that, as a result of the economic crisis of the early 1970s, the basic forces among elites were in place by the mid-1970s to move American politics to the right. Edsall (1984) also chronicles the rise of conservatism and the decline of liberalism at this same time.

The demise of PBJI can also be attributed to ineffective, or nonexistent, congressional and presidential leadership (Lynn and Whitman 1981: 238–40). The Carter administration was pushing three major legislative initiatives at once—energy, taxes, and welfare—and sent repeated messages indicating only lukewarm support for action on PBJI. The power of congressional leaders to control legislation was further weakened in the 1970s by the increased dispersion of power to subcommittees. In addition, Congress was reasserting its institutional independence from the executive branch and refused to consider fully the president's long agenda (Leman 1980).

How can these explanations inform our understanding of the passage of the TANF Block Grant? One recent study attempts to apply the lessons of earlier reform efforts to the current debate. Teles (1996) concurs with the earlier interpretations of welfare reform failure, pointing to an elite dissensus as the major factor preventing reform since the 1970s. That is, activist liberals and conservatives coalesced against a compromise policy from the center. He argues that the public has been consistently in favor of reform that offered more equitable standards and payments along with stricter work requirements for welfare recipients. Rather than act on this public consensus, elites have chosen to distort the welfare reform debate for their own political purposes.

Teles, though, does not view the 1996 devolution of welfare responsibility to the states as true welfare reform and, therefore, adamantly rejects the comparison driving this study. He characterizes such "process reform" as an unfortunate but natural consequence of the same elite dissensus over welfare politics that killed the earlier reform efforts.

Teles is correct to identify as noteworthy the different nature of welfare reform in 1996. The earlier reforms would have clearly established a national welfare policy, while the most recent version established broad national changes, passing responsibility for the details to the states. That is, however, precisely the best explanation for the successful passage of this plan in contrast with the failure of previous attempts at comprehensive welfare reform. The block grant plan reflected a strong consensus among both the public and elites. That consensus was for change, but more important, change created at the state and local level. The leaders of the parties and government, as well as significant portions of the activist and scholarly communities, recognized this consensus.

The public clearly favors welfare reform. They want the government to help those in need with the expectation that those able to work will do so in return for the aid. Increasingly, this has meant that the public favors such reforms as time limits, work requirements, and welfare spending limits.[9] Complementing these public views is the preference that many government responsibilities, welfare included, be transferred to the state and local level. Fully two-thirds of those sampled in a 1995 NBC–*Wall Street Journal* poll responded favorably to the following question: "Congress is considering eliminating certain federal spending programs and instead giving funds to state and local governments for them to provide services in those areas. Do you generally favor or oppose this change?" (*National Journal* 1995b: 572) While the question did not specify policy areas, the most prominent policy area in the devolution debate at that time was welfare. Thus, the public has clearly stated in recent years its preference for comprehensive welfare reform to come from the state and local level of government.[10]

More important, elite opinion has also shifted in that direction. While it is more difficult to measure the opinions of elites, conservative activists, excluding some social conservatives, have staked out a position unequivocally for devolving welfare policy responsibility to the states. How else can one account for the near unanimous support given the block grant approach by Republican presidential candidates in the 1996 primaries and by Republicans in the House and Senate?[11]

Even more significant is the increasing support given to devolution by liberals. The governors, acting through the National Governors' Association, have been pushing for greater control of welfare policy for several years, and this includes many Democrats. Rivlin's (1992) book, published by the liberal Brookings Institution, advocating a clearer division of responsibilities between the states and the federal government also indicated a turning point in traditional liberal thought.[12] Finally, the "reinventing government" concept developed by Osborne and Gaebler (1993) and adopted by those calling themselves "New Democrats" included strong elements of decentralization and devolution. Thus, while it remains true that many liberal activists and groups still favor a national welfare policy,[13] enough liberals and moderates have reconsidered the traditional approach so that half of the Democrats in the House and Senate voted in favor of the Personal Responsibility and Work Opportunity Reconciliation Act in 1996.

Some institutional factors can also help account for the passage of comprehensive welfare reform. Newt Gingrich emerged in the 104th Congress as one of the strongest leaders of the House of Representatives in decades, and he was influential in keeping the divisions between social conservatives and moderates from tearing the reform package apart. Similarly, President Clinton played an important leadership role in the welfare reform debate by forcing key changes in the Republican plan and providing political cover for Democrats in Congress who were reluctant to vote for the legislation.

CONCLUSION

Do elections have an impact on policy? In a democracy citizens must influence policy and elections are the means by which that happens. Welfare reform provides an insightful case study of the pitfalls of elections and their potential power over policy. Elections clearly help move issues of importance to the public high onto the policy agenda of government. Reform of AFDC has been on the national policy agenda for most of the past thirty years as a result of national presidential elections. For most of those years, however, reform floundered. The failure of reform is an indication of the high hurdle imposed by the policy process. Factors such as public and elite opinion, ideological divisions, organized interest opposition, and institutional obstacles combined to kill the FAP and the PBJI. But in 1996 a comprehensive welfare reform plan tapped into public and elite consensus, found ideological agreement, faced minimal interest group opposition, and took advantage of favorable institutional leadership. The seemingly never ending story of welfare reform illustrates the difficulty and, ultimately, the great potential that elections have to determine policy.

NOTES

1. This is from Maisel's (1993:1) study of elections and parties in America.

2. For the history of U.S. welfare policy, see Patterson (1981) and Trattner (1984).

3. See the most recent edition of the annual *Background Material and Data on Programs within the Jurisdiction of the Committee on Ways and Means*, popularly known as the *Green Book*, for a description of the AFDC program.

4. Clinton's welfare reform plan introduced in 1994, much like the 1967 WIN program and the 1988 Family Support Act, would have significantly changed the welfare system but left the existing structure intact. For a description of the Clinton plan and its failure in Congress, see Teles (1996).

5. For descriptions of the provisions of the FAP, see *Congress and the Nation*, vol. 3: 622–27; 1970 *Congressional Quarterly Almanac*: 1030–41; and 1971 *Congressional Quarterly Almanac*: 519–26. Descriptions of the proposal, its legislative history and politics can also be found in Allen (1972), Aaron (1973), Marmor and Rein (1973), Moynihan (1973), Burke and Burke (1974), Bowler (1974), and Leman (1980).

6. For descriptions of the provisions of the Program for Better Jobs and Income, see *Congress and the Nation*, vol. 5: V: 679–712; 1977 *Congressional Quarterly Almanac*: 471–78; 1978 Congressional Quarterly Almanac: 600–03; 1979 *Congressional Quarterly Almanac*: 509–11; and Storey et al. (1978). Descriptions of the proposal, its legislative history and politics can also be found in Anderson (1978), Weil (1978), Leman (1980), and Lynn and Whitman (1981).

7. For descriptions of the provisions, legislative history, and politics of the Personal Responsibility and Work Opportunity Act, see Jeffrey L. Katz (1996a, 1996b, 1996c).

8. See the *Gallup Opinion Index*. 1969: 51: 4, for the public support for Nixon's Family Assistance Plan. The public support for Carter's is reported in Lynn and Whitman (1981: 228–31).

9. The *National Journal* (1995a: 508) reported a recent ABC–*Washington Post* poll asking, "Do you favor or oppose a law limiting welfare recipients to a maximum of two years of benefits, after which those who are able to work would have to get a job or do community service?" Ninety-one percent of respondents answered yes. The *National Journal* (1996: 2140) also reported a recent Gallup poll for CNN–*USA Today* that asked, "Which of the following two statements better represents your views

about welfare? Government should limit the amount of money it spends on welfare programs, even if some poor people do not receive assistance, or government should provide a basic amount of assistance to all poor people, even if there are no limits on the amount of money the government spends." Fifty-one percent favored limiting welfare spending, while only 31 percent said there should be no limits on spending.

10. President Clinton's unwillingness to veto the welfare reform legislation is a strong, though unscientific, indicator of the public's support for the block grant approach.

11. Katz (1996c) reports that only two Republicans opposed the conference report, both Cuban-Americans from South Florida who objected to cuts in aid to legal immigrants.

12. In fairness to Rivlin, she called for AFDC to remain a shared state/federal responsibility. However, by proposing that several policy responsibilities be turned back to the states, she did encourage discussion of devolution among other liberals.

13. Edelman (1997) provides a passionate account of the traditional liberal position favoring national welfare policies.

REFERENCES

Aaron, Henry. 1973. *Why Is Welfare So Hard to Reform?* Washington, DC: The Brookings Institution.

Allen, Jodie T. 1972. *A Funny Thing Happened on the Way to Welfare Reform.* Washington, DC: The Urban Institute.

Anderson, Martin. 1978. "Why Carter's Welfare Reform Plan Failed." *Policy Review* 5: 37–39.

Asher, Herbert B. 1992. *Presidential Elections and American Politics: Voters, Candidates, and Campaigns Since 1952.* 5th ed. Belmont, CA: Wadsworth.

Bowler, M. Kenneth. 1974. *The Nixon Guaranteed Income Proposal: Substance and Process in Policy Change.* Cambridge: Ballinger Publishing.

Burke, Vincent J., and Vee Burke. 1974. *Nixon's Good Deed: Welfare Reform.* New York: Columbia University Press.

Congress and the Nation, 1969–1972. 1973, Vol. 3. Washington, DC: Congressional Quarterly Press.

———, 1977–1980. 1981, Vol. 5. Washington, DC: Congressional Quarterly Press.

Congressional Quarterly Almanac. 1970. Washington, DC: Congressional Quarterly Press.

———. 1971. Washington, DC: Congressional Quarterly Press.

———. 1977. Washington, DC: Congressional Quarterly Press.

———. 1978. Washington, DC: Congressional Quarterly Press.

———. 1979. Washington, DC: Congressional Quarterly Press.

Coughlin, Richard M. 1980. *Ideology, Public Opinion, and Welfare Policy Attitudes Toward Taxes and Spending in Industrialized Societies.* Berkeley: Institute for International Studies, University of California at Berkeley.

Edelman, Peter. 1997. "The Worst Thing Bill Clinton Has Done." *The Atlantic Monthly* (March): 43–58.

Edsall, Thomas Byrne. 1984. *The New Politics of Inequality.* New York: W.W. Norton.

Ferguson, Thomas, and Joel Rogers. 1986. *Right Turn: The Decline of the Democrats and the Future of American Politics*. New York: Hill and Wang.

Gallup Opinion Index. 1969. Vol. 51 (September): 4.

Gilder, George. 1981. *Wealth and Poverty*. New York: Basic Books.

Heclo, Hugh. 1986. "The Political Foundations of Antipoverty Policy." In Sheldon H. Danziger and Daniel H. Weinberg, eds., *Fighting Poverty: What Works and What Doesn't*. Cambridge: Harvard University Press.

Katz, Jeffrey L. 1996a. "Conferees May Determine Fate of Overhaul Bill." *Congressional Quarterly Weekly Reports* (July 20).

———. 1996b. "Welfare Showdown Looms As GOP Readies Plan." *Congressional Quarterly Weekly Reports* (July 27).

———. 1996c. "After 60 Years, Most Control Is Passing to States." *Congressional Quarterly Weekly Reports* (August 3).

Leman, Christopher. 1980. *The Collapse of Welfare Reform: Political Institutions, Policy, and the Poor in Canada and the United States*. Cambridge: The MIT Press.

Levitan, Sar A. 1990. *Programs in Aid of the Poor*. 6th ed. Baltimore: Johns Hopkins University Press.

Lynn, Laurence E., Jr., and David Whitman. 1981. *The President as Policymaker: Jimmy Carter and Welfare Reform*. Philadelphia: Temple University Press.

Maisel, L. Sandy. 1993. *Parties and Elections in America: The Electoral Process*. 2nd ed. New York: McGraw-Hill.

Marmor, Theodore R., and Martin Rein. 1973. "Reforming 'the Welfare Mess': The Fate of the Family Assistance Plan, 1969–1972." In Allan P. Sindler, ed., *Policy and Politics in America: Six Case Studies*. Boston: Little, Brown and Company.

Mead, Lawrence. 1992. *The New Politics of Poverty*. New York: Basic Books.

Moynihan, Daniel Patrick. 1973. *The Politics of a Guaranteed Income: The Nixon Administration and the Family Assistance Plan*. New York: Random House.

National Journal. 1995a (February 25): 508.

———. 1995b (March 4): 572.

———. 1996 (October 5): 2140.

Osborne, David, and Ted Gaebler. 1993. *Reinventing Government: How the Entrepreneurial Spirit is Transforming the Public Sector*. New York: Plume.

Patterson, James T. 1981. *America's Struggle Against Poverty, 1900–1980*. Cambridge: Harvard University Press.

Rivlin, Alice. 1992. *Reviving the American Dream: The Economy, the States, and the Federal Government*. Washington, DC: The Brookings Institution.

Salamon, Lester M., ed. 1978. *Welfare: The Elusive Consensus*. New York: Praeger.

Storey, James R., Robert Harris, Frank Levy, Alan Fechter, and Richard C. Michel. 1978. *The Better Jobs and Income Plan: Guide to President Carter's Welfare Reform Proposal and Major Issues*. Washington, DC: The Urban Institute.

Teles, Steven M. 1996. *Whose Welfare? AFDC and Elite Politics*. Lawrence: University Press of Kansas.

Trattner, Walter. 1984. *From Poor Law to Welfare State*. New York: Free Press.

Weil, Gordon L. 1979. *The Welfare Debate of 1978*. White Plains, NY: Institute for Socioeconomic Studies.

16

The Electoral Connection: Public Influence on Policy Output of the United States Supreme Court

Mark Kemper

INTRODUCTION

This article examines how electoral politics can influence the legal policies created by the U.S. Supreme Court. Such an analysis might sound odd to those who have been taught that the Court is an independent branch of the national government largely free from external political influence. After all, Article III of the U.S. Constitution grants the justices life tenure and prohibits the diminution of their salaries. Moreover, one can often view C-Span after a controversial Supreme Court decision and find members of Congress lambasting the Court's rulings and labeling the justices as undemocratic "Platonic Guardians." Indeed, the notion that the Supreme Court is unaccountable to the public via the electoral process is one of the most widely preached political "truths" in American political discourse.

But these views are quite misguided. The Court is not free from external political influence. The actions taken by Congress, the president, agencies in the vast federal bureaucracy, lower court judges, state government officials, and organized interest groups can all exert significant influence on the Supreme Court. And because many of these actors are elected by the public, this means that elections can have a tremendous impact on the policies enunciated by the Court. The voting public can dramatically alter the policies announced by the Supreme Court by electing state and federal officials who will, in an attempt to shape the formation of legal policy, exert pressure on the Court.

But in order to thoroughly understand how elections influence policies enacted by the Court, we need to understand the major criteria that the justices use when they decide how to vote in cases. Therefore, the first section of this article will review the dominant models of Supreme Court policy making. Following this, we will narrow our scope and focus directly on the linkages between public opinion and Supreme Court policy formation. We will develop a model that can be used to conceptualize how electoral politics provide the public with a means of influencing the Court and its policy output. In the third section we will analyze the correspondence between public opinion data and Supreme Court decisions. This analysis should help convince us that the policies handed down by the Court are normally closely aligned with the preferences of the public.

This will take us to the final topic of this article. Certainly one of the most intriguing (yet bedeviling) questions asked by those who study the Court is: "Will the Court's policies become more liberal, conservative, or moderate as we approach the turn of the century?" This issue will be briefly explored at the end of the article. We will analyze the current voting blocs among the justices on the Court, and attempt to gauge how these blocs might shift over the next decade as sitting justices retire and new members are appointed. This analysis will allow us to make some educated "guesses" about whether the Court's policies will change dramatically over this period and, if so, in what direction they might go.

MODELS OF SUPREME COURT DECISION MAKING

Within the field of judicial politics there are essentially three general models that have been used to explain the decision-making process of Supreme Court justices. The first model is the traditional legal model. This model contends that the justices decide cases by objectively evaluating and drawing conclusions from several sources of legal authority. In regard to the U.S. Supreme Court, the sources of legal authority will normally be one of the following: (1) the U.S. Constitution, (2) federal (and sometimes state) statutes, (3) national treaties, and (4) legal precedents.

According to the legal model, the personal preferences of the justices should not affect how they decide cases. Thus, liberal and conservative justices must be able to put aside their personal convictions and attempt to decide cases based on the written law. In this sense, the judicial decision-making process is a mechanical one, and the justices are deemed to exercise no personal discretion. The justices are simply the "conduits" through which the law flows. And, because "the law" is the single factor in the judicial decision-making equation, external stimuli such as the ideological preferences of the president, members of Congress, or the public should not influence case outcomes.

The second model of Supreme Court decision making is known as the attitudinal model. This model has its roots in the legal realist movement of the late nineteenth and early twentieth centuries, a movement that was a full-frontal assault on the traditional legal model. Attitudinalists strongly disagree with the legal model's maxim that the justices simply apply the law to the facts in legal disputes. Indeed, proponents of attitudinalism note that we should be skeptical of claims made by judges when they assert that they are merely applying legal rules and not their own personal predilections. As Shapiro (1994: 156) boldly asserts:

> Courts have decided, however, in all of the societies that have a modern judicial system, to avoid the appearance of deciding cases based on judicial whim. . . . [I]n all modern societies, and in all cases, judges tell the loser: 'You did not lose because we the judges chose that you should lose. You lost because the law required that you should lose.' That is the answer arrived at to satisfy the losers through hundreds of years of experimentation in numerous societies. This paradox means that although every court makes law in a few of its cases, judges must always deny that they make law. . . . That makes courts part of a distinctive subset of political institutions: one that must always deny that they are wielding political authority when they in fact *do* wield political authority. Such is the nature of courts. They must always deny their authority to make law, even when they are making law. One may call this justificatory history, but I call it lying. Courts and judges always lie. Lying is the nature of the judicial activity. (italics in original)

According to the attitudinal model, the fundamental goal sought by members of the Supreme Court is to promote legal policy that is consistent with their personal policy preferences (Segal and Spaeth 1993). To accomplish this task, proponents of the attitudinal model argue that the justices cast sincere votes when they decide cases. Casting a sincere vote simply means that justices cast votes so that the policy outcomes of cases are at their respective ideological ideal points (those points at which the satisfaction they derive from the policy is maximized). As a result, liberal justices will cast votes for liberal policies, moderate justices for moderate policies, and conservative justices for conservative policies.

The attitudinal theory posits that members of the Court are able to cast sincere votes for several reasons (Rohde and Spaeth 1976). First, the justices have life tenure and their salaries cannot be decreased during their stay in office. Second, supporters of the attitudinal model argue that the justices have no ambition to attain a higher office. A seat on the Supreme Court represents the pinnacle of a legal career and allows one to exercise great influence in the political system. Consequently, unlike lower court judges, Supreme Court justices have no reason to compromise their ideological beliefs (by casting votes for legal policies they do not like) in an effort to placate other actors (e.g., voters, executives, legislators) who have the authority to elevate them to some higher position in the political system.

A third reason the justices are able to cast sincere votes is that the primary sources of legal authority (e.g., the U.S. Constitution, federal statutes and treaties, and judicial precedents) are in many instances written in broad and majestic strokes. For example, the phrase "due process of law" found in the Fifth and Fourteenth Amendments is quite ambiguous in its meaning; similarly, judicial precedents often can be easily distinguished from subsequent cases that come to the Court, thus allowing the justices to establish legal policy in a manner relatively unconstrained from earlier decisions. Thus, because the legal materials relied upon by the justices when they decide cases are so spacious in their construction and ambiguous in their guidance, they are provided with a significant amount of discretion during the decision-making process. The net result is that the justices will be able to reach whatever legal policy results they prefer in their decisions.

Finally, the attitudinal model contends that the justices are able to cast sincere votes because they sit on the highest court in the land. Thus, unlike lower court judges, members of the Supreme Court do not have to tailor their decisions so that they comply with the legal dictates of a higher tribunal. Because there is no danger of being reversed by another court, the justices are able to create legal policy as they see fit. In the hierarchy of justice within the American political system, the "buck stops" at the U.S. Supreme Court.

The third and final model of judicial decision making is known as the rational choice model (Epstein and Knight 1998). The rational choice approach does not challenge the attitudinal model's assertion that the *main* goal of the justices is to design legal policy consistent with their ideological preferences. On this point the two models are in perfect agreement. Nevertheless, the models differ in their description of how the justices attempt to maximize their policy satisfaction when they decide cases.

According to advocates of the rational choice model, the attitudinal model fails to accurately describe the behavior of Supreme Court justices because it portrays the justices as unsophisticated policy maximizers who always cast sincere votes. In contrast, the rational choice model contends that judges are more sophisticated in their behavior. In particular, the model posits that the justices are strategic actors who might, under certain circumstances, seek to create legal policies that are *not* at their respective ideological ideal points. In other words, the rational choice model argues that members of the Court will not always vote based on their sincere preferences.

The rational choice model contends that members of the Court are often compelled to act strategically because there are many external constraints on the Court. For example, the model points out that the Constitution creates a separation-of-powers system in which the three coordinate branches of the national government share overlapping control. This sharing of power allows the political branches to challenge the Court in a variety of ways (Epstein and Knight 1998). For example, Congress and the president can work together to pass legislation that does any or all of the following: increase or decrease the number of members on the Court; restrict the Court's appellate jurisdiction; freeze the justices' salaries or cut the Court's operating budget; overturn a statutory decision of the Court. Similarly, Congress can attempt to impeach a member of the Court or propose a constitutional amendment, and the executive branch can refuse to implement a decision of the Court. Finally, the numerous lower federal courts can make life difficult for the Supreme Court if they choose to resist that institution's legal policies. Because these lower courts decide the vast majority of all legal disputes in the federal judicial system (of which 99.9 percent never reach the Supreme Court), the justices will want to make sure they do not create policies that unnecessarily cause tension between the Supreme Court and lower federal tribunals.

These external checks on the Supreme Court indicate that the other branches of the national government and lower federal courts have the potential to exert real influence on the Court's members. Indeed, some of the more powerful checks allow other political actors to actually overturn a policy of the Court. Given this scenario, the justices might realize that casting sincere votes for their most preferred policies could result in outcomes that, in the long run, are *worse* than would have been the case if they had "compromised" and voted for less desirable policies when they initially decided the cases. Indeed, few things could be worse for members of the Court than to adopt a policy that brings maximum policy satisfaction, only to see the political branches respond by overturning that policy and replacing it with one that brings the justices very little satisfaction. As a result, it is rational for the justices to act strategically and adopt policies that are as close as possible to their preferred policy positions, yet that do not lie unduly far from the ideological preferences of the political branches so as to trigger a detrimental response from those branches.

Thus, the rational choice model depicts the Court as an institution comprised of individuals who carefully scan the national political horizon before they decide cases; the justices are considered to have a powerful incentive in many instances to gauge the prevailing political winds that periodically gust through the nation's capital. But the model can also be readily applied to the federalist structure established by the Constitution. Indeed, the model predicts that the justices will alter their decision-making behavior as the ideological preferences of state actors change. After all, members of the Court might fear that state actors will refuse to implement decisions of the Court if the policies of those decisions are significantly distant from the policies preferred by state officials. If the Court adopts policies considered intolerable to state officials, then these actors may attempt to drastically shift policy away from the Court's preferred position during the implementation process. In order to prevent this, the justices will attempt to decide cases so that legal policy is tolerable to state officials, with the hope that those actors will then be more inclined to faithfully implement the Court's decisions.

Finally, the rational choice model maintains that the Court will be sensitive to the overall preferences of the public. After all, many scholars of the Court have argued that high levels of public support for the Court are essential if it wants to have its decisions followed by other political actors. In particular, elected officials will hesitate to challenge Court decisions that they personally dislike if the public is largely supportive of the policy results in those decisions. Consequently, in order to protect its legitimacy in the eyes of the public, the Court might modify policy away from its ideal point so that it is closer to the aggregate preferences of the body politic.

This concludes our discussion of the three models of Supreme Court decision making. We have seen that, according to the legal model, legal policy should remain relatively static over time since the justices only rely on the existing sources of legal authority when they decide cases. In contrast, the attitudinal model contends that legal factors are not important in the decision-making process. Instead, the attitudes of the justices drive how they vote. Thus, for this model, legal change is largely a product of changes in the ideological preferences of the Court's members. Finally, the rational choice model argues that the justices will—as the attitudinal model suggests—strive to accomplish their policy goals. However, in doing so, the justices will be sensitive to external political forces and will decide cases so as to maximize their policy satisfactions over the long run. Thus, a mix of the justices' personal policy preferences and the Court's external political environment will dictate the extent of legal change.

THE IMPACT OF ELECTIONS

Without a doubt, there is a "connection" between the Supreme Court and the preferences of the public. The connection comes in two types. First, the discussion of the rational choice model clearly demonstrates that as the preferences of actors in state and national institutions change, or as the public's overall opinion shifts, the justices may be more (or less) able to decide cases so that legal policy is at their most preferred locations. For example, as the public and political elites become more liberal in their views, then a liberal Supreme Court will—all things being equal—find it easier to enact policies that its members find acceptable. In such a scenario, the justices will be operating in a political environment that facilitates their quest to enact their most preferred policies.

This indicates that the public can have a meaningful direct and indirect impact on the Court's policies. After all, the Court will be responding to the preferences of the public (direct effect) and to the preferences of political elites (indirect effect) who represent the public. Because the Court is sensitive to political elites, and because the public is responsible for selecting those individuals, the public has an indirect means of influencing the Court's output. In short, the public's ability to elect state and national officers provides it with an important mechanism to hold the Court indirectly accountable.

But there is an even more important *electoral* connection between the public and the Court. As we saw when discussing the attitudinal and rational

choice models, both approaches posit that members of the Court will attempt
to maximize their policy views. The attitudinalists contend that the justices
take a short-term, nearsighted approach, whereas the rational choice theorists
contend that the justices take a more long-term, farsighted perspective. Nevertheless, both models are in agreement that the attitudes of the justices will exert tremendous influence on their behavior when they decide cases. In short,
the policy of the Court will closely track the ideological values of the Court's
membership.

This means that the selection of justices will have important ramifications
on the Court's policy output. Nearly all scholars of the American political system agree that elected officials attempt to appoint members to the Supreme
Court who share their political ideology (Abraham 1992; Segal and Spaeth
1993). Presidents and senators are wily politicians who realize that they can
have a lasting legacy by appointing individuals to the Supreme Court who
share their ideological beliefs. Consequently, we should expect that the
Court's policy output will dovetail nicely with the policy preferences of elected
officials and the citizenry who elect those officials (Dahl 1957).

Perhaps the model portrayed in Figure 16.1 will clarify our discussion up to
this point. The model is designed to depict how decisions of the Supreme
Court can be influenced by the public. The model attempts to incorporate all
of the major factors identified in the judicial politics literature that influence
the decision-making process of the justices. Obviously, as the model indicates,

Figure 16.1
Public Influence on Supreme Court Decisions

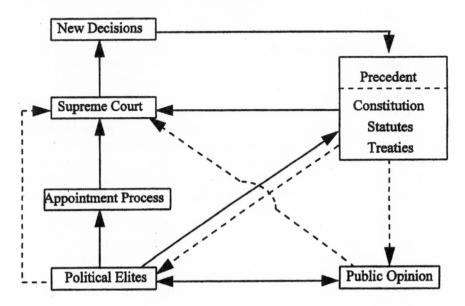

there are several pathways through which the preferences of the public are felt by the Court (the solid lines indicate stronger linkages than the dotted lines). Let's briefly discuss the model.

As noted, the legal model posits that the justices will cast votes that are consistent with legitimate sources of legal authority. In Figure 16.1 these sources are captured in the box that contains precedent, the Constitution, statutes, and treaties. At any point in time, one could consider these items to represent the legal policy status quo. If the justices adhere to the doctrine of *stare decisis* and the other facets of the traditional legal model, then the legal policy status quo should have a powerful impact on the outcome of later decisions.

However, as the Court decides new cases, the legal policy status quo will inevitably be altered. In particular, the mix of precedents in the box will have been changed, for now there will be new precedents added to the collection of previous decisions. Of course, if these new precedents are consistent with older precedents, one could safely argue that they will not significantly—if at all—alter the overall status of existing legal policy. However, if these new decisions are departures from earlier precedents (e.g., perhaps they overruled one or more of the existing precedents), one could persuasively contend that the state of legal policy has been altered. This means that if we are to understand legal policy change that is instigated by the Supreme Court, we need to understand those factors that shape the policies contained in decisions where the justices chose *not* to rely on existing case law.

As noted earlier, both the attitudinal and rational choice models contend that the policy preferences of the justices will be important factors that influence their decisions. These determinants are captured in the box labeled Supreme Court in Figure 16.1. It is at this point that we can consider the impact of elections on the Court. First, the model in Figure 16.1 indicates that political elites (e.g., members of Congress, the president, organized interest groups) will shape the attitudes of the justices through the appointment process. In this way, the mass public can have a very real impact on the Supreme Court when it goes to the polls in elections and chooses individuals for public office. Indeed, a Republican president and a Republican-controlled Senate will probably nominate and confirm justices who have attitudes that are quite different from those who would be appointed to the Court by Democrats. Moreover, the citizenry can also choose to participate in or financially support organized interest groups, and these groups can play a prominent role in the appointment process (Caldeira and Wright 1998). In short, democratic politics provide the public with several meaningful avenues to influence the appointment of Supreme Court justices.

But the model also indicates that the Court will be influenced by political elites in two other important ways besides the appointment process. First, political elites can write new statutes and treaties or alter the U.S. Constitution (only the Court can create judicial precedent, thus explaining the dotted line in Figure 16.1). Because these actions will alter the legitimate sources of legal authority, they can have tremendous consequences on Supreme Court policy. More important, political elites can directly influence the Court since the justices will, according to the rational choice model, be sensitive to the preferences of these actors. As the rational choice model argues, justices will scan the political terrain and attempt to design legal policies that are tolerable to political elites.

The model also indicates that public opinion might directly influence the Court's decisions. A number of scholars have tested for such effects and have concluded that the Court does seem to follow public opinion (Mishler and Sheehan 1993; cf. Norpoth and Segal 1994). However, the direct influence of public opinion on the Court certainly pales in comparison to the indirect influence that the public exerts via the election of political elites.

Finally, the model in Figure 16.1 indicates that legal policy enunciated by the Court may influence both political elites and members of the public (the model also indicates that political elites can influence members of the public). As the Court decides new cases that alter the existing legal order, political elites and the public might evaluate the Court's decisions and conclude that it is correct. In other words, the preferences of political elites and the public might be, in some small way, shaped by the Court. Although the evidence supporting such an effect is limited (Franklin and Kosaki 1989), it is a possibility that one should keep in mind when considering the relationship between the public and the Court.

TRENDS IN PUBLIC OPINION AND SUPREME COURT POLICY

So far we have discussed the possible linkages between the public and the Court, and have concluded that the strongest linkages are those fostered by the electoral process. However, we have not analyzed any empirical data to determine whether there is a close relationship between the preferences of the public and the Court's policy output. The data provided in Figure 16.2 are designed to address this deficiency. The solid line is a standardized measure of the percentage of civil liberties cases decided in a liberal direction by the Court during each term between 1952 and 1996. The dotted line is a standardized measure of the public's ideological mood based on public opinion polls conducted between 1952 and 1996 (Stimson 1998). The chart is constructed so that higher scores represent more liberal positions than lower scores.

Figure 16.2 depicts how the policies announced by the Supreme Court have, during most years, tracked quite nicely with the preferences of the public. Indeed, the data indicate that the Court has rarely been significantly out of step with the public. Beginning in the late 1950s, both the public and the Court became more liberal in their positions. This propensity for liberal policies peaked in the mid-1960s, and then began drifting downward until about 1980, at which point both the Court and the public were substantially more

Figure 16.2
Time Series of Supreme Court Policy and Public Mood, 1952–1996 Terms

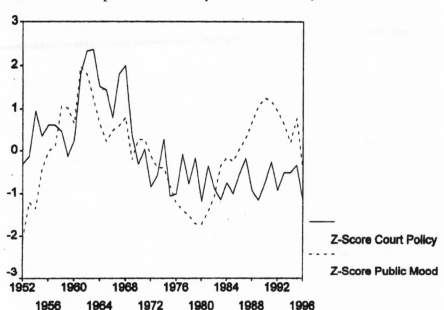

This data for the 1953–1994 terms was taken from Table 3-8 Epstein et al. (1996). The data for the
   1995–1996 terms was taken from the USSC Judicial Database (Spaeth 1998). Civil liberties
   cases contain all of the following issues: free speech, free press, religion, criminal, equal
   protection, privacy, and attorney discipline.

conservative. However, during the 1980s the public and the Court drifted
apart. The public became more liberal during this period, while the Court remained relatively stable at a fairly conservative position. By the mid-1990s,
though, the public and the Court once again have converged as the public has
become more conservative in its ideological leanings.

The results in Figure 16.2 support the thesis that the public has had a tremendous impact upon the policy output of the Supreme Court. The bulk of
this influence was probably exercised through the appointment of new justices
(Norpoth and Segal 1994). For example, the liberal appointments to the
Court made by Eisenhower, Kennedy, and Johnson resulted in a Court that
matched the liberalism of the public during the early and middle 1960s. However, as the public's liberalism faded in the late 1960s, the Court's policies also
became more conservative. This, most likely, was the result of the four conservative appointments made by President Richard Nixon. The election of Ronald Reagan and Senate Republicans in 1980 came on the heels of the
conservative 1970s, and so new appointments made to the Court during the
1980s made it difficult for that institution to adjust its policies and follow the

public in a more liberal direction. The result was a fairly wide gap between the Court and the public throughout the 1980s. However, the election of the moderate Democrat Bill Clinton in 1992, coupled with a decline in the public's liberalism, has once again resulted in a Court that is making policy more closely in tune with the public's desires.

But the close relationship between the public's preferences and Court policy could also be the result of external political pressure that is unrelated to the appointment of new members. For example, political elites might have pressured the Court to adopt policies that the elites found acceptable. And, because elites are elected, they would probably be pressuring for policies that the public also considers desirable. Moreover, the public might have had an effect on the Court independent of that exerted through political elites and the appointment process. Members of the Court are also members of society, and they certainly pay close attention to the current mores and values of the citizenry. Indeed, Chief Justice Rehnquist (1987: 40) has written that "[j]udges, so long as they are relatively normal human beings, can no more escape being influenced by public opinion in the long run than can people working at other jobs." Thus, one would expect that the justices will in many situations adopt policies that are not too distant from those the public considers appropriate.

The crux of this cursory analysis of trends in public opinion and Supreme Court decisions is that the public's attitudes certainly can and probably do influence the Court's policy output. Precisely how that occurs is complicated. Indeed, when evaluating the potential public-Court linkages by analyzing the correspondence between public opinion and the Court's policies, one should take Caldeira's (1991: 314) warning very seriously. He writes: "Congruence tells us only of a similarity between policy and opinion; it tells us nothing about the mechanisms that brought about this state of affairs. Ultimately, we want to unravel the causal linkages between our political institutions and public opinion."

With this warning in mind, I would argue that the most dominant public influence on the Court's policy is that exerted through the replacement of its members. After all, if judges are policy maximizers, then changing the mix of preferences held by the Court's membership will undoubtedly alter the state of existing legal policy. And, as we have seen, the public has a significant amount of control over who those new appointments will be.

However, one should not discount the effect that the public can have on the policy output of the Supreme Court in the absence of new appointments. If the justices are strategic actors who attempt to tailor their policies so as to maximize their long-term goals, then alterations in the policy preferences held by political elites in the wake of elections will surely have important ramifications on legal policy. The moral of the story is that the public has much more control over the actions taken by members of the Court than is commonly realized. Indeed, Mr. Dooley's succinct but profound statement that the Supreme Court "follows th' iliction returns" (Dunne 1938) seems to be right on target. And, given that we live in a representative democracy, maybe that is not such a bad thing.

SUPREME COURT POLICY BEYOND 2000

Where can we expect the legal policies of the Court to go as we approach the next millennium? Well, although forecasting the direction of future Court policy is a hazardous enterprise (Baum 1992), this is an intriguing question. In order to provide an answer, however, we need to examine the nature of policies currently emanating from the Court (see Figure 16.2), the voting blocs among sitting justices, and, finally, the potential impact of new appointments.

To examine the current voting blocs on the Court, I performed a multidimensional scaling analysis of all votes cast in all orally argued cases decided during the Court's 1994–1997 terms. This technique uses the votes to compute "distances" in two-dimensional space between the justices. Those justices who often vote in the same manner (e.g., they either both cast votes with the majority or they both cast dissenting votes) will be placed closer to one another in the two-dimensional space; in contrast, those justices who vote in different ways (e.g., one votes with the majority while the other dissents, or vice versa) will be placed farther apart.

The results of the dimensional analysis are presented in Figure 16.3. The findings indicate that there are basically two blocs of justices on the Court that are clearly separated along one major dimension (Dimension 1). First, Justices

Figure 16.3
Multidimensional Scaling of Justices' Votes, 1994–1997 Terms

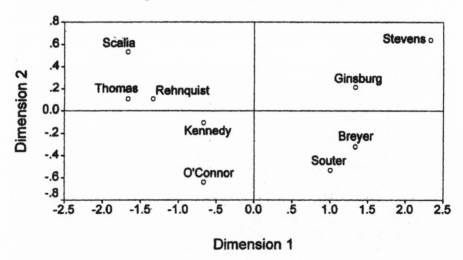

Data for 1994–1996 terms from USSC Judicial Database (Spaeth 1998). Data for 1997 term collected by author.

Thomas, Scalia, Rehnquist, Kennedy, and O'Connor frequently vote together and, thus, are very close to one another on dimension one. Because these justices cast mostly conservative votes, they clearly form a solid conservative voting bloc on the Court. In contrast, Justices Ginsburg, Stevens, Breyer, and Souter are fairly close to one another and tend to represent the Court's moderate-liberal bloc.

The second dimension more precisely separates the justices from one another according to their votes. It indicates that a simple liberal-conservative dimension does not perfectly capture the justices' voting behavior. For example, Justices O'Connor and Souter are equally distant on dimension two from Justices Scalia and Stevens. However, because dimension two explains much less of the variation in the justices' voting patterns than does dimension one, it is of much less interest. Dimension two simply indicates that, among both the liberal and conservative camps, the justices vary from one another in subtle and interesting ways.

To estimate the likely change in the Court's policies over the next few years, one needs to know which justices are likely to depart the Court—either through retirement or death. On average, a seat will become vacant on the Court every two years. But this is only an average, and one can readily identify instances throughout U.S. history when there were significant deviations from this average. In any case, many Court watchers believe that Justices Rehnquist and Stevens are the most likely to leave the bench. Justice Rehnquist and Stevens are seventy-four and seventy-eight years old, respectively, and both justices have had minor health problems. A less likely prospect for departure—but certainly a real possibility—is Justice O'Connor. Justice O'Connor is sixty-eight years old and has also suffered from some health problems over the past several years.

How might the Court's policy output change if any or all of these three justices leave the Court over the next decade? To estimate this one is forced to speculate on the probable ideology of their replacements, something that hinges squarely on electoral politics. If, for example, Chief Justice Rehnquist were to resign during the presidency of Bill Clinton, and the Senate remained in the hands of the Republican party, we would likely see an individual appointed to the Court with ideological views very similar to Justices Ginsburg and Breyer. The result of such a transaction would be a Court that would probably produce slightly more liberal policy pronouncements. If, however, Justice Stevens retired (which is probably more likely) and a Ginsburg-Breyer–like justice was appointed to replace him, the Court would probably become slightly more conservative. If both Chief Justice Rehnquist and Stevens were to retire, then we would probably end up with a Court that is, overall, more centrist in its position. After all, Rehnquist and Stevens would probably be replaced by two justices who would have ideological beliefs very similar to Clinton's other two appointments, Justices Ginsburg and Breyer.

In any event, given the current composition of the Court, it is unlikely that the Court's policies will change drastically any time soon. Only if Rehnquist, Stevens, and O'Connor were replaced en masse with either archconservatives or archliberals would the Court's policy output shift appreciably. That, however, is an unlikely scenario. Indeed, as Figure 16.2 indicates, the mood of the public is currently quite moderate in its ideological temperament (although it appears to be becoming more conservative). Thus, it is unlikely that political elites will be able to appoint ideological extremists to the Court in the near future. However, if the public's ideological mood abruptly shifts and becomes either more conservative or more liberal, and the citizenry elect more ideologically extreme political elites to match its preferences, then the Court might alter its policy direction (particularly if political elites have the opportunity to appoint several new members to the Court). Only time will tell the answer to this question, but, in the meantime, the best prediction would be that the Court will continue to follow a moderately conservative course and be deferential to the legal policy status quo.

CONCLUSION

This article has examined how electoral politics in America can shape the formation of policy on the United States Supreme Court. In doing so, we reviewed the major models of judicial decision making, highlighting how these models provide avenues for the public to influence the Court. In particular, we noted how political elites can shape legal policy by writing new statutes, amending the Constitution, revising treaties, refusing to implement Court decisions, or by overtly attacking the Court by cutting its budget or limiting its appellate jurisdiction. Second, political elites can appoint new members to the Court as justices depart, and thus attempt to shape the ideological preferences of the Court's membership.

In short, because of the tremendous leverage over the Court that is granted to political elites by our nation's constitutional structure, the Court is indirectly accountable to the public. Political elites are directly accountable to the public, and the Court is powerfully influenced by political elites. Sure, the public might be able in some instances to exert direct influence on the Court (and vice versa), but the strongest Court-public link is that provided by the election of political elites. Thus, those who bemoan that the Supreme Court is a collection of Platonic guardians who manipulate public policy according to their own desires are quite misguided. While the Court may not be as accountable to the public as, say, Congress and the president, it is still a fairly "democratic" institution. In other words, there is truly an electoral connection between the Court and the American people. While this might be shocking and troubling to some, it should not alarm intrepid democrats who believe that the governed ought to wield significant control over their governors.

REFERENCES

Abraham, Henry. 1992. *Justices and Presidents*. 3d ed. New York: Oxford University Press.

Baum, Lawrence. 1992. "On the Unpredictability of the Supreme Court." *PS: Political Science and Politics* 25: 683–88.

Caldeira, Gregory A. 1991. "Courts and Public Opinion." In John B. Gates and Charles A. Johnson, eds., *The American Courts: A Critical Assessment*. Washington, DC: Congressional Quarterly Press.

Caldeira, Gregory A., and John R. Wright. 1998. "Lobbying for Justice: Organized Interests, Supreme Court Nominations, and the United States Supreme Court." *American Journal of Political Science* 42, 2: 499–523.

Dahl, Robert A. 1957. "Decision-Making in a Democracy: The Supreme Court as a National Policy-Maker." *Journal of Public Law* 6: 279–95.

Dunne, F.P. 1938. *Mr. Dooley at His Best*. New York: Charles Scribner's Sons.

Epstein, Lee, and Jack Knight. 1998. *The Choices Justices Make*. Washington, DC: Congressional Quarterly Press.

Epstein, Lee, Jeffrey A. Segal, Harold J. Spaeth, and Thomas G. Walker. 1996. *The Supreme Court Compendium: Data, Decisions, Development*. Washington, DC: Congressional Quarterly Press.

Franklin, Charles H., and Liane C. Kosaki. 1989. "Republican Schoolmaster: The U.S. Supreme Court, Public Opinion, and Abortion." *American Political Science Review* 83: 751–71.

Mayhew, David. R. 1974. *Congress: The Electoral Connection*. New Haven: Yale University Press.

Mishler, William, and Reginald S. Sheehan. 1993. "The Supreme Court as a Counter-majoritarian Institution? The Impact of Public Opinion on Supreme Court Decisions." *American Political Science Review* 87: 87–101.

Norpoth, Helmut, and Jeffrey A. Segal. 1994. "Popular Influence on Supreme Court Decisions." *American Political Science Review* 88: 711–16.

Rehnquist, William H. 1987. *The Supreme Court: How It Was, How It Is*. New York: William Morrow.

Rohde, David W., and Harold J. Spaeth. 1976. *Supreme Court Decision Making*. San Francisco: W.H. Freeman.

Rosenberg, Gerald N. 1991. *The Hollow Hope: Can Courts Bring About Social Change?* Chicago: University of Chicago Press.

Segal, Jeffrey A., and Harold J. Spaeth. 1993. *The Supreme Court and the Attitudinal Model*. Cambridge: Cambridge University Press.

Shapiro, Martin. 1994. "Judges as Liars." *Harvard Journal of Law and Public Policy* 17: 155–56.

Stimson, James. 1998. Personal Homepage: www.unc.edu/~jstimson/time.html

PART THREE

RETHINKING ELECTION THEORIES AND PRACTICES

We have learned in Part One how American elections are conducted and the major influences on them, and have seen specific instances of the force of elections on public policies (but also of their non-effect) in Part Two. In conclusion, we turn in Part Three to an examination of electoral reform, perhaps the headiest topic of our study because it is the most unpredictable.

We have the work of five scholars to assist us in this pursuit, led off by Michael Lynch who, in his "The Myth of the Mandate," invites us to rethink our interpretation of elections based on an examination of what is (and what is not) in the minds of voters when they go to the polls.

Dennis Anderson then proposes a most dramatic change, replacing our system of electing only one legislator per district via plurality decision (the so-called "single-member district" system) with proportional representation, or multiple-member districts, with representatives chosen proportionally to the vote.

Everett Carll Ladd, in turn, takes a more cautious approach, calling our electoral system "not broken, but in need of prudent repair." Yet, for all of his caution, Ladd offers some novel and enticing proposals for change, both in campaign financing and in the way television presents candidates.

The theory and history of "political realignments" (dramatic and sudden political and policy shifts) get extended treatment in Daniel Shea's piece, in which he questions whether such realignments and their salutary results are any longer possible given recent developments in American politics.

Finally, Gerald Pomper offers the intriguing possibility, based on recent data, that American government, long regarded as a "presidential system," may be evolving into "parliamentary government" and what that evolution may signify for the effect elections will have on American public policy as we enter a new millennium.

Taken together, these articles encourage us to think deeply and creatively about our democracy, and to search for ways to improve it.

17

The Mandate Myth: Why Presidential Elections Are Not Public Policy Plebiscites

Michael E. Lynch, Sr.

Postmortems of American elections frequently contend that the outcome has provided the victorious candidate with a "mandate" (Kelly 1983: 126). The mandate thesis contends that "a clear majority of the voters prefer the winner because they prefer his policies and wish him to pursue his policies" (Dahl 1990: 361–62)—that is, that an electoral victory constitutes a manifestation of the electorate's "support for a political program" (Plano and Greenberg 1993: 82). Claims of mandates posit the superficially democratic notion that the *vox populi* has spoken via the election, both empowering and obliging the victor to implement the policies upon which she/he stood for (re)election. Thus, the mandate concept rationalizes victors' attempts to implement their public policy agendas.

Victorious candidates and their political parties routinely lay claim to mandates. Of his 1972 victory Richard Nixon told Americans "your votes were a mandate" (Kelly 1983: 99). Transmitting his Fiscal Year 1982–83 budget to Congress President Reagan admonished "members of Congress to remember that last November the American people's message was loud and clear. The mandate for change expressed by the American people was not my mandate; it was our mandate" (Cowan 1981). House Speaker Newt Gingrich interpreted Republican victories in the 1994 congressional elections as a mandate for his Contract with America. Journalists reiterate the mandate myth. In November

1994 Charles Krauthammer wrote of the "Republican Mandate" in the *Washington Post* (Krauthammer, *Washington Post* 1994: A31) and a November 1988 upstate New York newspaper headline read "Expert: Bush Has a Mandate from the People" (*The Daily Star* 1988). Even some scholars perpetuate the myth, for example, the *Dictionary of American Government and Politics* states, "U.S. Presidents who win elections by overwhelming majorities may rightfully feel the vote is a mandate to carry out their proposed policies" (Shafritz 1988: 340).

Despite the frequency with which mandates are claimed, scholars in the field of American voting behavior generally agree that the notion of an electoral mandate is specious. Fifty years of empirical research by political scientists has discredited the mandate thesis to the point that it is aptly termed a "myth"— an illusionary "fiction or half-truth . . . that forms part of the ideology of a society" (*American Heritage Dictionary* 1982: 827).

Scholars generally agree on a set of preconditions for an electoral policy mandate. First, voters must be both knowledgeable and concerned about an issue or set of issues. Second, candidates and/or parties must take clearly distinguishable positions on the issue(s). Third, the electorate must accurately perceive candidates' stands on the issue(s) (Flanigan and Zingale 1998: 187). Fourth, voters must be prospectively concerned with future policy, not retrospectively evaluating past policies. Fifth, the position of the majority of the electorate on specific policy questions must be ascertainable (Pomper and Lederman 1980: 212). In short, there is no potential for an electoral mandate unless the candidates have taken clearly distinguishable prospective stances on public policy issues, the public accurately perceives these stances and, in turn, cast their ballots prospectively, based upon the issues (Hill and Luttbeg 1983: 39).

A number of scholars agree that these preconditions are not "substantially satisfied" in American elections (Pomper and Lederman 1980: 212). This piece will explain *why* and *how* these preconditions are not met and, consequently, why the electoral mandate is only mythical in the United States.

THE PROBLEM OF NONVOTERS

In a majoritarian democracy a policy mandate requires the concurrence of more than 50 percent of the eligible electorate. In the United States the "nonvoter problem"—low voter turnout—presents an insurmountable problem in this regard. Presidential elections garner the highest turnout of any American popular elections. However, even in these "high stimulus" elections, turnout has generally hovered between some 52 and 62 percent of the eligible electorate over the past six and one-half decades (Luttbeg and Gant 1995: 94; Flanigan and Zingale 1998: 33), dipping to a forty-four-year low of 48.5 percent in 1996 (Ladd 1997: 5). Figure 17.1 portrays voter turnout in the seventeen presidential elections.

Figure 17.1
Voter Turnout, 1932–1996

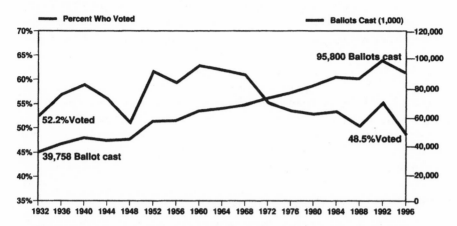

Source: Ladd, Everett C. "The Status-quo Election: Introduction," *The Public Perspective: A Roper Center Review of Public Opinion and Polling*, Volume 8, Number 1 (December/January 1997): 5.

These survey-based percentages even exaggerate turnout because some respondents report having voted when they did not do so. Such distortion is commonly attributed to "social desirability response-set bias" wherein respondents are uncomfortable admitting that they are not in conformity with prevailing social norms. Thus, either consciously or subconsciously, some seek to make themselves "look good" by falsely reporting that they voted (Alreck and Settle 1985: 112). Silver et al. reinforce this, observing that "respondents most inclined to overreport their voting are . . . those most supportive of the regime norm of voting and those to whom voting is the most salient" (Silver et al. 1986: 616).

The U.S. Census Survey data exaggerated presidential election turnout in 1992, but less than did the National Election Study (NES) survey conducted by the Survey Research Center (SRC) at the University of Michigan. The NES survey reported that 75 percent of the eligible electorate voted; the Census Survey recorded 61.3 percent turnout; official election records placed turnout at only 55 percent (Luttbeg and Gant 1995: 93). For 1996, Abramson et al. (1998: 69) reported 49 percent turnout and the SRC data, a 77 percent turnout. Similarly, Silver et al. observe that SRC data overestimated voter turnout in 1964, 1976, 1978, and 1980 by 27.4 percent, 31.4 percent, 22.6 percent, and 27.4 percent, respectively (Silver et al. 1988: 616).

With voter turnout ranging from 63 percent to 35 percent of the eligible electorate, victorious candidates routinely garner the support of far less than 50 percent of the eligible electorate. Victors cannot legitimately claim mandates because no majority has spoken. Voter turnout in congressional elections is invariably below that of presidential elections (Luttbeg and Gant 1995: 94; Flanigan and Zingale 1998: 36; Abramson 1994: 103). Figure 17.2 depicts voter turnout in both presidential and congressional elections since 1870. The 36 percent turnout for the 1998 congressional election was the lowest since 1942 (Wayne 1998). A member of Congress cannot claim an electoral mandate when "even a majority of voters would not include a majority of the total of the (district's) adult population" (Pomper and Lederman 1980: 214). Low voter turnout debunks the mandate thesis because the fifth precondition previously cited, ascertaining the position of the majority of the eligible voters, is not met. In this context Polsby and Wildavsky ask, "Is it right to ignore the multitudes who do not vote and whose preferences are not registered?" (Polsby and Wildavsky 1996: 318).

NONIDEOLOGICAL POLITICAL PARTIES

The nature of the American two-party system is among numerous additional reasons for casting aside the mandate myth. The American party system is nonideological in nature. Both major parties are parties of moderation, situated more toward the middle of the ideological spectrum than its extremities.

They have long been criticized by some for being too similar, an argument classically presented in the American Political Science Association's *Toward a*

Figure 17.2
Turnout of Eligible Voters in Presidential and Congressional Elections, 1868–1996

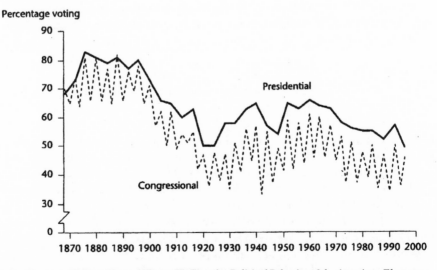

Source: Flanigan, William H., and Nancy H. Zingale. *Political Behavior of the American Electorate*, 9th edition. Washington, D.C., Congressional Quarterly, 1998: 36.

More Responsible Two-Party System (Committee on Political Parties 1950: 1). Rabid critics of this similarity might well label the two major American parties "tweedle dumb" and "tweedle dumber." The criticism concludes that political parties that do not offer sharply contrasting policy alternatives render it virtually impossible for the American electorate to cast issue-based votes. *Toward a More Responsible Two-Party System* contends that the two major political parties are not sufficiently ideologically separated to "provide the electorate with a proper range of choice between alternatives of [*sic*] action" (Committee on Political Parties 1950: 1). As Nie, Verba, and Petrocik write, even "citizens with issue positions cannot vote those positions unless they are given a choice" (Nie et al. 1976: 163).

So-called revisionist studies of American voting behavior hold political parties, not the electorate, responsible for the absence of issue-based voting and, thus, mandates. They fault political parties because of the "ambiguity" with which they present their platforms and candidates to the public (Niemi and Weisberg 1993: 110). Referring to the 1968 presidential election, Brody and Page observe that it is "quite hard to vote on the basis of the slight differences which actually existed" between Nixon and Humphrey (Niemi and Weisberg 1993: 112). Fiorina similarly asserts that there is too much variability in the differences between the parties' candidates from election to election (Abramson 1994: 182).

The revisionists' critique of American political parties undermines the contention that general elections provide policy mandates and points to another major problem with the mandate thesis—that is, the question of whether voters' issue orientations determine how they vote.

THE ISSUE-VOTING ISSUE

For decades social scientists have been intrigued by the causes of vote direction, especially the relationship between issue attitudes and vote direction. As previously stated, issue-based voting, or issue voting, is one precondition for an electoral mandate. Issue voting requires that voters carefully assess opposing candidates' stances on the issues, distinguish among them, and cast their ballots for the candidate whose issue stances most resemble their own. Like the mandate thesis, this model assumes that voters are politically knowledgeable and focused upon public policy issues. Vote direction is compelled neither by emotionally based allegiance to a political party nor superficial reactions to the candidates' general images. Rather, this model presumes that issues determine vote direction.

Campbell, Converse, Miller, and Stokes' 1960 publication of *The American Voter* set the stage for a debate among students of American voting behavior. Apropos of electoral mandates, the most noteworthy conclusion of *The American Voter* was that the American electorate is not primarily issue oriented. Rather, Campbell et al. concluded that party identification outstripped both issues and candidates as a determinant of vote direction. The "four horse-men" of the University of Michigan also observed that party identification tended to be very stable throughout life (Campbell et al. 1960: 165). They defined party identification as "a psychological identification, which can persist without legal recognition or evidence of formal membership and even without a record of consistent party support" (121). It represents "a psychological commitment or attachment to a political party that normally predisposes us to evaluate the party and its candidates in a favorable light" (Asher 1988: 41). *The American Voter* concluded that party identification, an enduring affective attribute, surpassed both evaluations of candidates and attitudes on public policy issues as a determinant of vote direction (Niemi and Weisberg 1993: 94). Campbell et al. conclude that the "psychological dimensions of voting . . . of greatest importance for the political system . . . [are] low emotional involvement of the electorate in politics; its slight awareness of public affairs; its failure to think in structured, ideological terms; and its pervasive sense of attachment to one or the other of the two major political parties" (Campbell et al. 1960: 541). Clearly, *The American Voter* concluded that the preconditions of issue voting did not exist in 1960. Neither then, could mandates exist.

A body of scholarly literature challenged *The American Voter*'s findings. The challengers were commonly known as "revisionists" and their late 1960s literature emphasized the significance of issues in determining vote direction (Niemi and Weisberg 1993: 137; Weisberg 1995: 10). Luttbeg and Gant summarize the "Revisionist Model of the American Voter" as follows:

1. The typical voter is capable of rationally deciding whether to participate and how to vote if he or she decides to vote. Sometimes most of the electorate cast rational votes that shape government.

2. Partisan identification is a running tally of prior (retrospective) judgments of which party has in the past behaved closest to one's preferences.

3. Politics is not a normal concern of Americans, but on occasion they express dissatisfaction in their choice among candidates for public office.

4. Many vote on the basis of issues. Even voter judgements that a candidate is more honest or likeable may be important to the competency of that candidate for public office. Thus, it is rational to assess the liability and honesty of candidates.

5. Strength of party identification is of little importance. (Luttbeg and Gant 1995: 26)

The revisionists' thesis is that the American electorate is rational, in part because it is issue oriented. However, to the revisionists, issue orientation simply meant that *some issues* are *sometimes* important to *some* voters. Furthermore, retrospective voting and voting by candidate image and party identification are rational. The revisionists conclude that elections may provide mandates only by relaxing the definition of rational voting to near meaninglessness. Decades later the "rational-choice" theorists would also place "greater emphasis on the issue side of voting" (Weisberg 1995: 11).

It can be argued that the revisionists' position is invalid in part because it is based upon an erroneous premise: that *The American Voter* contended voters were irrational. In the posthumously published *The Responsible Electorate*, V. O. Key, Jr., rather colorfully scored the revisionists' marching song.

The perverse and unorthodox argument of this little book is that voters are not fools.... [T]he electorate behaves about as rationally and responsibly as we should expect, given the clarity of the alternatives presented to it. In American presidential campaigns of recent decades the portrait of the American electorate is one of an electorate moved by concern about central and relevant questions of public policy, of governmental performance and of executive personality. (Key 1966: 7–8)

However, Campbell et al. did not label American voters "fools," as Key implies. They concluded neither that votes were cast randomly nor that party identification was the only variable which influenced vote direction.

The second reason to be skeptical of the revisionists' conclusions is that some have openly admitted their lack of scholarly objectivity. It is fundamental to all empirical social scientific research that findings must be uncontaminated by the scholar's personal political values. Social scientists are obliged to conduct objective, unbiased research (Frohock 1967: 147; Eulau 1966: 12). Valid empirical research cannot be akin to a legal brief or a position paper. Nonetheless, a number of the revisionists have openly admitted being troubled by the findings reported in *The American Voter* and intentionally embarking upon research to demonstrate that it was erroneous. Revisionists admitted a biased intent to demonstrate that vote direction is issue driven.

Revisionism apparently emerged as a spinoff of the Caucus for a New Political Science, itself conditioned by the "counterculture" of the late 1960s. This counterculture preached, among other things, that "if you are not part of the solution, you are part of the problem." The Caucus for a New Political Science held that political science should become much more "relevant," conducting research dedicated to improving the political system, according to the revisionist's value system (Bay 1969: 113). With regard to the debate over the determinants of vote direction, the revisionists feared that the future of American popular democracy would be jeopardized if public officials believed that voters were not issue oriented.

A number of revisionist scholars have openly acknowledged their bias. For instance, Gerald Pomper admits that he "attempted to argue on behalf of the competence of the average voter" (Pomper and Lederman 1980: xi). Key reflects such bias when he muses that "with a steady diet of buncombe the people may come to expect and to respond with the highest predictability to buncombe and those leaders most skilled in the propagation of buncombe may gain lasting advantage in the recurring struggles for popular favor" (Key 1966: 7). The June 1972 issue of the *American Political Science Review* contains a symposium on "Issue Voting," with articles by Gerald Pomper and Richard Boyd. Pomper alludes to V. O. Key's worry that politicians who perceive that voters are susceptible to delusion will attempt to delude them, to wit, "perhaps in response to Key's concern the contributors to this symposium and other writers have sought to discover, and frankly emphasize, the importance of issue voting" (Pomper 1972: 466). While Pomper's candor is laudatory, his admission, nonetheless, undermines the validity of his conclusions. The revisionist's research on issue voting is unpersuasive precisely because they set out to "discover" and/or to "emphasize" (466) the role of issues in determining vote direction. Even setting aside this fundamental breach of social scientific protocol, the revisionists do not present compelling evidence.

Pomper posits that (1) party loyalty is significantly correlated with attitudes on policies; (2) increasingly, the electorate is perceiving differences between the two major parties; (3) voters are increasingly showing more consistency across issue areas; and (4) with regard to vote direction, issues have become more important and party identification less important (Pomper 1975: Chapter 8). From his value system, Pomper sees the American electorate as "on the mend" from the scenario described in *The American Voter*, a recovery that he believes continued through the election of 1992 (Pomper 1993: 149). In any event, the mandate thesis is not validated by the revisionists' qualified conclusion that "policy concerns have contributed to voters' decisions, independent of the effects of partisanship, in presidential elections since 1964" (Luttbeg and Gant 1995: 36).

Much research on American voting behavior has focused upon the *relative* impact of independent variables—that is, "attempt[s] to decompose the vote statistically" (Weisberg 1995: 72). This decomposition is at the core of the debate between the revisionists and the traditionalists. It entails assessment of the relative influence of multiple independent variables, especially party identification, opinions on public policy issues, party image, and candidate image. Debunking the mandate myth simply requires evidence that variables other than issue orientations significantly influence vote direction. Research has clearly demonstrated the very significant influence of both party identification and candidate image.

The American Voter concluded that party identification was the independent variable that most influenced vote direction (Campbell et al. 1960: Chapter 6). Its influence is exercised both directly and indirectly. In the latter, party identification impacts political attitudes which, in turn, influence vote direction (Campbell et al. 1960: Chapter 6; Luttbeg and Gant 1995: 34). Even after the era of partisan "dealignment"—"decline of partisanship"—Luttbeg and Gant concluded in 1992 that "it is still the case, too, that most people's votes can be predicted by asking them their party identification or any question that at its root is asking them how they will vote" (Luttbeg and Gant 1995: 26). In 1993, Niemi and Weisberg boldly stated that partisanship had been "the most important causal factor" in the election of 1956 and that neither its decrease in impact nor the increased impact of issues changed this through 1976: "the issue factor was always the least important of the three, and party always first"

(Niemi and Weisberg 1993: 100). For the 1992 presidential election, Luttbeg and Gant observed, "most partisans voted for the candidate of their own party, and party 'switching' was very low. . . . [P]arty identification is still a strong predictor of the vote. More than 90 percent of strong partisans voted for their party's candidate and more than two-thirds of those categorized as weak partisans and 'leaning' independents remained loyal to their standard bearer" (Luttbeg and Gant 1995: 45). Luttbeg and Gant acknowledge, however, that the apparent impact of party identification would likely be diminished by controlling for candidate image and issue orientation (26).

In the midterm congressional elections of 1994 House Speaker Newt Gingrich forged the Contract with America, a set of campaign issues that he portrayed as a nationwide platform for Republican congressional candidates. Republicans gained fifty-two seats in the House, attaining a majority for the first time in forty-two years, and also assumed control of the Senate by capturing eight formerly Democratic seats (Jacobson 1996: 1). This emboldened Speaker Gingrich to boast that the Republican Congress had received an electoral mandate to fulfill its Contract with America. In analyzing the 1994 midterm elections Grant Reeher and Joseph Cammarano conclude that for their "whites only" sample "the only significant, independent influences on vote choice were party identification and the presence of a Democratic incumbent in the race (which increased Democratic support)" (Reeher and Cammarano 1996: 134). Even Gerald Pomper, a revisionist and an issue voting enthusiast, has concluded that the Contract with America was not a popular mandate (Pomper 1996). So much for the mythical mandate for the Contract with America.

"Candidate image," the third independent variable commonly employed to explain vote direction, is defined as "the personal characteristics of a candidate which the voter finds appealing or unappealing . . . unrelated to the candidate's policy or partisan views. [These include] . . . personal factors such as physical appearance, intelligence, schooling, family background, or speech" (Luttbeg and Gant 1995: 70). Candidate image is a nonissue variable that significantly impacts vote direction. It cuts both ways; a positive image is a benefit and a negative image is a liability. George Bush's negative image was a decided advantage for Bill Clinton in 1992 (Weisberg 1995: 99–108). Robert Dole apparently had a similar image problem. Clearly, votes based upon candidate image are neither issue based nor the foundation for a policy mandate. Although more important in some presidential elections than in others, candidate image routinely has substantial impact upon vote direction. It was the most important variable in 1972 (Luttbeg and Gant 1995: 71). Evidence that candidate image has a significant impact upon vote direction, independent of the voter's issue attitudes, discredits the mandate myth, even though candidate image is sometimes colored by party identification (Niemi and Weisberg 1993: 188).

Niemi and Weisberg do not attempt to decompose the factors influencing vote direction.

We suspect that any final determination of the relative importance of issue . . . and candidate factors should not be expected. When different theories are based on completely different paradigms for understanding politics it is virtually impossible to design a fair test between them. . . . Just as the Michigan approach was thought to emphasize partisanship at the expense of issues, the rational choice approach emphasizes issues at the expense of any attention to the candidate factor. (148)

Nonetheless, observations about vote direction being influenced by candidate image and party identification have made the point that American general elections are not plebiscites on public policy: they do not provide public policy mandates. However, additional rebuffs to the mandate myth may be made by explaining some methodological factors that exaggerate the *apparent* influence of issues upon vote direction, even in unbiased research.

MEASURING ISSUE VOTING

To repeat, the mandate concept presumes that votes are cast on the basis of issues, which further presumes that voters know of the candidates' positions on the issues (Flanigan and Zingale 1998: 187). Not a few studies have seriously challenged this placid assumption about the level of voter cognition. The cognitive stumbling block to issue voting led Carmines and Stimson (1995) to create two categories of issue-based voters, "easy-issue voters" and "hard-issue voters." According to Weisberg and Niemi, because "hard issues . . . are more difficult for voters to comprehend than are easy ones, so hard issues will be important only for voters with high levels of political information" (Niemi and Weisberg 1993: 98). Voting upon the basis of hard issues "presumes that issue voting is the final result of a sophisticated decision calculus; that it represents a reasoned and thoughtful attempt by voters to use policy preferences to guide their electoral decisions" (Carmines and Stimson 1995: 114).

Carmines and Stimson's "hard-issue voting" is simply "issue voting" as the latter term has long been employed. However, "easy-issue" voting is a debased issue voting because easy issues are not difficult to comprehend and are devoid of any "conceptual sophistication" (114). Easy issues are "symbolic rather than technical . . . deal with policy ends rather than means . . . [and have been] long on the political agenda" (115). They continue, "Easy issue voting . . . requires neither cognitive ability nor attention to politics. . . . When easy issues are present, . . . increases in issue voting are observed. When easy issues are absent, . . . issue voting is considerably more modest because it is concentrated among hard issues" (117–18). Since easy issues are "no-brainers," are easy-issue voters truly issue voters in any meaningful sense? Perhaps they should be called faux-issue voters or pseudo-issue voters? The cognitive stumbling block to the mandate thesis is that voters cannot meaningfully endorse issues of which they are unaware or which they do not comprehend.

Retrospective voting also undermines the mandate thesis, which presumes that ballots are cast prospectively, on the basis of the campaign promises proffered by candidates (Pomper and Lederman 1980: 212). Research has revealed that retrospective voting is fairly common—that is, a "candidate may get elected for a policy he pursued or preferred in the past that has no relevance to present circumstances" (Polsby and Wildavsky 1996: 318). Ronald Reagan's first electoral victory was attributable in no small part to the electorate's negative retrospective evaluation of President Jimmy Carter (22). Fiorina argues that retrospective voting is rational (Niemi and Weisberg 1993: 98–99). Nonetheless, retrospective voting, like antivoting, invalidates attempts to interpret election results as prospective policy mandates.

Additionally, those voters who actually cast prospective issue-based votes in any election are not all focused upon the same public policy issue(s). Observing that "numerous minorities compete for shares in the policy making," Polsby and Wildavsky conclude that the existence of multiple issues and issue publics, in and of itself, determines that "presidential elections are not referendums" (Polsby and Wildavsky 1996: 315), that is, they do not provide mandates.

Stanley Kelly, Jr., writes that "the sample survey has again given us the ability to discover the grounds of voters' choices" (1983: 136). However, one type of measurement error presents particular problems in this regard. The term "nonattitudes" was coined by Philip Converse (1964) to describe opinions that "are unstable over time, perhaps being formed only after respondents are asked their opinions by interviewers" (Luttbeg and Gant 1995: 18). In other words, some survey respondents are only faking attitudes.

A concept termed "social desirability response-set bias" largely explains such fabrication of "nonattitudes." In survey research, social desirability-based measurement error arises when answers to questions do not accurately portray respondents' attitudes but rather reflect their perceptions of which attitudes are "socially acceptable" (Alreck and Settle 1985: 112). Some respondents deliberately misrepresent their attitudes so they will appear to conform to cultural norms. The rationality-activist model of citizenship is an American cultural norm that dictates that the ideal/model citizen ought to be knowledgeable about public affairs. Consequently, survey respondents may perceive it to be socially undesirable/unacceptable to acknowledge that they lack either political knowledge or attitudes. This perception leads some respondents to conjure up "nonattitudes" during interviews, faking the possession of attitudes simply to cast themselves in the favorable light of being politically aware (Converse 1964: 245, 259–60). This reaction also occurs because Americans tend to perceive opinion surveys as IQ tests; "don't know" and "no opinion" responses are seen as self-deprecating confessions of ignorance (Asher 1992: 21–22). The measurement of nonattitudes contributes to the overestimation of issue-based voting, the foundation of the mandate thesis.

Issue-based voting is also overestimated because individuals strive for internal consistency among their political attitudes. Cognitive dissonance arises when an individual holds conflicting opinions, beliefs, attitudes, and/or perceptions. Because the modal American culture eschews inconsistency, attitudinal dissonance causes psychological stress. Consequently, individuals act to remove and/or avoid dissonance, displacing it with harmonious attitudinal consonance. One method of dissonance resolution is to change one's attitudes so they become consistent. However, when attitudes are firmly held and/or central to an individual, attitudinal change is the last recourse. This is true for inconsistent configurations of political attitudes, candidate images, party images, and/or party identifications (Flanigan and Zingale 1998: 139).

In addition to the more general psychological defense mechanisms (139), voters employ two dissonance-reduction strategies that do not entail changing their fundamental political attitudes and orientations. Projection and persuasion are adaptive strategies that exaggerate the number of issue voters. Projection entails a misperception of the issue positions of the candidate whom the voter is predisposed to support upon the basis of party identification and/or candidate image. The voter erroneously projects his/her own issue preferences onto the candidate. Cognitive dissonance is resolved by the voter's misperception that he/she is in agreement with his/her candidate of preference (139). *The American Voter* focused primarily upon party identification-based projections (Niemi and Weisberg 1993: 187). Because party identification is a long-term variable—it tends to be stable over time—it is not likely to be altered by candidate image(s) in a single election. On the contrary, projection removes dissonance by distorting candidate image and/or perceived issue positions. Individuals who engage in projection obviously cannot be labeled "policy voters" (Brody and Page 1993: 108). Projection was apparent in the election of 1972 (Miller and Levitin 1976: 141–44; Pomper 1975: 191). In 1972 significant portions of the electorate who comprised the "natural constituencies" of both McGovern and Nixon failed to accurately perceive which candidate agreed with them, even on some of the election's most salient issues. Astoundingly, 22 percent of the "doves" did not perceive themselves to be closer to McGovern than to Nixon on Southeast Asian foreign policy (Miller and Levitin 1976: 141).

Cognitive dissonance also can be resolved through a second process, persuasion. Here the voter changes his/her issue attitudes, rendering them consistent with the positions of the party and/or the candidate he/she is predisposed to support. However, this is only a pseudo conversion because it rarely endures for more than one election. Even Pomper acknowledges that "this possibility [persuasion] cannot be excluded" (1975: 191). Niemi and Weisberg confirm its existence by writing that "projection is more common than persuasion" (1993: 103). Apropos of the mandate as myth, Brody and Page write, "We cannot say that the voter who is persuaded is evaluating or voting on the basis of policy" (1993: 108). Persuaded voters' policy preferences are merely reflections of, or surrogate measures of, their candidate and/or party preferences.

Neither projection nor persuasion results in an issue-based vote. In each dissonance reduction strategy, issue orientations are *effects* of, not causes of, candidate and/or partisan preference. A mandate requires exactly the opposite causal pattern. Issue orientations must give rise to candidate and/or partisan preference and, hence, "cause" the vote direction decision. The existence of projection and persuasion further undermines the mandate thesis.

CONCLUSION

This piece has explained why mainstream scholars in the field of American voting behavior do not recognize claims to electoral mandates as being legitimate. And they do not! For instance, Flanigan and Zingale write, "It is very difficult to establish that the voters' (candidate) preferences have certain policy meanings or that the votes for a particular candidate provide a policy mandate" (1998: 187). Even V.O. Key, Jr., a revisionist who portrayed a rational, responsible electorate, agrees: "It thus can be a mischievous error to assume, because a candidate wins, that a majority of the electorate shares his view on public policy questions . . . , or has specific expectations about his future conduct" (1966: 2). Gerald Pomper, who also criticized *The American Voter*'s position on issue voting, unequivocally states, "The electorate does not mandate policy, but it accepts or rejects the officials who initiate it" (Pomper and Lederman 1980: 125). Similarly, Polsby and Wildavsky acknowledge that "elections do not transmit unerringly the policy preferences of electorates to leaders or confer mandates on leaders with regard to specific policies" (1996: 314). Most political scientists specializing in American voting behavior now agree that the notion of an electoral mandate is clearly a myth!

The absence of a plebiscite-style electoral mandate does not mean that popular elections have no impact upon public policy in the United States. A more appropriate conclusion is that the electoral linkage is not as direct and determinant as the simplistic mandate thesis posits, that there is slippage in the electoral linkage. It can be argued that this slippage is advantageous to American democracy in that it allows for enlightened deliberation (Dahl 1990: 370–72). Furthermore, disabusing citizens of the mandate myth may be functional for both systemic stability and political participation. It may defuse one source of political cynicism and political alienation among the citizenry, that arising from the misperception that unfulfilled electoral mandates are indicative that the system is undemocratic, dysfunctional, and, as such, unworthy of support.

REFERENCES

Abramson, Paul R., John H. Aldrich, and David W. Rohde. 1994. *Change and Continuity in the 1992 Elections.* Washington, DC: Congressional Quarterly Press.

———. 1998. *Change and Continuity in the 1996 Elections.* Washington, DC: Congressional Quarterly Press.

Alreck, Pamela L., and Robert B. Settle. 1985. *The Survey Research Handbook.* Homewood, IL: Richard D. Irwin, Inc.

American Heritage Dictionary, 2nd collected ed. 1982. Boston: Houghton Mifflin Co.

American Political Science Association. 1972. "American Voting Behavior Symposium." *American Political Science Review* (June): 415–70.

Asher, Herbert B. 1992. *Polling and the Public: What Every Citizen Should Know.* Washington, DC: Congressional Quarterly Press.

———. 1988. *Presidential Elections and American Politics.* Chicago: The Dorsey Press.

Bay, Christian. 1969. "Politics and Pseudopolitics: A Critical Evaluation of Some Behavioral Literature." In Heinz Eulau, ed., *Behavioralism in Political Science.* New York: Atherton Press: 109–40.

Boyd, Richard. 1972. "Popular Control of Public Policy: A Normal Vote Analysis of the 1968 Election." *American Political Science Review* (June): 429–49.

Brody, Richard A., and Benjamin I. Page. 1993. "The Assessment of Policy Voting." In Richard G. Niemi and Herbert F. Weisberg, eds., *Classics of Voting Behavior.* Washington, DC: Congressional Quarterly Press: 107–09.

Campbell, Angus, Philip E. Converse, Warren E. Miller, and Donald E. Stokes. 1960. *The American Voter.* New York: John Wiley & Sons, Inc.

Carmines, Edward G., and James A. Stimson. 1995. "The Two Faces of Issue Voting." In Richard G. Niemi and Herbert F. Weisberg, eds., *Classics of Voting Behavior.* Washington, DC: Congressional Quarterly Press: 114–18.

Committee on Political Parties, American Political Science Association. 1950. *Toward a More Responsible Two-Party System.* New York: American Political Science Association.

Converse, Philip E. 1964. "The Nature of Belief Systems in Mass Politics." In David E. Apter, ed., *Ideology and Discontent.* Glencoe, IL: The Free Press.

Cowan, Edward. 1981. "Fast Action Planned." *New York Times* 130, March 11, A1(2).

Dahl, Robert. 1990. "The Myth of the Presidential Mandate." *Political Science Quarterly* 105, No. 3.

Eulau, Heinz. 1966. *The Behavioral Persuasion in Politics.* New York: Random House.

"Expert: Bush Has a Mandate from the People." 1988. *The Daily Star,* Oneonta, NY November 15, 1

Flanigan, William H., and Nancy H. Zingale. 1998. *Political Behavior of the American Electorate,* 9th ed. Washington, DC: Congressional Quarterly Press.

Frohock, Fred M. 1967. *The Nature of Political Inquiry.* Homewood, IL: The Dorsey Press.

Hill, David B., and Norman R. Luttbeg. 1983. *Trends in American Electoral Behavior.* Itasca, IL: F.E. Peacock Publishers, Inc.

Jacobson, Gary C. 1996. "The 1994 House Elections in Perspective." In Philip A. Klinker, ed., *Midterm: The Elections of 1994 in Context.* Boulder, CO: Westview Press, Inc.: 1–20.

Kelly, Stanley, Jr. 1983. *Interpreting Elections*. Princeton, NJ: Princeton University Press.

Key, V. O., Jr. 1966. *The Responsible Electorate*. Cambridge: Harvard University Press.

Krauthammer, Charles. 1994. "Republican Mandate." *Washington Post*, November 11, A31.

Ladd, Everett C. 1997. "The Status-quo Election: Introduction." *The Public Perspective: A Roper Center Review of Public Opinion and Polling* 8.1 (December/January): 5.

Luttbeg, Norman R., and Michael M. Gant. 1995. *American Electoral Behavior, 1952–1992*. Itasca, IL: F. E. Peacock Publishers, Inc.

Miller, Warren E., and Theresa E. Levitin. 1976. *Leadership and Change*. Cambridge: Winthrop Publishers, Inc.

Nie, Norman H., Sidney Verba, and John R. Petrocik. 1976. *The Changing American Voter*, enlarged ed. Cambridge: Harvard University Press.

Niemi, Richard G., and Herbert F. Weisberg. 1993. "What Determines the Vote?" In Richard G. Niemi and Herbert F. Weisberg, eds., *Classics in Voting Behavior*. Washington, DC: Congressional Quarterly Press: 160–69.

Plano, Jack C., and Milton Greenberg. 1993. *The American Political Dictionary*, 9th ed. Fort Worth, TX: Harcourt Brace College Publications.

Polsby, Nelson W., and Aaron Wildavsky. 1996. *Presidential Elections*, 9th ed. Chatham, NJ: Chatham House.

Pomper, Gerald. 1972. "From Confusion to Clarity: Issues and American Voters, 1956–1968." *American Political Science Review* (June): 415–28.

———. 1975. *Voters' Choice*. New York: Dodd, Mead & Co.

———. 1996. "Parliamentary Government in the U.S.?" Address given at "The Impact of Elections on Governing" Conference, State University of New York College at Oneonta, October 25.

———, ed. 1993. *The Election of 1992*. Chatham, NJ: Chatham House.

Pomper, Gerald, and Susan S. Lederman. 1980. *Elections in America*, 2d ed. New York: Longman Press.

Rahn, Wendy M., John A. Aldrich, Eugene Borgida, and John L. Sullivan. 1993. "A Social-Cognitive Model of Candidate Appraisal." In Richard G. Niemi, ed., *Controversies in Voting Behavior*. Washington, DC: Congressional Quarterly Press: 99–113.

Reeher, Grant, and Joseph Cammarano. "In Search of the Angry White Male: Gender, Race, and Issues in the 1994 Elections." In Richard G. Niemi, ed., *Midterm: The Elections of 1994 in Context*. Boulder, CO: Westview Press, Inc.: 125–36.

Shafritz, Jay M. 1988. *The Dorsey Dictionary of American Government and Politics*. Chicago, IL: The Dorsey Press.

Silver, Brian D., Barbara A. Anderson, and Paul R. Abramson. 1986. "Who Overreports Voting?" *American Political Science Review* (June): 613–24.

Smith, Eric R.A.N. 1993. "Changes in the Public's Political Sophistication." In Richard G. Niemi and Herbert F. Weisberg, eds., *Controversies in Voting Behavior*. Washington, DC: Congressional Quarterly Press: 72–111.

Wayne, Leslie. 1998. "The Nation: The Price of the Vote." *New York Times*, November 8, 4: 4.

Weisberg, Herbert F., ed. 1995. *Democracy's Feast: Elections in America*. Chatham, NJ: Chatham House.

Weisberg, Herbert F., and David C. Kimball. 1995. "Attitudinal Correlates of the 1992 Presidential Vote: Party Identification and Beyond." In Herbert F. Weisberg, ed., *Democracy's Feast: Elections in America*. Chatham, NJ: Chatham House: 71–111.

18

Alternative Electoral Systems: An Answer to Our Governing Crisis

Dennis M. Anderson

"I've been in previews of *Independence Day* and definitely the biggest round of applause comes when the White House blows up. It's a perfect moment. It speaks volumes for the political tenor of the times."
— Robert J. Skall, author of *The Monster Show*, sociological history of horror in the movies (Borrelli 1996: G1).

Elections are supposed to express our social solidarity, legitimize the authority of those who govern us, and enable us to throw the rascals out. Increasing numbers of voters say that it makes no difference who is elected or that there is little meaningful choice. A Harris poll measuring alienation reached new quarter-century highs in the 1990s.[1] The belief that government was responsive fell from 62 percent to 30 percent between 1960 and 1988. Gordon S. Black and Benjamin D. Black report that over the past fifteen years in more than two hundred customer satisfaction studies. "We have never, not once, seen consumers in the private sector in the United States as unhappy with a business or a product as Americans are with their government and political leaders" (1996: 214). In addition, several major polls in the 1990s have found that roughly 60 percent of Americans support the establishment of a new party (Lowi 1994: 189).

As W. Lance Bennett has stated, "The steady decline of voter satisfaction and participation is probably the most important indicator that elections as rituals have become dangerously empty experiences. As the dramatic turn-about in the 1994 election indicated, voters have become increasingly impatient with the disconnection between elections and government" (1996: 162).

The theme of this volume poses the question: "We get what we vote for . . . or do we?" No, we do not. We do not get to vote for what many of us would want if we had a wider variety of choices. My argument is we would be much more likely to answer unequivocally "yes" to the question if we were to abandon the systems of election used in the United States and to adopt elections by proportional representation.

I suggest that the increasing distemper in Americans' attitudes toward their political system indicates failure in our system of representation.[2] Few Americans have known any system of election other than majority (or plurality) systems of voting. Two such familiar systems have dominated our history: election by the single-member district, where only one candidate can win; and "first-past-the-post" plurality at-large elections, where the first X number of finishers win, X being the number of candidates to be elected. If voting is polarized, the candidates from the larger faction or group in a multiseat election will win all the seats being filled. Under systems of proportional representation the threshold for election in multimember districts is lowered so that minorities of significant size may win a share of seats proportionate to their share of the total vote.

Majoritarian systems such as the single-member district (SMD) or plurality at-large elections in multimember districts have been the dominant mode of election in the English-speaking world (United States, United Kingdom, Canada). However, most other democratic nations including continental and Eastern Europe, Israel, the states of the former Soviet Union and emerging nations use proportional systems of voting.

There has also been significant use of proportional systems in the United States at state and local levels. Twenty-three municipalities and a few dozen school boards in Massachusetts and New York have used proportional representation (Weaver 1986: 144). A different form of proportional representation, cumulative voting, was used for 110 years to elect the lower house of the Illinois legislature until its abandonment in 1980 (Weaver 1984: 195). Cumulative voting has more recently been employed in counties and municipalities in Alabama and elsewhere as a remedy in civil rights suits (Still 1990).[3]

The version of proportional representation used in other nations has been a party list (PR/PL) system in which parties win a proportion of seats in their legislative bodies based on the percent of the popular vote a party's list of candidates receives. Because of Americans' proclivity to vote for individuals, another form of proportional representation has been used in the United States. This is the single transferable vote (PR/STV) system of proportional representation that is also called preference voting. PR/STV (preference voting) calls for voters to vote not for party slates but for individual candidates, rank-ordering their preferences with numbers instead of X's next to each preferred candidate on the ballot. For example, in a city council of nine members, first choice votes from roughly 10 percent of the electorate will elect a candidate. "Surplus" votes not needed by the first choice winners are redistributed to the second place candidates on these ballots. The candidates with the fewest first place votes are then eliminated in turn and their ballots are redistributed to their second choices. Ballots are transferred until nine candidates are elected. In contrast to plurality systems, preference voting typically results in 90 percent of the voters casting a vote that is effective in electing some candidate. Perhaps even more importantly 60 to 70 percent of the voters will see their first choice elected. A majority party or group will win a majority but its seat total will not be inflated out of proportion to its share of the total vote.[4]

Cumulative voting is a semiproportional system of voting where every voter has as many votes as there are candidates to be elected but, unlike majoritarian or plurality systems, the voter may cast (or "plump") all of his or her votes for one candidate or distribute equally his/her votes to any number of candidates between one and the number to be elected. Thus, if we have a seven-member council or commission the voter can "plump" all seven votes for one candidate, cast one vote for each of seven candidates, cast three and a half votes for each of two candidates, or distribute his or her votes equally to any number in between. This system is used to elect the county commissioners in Chilton County, Alabama, where, in elections to a seven-member county commission, it has enabled two minorities to receive representation for the first time (Blacks and Republicans).

SYSTEMS OF PROPORTIONAL REPRESENTATION

Many problems of American politics pertaining to empowerment and representation could be effectively addressed by substituting systems of proportional representation (PR) for systems that reward only majority or plurality victors.

An Electoral System That Makes It Possible for Minority Parties or Candidates to Win Representation Will Empower the Voters

Plurality election systems overrepresent the majority party. With two parties competing in a system of single-member districts the winning party will normally win a disproportionate share of the close races. This means that it may win 5 to 10 percent more seats in a legislative body than the percent share of its candidates' votes aggregated nationwide (or statewide) (see Taagepera and Shugart 1989). The winning party's bonus means the principal opposition party is somewhat underrepresented—that is, its percent of seats is lower than its share of the vote. Unless a third party's strength is concentrated in one region, its chances of winning representation anywhere are slim. Voters disillusioned with both major parties will be told by the second party: "Join us, we are closer to your position than the incumbent. Don't waste your vote by voting for your candidate who has no chance to win." This argument is apparently effective because third party candidates' support starts to hemorrhage as Election Day approaches. American voters have traditionally not seen the casting of a protest vote as an effective choice. In 1980, only 39 percent of the voters who liked John Anderson best in the preelection SRC-CPS Survey voted for him. Reagan and Carter received votes from 98 and 87 percent, respectively, of those who liked them best (Abramson et al. 1982: 174–75, 185).

Americans' willingness to give up their first choice in favor of a second choice who is more electable suggests a new slant on this book's theme. Instead of asking, "We Get What We Vote For . . . Or Do We?" we might say "We Vote for What We Want . . . Or Do We?" Answer: No, we don't always vote for what we really want. Evidently, many people feel it is fruitless to vote for their preferred but electorally hopeless candidate.

Not only is the majority or plurality party given disproportionate advantages in a two-way race but the party with a mere plurality receives an even bigger bonus when three parties are contesting seats under a single-member district (SMD) election system. In the United Kingdom, a third party with 23 percent of the national vote received only 3.5 percent of the seats in the 650-member House of Commons (Amy 1993: 34). In three elections (1983, 1987, and 1991) the Conservative party won large majorities of seats based on roughly 42 percent of the national vote. Should major policy changes rest on a mere 42 percent of the vote?

There are other problems in majority systems. Are you a Republican who lives in a large city who is "represented" in Congress by a liberal Democrat? Are you a Democrat living in a small town or rural area who is "represented" by a Republican? In a single-member district (SMD) as many as 49 percent of the voters in a two candidate race may be considered to have "wasted" their votes—that is, cast votes not effective in electing a candidate of their choice.

Plurality/majority systems set high thresholds that make the election of a third party or independent candidate highly unlikely. Lower thresholds for election would give minority candidates some chance to win a seat (or some seats) in legislative bodies. Electing a nine-person council at large or electing nine members to a legislative body from a multimember district under proportional representation with the single transferable vote would make it possible for a cohesive 10 percent of the population to elect one member. Under cumulative voting roughly 25 percent can elect one member in a three-member district. The first step in reestablishing the frayed connections between the rulers and the ruled in the United States should be to lower the threshold for election. Thus, voters who see that their votes are effective should have a greater sense of being represented.

Legislative Bodies Elected Under Preference Voting (PR) Will Look More Like America

The U.S. House of Representatives is 89 percent male and about 91 percent white. The high threshold for election under plurality/majority systems of election exacerbates the difficulties facing the candidacies of members of newly emergent groups. Countries using PR elections have two to three times as many women in their legislative bodies as those countries whose representatives are elected by the single-member district (SMD) (Rule 1987).

Proportional representation with the single transferable vote (PR/STV) in municipalities in the United States opened city councils to hitherto excluded groups. In the five case studies of Ohio cities using PR/STV examined in Kathleen Barber's *Proportional Representation and Election Reform in Ohio*, significant entry to city councils by racial and ethnic minorities was made possible by PR. The initial election of African Americans was made possible by PR in Cincinnati (Kolesar 1955: 188), Hamilton (Weaver and Blount 1995: 223), and Toledo (Anderson 1995: 274). Token black representation under ward elections increased in Cleveland when it changed to PR/STV (Barber 1995: 141).

White ethnics fared well in these early experiments with PR in this country. Irish Catholics in Ashtabula gained representation under PR (Busch 1995: 108–9) and Polish voters in Toledo won one or two seats in all but one of eight PR elections (Anderson 1995: 275). Many of these minorities lost their handhold on power for a time after the abandonment of PR in these cities.

Women won significant representation on the PR councils in Cleveland elected in the 1920s. After the abandonment of PR in Cleveland it was ten years before women won election to council again (Barber 1995b: 142).

Descriptive representation asks the question: Does it really matter that Congress does not mirror the people it represents? The Black Caucus's distinctive policy stands clearly suggest that a Congress with more black members would be more liberal. If 50 percent of Congress were women, would it make any difference? The literature indicates that women officials are more liberal than their male colleagues and are more likely to support legislation concerned with women, children, and family issues (Thomas 1994). A study measuring female legislators' attitudes found that women were "more predisposed to the idea of representing women's concerns than . . . their male colleagues" (Reingold 1996: 184). In summary, PR makes a difference in the proportion of women and minorities in legislative bodies and these differences are likely to have a substantive policy impact.

Service Representation Would Be Strengthened by PR

Service representation, or constituent service, refers to the effectiveness of representatives in responding to communications from constituents. How well the constituents are served may depend on the extent to which those constituents feel that "their" representative is approachable. Constituents are most likely to write representatives with whom they agree or who are their fellow partisans. The evidence for gender, race, and ethnicity is both systematic and anecdotal. Rosenstone and Hansen have found that members of underrepresented groups are less likely to write their representative in Congress. Controlling for all other variables they found women were 3.7 percent less likely than men, blacks 7.3 percent less likely than whites, and Hispanics 14.4 percent less likely than non-Hispanics to write a letter to their congressman (1993: 75, 77–79). At the time these data were gathered there were 5 percent black members of Congress and 6 percent women. At that time, 80 percent of blacks in this country were not represented in Congress by a black member.

Only 5 percent of American women were represented in the U.S. House of Representatives by a woman. Rosenstone and Hansen suggest that blacks and women face an "ascriptive barrier" to communication with white male legislators. "Psychologically . . . we suspect women doubt that white [male] politicians will be sympathetic to their views, and they therefore hesitate to offer them" (1993: 77–8). Recently, U.S. Representative Cynthia McKinney (D-Ga.) reported in an interview (Nichols 1996: 34) that shortly after her election "women started showing up at my office to tell me they had problems 'of a personal nature'. . . but what they were really talking about was sexual harassment." Representative McKinney noted that she was the first woman representative from Georgia in thirty years. "Before I was sworn in, they hadn't felt there was anyone they could come to because they hadn't felt comfortable talking about what these men were doing to them." She also noted that her caseload of child support complaints reflected "such a serious problem for women that we have found that we've had to become specialists in child support issues." The poor connectivity across gender, race, and ethnicity in the links between constituents and representatives appears to be another factor contributing to the popular feeling, at least among women and minorities, that the government is not there for them.

Preference Voting (PR) Will Put an End to Gerrymandering

Gerrymandering is engineered by "packing" and "cracking." By "packing" opposition supporters in a few districts so they waste their votes, and/or dividing up a group the dominant party wants to prevent from electing one of its own ("cracking"), that party can greatly increase its number of seats, often creating a gross disproportion between the percentage of seats won and that party's aggregate support level in the national or statewide electorate. Bipartisan gerrymanders are also frequently used to enhance the reelection possibilities of incumbents. Safe seats undermine responsiveness and accountability (Amy 1993: 48–53). Abolishing single-member districts in favor of multi-member districts with PR will essentially eliminate gerrymandering.

One arguably benign form of gerrymandering is racial gerrymandering: establishing districts in which racial minorities are a majority.[5] Lani Guinier (1993) has argued that there are inherent problems with majority/minority single-member districts. The first is that race conscious districting "fails to mobilize sustained voter participation" (Guinier 1992: 33). The mobilization of poor black and Latino voters in the "break-through elections are generally not repeated; the black pioneer becomes the incumbent, turnout drops." The second is that when most blacks live in majority black districts the "electoral success of white legislators in white districts is not dependent on black voters." Without white allies, black representatives become isolated and they lose "proportional legislative influence" (Guinier 1992: 34).

Most of our interests are not geographically defined. Only PR gives groups of voters the opportunity to decide for themselves what demographic characteristics, cultural or economic interests, or lifestyle choices are their most salient defining characteristics. Drawing district lines on maps is not an effective way to represent people's interests and is never a neutral activity. Lani Guinier has argued, "[A]lternative nonterritorially based cumulative voting schemes avoid this problem to the extent that groups are self-defined and changeable, allowing 'continuous redistricting by the voters themselves,' with any differences in voting-group composition being chosen by the voters rather than being imposed externally 'based on assumptions about demographic characteristics'" (Issacharoff 1995 citing Guinier 1993: 225). With PR, voters themselves, not activist judges nor gerrymander-prone legislators, define what constitutes meaningful communities. In addition, with PR, voters choose their representatives rather than having incumbent legislators choose their voters.

PROPORTIONAL SYSTEMS OF VOTING WILL (A) ENCOURAGE MORE ISSUE-ORIENTED CAMPAIGNS, (B) FACILITATE THE EXPRESSION OF A GREATER RANGE OF ISSUE POSITIONS AND PUT NEW IDEAS ON THE NATIONAL AGENDA

Proportional Systems of Voting Will Encourage More Issue-Oriented Campaigns

The candidate seeking office under plurality systems must attempt to build a very broad coalition that normally is heterogeneous and likely to contain antithetical elements. Often any such "coalition of minorities" will have single-issue voters whom a candidate offends at her peril. The loss of any part of that coalition could spell the difference between a majority or plurality victory or a near miss. However, when the threshold for election becomes, for example, 20 percent, a candidate is liberated from the constraints of maintaining a large "coalition of minorities" (Lowi 1994: 190).

Honesty and candor suddenly become less risky. Issues that have been too controversial to mention or difficult to explain in a majority or plurality race may be introduced by one or more candidates in an election conducted under preference voting. A politician is free to talk more fully about issues she cares about with less temptation to concentrate on image and personality. Because the candidate now needs to give people more substantive reason to vote for her, personalized appeals may be less a temptation (Amy 1993: 63).

Proportional Systems of Voting Will Improve the Quality of the Political Dialogue, Facilitate the Expression of a Greater Range of Issue Positions, and Put New Ideas on the National Agenda

European nations with some form of PR have multiparty systems offering a range of choice vastly broader than the range from this country's most liberal Democrats to conservative Republicans (Reiter 1993: 32–33). With more parties having a chance to win representation, new policy proposals not even on the agenda of the two major parties would be more likely to receive attention. The lavish fund-raising practices of both parties betray the elite character of the interests served by these parties.

When the office seeker must seek pluralities every unfamiliar idea becomes a dangerous idea. And for plurality-vote-seeking politicians, every dangerous idea becomes unmentionable. Because campaigns are relatively short, candidates do not offer uncomfortable truths that require time for gestation. As Bruce Babbitt once observed: "He who would tell the truth needs to keep one foot in the stirrup." Under plurality systems, no one has an incentive to speak truths that are jarring enough to engender skepticism and hostility when first offered. Such difficult "truths" are impossible to defend in a sound bite.

Let us consider some examples of issues or policy positions that both major parties would prefer to keep off the agenda and consider them in the context of the October 1996 Clinton-Dole "debate." Because the electoral system makes it virtually impossible for third party candidates to compete effectively in legislative elections, third parties and independent candidates are usually too weak to surmount the barriers to inclusion in the presidential debates. Any issues that were inconvenient or embarrassing to either President Clinton or Senator Dole were excluded.

No one was present to ask of the "welfare reform" bill: "Where are the jobs for which former welfare mothers are qualified?" "What transportation is available to get them to work?" "Who will care for their children?" Neither major party candidate confronted the widening gap between rich and poor and the stagnation of workers' wages and the downward mobility of millions.[6] No one was there to ask, "What are you going to do about job loss when corporations move to Mexico or Taiwan?"

Neither Clinton nor Dole questioned the assumptions underlying our drug policies. What might the audience have heard had the Libertarian party candidate for president not been excluded from the debates? "What do you two have to show for 30 billion dollars spent in America's 'war on drugs?' " "Why not define the 'drug problem' as a medical/public health problem rather than fill the jails with minor drug offenders?"

Had he been there, Ralph Nader probably would have asked us to consider the implications of the fact that four trillion dollars in workers' pension funds are invested in stocks of American corporations. "Workers have no voting mechanism regarding this money" (1996: 20). "Why shouldn't they have power commensurate with their ownership?"

Several decades ago the United States mandated a forty–hour work week. Occasional feature stories on family life (see Pakulski 1998) have reported complaints from parents and children on how hard it is to have time together because of parents working mandatory overtime. Encouraging new hiring by making overtime more costly to corporations would be one way to enhance family life. Would Dole or Clinton have conceded that family values could be threatened not by government but by corporations?

Add your own favorite undiscussed issues. You will more likely hear them discussed in an electoral system that provides voters more choices, and candidates and parties incentives to talk about hard issues and solutions. Failing to provide sufficient issue content, offering a narrow range of solutions, keeping many issues entirely off the national agenda, and dumbing down the political debate are all effects of the U.S. electoral and party system. By opening the "conventional wisdom" to challenge, all kinds of new approaches become mentionable and thus politically feasible.

Many voters in post-debate surveys complained about what they had heard. A retired businessman said the questions "were not pointed and we've heard them a hundred times before." A young, single welfare mother said of the questions, "Where do I fit in? I didn't see any of my kind asking questions." A young woman employed by a nonprofit agency was angry. "What ticked me off was there was no direct answer to any question" (Tanber 1996: 8). It was not difficult to see the basis of the dissatisfaction with the candidates' statements. The format of the debate and the exclusion of third, fourth, and fifth candidates left the two major party candidates free to give their safe and rehearsed answers to the citizens' questions. Soundbite answers of ninety, sixty, and thirty seconds each fit Clinton's and Dole's purposes neatly. Candidates probably do not need more than a minute if they have no unfamiliar thoughts to utter.

PREFERENCE VOTING (PR) SHOULD FACILITATE A CLOSER RELATIONSHIP BETWEEN CAMPAIGNING AND GOVERNING

When campaigns are largely meaningless, the ability to govern is at issue. As Douglas Amy (1993: 60) has pointed out, "Campaigns that neglect issues tend to sever the lines of control between the public and elected officials." If a winning candidate's "campaign is devoid of policy content, it will be hard to govern successfully" (Weko and Aldrich 1990: 263). The success of President Reagan's legislative agenda in 1981 depended in significant measure on his having incorporated elements of his campaign into his legislative program. Subsequently, avoidance of policy discussion during the campaigns of 1984, 1988, and 1996 was followed after the election by sparse legislative agendas and little legislative productivity. If the winning candidate has not talked about some issues, he has no basis for claiming popular support for them.

PROPORTIONAL REPRESENTATION WILL ENCOURAGE MORE POSITIVE AND MORE CIVIL CAMPAIGNS

Another reason for the dissatisfaction of the citizenry with their political leaders and with politics is negative campaigning. Negative attack commercials are used because they work. Candidates initiate attack ads to deliberately drive down turnout among voters who might be more inclined to vote for one's opponent. In their book *Going Negative* (1996), Stephen Ansolabehere and Shanto Iyengar found that voters who are not partisan are offended by the ads and come to hate politics as well as the candidates, withdraw from politics, and drop out of the electorate.

In a two-person race in SMDs the shortest route to victory is to raise your opponents' negatives by attack ads. Proportional and semi-proportional systems of election change the incentives for politicians. A candidate running for office under the single-transferable vote system of PR has every incentive to steer clear of personal attacks on his fellow candidates because he needs to try to get second or third choices from the voters whose first choice votes go to one of his opponents. When the competition is not a zero-sum game the incentives are for each candidate to emphasize his/her own program and avoid personal attacks. Similarly, under cumulative voting negative attacks would be irrational for a candidate who would like to share a part of a voter's divisible block of individual votes. In these ways a potent antidote to petty and personalized appeals is built directly into the electoral system. Ansolabehere and Iyengar (1996) found that positive campaigns elicited higher turnouts than negative campaigns. In the case studies of the use of PR in five Ohio cities, the lack of rancor in these city council campaigns was noteworthy (Busch 1995: 111; Weaver and Blount 1995: 239).

In a similar way, a third party block of legislators in Congress, acting as honest brokers, could constitute a vehicle for ending gridlock and working out compromises between the two major parties (Lowi 1994: 188, 194).

PROPORTIONAL REPRESENTATION SHOULD
INCREASE VOTER TURNOUT

With 50 percent turnout in presidential elections (33 to 38 percent in mid-term elections), the United States ranks seventeenth among eighteen industrial democracies in voter turnout. Of the sixteen nations ranking ahead of the United States, thirteen use proportional systems (Amy 1993: 141). The very highest turnout countries, all of which have PR, lead the United States' presidential voter turnout by forty percentage points.

PR, unlike majoritarian systems, gives promise of addressing the primary cause of low voter turnout—low motivation due to the voter's paucity of choices. In examining the effect of the caliber of the choices voters have had historically, Walter Dean Burnham has demonstrated that the massive decline in voter turnout after 1896 can be attributed primarily to a deterioration in the quality of choices offered to voters and decline in the ability of parties, particularly the Democratic party, to mobilize voters (1974: 1009, 1012). The definitive study of recent participation rates by Rosenstone and Hansen (1993) found that over half of the 1960 to 1988 decline in turnout must be attributed to failure of electoral mobilization by parties, unions, and social movements. These findings are important because they point to systemic, not individual, causes of low voter motivation.

Voter turnout is affected positively or negatively by the incentives provided by each particular election system. In most congressional districts in the United States, the biennial elections in the 435 SMDs are noncompetitive ("Dubious Democracy . . . " 1995: 47–50). Neither the majority whose victory is assured nor the opposition whose plight is hopeless have much incentive to get out a larger vote (Amy 1993: 147).[7]

All races under PR are likely to be close. Elections that are perceived to be close have higher turnouts. In addition, the wasted votes under plurality systems are disincentives to voters. The closer relation between a party's vote turnout and the number of seats won under PR means every vote really does count. Consequently every contestant has incentives to mobilize his/her followers.

By lowering the threshold for victory, proportional voting should lead to an increase in parties and candidates. More choices should also lead to greater voter enthusiasm because the voter is more likely to find a party or candidate he/she can identify strongly with. The presence of Ross Perot in the 1992 presidential race, and his more clearly defined stand on the budget and the deficit, provided a choice with clarity on some salient issues for many voters. Perot's presence in the race certainly was a positive factor in the 5 percent increase in turnout in 1992, the first significant upturn in presidential turnout in thirty-two years.

Having more than two parties or candidates should lead to greater issue clarity for voters. Where candidates' stands are distinguishable, voters' utility calculations are easier (Page and Brody 1972). In a study of presidential elections from 1968 to 1980 John Zipp found that "in general, if one has a clear choice among the candidates and one's policy preferences are close to at least one candidate, one is much more likely to vote." The conclusion he drew from his study was that "one reason that individuals do not vote is that their interests are not represented by any of the major candidates" (Zipp 1985: 58, 50; Amy 1993: 148).

WAYS OF APPLYING PR TO THE UNITED STATES

Where should PR be applied in the United States? Certainly PR is suitable for small cities on an at-large basis and for larger cities using a few large four- or five-member districts. In state legislatures preference voting with large districts of varying size could be used. Such arrangements could also be used for the election of many states' congressional delegations. Kevin Phillips (1994: 192) has suggested how PR might play out in a fifteen member district:

In large states, the effect of proportional selection would be considerable. For example, in California, where minor parties are already making some impact in congressional races, a changeover would make the state's potentially enlarged House membership of seventy-five House members elected in 2002 come in a wider variety of flavors. As one hypothetical approach, the state could be divided into five large regional districts, each of which would elect fifteen House members. Any party that crossed (say) a 7 percent threshold would get one House member. So the San Francisco Bay region, for example, might elect eight Democrats, three Republicans, one Nationalist, one Rainbow/Peace and Freedom, one Green, and one Gay Rights. Diversity would flourish. The nature of interest-group access to the House would change: voters and voter blocs would at least partially replace lobbies and hired guns.

Plans have already been suggested for ways medium-sized states might be divided into three-, four-, or five-member districts. The invalidation of racially gerrymandered districts in North Carolina and Georgia has given rise to plans with three multimember districts (Applebome 1994: sec. 4) in both states.

There are no constitutional obstacles to states that may choose to try PR for electing their state legislatures. There is, however, one statutory obstacle to using preference voting for states' U.S. House delegations. In 1967 Congress banned multimember districts and required states to use single-member districts. Representative McKinney has introduced a bill to restore discretion to the states.

CONCLUSION—A NEW DYNAMIC

For ameliorating our political woes, reform of our electoral system is more important than lobbying reform, gift bans, or campaign finance reform. Preference voting holds the promise of introducing a new dynamic into electoral competition. While I have suggested that PR opens new incentives to politicians, activists with the political will must seize the opportunities that will arise from altering institutional structures. The history of "reform" is festooned with unintended consequences. However, proportional representation in American elections is not like other "reform" proposals that bear little or no logical connection to the ills of our times. Unlike other such nostrums as term limits, PR is not designed to weaken legislative institutions or to take power away from voters. Systems of proportional voting not only enhance the power of individual voters but introduce a new dynamic into the relationship between the voters and those who speak for them in the councils of power. The result promises to be new possibilities for the governance of a troubled polity.

NOTES

1. The five questions on alienation were: "the rich get richer . . . poor get poorer"; "what you think doesn't count . . . "; the powerful "try to take advantage . . . "; rulers "don't really care . . ."; and "you're left out" (Black and Black 1996: 213).

2. Unhappiness with the nature of representation in Congress has been found to be one of the most powerful variables associated with disapproval of Congress (Hibbing and Theiss-Morse 1995).

3. Another semiproportional system of voting called "limited voting" was used in roughly two hundred jurisdictions for state boards and commissions and city councils, principally in Connecticut and Pennsylvania (Weaver 1984: 195–96). Voters are limited to voting for fewer candidates than are to be elected. For example, in elections for nine at-large members of a city council, the voters may be allowed to vote for only six candidates. Limited voting will normally render a majority incapable of winning all of the seats.

4. Another preferential vote is the alternative vote, which is used when only one candidate can win. The alternative vote rather than the plurality vote could be used in presidential elections. By eliminating also rans in order, it would result in a majority winner (Amy 1993: 193). The "alternative vote" is like PR with single transferable vote but with only one winner. Using any form of preference voting in presidential elections obviously would require constitutional amendments.

5. Where voting is polarized, creating majority/minority districts is the only way in which minorities will have a reasonable chance to gain representation under plurality systems of election. As a result of the redistricting after the 1990 census, the number of majority/minority districts was doubled, resulting in 1992 in an increase in the combined number of black and Hispanic members in the U.S. House of Representatives from thirty-nine to fifty-seven (Parker 1995: 47). "All of the 13 new black members were elected from the South." None came from districts in which blacks were not a majority (Grofman 1995: 34). The Supreme Court has held (*Miller vs. Johnson,* 1996) that racial factors may not be the primary consideration in districting decisions. Preference voting provides an obvious solution to a Supreme Court that is hostile to single-member districts drawn to give minorities representation.

6. Recent studies have shown that the gap is even worse than previously believed because of inequities in fringe benefits between the higher and the lowest paid workers (Passell 1998).

7. In addition, many are not contested at all. In the spring of 1998, with more than half of the filing dates still in the future, 10 percent of the membership of the U.S. House of Representatives had no opposition (Scripps 1998).

REFERENCES

Abramson, Paul R., John H. Aldrich, David W. Rohde. 1982. *Change and Continuity in the 1980 Elections.* Washington, DC: Congressional Quarterly Press.

Amy, Douglas J. 1993. *Real Choices/New Voices: The Case for Proportional Representation Elections in the United States.* New York: Columbia University Press.

Anderson, Dennis M. 1995. "PR in Toledo: The Neglected Stepchild of Municipal Reform." In Kathleen L. Barber, ed., *Proportional Representation and Election Reform in Ohio.* Columbus: Ohio State University Press: 241–81.

Ansolabehere, Stephen, and Shanto Iyengar. 1996. *Going Negative: How Attack Ads Shrink and Polarize the Electorate.* New York: The Free Press.

Applebome, Peter. 1994. "Guinier Ideas, Once Seen as Odd, Now Get Serious Study." *The New York Times,* April 3: E5.

Barber, Kathleen L. 1995a. *Proportional Representation and Election Reform in Ohio.* Columbus: Ohio State University Press.

———. 1995b. "PR and Boss Rule: The Case of Cleveland." In Kathleen L. Barber, ed., *Proportional Representation and Election Reform in Ohio.* Columbus: Ohio State University Press: 116–59.

Bennett, W. Lance. 1996. *The Governing Crisis: Media, Money, and Marketing in American Elections,* 2d edition. New York: St. Martin's Press.

Black, Gordon S., and Benjamin D. Black. 1996. "The Despair of the American Voter." In William F. Grover and Joseph G. Peschek, eds., *Voices of Dissent.* New York: HarperCollins.

Borrelli, Christopher. 1996. "Apocalypse Sells." *The (Toledo) Blade,* June 30, G1–2.

Burnham, Walter Dean. 1974. "Theory and Voting Research: Some Reflections on Converse's Change in the American Electorate." *American Political Science Review* 68, 3 (September): 1002–23.

Busch, Ronald J. 1995. "Ashtabula: The Pioneer Community." In Kathleen L. Barber, ed., *Proportional Representation and Election Reform in Ohio.* Columbus: Ohio State University Press: 83–115.

"Dubious Democracy and the 1994 Elections." 1995. *Voting and Democracy Report.* Washington, DC: The Center for Voting and Democracy.

Grofman, Bernard. 1995. "Shaw v. Reno and the Future of Voting Rights." *PS: Political Science and Politics* 28, 1 (March): 27–36.

Guinier, Lani. 1993. "Groups, Representation, and Race-Conscious Districting: A Case of the Emperor's Clothes." *Texas Law Review* 71: 1589.

Guinier, Lani. 1992. "Second Proms and Second Primaries: The Limits of Majority Rule." *Boston Review* (September).

Hibbing, John R., and Elizabeth Theiss-Morse. 1995. *Congress As Public Enemy: Public Attitudes Toward American Political Institutions.* Cambridge: Cambridge University Press.

Issacharoff, Samuel. 1995. "Supreme Court Destabilization of Single-Member Districts." *Voting Rights and Elections.* The University of Chicago Legal Forum.

Kolesar, Robert J. 1995. "PR in Cincinnati: From Good Government to the Politics of Inclusion?" In Kathleen L. Barber, ed., *Proportional Representation and Election Reform in Ohio*. Columbus: Ohio State University Press: 166–208.

Lowi, Theodore J. 1994. "The Party Crasher." In T. Lowi, B. Ginsberg, A. Hearst, eds., *Readings for American Government*. New York: W.W. Norton: 188–92.

Nader, Ralph. 1996. "Ralph Nader Says Free Enterprise Runs Too Free." *The Washington Spectator* 22, 14 (August): 1–3.

Nichols, John. 1996. "Cynthia McKinney." *The Progressive* 60, 7 (July): 33–36.

Page, Benjamin I., and Richard A. Brody. 1972. "Policy Voting and the Electoral Process: The Vietnam War Issue." *American Political Science Review* 66 (September): 979–95.

Pakulski, Gary T. 1998. "Overtime at Strike's Heart: Single Parents Protest Mandatory Job Hours." *The (Toledo) Blade*, March 8, E1, 2.

Parker, Frank R. 1995. "Shaw v. Reno: A Constitutional Setback for Minority Representation." *PS: Political Science and Politics* 28 No. 1 (March): 47–50.

Passell, Peter. 1998. "Working Poor Gap Grows, Data Study: Lack of Benefits Adds to Chasm." *(Toledo) Blade*, June 14: 1, 14.

Phillips, Kevin. 1994. *Arrogant Capitol: Washington, Wall Street, and the Frustration of American Politics*. Boston: Little Brown and Co.

Reingold, Beth. 1996. "State Legislators' Attitude About Representing Women: Comparing Men and Women, Arizona and California." In Jack Van der Slik, ed., *Politics in the American States and Communities: A Contemporary Reader*. Boston: Allyn and Bacon: 174–200.

Reiter, Howard S. 1993. *Parties and Elections in Corporate America*. White Plains, NY: Longman.

Ripley, Randall. 1988. *Congress*. New York: W.W. Norton and Co.

Rosenstone, Steven J., and John Mark Hansen. 1993. *Mobilization, Participation, and Democracy in America*. New York: Macmillan.

Rule, Wilma. 1987. "Electoral Systems, Contextual Factors and Women's Opportunity for Election to Parliament in Twenty-three Democracies." *Western Politics Quarterly* 40, 3 (September): 477–98.

Scripps Howard News Service. 1998. "27 in GOP, 17 Democrats Unopposed for House Seats." *The (Toledo) Blade*, April 13, 3.

Still, Edward. 1990. "Cumulative and Limited Voting in Alabama." Paper delivered at Congress on Representation, Reapportionment, and Minority Empowerment. Pomona College, Claremont, California.

Taagepera, Rein, and Mathew S. Shugart. 1989. *Seats and Votes: The Effects and Determinants of Electoral Systems*. New Haven: Yale University Press.

Tanber, George J. 1996. "Confusion Reigns Among Undecided." *(Toledo) Blade*, October 18, section 1, page 8.

Thomas, Sue. 1994. *How Women Legislate*. New York: Oxford University Press.

Weaver, Leon. 1986. "The Rise, Decline and Resurrection of Proportional Representation in Local Government in the United States." In Bernhard Grofman and Arend Lijphart, eds., *Electoral Laws and their Consequences*. New York: Agathon Press, Inc.: 139–53.

————. 1984. "Semi-Proportional and Proportional Representation Systems in the United States." In Arend Lijphart and Bernhard Grofman, eds., *Choosing an Electoral System: Issues and Alternatives*. New York: Praeger: 191–206.

Weaver, Leon, and James L. Blount. 1995. "Hamilton: PR Defeated by Its Own Success." In Kathleen L. Barber, ed., *Proportional Representation and Election Reform in Ohio*. Columbus: Ohio State University Press: 209–40.

Weko, Thomas, and John H. Aldrich. 1990. "The Presidency and the Election Campaign: Framing the Choices in 1988." In Michael Nelson, ed., *The Presidency and the Political System*, 3d edition. Washington, DC: Congressional Quarterly Press: 263–286.

Zipp, John F. 1985. "Perceived Representation and Voting: An Assessment of the Impact of 'Choices' and 'Echoes.'" *American Political Science Review* 79 (March): 30–61.

19

The American Electoral System at Century's End: Not Broken, but in Need of Prudent Repair

Everett Carll Ladd

Are we Americans losing confidence in our political system, and in particular in the way we run our election campaigns and choose leaders? A slew of books and articles in recent years have concluded that we are. Low voter turnout is often cited as a prime manifestation of the public's dissatisfaction. Interpretations of what's wrong vary, but the tone of much of the commentary is captured by the title of E. J. Dionne's widely read *Why Americans Hate Politics* (1991).

As director of The Roper Center for Public Opinion Research, I have been examining survey data on the public's opinions on politics and government for the last two decades.[1] These data show clearly (1) that most Americans remain strongly supportive of their basic political institutions; (2) that they aren't absorbed in politics, devoting themselves instead, outside of their family life, to religious and nonpolitical civic activities (Ladd 1996a: 1, 5–22); (3) that their relative indifference to contemporary politics doesn't mean they "hate it" or are alienated from it; but (4) that they do have specific complaints that are substantial—and that I think deserve attention. Here, I will address some of the latter—and offer a modest proposal to meet these concerns.

TWO CHEERS FOR THE U.S. ELECTORAL SYSTEM

Before turning to some key aspects of what seems to be troubling many Americans about contemporary electoral politics, I want to emphasize that the perceived problems reside in a generally successful system. The 1998 vote was the 106th consecutive election—including two during the Civil War—in which Americans have gone to the polls freely. It's an unmatched record of democratic participation. We lose sight of this sometimes amid the complaining that some in journalism, political science, etc., have engaged in about the process. In fact, our system of choosing leaders works remarkably well. Is there any alternate system in any other democracy that we should want to put in place of our own?

My Roper Center colleagues and I pay a good deal of attention to the electoral systems of other industrial democracies—such as France, Germany, Italy, United Kingdom, Canada, and Japan—and we have strong polling connections with organizations in all of these countries. It's striking to see how much more open the American electoral system is. The French system, for example, is still incredibly closed—dominated by party elites—and a source of enormous frustration to many citizens. America, in the Progressive Era, managed to open up its system to individual participation through direct primaries, referenda, and other direct democracy devices. Political science, my own field, has long complained about what the Progressives bequeathed us and its impact in the weakening of political party organizations. Yet, as we come to the end of the twentieth century, the whole world is striving to a greater individuation and more direct democracy. America's electoral system for all of its faults is well positioned. It is moving in the right direction. I expect we will see a continuation into the twenty-first century of the trends to which the Progressives early in the twentieth century gave leadership and direction.

There are, of course, a litany of complaints about how we elect our political leaders. Most of them are grossly misstated, I would submit, or overstated. Consider, for example, the argument about money in politics—that there is too much of it in the hands of parties and candidates. In fact, I'd argue that there is too little overall. That isn't to say that the money isn't often misused, or gotten through improper means. But if one takes the resources that the news media have to publicize their view of electioneering and sets it against the resources that the parties have to get their view out, there is a striking lack of parity. We've moved far from the early days of the Republic when the press was a party press to a situation where the parties have to operate in an adversarial environment. They have remarkably meager resources to get their message out unfiltered. Yet, in this environment the press often leads the cheerleading for means to restrict candidate and party spending even further.

We hear, also, that campaigns generally are too staged. That presidential nominating conventions are now overly choreographed was, for example, a common complaint during the 1996 Republican National Convention. There is something to this charge, but were you in a situation where you had only five and a half hours of air time for the total convention—and a large part of it dominated by someone else's commentary on what you said—you would be foolish not to try to get a message out in your limited time.

As far as polls are concerned, as someone in that business, I do think we've gone too far. In 1996, four *daily* tracking polls were being conducted in the public domain—the most ever. And 1998 saw more political polls than any previous off-year election. I looked back to the 1968 campaign between Nixon and Humphrey, and from September 1 through Election Day, there were just ten public-domain polls released in the news media (as opposed to what candidates may have done) that asked people how they would vote. Ten in the whole span! In 1996, national-level polls asked the "How would you vote?" question over two hundred times. It's my sense that this is probably unfortunate for the candidates and the electorate alike—since the question that needs attention isn't who *will* win, but who *should* win (Ladd 1996b: 4–6).

On the other hand, when you look at polling and its overall use in American politics, I think it has played an important democratizing function. The Washington press corps has become encapsulated, talking to itself and dominating Washington political discourse. Polls force the journalist community to reach out and ask cross sections of Americans what they think.

We do in fact have a highly pluralistic polling business. It's true that those conducting the public polls tend personally to be on the Democrats' side, and it's silly to suggest that such feelings have no influence on their work. It does. We need to acknowledge that the views we hold when we care deeply about elections inevitably manifest themselves in our understanding of them. Still, a variety of checks are present in election polling, including the great number of competing firms and a high measure of professionalization.

Among other criticisms about the electoral process, we often hear that today's candidates just aren't up to it. The past often looks better: Jefferson and Adams in 1800; McKinley and Bryan in 1896; and Eisenhower and Stevenson in 1952 and 1956. But there was also the race between Zachary Taylor and Lewis Cass in 1848, and that between James Garfield and Winfield Hancock in 1880. Ah, for those good old days! Many past contests left much to be desired.

We also hear, by way of criticisms, that the electorate chooses divided government too often, giving us "gridlock" as a result.[2] The United States historically has had two prolonged periods when divided government has been the rule: the half century or so from the early 1840s through the mid-1890s, and then from the mid-1950s to the present. In both eras major realignment was occurring. And in both, neither of the major parties had attained majority status. The first was a time of slow, incomplete realignment that left both parties at rough parity for an extended span. By the time of the Civil War, although the new Republican party had come far, the Democrats had "won" a truly solid South and retained substantial Jacksonian-era-type backing outside Dixie. Not until industrialization had progressed far enough to erode the socioeconomic fabric of Jacksonian America did national Republican ascendancy become possible.

Divided government of our era also reflects the fact that changes in party strength have been occurring slowly. The Republicans have again gained ground (not, of course, as a new party but by progressing from a weak number two position during most of the New Deal/Great Society years), but they have climbed only to parity. This relatively even two-party balance doesn't mandate that control of government will be divided, but it makes split results more likely.

Today, in contrast to the late nineteenth century experience, a growing segment of the electorate really doesn't belong to any party and is disinclined to place much long-term faith in either party's leadership or direction. One part of the story almost certainly involves the extraordinary degree of ambivalence that this electorate manifests about the role of the modern state. We have gone through a real revolution in the last twenty-five years in thinking about government, and if you track "role of government" questions in the polls, you see a powerful move away from the idea that was so strong at the height of the Great Society—that more government was progress. Today's electorate is much more skeptical about the idea that more government can solve our problems. But, at the same time, it wants a lot of services.

Ambivalent about the modern state, Americans take advantage of their historic legacy of separation of powers to divide political authority. William Schneider, a political scientist who taught at Harvard and now works for CNN (Cable News Network), quipped a few years ago that the Republicans would never win control of Congress until the Democrats won the presidency. There's much to this insight, given the electorate's mood. The American system allows an ambivalent electorate to give some power to one party and some to the other. It works, I think.

On this point I'd add one final observation: What's wrong with gridlock? Take a look at political systems that haven't had it. In the British system, the government of the day can do almost anything it wants as long as it can hold its House of Commons majority. Would one really argue that British public policy is superior to that of the United States? Surely many other things separate British policy results from those in the United States, so in one sense the comparison isn't fair. But if in setting policy direction we are often uncertain as to what will work, perhaps it's a good idea not to move too decisively. Dividing authority may not be a bad idea.

THE NEED FOR A MODEST REFORM AGENDA

If we spend too much time complaining about everything connected with how we choose our leaders, we are apt to spread our energy too thin and fail to focus on areas where perhaps carefully orchestrated changes would really be helpful. Quite clearly, the large elements of the American electoral system aren't going to be changed. For example, if one thinks that the way we picked presidential nominees prior to the 1960s was better than the way we do it now—try going back. I read recently a new biography of Harry Truman, which reviews in detail the contest for the 1952 Democratic presidential nomination (Hamby 1995). Senator Estes Kefauver got most of the votes in the primaries, but that didn't particularly matter. Party leadership ran the convention, and the leadership believed Kefauver would be a poor candidate. Leadership thought Adlai Stevenson a better candidate and nominated him. Stevenson was indeed a better candidate, and had he become president he probably would have done better in the job than Kefauver ever could. The planning role given party leadership in the old system clearly had merits. But we're not going back to that system. To the extent that we spend time pining for it, we dissipate energy. I suggest strongly that we try to concentrate on a few areas where we might get agreement across party lines and where achievable changes might really improve things.

If one lives and writes long enough, he is likely to find himself looking back on some things that he wrote that he subsequently would take issue with. For example, I wrote a piece for *Fortune Magazine* in 1980 on "A Better Way to Pick our Presidents." It was a magnificent blueprint for electoral change, with all kinds of bells and whistles (Ladd 1980: 86–89). Some of those ideas might actually have something to commend them, but their prospects of going anywhere were nil. I no longer have much patience with dissipating energy through such sweeping calls.

The question we need to pose is: If one believes that the way we pick our political leaders has flaws, what is the main source of these flaws and what are the several areas where it might be possible to build coalitions across party lines to find solutions? Little reform will come without an important element of bipartisanship—as all of the jockeying on campaign finance in recent years has shown. What are some things on which we might actually be able to get significant proportions of Democrats and Republicans to agree?

FINANCING CAMPAIGNS

I am going to suggest two related areas of change that I believe accord with the public's wishes and could have major impact if we could get them through, even though they might seem on the surface not too momentous. One involves how we finance our elections. Here I'm focusing on national-level financing, although aspects could apply at the state level. It has been clearly established, by experience under the Federal Election Campaign Act and its amendments, that efforts to centrally regulate the flow of money into campaigns are overturned with abandon. Michael Malbin, a professor at the State University of New York at Albany and probably the leading scholar in the country on money and politics, has shown that money is going to find its way into the process even over the most determined regulation.[3]

I would suggest, instead of such efforts at curbing the flow, an alternate approach that would greatly enlarge the base of contributors—a nonbureaucratic form of public finance. Every taxpayer would receive a 100 percent tax credit for contributions up to $100 a year (up to $200 a year for couples filing jointly). All he/she would need in order to give the money would be the interest in doing so—because it wouldn't cost him/her anything monetarily. Thus, it wouldn't be discriminatory against lower-income people. The contributor would only have to care enough to go through a particular process of identifying the candidate or the party and giving the money and keeping adequate records. Such a measure would likely increase dramatically the resources available to parties and candidates—again in a largely nonbureaucratic fashion. (It is public financing, of course, because it would involve using tax resources.) It could significantly reduce the impact of the special interest money—and the substantial frustration that many Americans feel about the impact of these funds—on the nation's politics.

A NEW PROGRESSIVE ERA

My second proposal is designed to address a different source of the frustrations felt about contemporary electioneering. In 1996, the Roper Center conducted polls for a media foundation called The Freedom Forum. We did a panel study, interviewing large numbers of potential voters at the beginning of the campaign and then coming back and reinterviewing them at later stages. Thus we not only had readings over time, but we could see what the same people were saying as they experienced the campaign. Respondents clearly indicated their deep concern that the press, as a special interest, has an excessive hold on present-day electioneering. The extent to which cross sections of Americans, without any prompting, came down so decisively, frankly surprised us.

Large sections of the public during the original Progressive Era were frustrated by special interests, "the Trusts," corrupt politicians, and political party machines. We don't know this from polling, of course, but we certainly know from their behavior and other types of data. There was strong support for opening the system up—through direct primaries, referenda, etc.—to help take control of elections from the interests and "return it to the people." While the Progressive reforms were imperfect and limited in their reach (as any set of changes are bound to be), on the whole they accomplished what was intended. They led to a reduction of public skepticism about the governmental process.

From the 1930s through the 1960s, the public at large displayed little by way of concern about how the game of politics was being conducted. Political scientists, journalists, and others discussed perceived problems in this area, but this discussion didn't reach outside political circles. Looking back at poll data from this period, it's striking that one can't find a trace of substantial general concern about how elections were conducted or any other "process" issue.

But broad concern has been building since the 1960s. Much of the public now believes that a new set of special interests wield excessive control over the political system—yet they don't know what to do about the problem. The mass media are one of these special interests. In the Freedom Forum polls we posed this statement: "I'm more likely to believe what the news media say about the candidates than what the candidates say about themselves." A majority (51 percent) disagreed. We're told—and there's certainly something to this—that politicians don't have the highest standing in terms of believability. Nonetheless, the public declared itself more inclined to trust what the candidates say than the media's interpretation of what they say. Almost 80 percent of our interviewees responded that the news media have too much control in defining the issues of the campaign. Seventy-three percent said that the news media should carry the party conventions live in their entirety, while 55 percent of those who followed the convention said that they preferred watching them without press commentary (Lado 1996b: 14). We want to get it straight, rather than through filtration.

The press is a special interest. It has a great political resource, the communications system, especially the vast reach of electronic communications. There is nothing sinister here. Rather, the point is that interests sometimes get too strong—not necessarily through some malevolent intent—but because they control decisive resources in a vital sector.

I make a sharp distinction between the "constitutional press" on the one side and the "opinion press" on the other. Writing for *The Weekly Standard* or *The New Republic* or *The Nation*, for example, one says what he wants. Such magazines are recognized as part of the opinion press. One turns to them for a point of view. But when Americans turn on the evening news, they are looking at a part of the constitutional media: This is where they get their basic information. Whatever comes through in these media needs to be "the news," not opinion. The constitutional press must be a vehicle for direct interaction between leaders and publics—a neutral conduit in the electronic age.

Back in 1858 when Lincoln and Douglas debated across seven communities in Illinois, a candidate could only reach directly an audience defined by the power of his unamplified voice. Media were not irrelevant, but they were vastly less important. Today, a candidate can't begin to communicate without access to the airwaves, and candidates now get that access in smaller and smaller bites. Try sounding brilliant, like Abraham Lincoln, in seven seconds. What Lincoln said in those seven debates had the force, the power, and the brilliance to rally a nation. In fairness, few could do it then, and few can do it now. But at least the form of communication permitted the candidate to attempt it. And if the results were rarely Lincolnesque, they were what the candidate could muster.

Increasingly, the press—and I include here on-air journalists, producers, and others—have become the gatekeepers of contemporary American electioneering to a degree without precedent in any previous time. Since the public doesn't like it, and since in certain substantial ways it challenges an open democratic process, we need to find some practical way, consistent with freedom of the press and the Bill of Rights generally, for changing it. I would submit that such a means is quite readily available. It would involve giving large blocks of air time to the candidates.

This could be done in one of two ways. Some have long argued that since the electronic media (in contrast to the print media) use a public resource—the air waves—they should be required as part of their licensing to give blocks of time for public service. If one rejects this approach, believing that it doesn't square with the free market tradition where, after all, television stations are private businesses, then one could use the public treasury to pay for the air time. Either way, give all qualifying candidates large blocks of free air time without intermediation. Let the candidates say what they want to on their own terms. Return constitutionally guaranteed communications to candidates by giving them sufficient access to the media that are essential for them to reach contemporary audiences. Various bills have been introduced into Congress to achieve this. Back in 1986, for example, Congressman Andrew Jacobs of Indiana introduced a bill that is interesting to look at in terms of the mechanics that it envisioned.[4] There are a range of mechanical problems in how to make it work—but none seem insurmountable.

Proposals were made in the last presidential contest to give the candidates more air time. A group chaired by Paul Taylor of the *Washington Post*, which included Senators Alan Simpson, Claiborne Pell, John McCain, and Bill Bradley, and former TV anchor Walter Cronkite, sought to persuade, rather than try to force, the networks to move in this area. But what was sought was so modest as to be largely inconsequential, except symbolically, and the network response failed to meet even the limited call.

Nonetheless, what Taylor said in introducing the idea at a press conference is extremely interesting and important. He argued that what needs fixing is the way we hold our "political conversation" on television. Democracy is indeed a political conversation, a process of discussion. In his brilliant essay, *Reflections on Government* (1942), political theorist Ernest Barker describes stages of discussion, from publics to legislatures, as the very core of the democratic process. What needs fixing, Taylor argued, is the way we're holding this discussion. His depiction is strikingly forceful:

I won't bother laying out the case that it's broken. Everybody in this room knows it's broken. Everybody in America knows it's broken. It needn't be that way. The nation's airways have been given to Misters Eisner, Jordan, and Welch [CEOs of the parent companies of three major networks] and their fellow broadcasters as a public trust. . . . Surely we can find our way out of the vicious cycle in which all of the great actors in the pageant of democracy—the citizens, the candidates and the journalists—bring out the least in one another. (Taylor 1996)

As noted, survey data show how decisively the general public believes key parts of the process are broken. We can fix them, as the Progressives did, by opening the system up. Doing so requires that we recognize the transformation of political speech that has occurred in modern-day electioneering. We have in effect altered the constitutional intent without ever saying so. Electronic technology has dramatically changed the nature of speech in the political domain.

CONCLUSION

Opening up the structure of campaign finance, by giving citizens tax credits for contributions they make to the candidates and parties of their choice, and restoring a more unmediated discussion between candidates and voters by permitting candidates to take their case directly to the voters through extensive free air time, aren't panaceas. But they can be important steps in our second generation of Progressive-type reform. They can reduce the role of special interests, and enhance that of the public at large.

(Based on an address given by Everett Carll Ladd at the conference on "The Impact of Elections on Governing," October 25–26, 1996, at SUNY College at Oneonta.)

NOTES

I wish to express my deep appreciation to Cathy Cuneo and Regina Dougherty for their valuable contributions to this chapter.

1. I've discussed the results of these inquiries in a number of publications. See, for example, Ladd and Keene 1988: 11–16; Ladd 1990: 1–11; Ladd and Bowman 1994; Ladd 1996a; and Ladd 1996c: 14–46.

2. See, for example, Cutler 1989: 485–92 and Sundquist 1988: 613–35.

3. See, for example, Malbin 1984: 232–76.

4. The Jacobs' bill called for an allotment of ninety minutes of television time to House candidates, to be divided as the candidate wished, provided that each appearance was at least five minutes long; and an allotment of 125 minutes of radio time, again to be used as the candidate chose, as long as the appearance lasted at least five minutes. See Ladd 1986: 34.

REFERENCES

Barker, Ernest. 1942. *Reflections on Government.* Oxford: Clarendon Press.

Cutler, Lloyd. 1989. "Some Reflections About Divided Government." *Presidential Studies Quarterly* (summer): 485–92.

Dionne, E.J., Jr. 1991. *Why Americans Hate Politics.* New York: Simon and Schuster.

Hamby, Alonzo L. 1995. *Man of the People: A Life of Harry S. Truman.* New York: Oxford University Press.

Ladd, Everett Carll. 1996a. "Political Parties and Presidential Elections in the Postindustrial Era." In Harvey Schantz, ed., *American Presidential Elections: Proc-*

ess, Policy and Political Change. Albany, NY: State University of New York
Press.

———. 1996b. "The Polls and the Election." *The Public Perspective* (October/No-
vember): 4–6.

———. 1996c. "Electoral Setting: The Public's Views of National Performance." *The
Public Perspective* (October/November): 15–46.

———. 1996d. "The Data Just Don't Show Erosion of America's 'Social Capital.'"
The Public Perspective (June/July): 1, 5–22.

———. 1990. "Public Opinion and the 'Congress Problem.'" *The Public Interest*
(summer): 1–11.

———. 1986. "Money, Campaigns, and American Democracy." *Ladd Report* 4: 34.

———. 1980. "A Better Way to Pick Our Presidents." *Fortune* (May 5): 86–89.

Ladd, Everett Carll, with Karlyn Bowman. 1994. "Public Opinion Toward Congress:
A Historical Look." In Thomas E. Mann and Norman J. Ornstein, eds.,
Congress, the Press, and the Public. Washington, DC: American Enterprise
Institute and the Brookings Institution.

Ladd, Everett Carll, with Karlyn H. Keene. 1988. "Attitudes Toward Government:
What the Public Says." *Government Executive* (January): 11–16.

Malbin, Michael. 1984. "Looking Back at the Future of Campaign Finance Reform:
Interest Groups and American Elections." In Michael Malbin, ed., *Money
and Politics in the United States.* Chatham, NJ: Chatham House: 232–76.

Sundquist, James. 1988. "Needed: A Political Theory for the New Era of Divided
Government in the United States." *Political Science Quarterly* (winter
1988–89): 613–35.

Taylor, Paul. 1996. "Free TV for Straight Talk Coalition." News conference, Washington, DC (April 18.) In *The Public Perspective.* 1996. (October/Novem-
ber): 14.

20

Realignments, the Atomization of Politics, and What We Don't Get from Elections

Daniel M. Shea

INTRODUCTION

In a seminal article published in 1955, V. O. Key introduced students of American politics to "critical realignment theory." Refined by hosts of scholars, at its core realignment theory posits important, long-term shifts in partisan cleavages among the electorate, and accordingly, the balance of power within government. To Burnham (1970), these events represent the true "mainsprings" of American governance, something that brings the political process back to its popular roots and forces the system to respond to the needs of average citizens. It is, he writes, "a mode of behavior by which the electorate seeks to exercise its sovereignty over government" (Trilling and Campbell 1980: 3, citing Burnham 1970).

This paper examines the prospects of realignments given contemporary conditions. The first section reviews the basic tenets of this model and several refinements offered over the years. It also highlights elections traditionally cited as "critical" or "realigning." It then moves to what might be termed the "missing realignment," where I offer reasons why this change did not occur as scheduled and is unlikely to happen in the near future. This is followed by a discussion of what post-realignment politics implies about the nature of the American system—what I term the *age of atomized politics*. At its core, this article argues that the atomization of politics has made realignments impossible, and without significant changes in the structure of government or the way citizens think about politics, the prospects for vibrant, popular democracy are disheartening.

A THEORY OF CRITICAL REALIGNMENT

The Political Organizations and Parties section of the American Political Science Association (APSA) broke a long standing tradition in 1996 and presented their "Outstanding Article" award to a deceased scholar. It was given to V. O. Key for his 1955 piece, "A Theory of Critical Elections." Key's analysis in this seminal article is rather simple. He first examines the rapid growth of Democratic voters in two towns in Massachusetts (Somerville and Ashfield). He finds that a "reshuffling of voters" peaked in 1928 and remained stable until the writing of the article. He then expands his analysis to an additional twenty-nine towns in Massachusetts, again finding the same pattern. Finally, Key enlarges his sample to four additional New England states, all suggesting the same pattern; Republicans were the majority party prior to 1928, but after this became the minority party. Key leaves open a number of questions regarding the import of these sharp and durable partisan shifts—namely the consequences for public administration, the legislative process, and the operation of the economy. But there is little doubt in the reader's mind that he is up to something quite important.

Accepting the award on Key's behalf at the APSA meeting was one of his students, Walter Dean Burnham. Burnham, along with scores of additional scholars, have fine-tuned Key's original theory and, to a great extent, answered many of his questions. A brief summary of the traditional critical realignment theory is as follows:[1] (1) a social and/or economic crisis arises, one that supersedes existing partisan lines of cleavage; (2) the crisis intensifies political debate and politicizes society; (3) this "cross cutting issue" and mobilization of voters manifests itself electorally in a relatively sudden, massive transformation of the coalitional bases of the party system; (4) an unusually large number of elected officials are thrown from office throughout the branches and levels of government (and, to a lesser extent, from party leadership, bureaucracies, and the courts); (5) government institutions implement policies designed to resolve the original crisis in accordance with the interests of the new majority; (6) and finally, this change in the direction of government and coalitional composition of the parties is durable—it lasts for at least several elections. To put it succinctly, realignments represent "a general, comprehensive, partisan shift, across vertical and horizontal boundaries of the constitutional system connected with large-scale and durable shifts in electoral behavior" (Burnham 1989: 16).

A few additional points are worth brief mention. First, there appears to be a significant weakening of partisan loyalties just prior to realignments. A number of studies have discerned, for instance, increased ticket splitting prior to these elections (i.e., Clubb, Flanigan, and Zingale 1980). We also see a rise in third-party activity prior to realignments—again suggesting a weakening of partisan loyalties among voters (Sundquist 1983). In short, partisanship enters a "decay phase" prior to critical elections (Beck 1974).

What makes critical realignment theory intuitively exciting, among other things, is the regularity with which the changes seem to have occurred. With the debate aside over whether the election of 1800 was the first realignment or simply an "aligning" election,[2] most agree that roughly speaking 1828, 1860, 1896, and 1932 were "critical" elections.[3] An obvious query is why they seem to occur every thirty to forty years. The strongest argument in this regard has been afforded by Paul Allen Beck (1974). His "generational theory" posits that realignments occur at about the length of time required for a generation *not* able to vote during the prior realignment to become a majority of the electorate.[4] Others have taken exception to the thirty to forty-year generational approach. If it is true that the election of 1896 marked a realigning election, giving the Republicans the clear majority, how might one explain the ascendance of Woodrow Wilson and a Democratic Congress just sixteen years later? And what about the election of Eisenhower, a Republican, just twenty years after the New Deal realignment? To Angus Campbell (1966) and other traditional realignment theorists, these elections are merely "deviating," centered only in the executive and short-lived. But to others the time between realignments has been misread. Arthur Schlesinger, Jr.(1986), for instance, maintains that the direction of our government shifts every sixteen years or so—corresponding to alterations between cycles of liberalism and conservativism (the former refers to a commitment to the "public purpose," and the latter to "private interests"). A. James Reichley (1996) has argued that sixty to seventy year "super cycles" more appropriately describe the ideological shifts in public policy.

The policy component of realignment theory is worth brief discussion as well. Realignment theory has become a growth industry in political science since Key's 1955 article *not* simply because it affords a neat conceptual paradigm, but because these elections appear to matter when it comes to what government does. Realignments are believed an opportunity for the electorate to rise up and change the direction of government. They afford average citizens the ability to make clear choices and to make accountability judgments. In a sense, realignments are the elastic that snaps government back to the will of the people.

THE MISSING REALIGNMENT

Has there *not* been a critical election or comprehensive shift in government since the New Deal? The answer to this question has occupied much scholarly time and is hotly debated. The late 1960s had many of the markings of a traditional realignment period. For one, it was on track with the generational change view. If 1930/32 was a realignment, as few would dispute, then 1968 would seem to fit nicely—thirty-six years later. Second, 1968 marked a clear shift in voter preferences for GOP presidential candidates. From 1968 to 1988, the Republicans took control of the White House in five out of six elections. And it can be argued that Carter's election in 1976 was an anomaly caused by Watergate. In at least half of these elections the Republican candidate swamped his Democratic opponent (1972, 1980, and 1984). Third, an historically Democratic region (i.e., the South) moved away from Democratic presidential candidates by 1968. George Wallace might have been the impetus that pushed white voters away from the Democrats, but they have yet to come back. Carmines and Stimson (1989) have argued the 1960s marked a realigning period because the Democrats became less tied to their segregationist southern wing; the South became more Republican and African Americans became solidly Democratic. Finally, it can be argued that 1968 marked a modest redirection of public policy.

Yet, the House of Representatives remained in the hands of Democrats from 1932 until 1994, with the brief exceptions of 1947–48 and 1953–54. The Senate followed a similar pattern, being controlled by the GOP in 1947–48, 1953–54 and 1981–86. Congress clearly did *not* "realign." On top of this, most governorships and state legislatures, as well as most municipal offices, remained in Democratic control. The model also suggests that voters will develop a new partisan attachment—at least in the aggregate. This has not occurred either; in fact, Republican identifiers are no more common in the 1960s, 1970s or 1980s, than they were in the 1950s (Wattenberg 1996). Electoral mobilization, a characteristic of traditional realignments, has not been seen during this period. If anything we have seen a more or less steady drop in voter turnout and a movement away from other forms of political participation since the 1960s. Finally, it is debatable that the public agenda shifted all that much. One would be hard-pressed to stack up Nixon's New Federalism with the rise of Jacksonian democracy in 1828, the abolition of slavery in the 1860s, the probusiness move in 1896, or the New Deal in 1932.

Others have suggested 1980 or perhaps 1994 have been realignments. On the surface, the case for 1980 has merit: Reagan came into office with a very different view of government than his Democratic predecessors (i.e., "Reagan Revolution"), the Senate changed to a Republican majority, and the GOP made substantial gains in the House. The election also marked the breakdown of the New Deal coalition with, for example, a majority of blue-collar workers supporting Reagan. There was an upward "blip" in voter turnout. On the other hand, even though Reagan's idea of government was modestly successful in the early 1980s, by 1983 much of what he sought was checked by Tip O'Neill and the Democrats in the House. Wattenberg notes that the apparent decline of split-ticket voting in 1980 was merely an "optical illusion" reflecting a mere deviation from the norm (1996: 22). And even though Reagan was reelected in a landslide in 1984, the GOP lost the Senate and a host of House seats two years later. The Reagan realignment, if there was any at all, was short-lived.

As for 1994, a case can be made that the Republican sweep into the House and Senate marked a dramatic sea change in American politics. Roughly 10 percent of House incumbents were thrown from office—a massive number compared to prior years—and every one was a Democrat. Many would argue that realignment in the South had finally crystallized and spread to the congressional level (Burnham 1995). Republican gains were also quite evident at the state and local levels throughout the nation. The idea that 1994 marked a realignment is further reinforced by the coherent, distinct policy platform the GOP carried with them into power, the Contract with America. Declarations of a long-awaited realignment could be heard among media pundits, those in the ivory towers, and especially from the halls of Congress.

But the proclamations of a 1994 realignment have been greatly exaggerated. The Contract appeared to be a catalyst for a new direction in government, but most of its provisions went no further than the House (Kolodny 1996). More to the point, voters did not seem all that convinced that the Republican view of government was the proper course, and by a clear majority sent Bill Clinton back to the White House. Since his reelection, the Republican leadership in Congress seems quite willing to set a middle-of-the-road course, frustrating many of the more conservative activists in their ranks. Shortly after Clinton's reelection Gingrich commented, "Our goal is to find common ground [with Clinton]. . . . We don't have to live in a world of confrontation. We ought to work with him and give him a chance to lead in the direction he campaigned on" (Clymer 1996). While this is perhaps good politics considering the realities of divided government, few bold GOP initiatives are likely. Finally, according to the Pew Research Center for the People and the Press, by 1996 more Americans considered themselves independent than either a Democrat or a Republican. This was especially true for folks under thirty (45 percent of whom consider themselves independent). In brief, the case for a 1994 realignment appears tenuous at best.

WHY A REALIGNMENT HAS NOT OCCURRED SINCE 1932

It seems clear, then, that realignment, at least in the traditional sense, has not occurred since 1932. But if this change has not taken place, what has been going on? Many speculate we have moved into a persistent state of "dealignment" (Nie, Verba, and Petrocik 1979; Wattenberg 1984, 1996). Instead of crosscutting issues forging new partisan alliances, voters have moved away from party labels. As for self-identification, roughly 75 percent of Americans considered themselves either a Democrat or Republican in 1952, but by the late 1990s this number had shrunk to roughly 60 percent (Ladd 1997). And the number of "pure independents" during this same period has gone from 5 to 12 percent of the electorate (Weisberg and Kimball 1995: 75–80).

Party voting has shifted more dramatically than partisanship. This has led to highly unstable electorates and an enormous rise in split-ticket voting. Whereas only about 10 percent of the electorate reported that they had split their vote choice in the 1950s (between presidential candidate and House candidate), this figure is now around the 50 percent mark (Wattenberg 1996). This has, of course, led to near persistent divided government—not only at the national level, but in most states as well. We have also seen an overall decline in political participation. Turnout during presidential contests, for example, has dropped from about 65 percent in the 1960s, to roughly 50 percent in recent elections.

Finally, dealignment has led to new interest in third party candidates. Ross Perot's 19 percent showing in 1992 highlights this development, but it can be seen elsewhere. Collet and Hansen (1996) find the number of third party candidates for governor and Congress doubled from 1970 to 1994, and there has been an even more dramatic increase in the number of races with three, four, and five or more candidates. They also note that in survey after survey roughly 65 percent of Americans would like to see a viable third party candidate join the act.

THE ATOMIZATION OF POLITICS

Perhaps dealignment is a recurring theme in American history. Beck's notion that the electorate becomes ripe prior to critical elections is analogous with what has been going on lately. The real question is why our system has not realigned since 1932 given its "ripeness." Put a bit differently, unlike prior periods where dealignment was a temporary condition, why do we confront a persistent state of dealignment?

The most frequently cited perspective is the shift toward candidate-centered elections. Candidates and their handlers have learned that they can run for office more effectively by discarding their overt party affiliation. New-style campaign consultants are also eager to use the most efficient means to win, which often implies encouraging their candidates to run *away* from partisan links when it best suits their needs. And given that the electorate is increasingly dealigned, this strategy makes more and more sense. Voters are afforded little reason to coalesce around a party label because candidates rarely mention their party during the campaigns (or after the election, for that matter). In his fifty-seven minute nomination acceptance speech in 1996, Bob Dole mentioned his own party by name only twice.

The candidate-centered explanation is compelling and explains much of the puzzle. A more inclusive perspective, however, might be termed the *atomization of politics*. This notion suggests that government and politics are now perceived as conflict among individual actors. Unlike candidate-centered politics, it denotes more than the strategic actions of candidates and campaign consultants. We can break this phenomenon into four parts: the nature of campaigns, the nature of news coverage, the activities of the parties, and the changing value preferences of voters. Given that the candidate-centered perspective has already been reviewed, let us turn to the media.

The press now covers politics as if it were a contest among individuals, rather than between parties or sets of ideas. This may have begun with John Kennedy and "Camelot," but it certainly was the name of the game played by the Reagan administration. Reagan's adversary was not the Democrats, but rather Tip O'Neill. More recently, even the Contract was not about Republican ideas, but Newt Gingrich's personal "radical" platform. The 1996 presidential campaign has been disparaged by media pundits due, of all things, to its civility. Because Dole and Clinton refused to attack each other on a personal basis, the race was dubbed "boring." Perhaps the pundits are correct—there seems to be less interest in the campaign, as compared to 1992, a very "personal" race.

There is much speculation in the wake of the 1996 presidential nomination process that the television networks will no longer cover national conventions. Their rationale is that these events no longer make "news." Ironically, many of the reforms suggested in the acclaimed 1950 American Political Science Association report, *Toward a More Responsible Two Party System*, dealt with convention-centered activities (White 1992: 4). This shift by the media clearly reflects the individual-centered nature of contemporary news coverage. We knew Dole and Clinton would be the candidates, but how did the Democratic platform differ from the Republican plan? Even when viewers are afforded *some* policy-based coverage during the conventions, it is quickly turned into a battle between individuals. The abortion fight in the GOP, for instance, was converted into a battle between Pat Buchanan and Bob Dole, or between Dole and Christine Todd Whitman. Few in the media seemed concerned with the policies Jesse Jackson might outline in his Democratic convention speech, but there was great speculation as to whether or not he would attack Clinton.

The media has also turned to what Sabato (1991) has coined "feeding frenzies." A premium is placed on character-based transgressions (often based on mere rumor and gossip). The outcome has been a reconfiguration of political news from partisan skirmishes into personal breaches. To many voters, the best party is the one with the fewest feeding frenzies pitted against its players. Politicians have caught on to this media preoccupation and see the politics of scandal as more effective than slugging it out in the trenches of ideas and policy alternatives. Ginsberg and Shefter (1990) have termed this development "politics by other means," where "revelation, investigation, and prosecution" have replaced partisan-based electoral politics. Recent examples abound: When Gingrich was elected Speaker in 1994, the Democrats' first attack was not over elements of the Contract, but rather his lucrative book contract and possible illegalities by his political action committee, GOPAC. When the Republicans became frustrated with Clinton, they simply turned up the heat on Whitewater, "Travelgate," and "Filegate." During the waning days of the 1996 presidential race, Gingrich emerged from the shadow—*not* as an avid supporter of Dole, or a GOP supply-side advocate, but to level new charges against Clinton, this time for accepting "illegal" campaign contributions from an Indonesian couple. "This scandal," suggested Gingrich on *Meet the Press,* October 13, 1996, "will make Watergate look tiny." And of course "Monica-gate" has been the big political story of 1998. A frustration commonly aired by Democratic congressional candidates was that the media seemed fixed on the Clinton sex scandal, at the expense of what most voters were concerned about—such as saving Social Security, education, and protecting the environment. Partisan politics is now individual-centered scandal politics. This clearly does nothing to bind voters to a partisan badge.

The parties have contributed to the atomization of politics in a number of other ways as well. By placing a premium on primaries and caucuses, a response to the intraparty democratic movement of the early 1970s, candidates now appeal directly to the voters—again as "independents." Jimmy Carter's ascendance in 1976 speaks volumes about the individualistic nature of party politics—as does the early success of relatively unknown millionaire Steve Forbes during the 1996 GOP primaries. Candidates at every level need not carry the party banner or work their way up the ranks. Money, exposure, and campaign prowess have replaced party screening mechanisms.

The parties have also created office- and level-specific campaign organizations. In an effort to stay ahead of the campaign technology wave, both parties have devised operations specifically geared to a single branch of the legislature. At the national level these units are called the "Hill committees" (Herrnson 1998), and at the state level "legislative campaign committees" (LCCs) (Shea 1995). These organizations utilize cutting edge techniques and top-notch professionals to get *their* members elected—but care little about what happens to other members of the ticket. These units rarely transfer money, share information, or even conduct joint activities with members of their party running for different offices. Broad-based television, radio, or mail advertisements are highly unusual. It is also common for these units to encourage their "clients" to run in opposition to unpopular candidates of the *same* party. Perhaps realizing George Bush was in deep trouble, the director of the National Republican Congressional Committee (NRCC), Ed Rollins, sent a letter early in 1992 to all Republican House candidates telling them "not [to] hesitate to oppose the President" (Shea 1995: 16).

The shift away from broad-based party appeals took a new turn in 1996. During the waning weeks of the election the National Republican Campaign Committee decided to essentially abandon the head of their ticket (Dole) in hopes of maintaining their grasp on the House. They ran a series of ads subtly encouraging voters to split their vote choices. The operatives who devised the commercials would surely argue they were not abandoning Dole, just seeking support for GOP House candidates. There is no question, nonetheless, that these commercials were very different than any prior party activity, as they did *not* encourage support for the GOP slate—only for House candidates. Commenting on the "blank check" he gave GOP House candidates to declare their independence from Dole, Gingrich suggested, "It's better to have a majority that's slightly confused than a minority that is thoroughly solid."

As for which candidates to support, the "Hill committees" and state LCCs provide assistance based solely on a candidate's ability to win elections; there is no concern for policy/party solidarity. Two comments by party leaders are illustrative in this regard. Tom Loftus, former Speaker of the Wisconsin House of Representatives, noted: "Our only test is that the candidate is in a winnable seat and he or she is breathing, and those two requirements are in order of importance" (Shea 1995: 29). Regarding "Hill committee" concerns, Deborah Falvin, formerly a GOP official notes, "At the NRCC, our only ideology is that you have a 'big R' by your name. There is no litmus test on any issue" (as cited in Herrnson 1998: 78).

Finally, John White (1992, 1998) has argued our nation's party fabric has been woven out of a deep-seated rivalry of "us" versus "them." During the Cold War, this idea was especially strong—driving most candidate and party appeals. Eisenhower was elected despite Democratic brawn because he was clearly one of "us." With the end of the Cold War, this organizing principle has become less powerful. At the very least, it has been transformed; candidates still use "us" and "them," but the meaning has been narrowed. The Soviet Union does not represent "them"; instead the opponent is "out of step," "part of the Washington establishment," or does not represent "mainstream values."

In sum, not unlike the scores of sociological studies that have suggested Americans have moved away from community-based activities, American politics has become privatized. E. J. Dionne has recently termed this "the abandonment of public life" (1991: 10). Unions are in trouble, the ten million jobs Clinton boasts of having created are mostly in the service industry and promote individualism, small towns are in decline, and so too are the old urban ethnic enclaves. Certainly the rise of the Internet will keep citizens at home even more in the years ahead. Politics, like the rest of our world, is now about the individual.

THE ALL-IMPORTANT "SO WHAT?" QUESTION

It has become commonplace to hear scholars bemoan the passing of party-centered politics. These lamentations are, at times, grounded in carefully constructed arguments, and at other times simply echo the responsible party doctrine preached at most universities since the 1950s. A logical query is *why* we should be concerned with periodic shifts in the balance of power. Perhaps, as Everett Carll Ladd has argued, our preoccupation with realignment has been mostly unfortunate, counterproductive, and serves to minimize other important changes in the party system (1991).

Unlike the party scholars Ladd suggests are "waiting for Godot,"[5] I am not optimistic that a realignment in the traditional sense will occur any time soon, if ever again. But our distress over the "end of realignment" should extend beyond the need to merely reconceptualize party adjustments. Persistent dealignment implies coming to grips with a vastly different political process and questioning whether the democratic character of our nation will endure into the next century.

The first implication is the frequent, nearly persistent state of divided government—at both national and state levels. Among other implications, accountability judgments become arduous. The voter finds it difficult to determine which party or politician is responsible for a good or bad development. Clinton signed the welfare reform bill, but the Republicans passed it through Congress. The deficit mushroomed under Reagan, but the Democrats approved his budget plans. At the very least, this leaves the electorate confused—but more likely this leads to frustration and cynicism.

It is indeed a marvel of modern electioneering that the Clinton reelection team turned the 1996 election into an accountability judgment on the "Dole/Gingrich" platform. Voters rejected Dole because, among other things, they disapproved of what the Republicans had done in Congress during the prior two years. It might be argued, in this light, that accountability judgments *are* possible during divided government. Nevertheless, this line of reasoning falls flat on closer inspection. It is *only* because the Republicans entered the House in 1994 proclaiming a "mandate" and offering a coherent, highly publicized program that an accountability judgment was made possible. In other words, 1994 represented, at least when it comes to policy, the makings of a traditional realignment. The only problems are that these issues did not truly reflect the majority will, and the pull of individual politics was too strong; as soon as Republicans discerned that their program was a bit unpopular, they began to jump ship.

But what about policy outputs? Burnham, as noted, believes periodic realignments redirect government policy. History seems to be on his side. Yet Mayhew (1991) among others suggests that significant shifts in policy *are* possible during periods of divided government. Reagan's achievements during his first two years are cited as a case in point. Clinton's accomplishments, including significant deficit reduction, are also suggestive.

Others argue, however, that while incremental changes in public policy might occur during divided government, these changes are not the type of policy shifts that draw the public into the governing process in a meaningful way. In fact, just the opposite has been occurring. Policy disputes are quickly reduced to middle-of-the-road measures that appease some constituencies without affording long term solutions. The public remains dissatisfied with government outputs, but not irate. Dionne, in his powerful book *Why Ameri-*

cans Hate Politics (1991), puts it a bit differently: "Wracked by contradiction and responsive mainly to the needs of their various constituencies, liberalism and conservativism *prevent* the nation from settling the questions that most trouble it" (1991: 11). The voters are afforded, he argues, a set of false choices.

We might inquire, if government is indeed responsive under divided government control, why has the level of distrust, cynicism, and apathy among the electorate skyrocketed during precisely the same time period. According to Stanley and Niemi's calculations, confidence in government, measured by a number of indicators (including trust in government to do the right thing), has plummeted since the early 1960s (1994: 169). Most Americans do not trust government to do the right thing. Surely other forces have been at work, and one would be hard-pressed to pin the blame for these developments on the doorstep of divided government, but this certainly puts the "responsiveness" of government in a new light.

Which brings us to a second, arguably more important, consequence of atomized politics. Students of American government have long ago identified two strains of democratic theory that have battled it out in our system. The "elite democracy" model holds that so long as there are guarantees of fairness and political opportunity, a democratic system is healthy. After competitive elections, public officials should be left to conduct the business of government. This view holds that it is best for average citizens to stay out of the way because governance is complex business. Alexander Hamilton was an especially strong advocate of this view. "Popular democracy," on the other hand, is based on the Rousseauvian model and places a premium on civic involvement in the conduct of government. This implies an ongoing, meaningful involvement in the affairs of the state. When this occurs, citizens develop an affinity for the system because they have a stake in the outcome. Jeffersonians more closely adhere to this approach.

Those who play down the effects of divided government (and those who see realignment as irrelevant) must surely adhere to an elite democratic perspective. Popular democrats would argue that realignment provides citizens a means of becoming involved in the policy direction of the government—albeit sporadically. During these elections, voters head to the polls with a clear view of what should be done and which party is best suited to accomplish it. Even if their side loses on election day, the voters feel assured because they have been meaningful players in the process. It matters little how truly informed they are on the intricacies of the policy debate, or what actual bearing their vote has on the outcome of the election, only that they believe their involvement has the *potential* to shape the direction of the nation.

It can be argued that periodic realignments shift policy and bring government back to "the people." And they might also be credited with making accountability judgments easier. But a stronger case can be made that these events bring voters into the political process in a meaningful way. Realignments give citizens a sense of true involvement that leads them to believe that their effort will make a difference. Realignment scholars and students of American government have rarely looked down this normative path. Considering the state of the American polity, it makes sense that the role of the citizen in the governing process receive more attention.

PROSPECTS FOR THE FUTURE

One could not help but be pessimistic about the prospects of realignment in the future, as noted above. The pull of atomized politics is too powerful. We might consider, nevertheless, two broad suggestions for making party-centered government, and thus a recurring realigning process, a bit more possible.

The first option would be to enact measures that strengthen the position of parties in the electoral process. This idea is certainly nothing new, but perhaps some different approaches are worth considering. For example, the parties might be granted state and federal monies or be given free air time on television/radio throughout the year. It should be mandated that this assistance be restricted to non-candidate activities. We might require, for instance, that television spots be no shorter than five minutes and never mention the name of a politician. Ralph Goldman (1996), a longtime champion of responsible parties, suggested a number of "public relations" measures designed to strengthen the place of parties in the minds of voters, such as a "parties day" and even a "bill of rights for parties." This makes a great deal of sense. Theodore Lowi (1996) has argued that we should work to reduce the barriers to third party success and that this will revitalize the party system. The point is that if we are anxious to undermine the movement toward atomized politics, then innovative ideas must be explored to strengthen the parties.

Second, and certainly more radical, we might consider adjustments to the structure of our government. If we are serious about accountability, responsiveness, and popular democracy, it makes sense to rethink the separation of powers. If merging the executive and legislative branches is a tad too draconian, at the least we should begin to consider ways to better link the president to Congress. One option might be to require the president to appoint leaders of his/her party in Congress to the cabinet. Another possibility would be to bring Senate and House elections in line with presidential elections—every four years. Not only would this lead to party-centered thinking about politics but would reduce the pull of candidate-centered politics we see every two years. A host of other possibilities await exploration. The process can only begin, however, when we come to grips with what we truly do *not* get from elections.

NOTES

Portions of this chapter appeared in Shea (1999).

1. This summary closely parallels Trilling and Campbell's review (1980: 4).

2. Fulfilling many of the tenets of a classic realignment—especially with regard to the change in the direction of government—many would argue this election begins the chronology. Yet others argue it could not possibly fit the bill because partisan cleavages had not yet developed. Simply put, how could there be a realignment without first having an alignment?

3. There is some debate as to when, precisely, the realignments took place. That is, those who adhere to a "secular realignment" approach argue this process of change occurs at a steady, albeit gradual pace. They take exception to defining just one election as *the* critical election. Nevertheless, there is a good deal of consensus that these five periods, give or take an election, witnessed fundamental changes in the party system.

4. Simply put, the "children of realignment," whose partisan orientations were garnered from their parents, will be somewhat resistant to change; they will know why they are Democrats/Republicans because their parents, having been active during the last upheaval, will have instilled their values in them. Yet, as the third generation replaces the first, the rationale for party loyalty becomes less obvious. The electorate, argued Beck, becomes "ripe" for a realignment.

5. This is a reference to Samuel Beckett's play, *Waiting for Godot.*

REFERENCES

Axelrod, Robert. 1982. "Communication." *American Political Science Review* 76: 393–96.

Beck, Paul Allen. 1974. "A Socialization Theory of Partisan Realignment." In Richard D. Niemi and Associates, eds., *The Politics of Future Citizens*. San Francisco: Jossey-Bass.

———. 1996. *Party Politics in America*, 8th ed. New York: Longman.

Bibby, John F. 1996. Politics, Parties, and Elections in America, 3rd ed. Chicago: Nelson-Hall.

Burnham, Walter Dean. 1970. *Critical Elections and the Mainsprings of American Government*. New York: Norton.

———. 1989. "The Reagan Heritage." In Gerald Pomper, ed., *The Election of 1988*. Chatham, NJ: Chatham House.

———. 1995. "Critical Realignment Lives: The 1994 Earthquake." In Colin Campbell and Burt A. Rockman, eds., *The Clinton Presidency: First Appraisals*. Chatham, NJ: Chatham House.

Campbell, Angus. 1966. "A Classification of Presidential Elections." In Angus Campbell, Philip E. Converse, Warren E. Miller, and Donald E. Stokes, eds., *Elections and the Political Order*. New York: John Wiley and Sons.

Carmines, Edward G., and James A Simpson. 1989. *Issue Evolution: Race and the Transformation of American Politics*. Princeton, NJ: Princeton University Press.

Chambers, William N., and Walter Dean Burnham. 1975. *The American Party Systems*. New York: Oxford University Press.

Clubb, Jerome M., William H. Flanigan, and Nancy H. Zingal. 1980. *Partisan Realignment: Voters, Parties and Government in American History*. Beverly Hills: Sage.

Clymer, Adam. 1996. "Top Republicans Say They Seek Common Ground with Clinton." *New York Times*, November 7, A-1.

Collet, Christian, and Jerrold Hansen. 1996. "Minor Parties and Candidates in Sub-Presidential Elections." In John C. Green and Daniel M. Shea, eds., *The State of the Parties: The Changing Role of Contemporary American Parties*, 2nd ed. Lanham, MD: Rowman and Littlefield.

Dionne, E. J. 1991. *Why Americans Hate Politics*. New York: Simon & Schuster.

Fiorina, Morris P. 1977. *Congress: Keystone of the Washington Establishment*. New Haven, CT: Yale University Press.

———. 1991. "Divided Government in the States." In Gary W. Cox and Samuel Kernell, eds., *The Politics of Divided Government*. Boulder, CO: Westview Press.

———. 1992. *Divided Government*. New York: Macmillan.

Gingrich, Newt. 1996. NBC *Meet the Press* Interview, October 13.

Ginsberg, Benjamin, and Martin Shefter. 1990. *Politics by Other Means: The Declining Importance of Elections in America*. New York: Basic Books.

Goldman, Ralph M. 1996.. "Who Speaks for the Political Parties on, Martin Van Buren, Where Are You When We Need Your?" In *The State of the Parties: The Changing Role of American Parties*. John C. Green and Daniel M. Shea, eds., Lanham, MD: Rowan and Littlefield.

Herrnson, Paul S. 1988. *Party Campaigning in the 1980s*. Cambridge, MA: Harvard University Press.

———. 1998. *Congressional Elections: Campaigning at Home and In Washington*, 2nd ed. Washington, DC: Congressional Quarterly Press.

Inglehart, Ronald. 1971. "The Silent Revolution in Europe: Intergenerational Change in Post-Industrial Societies." *The American Political Science Review* 67 (November): 1194–1203.

Jacobson, Gary. C. 1990. *The Electoral Origins of Divided Government*. Boulder, CO: Westview Press.

Key, V.O. 1955. "A Theory of Critical Elections." *Journal of Politics* 18 (September): 3–18.

———. 1964. *Politics, Parties and Pressure Groups*, 5th ed. New York: Thomas E. Crowell Company.

Kolodny, Robin. 1996. "The Contract With America in the 104th Congress." In John C. Green and Daniel M. Shea, eds., *The State of the Parties: The Changing Role of Contemporary American Parties*, 2nd ed. Lanham, NJ: Rowman and Littlefield.

Ladd, Everett Carll. 1997. "1996 Vote: The 'No-Majority' Realigment Continues." *Political Science Quarterly* 112: 112–28.

———. 1991. "Like Waiting for Godot: The Uselessness of 'Realignment' for Understanding Change in Contemporary American Politics." In Byron E. Shafer, ed., *The End of Realignment? Interpreting American Electoral Eras*. Madison, WI: University of Wisconsin Press.

Lowi, Theodore J. 1996. "Toward a Responsible Three-Party System: Prospects and Obstacles." In John C. Green and Daniel M. Shea, eds., *The State of the Parties: The Changing Role of Contemporary American Parties*, 2nd ed. Lanham, MD: Rowman and Littlefield.

Mayhew, David R. 1974. *Congress: The Electoral Connection*. New Haven, CT: Yale University Press.

———. 1991. *Divided We Govern: Party Control, Law Making, and Investigations, 1946–1990*. New Haven, CT: Yale University Press.

Nie, Norman H., Sidney Verba, and John Petrocik. 1979. *The Changing American Voter*. Cambridge, MA: Harvard University Press.

Reichley, James A. 1996. "The Future of the American Two-Party System After 1994." In John C. Green and Daniel M. Shea, eds., *The State of the Parties: The Changing Role of Contemporary American Parties*, 2nd ed. Lanham, MD: Rowman and Littlefield.

Sabato, Larry. 1991. *Feeding Frenzy: How Attack Journalism Has Transformed American Politics*. New York: The Free Press.

Schlesinger, Arthur, Jr. 1986. *The Cycles of American History*. Boston: Houghton Mifflin.

Shafer, Byron E., ed. 1991. *The End of Realignment? Interpreting American Electoral Eras*. Madison: University of Wisconsin Press.

Shea, Daniel M. 1995. *Transforming Democracy: Legislative Campaign Committees and Political Parties*. Albany: State University of New York Press.

———. 1996. *Campaign Craft: The Strategy, Tactics and Art of Political Campaign Management*. Westport, CT: Praeger.

———. 1999. "The Advent of Realignment and the Passing of the 'Base-Less' Party System." *American Politics Quarterly* 27, 1 (January): 33–57.

Silbey, Joel H. 1991. "Beyond Realignment and Realignment Theory: American Political Eras, 1789–1989." In Byron E. Shafer, ed., *The End of Realignment? Interpreting American Electoral Eras*. Madison: University of Wisconsin Press.

Stanley, Harold W., and Richard G. Niemi. 1994. *Vital Statistics on American Politics*, 4th ed. Washington, DC: Congressional Quarterly Press.

Sundquist, James L. 1983. *The Dynamics of the Party System: Alignments and Realignments of the Parties in the United States*. Washington, DC: The Brookings Institution.

Trilling, Richard J., and Bruce A. Campbell. 1980. "Toward a Theory of Realignment: An Introduction." In Bruce A. Campbell and Richard J. Trilling, eds., *Realignment in American Politics: Toward a Theory*. Austin: University of Texas Press.

Wattenberg, Martin P. 1991a. "The Republican Presidential Advantage in the Age of Party Disunity." In Gary W. Cox and Samuel Kernell, eds., *The Politics of Divided Government*. Boulder, CO: Westview Press.

———. 1991b. *The Rise of Candidate-Centered Politics*. Cambridge, MA: Harvard University Press.

———. 1996. *The Decline of American Political Parties: 1952–1994*. Cambridge, MA: Harvard University Press.

Weisberg, Herbert F., and David C. Kimball. 1995. "Attitudinal Correlates of the 1992 Presidential Vote: Party Indentification and Beyond." In Herbert F. Weisberg, ed., *Democracy's Feast: Election in America*. Chatham, NJ: Chatham House.

White, John Kenneth. 1992. *The New Politics of Old Values*, 2nd ed. Hanover, NH: University Press of New England.

———. 1998. *Still Seeing Red: How the Cold War Shapes the New American Politics*. Boulder, CO: Westview Press.

21

Parliamentary Government in the United States?

Gerald M. Pomper

In 1996, the important political decision for American political warriors was not the contest between Bill Clinton and Robert Dole. "For virtually all of the powerful groups behind the Republican Party their overriding goal of keeping control of the House stemmed from their view that that was where the real political power—near- and long-term—lay." And, "Sitting in his office on the sixth floor of the AFL-CIO building on 16th Street, political director Steve Rosenthal said that labor, too, saw the House elections as the most important of 1996—more important than the contest for the Presidency" (Drew 1997: 2, 72).

These informed activists alert us to a major shift in the character of American politics. To baldly summarize my argument, I suggest that the United States is moving toward a system of parliamentary government, a fundamental change in our constitutional regime. This change is not a total revolution in our institutions, and it will remain incomplete, given the drag of historical tradition. Nevertheless, this trend can be seen if we look beyond the formal definition of parliamentary governments, the union of legislature and executive.

The parliamentary model is evident in both empirical and normative political science. Anthony Downs begins his classic work by defining a political party virtually as a parliamentary coalition, "a team of men seeking to control the governing apparatus by gaining office in a duly constituted election" (Downs

1957: 25). Normatively, for decades, some political scientists have sought to create a "responsible party system" (American Political Science Association 1950) resembling such parliamentary features as binding party programs and legislative cohesion.

Significant developments toward parliamentary government can be seen in contemporary American politics. The evidence of these trends cannot be found in the formal institutions of the written (capital letter C) Constitution. Institutional stability, however, may disguise basic change. For example, in formal terms, the president is not chosen until the Electoral College meets in December, although we know the outcome within hours of the closing of the polls in early November.

Let us go beyond "literary theory"[1] and compare the present reality of United States politics to more general characteristics attributed to parliamentary systems. In the ideal parliamentary model, elections are contests between competitive parties presenting alternative programs, under leaders chosen from and by the parties' legislators or activists. Electoral success is interpreted as a popular mandate in support of these platforms. Using their parliamentary powers, the leaders then enforce party discipline to implement the promised programs.

The United States increasingly evidences these characteristics of parliamentary government. This fundamental change is due to the development of stronger political parties. In particular, I will try to demonstrate transformation of American politics evident in the following six characteristics of the parties:

- The parties present meaningful programs;
- They bridge the institutional separations of national government;
- They reasonably fulfill their promises;
- They act cohesively under strong legislative leadership;
- They have assumed a major role in campaigning; and
- They provide the recruitment base for presidential candidates.

PARTY PROGRAMS

A parliamentary system provides the opportunity to enact party programs. By contrast, in the American system, observers often have doubted that there were party programs, and the multiple checks and balances of American government have made it difficult to enact any coherent policies. To look for evidence, I examine the major party platforms of 1992–96, the 1994 Republican Contract with America, and the 1996 Democratic Families First Agenda.

In previous research (Pomper and Lederman 1980: chapters 7, 8), we argued that party platforms were meaningful statements and that they were good forecasts of government policy. We found, contrary to cynical belief, that platforms comprised far more than hot air and empty promises. Rather, a majority of the platforms were relevant defenses and criticisms of the parties' past records and reasonably specific promises of future actions. Moreover, the parties delivered: close to 70 percent of their many specific pledges were actually fulfilled to some degree.

Furthermore, parties have differed in their programs. Examining party manifestos in the major industrial democracies over forty years, 1948–88, Budge concludes: "American Democrats and Republicans . . . consistently differentiate themselves from each other on such matters as support for welfare, government intervention, foreign aid, and defence, individual initiative and freedom. . . . Indeed, they remain as far apart as many European parties on these points, and more so than many" (Budge 1993: 696ff.).

In recent years, we might expect platforms to be less important. National conventions have become television exercises rather than occasions for party decision making. The expansion of interest groups has made it more difficult to accomplish policy intentions. Candidate-centered campaigning reduces the incentives to achieve collective, party goals and appears to focus more on individual characteristics than on policy issues.

The party platforms of 1992 provide a test. An independent replication confirms previous research on platform content. Perhaps surprisingly, this new work indicates that the most recent platforms, like those of previous years, provide significant political and policy statements. These manifestos meet one of the tests of a parliamentary system: meaningful party programs.

The 1992 platforms[2] can be divided into three categories: puff pieces of rhetoric and fact, approvals of one's own party policy record and candidates or disapproval of the opposition, and pledges for future action. The pledges, in turn, can be categorized as being simply rhetorical or general promises, or more useful statements of future intentions—such as promises to continue existing policies, expressions of party goals, pledges of action, or quite detailed promises.[3]

As seen in Figure 21.1, there is much in the platforms that induces yawns and cynicism. The Democrats were fond of such rhetorical statements as "It is time to listen to the grass roots of America" (actually a difficult task, since most plants are speechless). The Republicans were prone to vague self-congratulation, as when they boasted, "Republicans recognize the importance of having fathers and mothers in the home." (Possibly even more so if these parents are unemployed, not distracted by jobs?)

Nevertheless, these documents—while hardly models of rational discussion—did provide useful guides to party positions. When the Democrats criticized "the Bush administration's efforts to bankrupt the public school system . . . through private school vouchers," and the Republicans declared that "American families must be given choice in education," there was an implicit policy debate. Comparison was also facilitated by the similar distributions of platform statements across policy areas. Each party tended to devote about as much attention to particular or related policies as its opposition. The only im-

Figure 21.1
Platform Content, 1992 (By Party)

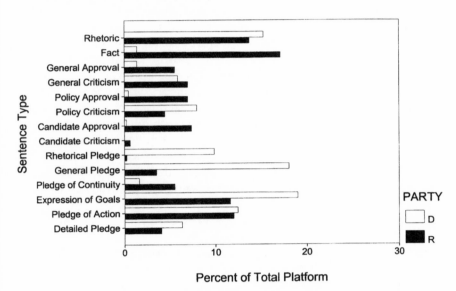

Percent of Total Platform

portant difference is that Democrats gave far more attention to issues involving women and abortion. Overall, about half of the platforms were potentially useful to the voters in locating the parties on a policy continuum.[4]

The 1994 Contract with America was even more specific. It consisted entirely of promises for the future, potentially focusing attention on public policy. Moreover, the large majority of its fifty-five sentences were reasonably specific promises. Pledges of definite action comprised 42 percent of the total document, and detailed pledges another 27 percent, while less than 4 percent consisted of only vague rhetoric. From the promise of a balanced budget amendment to advocacy of term limits, the Republicans foreshadowed major innovations in American institutions and law. This high degree of specificity can facilitate party accountability to the electorate.

PARTY AS PROGRAMMATIC BRIDGE

The great obstacle to party responsibility in the United States has always been the separation of national institutions, the constitutional division between the executive and legislative branches. Party has sometimes been praised as a bridge across this separation (Ford 1914), and party reformers have often sought to build stronger institutional ties, even seeking radical constitutional revision to further the goal (Ranney 1954). Despite these hopes and plans, however, the separation has remained. Presidential parties make promises, but Congress has no institutional responsibility to act on these pledges.

In a parliamentary system, the most current research argues—contrary to Downs—that "office is used as a basis for attaining policy goals, rather than that policy is subordinated to office" (Budge and Keman 1990: 31, chapter 2). In the United States as well, party program rather than institutional discipline may provide the bridge between the legislature and its executive. In previous years, however, we lacked a ready means to compare presidential and congressional programs. Now we have authoritative statements from both institutionalized wings of the parties. The Republican Contract with America marks a major first step toward coherent, interinstitutional programs.

The 1994 Contract was far more than a campaign gimmick, or an aberational invention of Newt Gingrich. It was actually a terse condensation of continuing Republican party doctrine, as can be seen in the left-hand columns of Table 21.1, a comparison of its specific pledges with the 1992 and 1996 Republican platforms. A majority of these promises had already been anticipated in 1992, and the party endorsed five-sixths of its provisions in 1996.

For example, the 1992 national platform criticized the Democratic Congress for its refusal "to give the President a line-item veto to curb their self-serving pork-barrel projects" and promised adoption of the procedure in a Republican Congress. The 1994 Contract reiterated the pledge of a "line-item veto to restore fiscal responsibility to an out-of-control Congress," while the 1996 platform reiterated that "a Republican president will fight wasteful spending with the line-item veto which was finally enacted by congressional Republicans this year over bitter Democrat opposition."[5] Republicans built on traditional party doctrine, specified the current party program, and then affirmed accountability for their actions. Building on this achievement in party building and their claims of legislative "success," the Republicans have already promised to present a new Contract for the elections at the turn of the century.

The Democrats imitatively developed a congressional program, the Families First Agenda, for the 1996 election. Intended primarily as a campaign

Table 21.1
Inclusion of Congressional Pledges in National Party Platforms

	Republican "Contract" (N=42) Party Platform of		Democratic "Agenda" (N=90) Party Platform of	
	1992	*1996*	*1992*	*1996*
Mentioned only	5 (12%)	3 (7%)	5 (6%)	1 (1%)
Took credit	2 (5%)	16 (38%)	0 (0%)	16 (18%)
Future Promise	16 (38%)	16 (38%)	36 (40%)	48 (53%)
No mention	19 (45%)	7 (17%)	49 (54%)	25 (28%)

document by the minority party, it is less specific than the Republican Contract. Still, ninety of its 204 statements were reasonably precise promises. The legislative Democrats also showed significant and increasing agreement with their presidential wing and platform. By 1996, as detailed in the right-hand columns of Table 21.1, three-fourths of the congressional Agenda was also incorporated into the Clinton program, and the platform specifically praised the congressional program. Its three sections—"security," "opportunity," and "responsibility"—paralleled those of the national platform (which added "freedom," "peace" and "community"—values presumably shared by congressional Democrats), and many provisions are replicated from one document to another.

The Republican Contract and the Democratic Agenda, then, can be seen as emblems of party responsibility and likely precedents for further development toward parliamentary practice in American politics. Party doctrine has become a bridge across the separation of institutions.

PROGRAM FULFILLMENT

Both Democrats and Republicans, as they held power, followed through on their election promises, as expected in a parliamentary model. Despite the clumsiness of the Clinton administration, and despite the Democrats' loss of their long-term control of Congress in their catastrophic election defeat in 1994, they actually fulfilled most of the 167 reasonably specific pledges in their 1992 manifesto.

A few examples illustrate the point. The Democrats promised negative action, in opposing major change in the Clean Air Act—and they delivered. In their 1993 economic program, the Democrats won action similar to their platform pledge to "make the rich pay their fair share in taxes." Through executive action, the Clinton administration redeemed its promise to reduce U.S. military forces in Europe. The Democrats achieved full action on their promise of "a reasonable waiting period to permit background checks for purchases of handguns."

To be sure, the Democrats have not become latter-day George Washingtons, unable to tell an untruth. There clearly has been no action on the pledge to "limit overall campaign spending and . . . the disproportionate and excessive role of PACs." In other cases, the Democrats did try, but were defeated, most notably in their promise of "reform of the health-care system to control costs and make health care affordable." (It is obviously too early to judge fulfillment of 1996 Democratic pledges, made in either the presidential platform or the congressional party Agenda.)

Most impressive are not the failures, but the achievements, illustrated in Figure 21.2. Altogether, Democrats did accomplish something on nearly 70 percent of their 1992 promises, in contrast to inaction on only 19 percent. In a completely independent analysis, another researcher came to remarkably simi-

Figure 21.2
Fulfillment of 1992 Democratic Platform

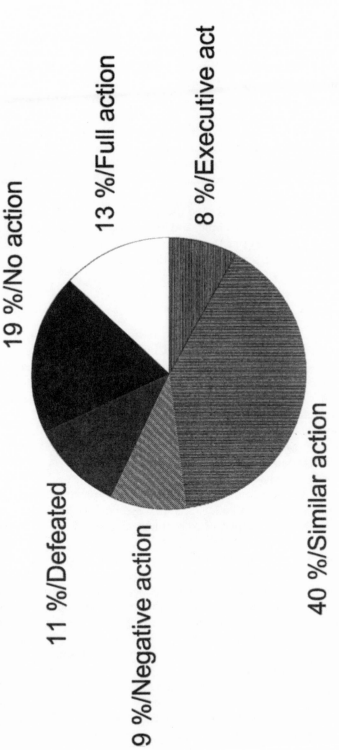

19 %/No action

13 %/Full action

8 %/Executive act

11 %/Defeated

9 %/Negative action

40 %/Similar action

lar conclusions, calculating Clinton's fulfillment of his campaign promises at the same level, 69 percent (Shaw 1996).[6] I do not believe this record is the result of the virtues of the Democratic party, which I use for this analysis simply because it controlled the government, nor can this record be explained by Bill Clinton's personal qualities of steadfast commitment to principle. The cause is that we now have a system in which parties, whatever their names or leaders, make and keep promises.

This conclusion is strengthened if we examine the Republicans. While the GOP of course did not hold the presidency, it did win control of Congress in 1994. In keeping with the model of parliamentary government, Republicans interpreted their impressive victory as an endorsement of the Contract with America and then attempted to implement the program. We must remember that the 1994 election cannot be seen as a popular mandate for the Republican manifesto: two-thirds of the public had not even heard of it in November, and only 19 percent expressed support. The Contract expressed party ideology, not voter demands.

Despite its extravagant tone and ideological character, the Republicans delivered on their Contract, just as Democrats fulfilled much of their 1992 platform. Of the more specific pledges, 69 percent were accomplished in large measure[7] (coincidentally, perhaps, the same success rate as the Democrats'). Even if we include the rhetorical and unspecific sentences in our test, as in Figure 21.3, more than half of this party program was accomplished.

Despite the heroics of vetoes and government shutdown, despite bicameralism and the vaunted autonomy of the Senate, and despite popular disapproval, the reality is that most of the Contract was implemented. The Republicans accomplished virtually all that they promised in regard to congressional reform, unfunded mandates, and welfare, as well as substantial elements of their program in regard to crime, child support, defense, and the social security earnings limit. Defeated on major economic issues, they later achieved many of these goals, including a balanced budget agreement in place of a constitutional amendment, a children's tax credit, and a reduction in capital gains taxes. On these questions, as indeed on the general range of American government, they won the greatest victory of all: they set the agenda for the United States, and the Democratic president eventually followed their lead. Such initiative is what we would expect in a parliamentary system.

Congressional performance on the Contract also carries significant implications for the theory of political parties. Monroe and Bernardoni (1995) test its implementation against two party concepts: responsible parties and a Downsian spatial model. Overall, the implementation of the Contract lends support to a different "cleavage" model developed by Page (1978), in which the parties "offer ideologically distinct positions . . . on those issues which have historically divided the parties and are related to support from voting blocs and interest groups" (Monroe and Bernadoni 1995:2). This model fits well with that developed through the Manifestos Research Project, comparing party

Figure 21.3
Fulfillment of 1994 Republican "Contract" Pledges

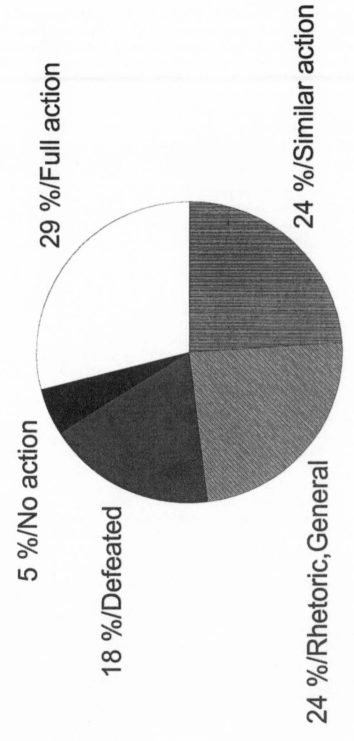

29 %/Full action

24 %/Similar action

24 %/Rhetoric, General

18 %/Defeated

5 %/No action

programs across western democracies. In this model, "what parties offer electors thus seems to be a choice between selective policy agendas, not between specific alternative policies addressed to items on a universal agenda" (Klingemann, Hofferbert, and Budge 1994: 25).

PARTY COHESION

Program fulfillment results from party unity. The overall trend in Congress, as expected in a parliamentary system, is toward more party differentiation.[8] One indicator is the proportion of legislative votes in which a majority of one party is opposed to a majority of the other—that is, "party unity" votes. Not too long ago, in 1969, such party conflict was evident on only about a third of all roll calls. By 1995, nearly three-fourths of House votes, and over two-thirds of Senate rollcalls, showed these clear party differences.

Figure 21.4 shows the increasing commitment of representatives and senators to their parties. The average legislator showed party loyalty (expressed as a "party unity score") of less than 60 percent in 1970. In 1996, the degree of loyalty had climbed to 80 percent for Democrats, and to an astounding 87 percent for Republicans. Cohesion was still greater on the thirty-three House roll calls in 1995 on final passage of items in the Contract. Republicans were unanimous on sixteen of these votes, and the *median* number of Republican dissents was but *one*. Neither the British House of Commons nor the erstwhile Supreme Soviet could rival this record of party unity.

The congressional parties now are ideologically cohesive bodies, even with the occasional but significant split among Democrats on such issues as trade and welfare reform. We need to revise our political language to take account of this ideological cohesion. There are no more "Dixiecrats" or southern conservative Democrats, and therefore there is no meaningful "conservative coalition" in Congress. Supportive evidence is found in the same roll call data: the average Southern Democrat supported his party 71 percent of the time in 1996 , and barely over a tenth of the roll calls found Dixie legislators in opposition to their own party and in alliance with a majority of Republicans. It also seems likely that "liberal Republican" will soon be an oxymoron restricted to that patronized minority holding a pro-choice attitude on abortion, confined to the back of the platform or, so to speak, to the back of the party bus.

Republicans have been acting like a parliamentary party beyond their ideological unity on a party program. The "central leaders' efforts during the Contract period were attempts to *impose* a form of party government" that succeeded in winning cooperation from committee chairmen and changed roll call behavior as "many Republicans modified their previous preferences in order to accommodate their party colleagues" (Owens 1997: 259, 265). Beyond programmatic goals, the Republicans have created strong party institutions in Congress, building on previous Democratic reforms (Rohde 1991).

Figure 21.4
Partisan Unity in Congress

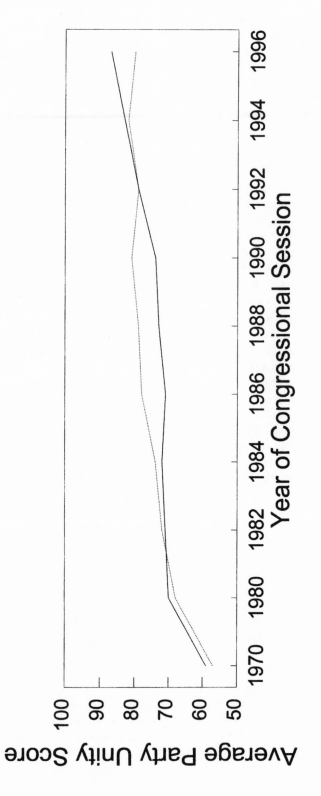

Even after the Contract with America is completely passed or forgotten, these institutions will likely remain. In their first days in power, as they organized the House, the Republicans centralized power in the hands of the Speaker, abolished institutionalized caucuses of constituency interests, distributed chairmanships on the basis of loyalty to the party program and in disregard of seniority, and changed the ratios of party memberships on committees to foster passage of the party program. Instruments of discipline have become more prevalent and more exercised, including caucus resolutions, committee assignments, aid in securing campaign contributions, and disposition of individual members' bills.

The building of parliamentary party institutions continues. Some of the structural changes in the House have now been adopted by both the Senate and the Democrats, perhaps most significantly the rotation of committee chairmanships, curbing the antiparty influence of seniority. The Republicans have insisted that committees report party bills, even when opposed by the chairman, as in the cases of term limits and telecommunications. The party record became the major issue in the 1996 congressional elections, with party leaders Newt Gingrich and Richard Armey doing their best to aid loyalists—but only loyalists—through fund-raising and strong-arming of ideological allies among political action committees.

The party differences and cohesion in Congress partially reflect the enhanced power of legislative leaders. The more fundamental reason for congressional party unity—as in parliamentary systems—is not discipline as much as agreement. Party members vote together because they think the same way. Republicans act as conservatives because they *are* conservatives; Democrats act like liberals or, as they now prefer, progressives, because they believe in these programs.

Supportive evidence on the ideological consistency of party elites can be found in studies of other partisans. In research conducted nearly forty years ago, Herbert McClosky and his students (1960: 406–27) demonstrated the large ideological differences among the two major parties' national convention delegates. Continuing party differences are also shown in more recent studies of convention delegates. John Kessel and his students (Bruce, Clark, and Kessel 1991: 1089–1106) have drawn the ideological structures of these party representatives. Though not monolithic, they are sharply distinct between the parties. These divisions persist among broader layers of party activists, such as contributors and campaign workers (Bruzios 1990: 581–601). Similarly, extensive surveys of state party convention delegates show consistent ideological differences, independent of state cultures (Abramowitz, McGlennon, and Rapoport 1986: chapter 3). There is a difference, consistent with the expectations of a parliamentary system.

The most recent nominating conventions provide further support for the ideological cohesion of the national parties. The CBS/*New York Times* poll found massive differences between Republican and Democratic delegates on questions involving the scope of government, social issues, and international affairs (see Table 21.2). A majority of these partisans opposed each other on *all* of ten questions; they were remotely similar on only one issue—international trade—and were in essentially different political worlds (fifty or more percentage points apart) on issues of governmental regulation, the environment, abortion, assault weapons, civil rights, affirmative action, and immigration.

PARTY ORGANIZATION

Party unity has another source, related to the recruitment of individual candidates with a common ideology. Unity is also fostered by the development of strong national party organizations, precisely measured by the dollars of election finance. Amid all of the proper concern over the problems of campaign

Table 21.2
1996 Convention Delegates' Issue Attitudes (in Percentages)

	Democratic Delegates	Democratic Voters	All Voters	G.O.P. Voters	G.O.P. Delegates
Scope of Government					
Government should do more to					
...solve the nation's problems	76	53	36	20	4
...regulate the environment and safety practices of business	60	66	53	37	4
...promote traditional values	27	41	42	44	56
Social Issues					
Abortion should be permitted in all cases	61	30	27	22	11
Favor a nationwide ban on assault weapons	91	80	72	62	34
Necessary to have laws to protect racial minorities	88	62	51	39	30
Affirmative action programs should be continued	81	59	48	28	9
Organized prayer should be permitted in public schools	20	66	66	69	57
International					
Trade restrictions necessary to protect domestic industries	54	65	60	56	31
Children of illegal immigrants should be allowed to attend public school	79	63	54	46	28

Source: CBS News/*New York Times* Poll, *The New York Times*,: August 26, 1996, A12.

contributions and spending, we have neglected the increasing importance of the parties in providing money, "the mother's milk of politics."

There are two large sources of party money: the direct subsidies provided by the federal election law, and the "soft money" contributions provided for the parties' organizational work. Together, even in 1992, these funds totaled $213 million for the major candidates and their parties.[9] Underlining the impact of this party spending, the Republican and Democratic presidential campaigns in 1992 each spent twice as much money as did billionaire Ross Perot, whose candidacy is often seen as demonstrating the decline of the parties.

An enhanced party role was also evident in the other national elections of 1992. Beyond direct contributions and expenditures, the parties developed a variety of ingenious devices, such as bundling, coordinated spending, and agency agreements, to again become significant players in the election finance game. Overall, in 1992, the six national party committees spent $290 million. (For comparison, total spending in all House and Senate races was $678 million.)[10] The party role became even more evident in 1994, with the victory of a Republican majority originally recruited and financed by Newt Gingrich's GOPAC, a party body disguised as a political action committee.

The party role expanded hugely in 1996, bolstered by the Supreme Court in its 1996 *Colorado* decision.[11] The Court approved unlimited "independent" spending by political parties on behalf of their candidates. Moreover, four justices explicitly indicated that they were even prepared to approve unlimited direct expenditures by parties, and three other justices are ready to rule on that issue in a future case.

The parties quickly took advantage of the Court's opening. Together, Republican and Democratic party groups spent close to a billion dollars, conservatively 35 percent of all election spending, without even counting the $160 million in federal campaign subsidies for the presidential race.[12] Despite the commonplace emphasis on "candidate-centered" campaigns, the parties' expenditures were greater than that of all individual House and Senate candidates combined. In discussions of election finance, political action committees (PACS) receive most of the attention, and condemnation, but the reality is that PACs are of decreasing importance. PACs' money has barely increased since 1988, and they were outspent two-to-one by the parties in 1996.[13] The parties now have the muscle to conduct campaigns and present their programs, to act as we would expect of parliamentary contestants.

PARTY LEADERSHIP

Parties need leaders as much as money. In parliamentary governments, leaders achieve power through their party activity. That has always been the case even in America when we look at congressional leadership: a long apprenticeship in the House and Senate has usually been required before one achieves the positions of Speaker, majority and minority leader, and whip. A strong indication of the development of parliamentary politics in the United States is the unrecognized trend toward party recruitment for the presidency, the allegedly separated institution.

The conventional wisdom is quite different. Particularly since the "reforms" of the parties beginning with the McGovern-Fraser Commission after 1968, presidential nominations have apparently become contests among self-starting aspirants who succeed by assembling a personal coalition that appeals directly to the voters in a series of uncoordinated state primaries. We have come to assume the disappearance of party influence in presidential nominations.

In reality, however, the parties have become important sources of leadership recruitment. Since 1980, as specified in Table 21.3, we have seen ten major party presidential nominations, all of them the choice of an established party leader, even in the face of significant insurgencies. These selections include four renominations of the sitting party leader, with only one facing a strong challenge (Carter in 1980); four selections of the leader of the established dominant faction of the party; and two selections of the leader of a major party faction.

Presidential nominations certainly have changed, but the trend is toward different, rather than less, party influence. Look back at the "traditional" convention system, as analyzed by Paul David and associates in 1960 (David, Goldman, and Bain 1960). Historically, some presidents retired voluntarily or involuntarily after one term, but every chief executive since 1972 has been renominated, including Gerald Ford, never elected to national office. When

Table 21.3
Recent Presidential Nominations

Year	Party	Candidate	Type
1980	Democrat	Carter	Renomination of incumbent
1980	Republican	Reagan	Dominant factional victory
1984	Democrat	Mondale	Dominant factional victory
1984	Republican	Reagan	Renomination of incumbent
1988	Democrat	Dukakis	Factional victory
1988	Republican	Bush	Dominant factional victory
1992	Democrat	Clinton	Factional victory
1992	Republican	Bush	Renomination of incumbent
1996	Democrat	Clinton	Renomination of incumbent
1996	Republican	Dole	Dominant factional victory

nominations have been open, inheritance and factional victory have become the universal paths to success, as they were historically. In contrast, past patterns of inner group selection or compromise in stalemate have disappeared.[14]

The selection of presidential nominees still evidences influence by leaders of the organized parties or its factions, even if these choices have not been made primarily by the formal party leadership (such as Democratic "super-delegates" and similar Republican officials). These decisions are quite different from the selection of such insurgents as Goldwater in 1964 or McGovern in 1972, the typical illustrations of the asserted decline of party. While insurgents do now have access to the contest for presidential nominations, the reality is that they fail in that contest, as shown by the examples of Democrats Edward Kennedy in 1980, Gary Hart in 1984, and Jesse Jackson in 1988, and the virtual absence of any Republican insurgents throughout the period until 1992.

The presidential nominations of 1992 and 1996 particularly evidence the party basis of recruitment. There were notable insurgent candidates: Republican Pat Buchanan twice attempted to reincarnate Barry Goldwater, Jerry Brown imitated McGovern, and Paul Tsongas eschewed partisanship. In contrast to earlier years, however, all were soundly defeated by established party figures. George Bush was not only the incumbent leader but also typified the career of a party politician, securing his nomination as the heir of the retiring leader, Ronald Reagan. Robert Dole is the quintessence of a parliamentary party leader, achieving nomination on the basis of his past service as national chairman, vice-presidential candidate, and legislative leader of the Senate and, moreover, against very pallid opposition, including a Buchanan insurgency even weaker than in 1992.

Bill Clinton came to party leadership from the position of governor, reflecting the variety of career opportunities available in a federal system, but Arkansas was hardly a robust power center. Clinton's real base was the Democratic Leadership Council, which provided much of his program, his source of contacts and finances, and his opportunity for national exposure. The DLC, composed of party officials and officeholders, is an organized party faction (Hale 1994: 249–63). Clinton's 1992 success is a testament to the influence of that faction, far more than evidence of the decline of party and the substitution of unmediated access to the voters. The absence of any challenge to the president in 1996 underlines the renewed importance of party leadership, despite his political vulnerabilities and intraparty discontent with his turn away from party orthodoxy.

Contrary to the fears of many observers (Polsby 1983) the new presidential nominating system has developed along with new institutions of party cohesion. Front-runners have great advantages in this new system (Mayer 1995: chapter 2), but that means that prominent party figures—rather than obscure dark horses stabled in smoke-filled rooms—are most likely to win nomination. Contrary to fears of a personalistic presidency, the candidates chosen in the post-reform period tackle tough issues, support their party's program, and agree with their congressional party's leaders on policy positions as much, or even more, than in the past (Patterson and Bice 1997).

Contemporary presidential nominations have become comparable—although not identical—to the choice of leadership in a hypothetical U.S. parliamentary system. Is the selection of Reagan in 1980 that different from the British Tories' choice of Margaret Thatcher to lead the party's turn toward ideological free-market conservatism? In a parliamentary system, would not Bush and Dole, Reagan's successors, be the ideal analogues to Britain's John Major? Is the selection of Mondale as the liberal standard bearer of the liberal Democratic party that different from the lineage of left-wing leaders in the British Labour party? Is the Democratic turn toward the electoral center with Clinton not analogous to Labour's replacement of Michael Foot by Neil Kinnock, John Smith, and Tony Blair?

To be sure, American political leadership is still quite open, the parties quite permeable. Presidential nominations do depend greatly on personal coalitions, and popular primaries are the decisive points of decision. Yet it is also true that leadership of the parties is still, and perhaps increasingly, related to prominence within the parties.

TOWARD PARLIAMENTARY GOVERNMENT?

Do these changes amount to parliamentary government in the United States? Certainly not in the most basic definitional sense, since we will surely continue to have separated institutions, in which the president is elected differently from the legislature, and the Senate differently from the House. Unlike a formal parliamentary system, the president will hold his office for a fixed term, regardless of the "votes of confidence" he wins or loses in Congress. By using his veto and the bully pulpit of the White House, Bill Clinton has proven that the president is independent and still "relevant." It is also true that we will never have a system in which a single political party can both promise and deliver a complete and coherent ideological program. As Charles Jones (1996: 19) correctly maintains, American government remains a "separated system," in which "serious and continuous in-party and cross-party coalition building typifies policy making." These continuing features were strikingly evident in the adoption of welfare reform in the 104th Congress.

But parliaments also evidence coalition building, particularly in multiparty systems. British parliamentarians can be as stalemated by factional and party differences on issues such as Northern Ireland as the Democrats and Republicans were on health care in the 103rd Congress. Achieving a consensual policy on the peace process in Israel's multiparty system is as difficult as achieving a consensual policy on abortion among America's two parties.

In the 105th Congress, we have already seen more open coalition building. With a close division among the parties in the House, more frequent use of filibusters in the Senate, and the president's veto threats, the necessities of politics and government have forced compromise, most notably in the budget-balancing agreement. Nevertheless, the party basis of parliamentary government will continue, because the ideological basis of intraparty coherence and interparty difference will continue, and even be increased with the ongoing departure of moderate legislators of both parties. The need for strong party institutions in Congress will also be furthered by new policy problems, more rapid turnover of membership, and the continuation of split-party control of government (Owens 1997: 269–72).

Of course the presidency will remain relevant, yet it may also come to be seen as almost superfluous. A principal argument on behalf of Bob Dole's candidacy was that he would sign the legislation passed by a Republican Congress—hardly a testament to presidential leadership. President Clinton fostered his reelection by removing himself from partisan leadership, "triangulating" the White House between congressional Democrats and Republicans, and following the model of patriotic chief of state created by George Washington and prescribed in *The Federalist*: "to guard the community against the effects of faction, precipitancy, or of any impulse unfriendly to the public good" (Madison 1941: 477).

In keeping with this restrictive model, he has become less involved in controversial issues, newly emphasizing the less partisan area of foreign policy, while appealing to consensual attitudes such as "family values" and school achievement. He adopted Republican programs, even changing previous positions on many issues, most prominently the balanced budget and welfare reform. He succeeded in winning re-election, but at the cost of the loss of policy initiative.

Political ambition, immodestly evidenced by President Clinton, Senator Dole, and their peers, is no sin. But the implications of the 1996 election campaign for American government remain important. The presidency is already a diminished office because the end of the Cold War has removed a principal support of its power, the predominance of foreign and defense policy. The limits on federal funds, created by the emphasis on budget balancing and the burden of middle-class entitlements, restrict the energy of the executive. Clinton's pieties on children and Dole's condemnation of drugs and pornography evoked no mandate for meaningful policy initiatives.

The absence of presidential initiative is more than a problem of the Clinton administration. Throughout American history, the president has persistently provided the energy of American government, the source of new "regimes" and policy initiatives (Skowronek 1993). Perhaps the lassitude of contemporary politics is only the latest example of the recurrent cycle of presidential initiative, consolidation, and decline. Or, more seriously, perhaps it marks the decline of the executive office itself as a source of creativity in the government of the United States.

America needs help. It may well be time to end the fruitless quest for a presidential savior and instead turn our attention, and our support, to the continuing and emerging strengths of our political parties. We are developing, almost unnoticed, institutions of semiparliamentary, semiresponsible government. To build a better bridge between the past and the future, perhaps this new form of American government is both inevitable and necessary.

NOTES

I gratefully acknowledge the help of Andrea Lubin, who performed the content analyses reported in this essay.

1. The phrase is from Walter Bagehot's classic analysis (1928: 1) of the realities of British politics.

2. The texts are found in *The Vision Shared* (Washington: Republican National Committee 1992) and, for the less loquacious Democrats, *Congressional Quarterly Weekly Report* 1992: 2107–13.

3. Each sentence, or distinct clause within these sentences, constituted the unit of analysis. Because of its great length, only alternate sentences in the Republican platform were included. No selection bias is evident or, given the repetitive character of platforms, likely. In total, there are 426 units of analysis in the Democratic platform, 758 in the Republican. For further details on the techniques used, see Pomper and Lederman: 235–48. To avoid contamination or wishful thinking on my part, Ms. Lubin (an undergraduate researcher at Rutgers University at the time) did the analysis independently. My later revisions tended to classify the platform sentences as less specific and meaningful than she did, contrary to my optimistic predisposition.

4. The "useful" categories are: policy approval and policy criticism, candidate approval and candidate criticism, and future policy promises classified as pledges of continuity, expressions of goals, pledges of action, and detailed pledges.

5. "The Vision Shared" (1992 Republican Platform): 46; Contract with America. In Wilcox (1995: 70); *Restoring the American Dream* (1996 Republican Platform): 25.

6. Using the same content categories, Carolyn Shaw (1996) of the University of Texas lists 150 presidential campaign promises of 1992 in the more specific categories. In regard to fulfillment, she employs the methods of Fishel (1985). With this method, she finds that there was "fully comparable" or "partially comparable" action on 69 percent of Clinton's proposals. This record is higher than that found by Fishel for any president from Kennedy through Reagan.

7. Even this figure underestimates the impact of the Contract. I have counted the failure to pass term limits as a defeat, although the Republicans actually promised no more than a floor vote, and I have not given the party credit for achievements in the following Congress.

8. These data are drawn from *Congressional Quarterly Weekly Report* 1996: 3461–67.

9. *Congressional Quarterly Weekly Report* 1993a: 1197.

10. *Congressional Quarterly Weekly Report* 1993b: 691; Federal Election Commission, *Record* 1993: 22.

11. *Colorado Republican Federal Campaign Committee v. Federal Election Commission* (No. 95–489, 1996 U.S. LEXIS 4258).

12. The parties spent $628 million directly, plus at least $263 million and up to $400 million in "soft money." For detailed figures, see *Congressional Quarterly Weekly Report* 1997: 767–73.

13. For an excellent discussion of 1996 election spending, see Corrado (1997).

14. The only exception to the trend away from inner party selection or compromise since 1924 is Alf Landon's designation as the Republican candidate in 1936.

REFERENCES

Abramowitz, Alan, John McGlennon, and Ronald Rapoport. 1986. "An Analysis of State Party Activists." In Rapoport et al., *The Life of the Parties*. Lexington: University Press of Kentucky.

American Political Science Association, Committee on Political Parties. 1950. "Toward a More Responsible Two-Party System." *American Political Science Review* 44: Supplement.

Bagehot, Walter. 1928 [1867]. *The English Constitution*. London: Oxford University Press.

Bruce, John M., John A. Clark, and John H. Kessel. 1991. "Advocacy Politics in Presidential Parties." *American Political Science Review* 85: 1089–1106.

Bruzios, Christopher. 1990. "Democratic and Republican Party Activists and Followers." *Polity* 22: 581–601.

Budge, Ian. 1993. "Parties, Programs and Policies: A Comparative and Theoretical Perspective." *American Review of Politics* 14: 696.

Budge, Ian, and Hans Keman. 1990. *Parties and Democracy*. Oxford: Oxford University Press.

Colorado Republican Federal Campaign Committee v. Federal Election Commission (No. 95–489, 1996 U.S. LEXIS 4258).

Congressional Quarterly Weekly Report. 1997. 55 (April 5): 767–73.

———. 1996. 54 (December 21): 3461–67.

———. 1993a. 51 (May 15): 1197.

———. 1993b. 51 (March 20): 691.

———. 1992. 50 (July 18): 2107–13.

Corrado, Anthony. 1997. "Financing the 1996 Elections." In Gerald M. Pomper, ed., *The Election of 1996*. Chatham, NJ: Chatham House: chapter 4.

David, Paul T., Ralph M. Goldman, and Richard C. Bain. 1960. *The Politics of National Party Conventions*. Washington DC: The Brookings, Institution.

Downs, Anthony. 1957. *An Economic Theory of Democracy*. New York: Harper.

Drew, Elizabeth. 1997. *Whatever It Takes: The Real Struggle for Political Power in America*. New York: Viking Penguin.

Federal Election Commission. 1993. *Record* 19 (May): 22.

Fishel, Jeff. 1985. *Presidents and Promises*. Washington DC: Congressional Quarterly Press.

Ford, Henry Jones. 1914. *The Rise and Growth of American Politics*. New York: Macmillan.

Hale, Jon F. 1994. "The Democratic Leadership Council: Institutionalizing Party Faction." In Daniel Shea and John Green, eds. *The State of the Parties*. London: Rowan and Littlefield: 249–63.

Jones, Charles O. 1996. "The Separated System." *Society* 33.

Klingemann, Hans-Dieter, Richard Hofferbert, and Ian Budge. 1994. *Parties, Policies, and Democracy*. Boulder, CO: Westview Press.

Madison, James. 1941 [1787]. *The Federalist*. New York: Modern Library.

Mayer, William. 1995. *In Pursuit of the White House*. Chatham, NJ: Chatham House.

McClosky, Herbert. 1960. "Issue Conflict and Consensus among Party Leaders and Followers." *American Political Science Review* 54: 406–27.

Monroe, Alan D., and Brian A. Bernardoni. 1995. "The Republican 'Contract' with America: A New Direction for American Parties?" Atlanta: Southern Political Science Association.

Owens, John E. 1997. "The Return of Party Government in the US House of Representatives." *British Journal of Political Science* 27.

Page, Benjamin. 1978. *Choices and Echoes in Presidential Elections*. Chicago: University of Chicago Press.

Patterson, Kelly, and Amy Bice. 1997. "Political Parties, Candidates, and Presidential Campaigns: 1952– 1996." Washington, DC: American Political Science Association.

Polsby, Nelson. 1983. *Consequences of Party Reform*. New York: Oxford University Press.

Pomper, Gerald M., with Susan L. Lederman. 1980. *Elections in America*, 2nd ed. New York: Longman.

Ranney, Austin. 1954. *The Doctrine of Responsible Party Government*. Urbana: University of Illinois Press.

Rohde, David. 1991. *Parties and Leaders in the Postreform House*. Chicago: University of Chicago Press.

Shaw, Carolyn. 1996. "Has President Clinton Fulfilled His Campaign Promises?" San Francisco: American Political Science Association.

Skowronek, Stephen. 1993. *The Politics Presidents Make*. Cambridge: Belknap Press.

Wilcox, Clyde. 1995. *The Latest American Revolution?* New York: St. Martin's Press.

For Further Reading

ARTICLES

American Political Science Association, Committee on Political Parties. 1950. "Toward a More Responsible Two-Party System." *American Political Science Review* 44: Supplement.

Brauer, Carl M. 1983. "Women Activists, Southern Conservatives, and the Prohibition of Sex Discrimination in Title VII of the 1964 Civil Rights Act." *Journal of Southern History* 49 (February).

Freeman, Jo. 1991. "How 'Sex' Got Into Title VII: Persistent Opportunism as a Maker of Public Policy." *Law and Inequality: A Journal of Theory and Practice* 9:2 (March).

Heclo, Hugh. 1986. "The Political Foundations of Antipoverty Policy." In Sheldon H. Danziger and Daniel H. Weinberg, eds., *Fighting Poverty: What Works and What Doesn't*. Cambridge: Harvard University Press.

Hicks, Alexander M., and Duane H. Swank. 1992. "Politics, Institutions, and Welfare Spending." *American Political Science Review* 86, 3.

Key, Jr., V.O. 1995. "A Theory of Critical Elections." *Journal of Politics* 17 (February).

Mishler, William, and Reginald S. Sheehan. 1993. "The Supreme Court as a Countermajoritarian Institution? The Impact of Public Opinion on Supreme Court Decisions." *American Political Science Review* 87.

Norpoth, Helmut, and Jeffrey A. Segal. 1994. "Popular Influence on Supreme Court Decisions." *American Political Science Review* 88.

Page, Benjamin I., and Richard A. Brody. 1972. "Policy Voting and the Electoral Process: The Vietnam War Issue." *American Political Science Review* 66 (September).

Sundquist, James. 1988. "Needed: A Political Theory for the New Era of Divided Government in the United States." *Political Science Quarterly* (winter 1988–89).

BOOKS

Abramson, Paul A., John H. Aldrich, and David W. Rohde. 1998. *Continuity and Change in the 1996 Elections*. Washington: Congressional Quarterly Press.

Amy, Douglas J. 1993. *Real Choices/New Voices: The Case for Proportional Representation Elections in the United States*. New York: Columbia University Press.

Bennett, W. Lance. 1996. *The Governing Crisis: Media, Money, and Marketing in American Elections*, 2nd ed. New York: St. Martin's Press.

Brecher, Charles, Raymond D. Horton, with Robert A. Cropf and Dean Michael Mead. 1993. *Power Failure: New York City Politics and Policy Since 1960*. New York and Oxford: Oxford University Press.

Burnham, Walter Dean. 1970. *Critical Elections and the Mainsprings of American Politics*. New York: Norton.

Campbell, Angus, Philip E. Converse, Warren E. Miller, and Donald E. Stokes. 1960. *The American Voter*. New York: Wiley.

Conway, M. Margaret, David W. Ahern, and Gertrude A. Steuernagel. 1995. *Women and Public Policy: A Revolution in Progress*. Washington, DC: Congressional Quarterly Press.

Darcy, R., Susan Welch, and Janet Clark. 1994. *Women, Elections, and Representation*. Lincoln: University of Nebraska Press.

Drew, Elizabeth. 1997. *Whatever It Takes: The Real Struggle for Political Power in America*. New York: Viking Penguin.

Edsall, Thomas Byrne. 1984. *The New Politics of Inequality*. New York: W.W. Norton & Company.

Edwards, George C., and Stephen J. Wayne. 1997. *Presidential Leadership: Politics and Policy Making*. New York: St. Martin's Press.

Fishel, Jeff. 1985. *Presidents and Promises: From Campaign Pledge to Presidential Performance*. Washington, DC: Congressional Quarterly Press.

Germond, Jack, and Jules Witcover. 1989. *Whose Broad Stripes and Bright Stars? The Trivial Pursuit of the Presidency 1988*. New York: Warner Books.

Gimpel, James, 1995. *Legislating the Revolution: The Contract With America in its First 100 Days*. Boston: Allyn and Bacon.

Ginsberg, Benjamin, and Martin Shefter. 1990. *Politics by Other Means: The Declining Importance of Elections in America*. New York: Basic Books.

Ginsberg, Benjamin, and Alan Stone, eds. 1996. *Do Elections Matter?* 3d ed. Armonk, NY: M.E. Sharpe.

Graber, Doris A. 1997. *Mass Media and American Politics*, 5th ed. Washington, DC: Congressional Quarterly Press.

Guth, James L., and John C. Green, eds. 1991. *The Bible and the Ballot Box: Religion and Politics in the 1988 Election*. Boulder, CO: Westview Press.

Hunter, James Davison. 1991. *Culture Wars: The Struggle to Define America*. New York: Basic Books.

Jones, Charles O., ed. 1988. *The Reagan Legacy, Promise and Performance*. Chatham, NJ: Chatham House.

Keefe, William J. 1994. *Parties, Politics, and Public Policy*. 7th ed. Washington, DC: Congressional Quarterly Press.

King, Anthony. 1997. *Running Scared, Why America's Politicians Campaign Too Much and Govern Too Little*. New York: The Free Press.

Leman, Christopher. 1980. *The Collapse of Welfare Reform: Political Institutions, Policy, and the Poor in Canada and the United States*. Cambridge: The MIT Press.

Loomis, Burdett A. 1998. *The Contemporary Congress*. 2d ed. New York: St. Martin's Press.

Maisel, L. Sandy. 1994. *The Parties Respond: Changes in American Parties and Campaigns*, 2d ed. Boulder, CO: Westview Press.

Malbin, Michael, ed. 1984. *Money and Politics in the United States*. Chatham, NJ: Chatham House.

Mayhew, David R. 1974. *Congress: The Electoral Connection*. New Haven: Yale University Press.

Nelson, Michael, ed. 1989. *Elections of 1988*. Washington, DC: Congressional Quarterly Press.

———, ed. 1997. *The Election of 1996*. Washington, DC: Congressional Quarterly Press.

Page, Benjamin I. 1978. *Choices and Echoes in Presidential Elections, Rational Man and Electoral Democracy*. Chicago: University of Chicago Press.

Parenti, Michael. 1986. *Inventing Reality: The Politics of the Mass Media*. New York: St. Martin's Press.

Patterson, Thomas E. 1993. *Out of Order*. New York: Knopf.

Phillips, Kevin. 1994. *Arrogant Capitol: Washington, Wall Street, and the Frustration of American Politics*. Boston: Little Brown and Co.

Piven, Frances Fox, and Richard Cloward. 1988. *Why Americans Don't Vote*. New York: Pantheon.

Pomper, Gerald, ed. 1993. *The Elections of 1992: Reports and Interpretations*. Chatham, NJ: Chatham House.

———, ed. 1997. *The Election of 1996*. Chatham, NJ: Chatham House.

Reichley, A. James. 1992. *The Life of the Parties: A History of American Political Parties*. New York: The Free Press.

Reiter, Howard L. 1993. *Parties and Elections in Corporate America*. New York: Longman.

Rosenstone, Steven J., and John Mark Hansen. 1993. *Mobilization, Participation, and Democracy in America*. New York: Macmillan Publishing Company.

Schantz, Harvey, ed. 1996. *American Presidential Elections: Process, Policy and Political Change*. Albany: State University of New York Press.

Sorauf, Frank J. 1992. *Inside Campaign Finance: Myths and Realities*. New Haven: Yale University Press.

Sundquist, James. 1983. *Dynamics of the Party System: Alignment and Realignment of Political Parties in the United States.* Washington, DC: The Brookings Institution.

Vig, Norman J., and Michael E. Kraft, eds. 1994. *Environmental Policy in the 1990s.* Washington: CQ Press.

Weisberg, Herbert F., ed. 1995. *Democracy's Feast: Elections in America.* Chatham, NJ: Chatham House.

Index

About the Contributors

DENNIS M. ANDERSON is Associate Professor of Political Science at Bowling Green State University. Recent publications include "Proportional Representation in Toledo: The Neglected Step-child of the Municipal Reform Movement" in Kathleen Barber, ed., *Proportional Representation and Election Reform in Ohio* (1995); and "One Way to Run a Legislative Body: The End of an Era in Ohio" in Jack R. Van Der Slik, ed., *Politics in the American States and Communities* (1995).

RICHARD P. BARBERIO is Adjunct Professor both in the Graduate Studies Program of SUNY Empire State College and the Interdisciplinary Studies Department of SUNY Ulster Community College. His main fields of interest are American political institutions, public policy, and political behavior, with primary research interests in American values and political ideology.

MONICA BAUER is Assistant Professor of Political Science at Metropolitan State College of Denver, and is coauthor (with Herbert E. Alexander) of *Financing the 1988 Elections*, Boulder, CO: Westview (1991). Her most recent publication is "Campaign Finance and Reform," an article in George Kurian, ed., *Encyclopedia of American Political Parties* (1996).

JOSEPH CAMMARANO is Assistant Professor of Political Science at Providence College. He is coeditor (with Grant Reeher) of *Education for Citizenship: Ideas and Innovations in Political Learning* (1997). His research focuses chiefly on how politicians provide accountability to citizens in an era of weakened party ties, and how citizens perceive politicians.

JEAN-PHILIPPE FALETTA is a doctoral candidate in Political Science at Wayne State University. His research interests lie primarily in presidential and legislative studies and political parties, and he has written on the presidency, campaign rhetoric, and elections.

JO FREEMAN is an independent scholar who practices law in New York City. She holds a Ph.D. from the University of Chicago and a J.D. from New York University Law School. She has written "Change and Continuity for Women at the Republican and Democratic Conventions" in *American Review of Politics* 18 (fall 1998); edited *Women: A Feminist Perspective* (1975, 1995); and is writing a book *A Room at a Time: Women's Entry Into Politics from the Mid-Nineteenth Century to the Mid-1960s*.

RODD FREITAG is Assistant Professor of Political Science at the University of Wisconsin–Eau Claire. His major academic interests are legislative politics, state and local politics, and political interest groups and the politics surrounding them.

JEAN WAHL HARRIS is Associate Professor of Political Science at the University of Scranton. She has written "Introductory Public Administration Textbooks: Integrating Scholarship on Women," in *Women and Politics* 14, 1 (1994); and "Comparison of Female and Male Prison Stressors," in *Journal of Offender Rehabilitation* 19, 1 (1993).

SAMUEL B. HOFF is ROTC Director and Professor of History and Political Science at Delaware State University. A specialist on the presidency, he has also served in three staff positions in the U.S. Congress. Recent publications include "A Positive Negative: Veto Strategy and Success by the Reagan Administration" in Eric J. Schmertz, Natalie Datlof, and Alexej Ugrinsky, eds., *Ronald Reagan's America* (Greenwood, 1997); and "Branch Battles: Nixon, Congress, and the Veto Power," *The Political Chronicle* (fall 1996).

MARK KEMPER is Instructor of Political Science at Miami University. He is coauthor (with Lawrence Baum) of "The Ohio Judiciary" in Alexander P. Lamis, ed., *Ohio Politics* (1994). His primary research focus is the U.S. Supreme Court.

JEFFREY KRAUS is Professor of Political Science at Wagner College, a political consultant, and past president of the New York State Political Science Association. He is a contributor to the forthcoming *Encyclopedia of American Third Parties*. His most recent publications include book reviews in the *American Political Science Review* and the *Southeastern Political Review*.

EVERETT CARLL LADD is Director of the Institute for Social Inquiry, University of Connecticut, and Executive Director and President of the Roper Center for Public Opinion Research. The author of scores of books and articles, Professor Ladd most recently coauthored (with Karlyn H. Bowman) the monographs *What's Wrong* and *Attitudes Toward Economic Inequality* (both 1998). He is editor of the Roper Center's election reviews *America at the Polls 1994, America at the Polls 1996,* and *America at the Polls 1998.* His latest book, *The Ladd Report on Civic America*, will be published in spring 1999.

STEPHANIE GRECO LARSON is Associate Professor of Political Science at Dickinson College. She is the author of "ABC's 'Person of the Week': American Values in Television News," in *Journalism and Mass Communication Quarterly* 75 (fall 1998); and *Creating Consent of the Governed: A Member of Congress and the Local Media* (1992).

MICHAEL E. LYNCH, SR., is Professor and Chair of Political Science at SUNY College at Oneonta. He is coauthor (with Dennis R. DeLong) of "The Policy Process and the Bureaucracy" in Peter Colby, ed., *New York State Today*, (2d edition, 1989). His research and teaching concentrations are in computer-assisted instruction and full-time public service internships, with a continuing focus on American political behavior.

ERIKA E. PILVER is Professor of Political Science at Westfield State College and member and past director of the college's Women's Studies Program, which she helped develop. She writes on public administration, state and local government, and women's studies.

WILLIAM C. PINK is Research Analyst, Global Tracking Programs, Worldwide Market Intelligence Department of IBM. He is the author of "The (In)compatibility of Rousseau and Olson," in *Conference* 8 (fall 1998); and "Candidate Ambiguity in American Presidential Elections" (in progress).

GERALD M. POMPER is Board of Governors Professor of Political Science at Rutgers University. His most recent of many publications include *The Election of 1996*, Chatham, NJ: Chatham House (1997); *Passions and Interests* (1996); and "The Alleged Decline of American Parties," in John Geer, ed., *Politicians and Party Politics* (1998). His article in this reader also appears in John C. Green and Daniel M. Shea, eds., *The State of the Parties*, 3d edition, 1999).

PAUL E. SCHEELE is Professor Emeritus of Political Science at SUNY College at Oneonta. His chief research interests have been American national public policy and policy making focusing especially on natural resource issues.

DANIEL M. SHEA is Associate Professor of Political Science at Allegheny College. He has written or edited a number of books on parties and elections, including *Campaign Craft: The Strategy, Tactics and Art of Political Campaign Management* (Praeger, 1996); and (with John C. Green) *The State of the*

Parties: The Changing Role of American Parties (3d edition, 1999). Forthcoming in 1999 (with John K. White) is *Parties in the Information Age.*

JUNE SAGER SPEAKMAN is Associate Professor of Political Science at Roger Williams University. Her chief research interests are congressional decision making with a focus on policy change; the impact of individual legislators on the legislative process; and the role of the media in politics, with emphases on campaign advertising and images of women in the media.

JEFFREY M. STONECASH is Professor of Political Science in the Maxwell School of Citizenship and Public Affairs at Syracuse University. A prolific writer, he is the author of the forthcoming *Governing New York State* (4th edition); "Emerging Party Cleavages in the House of Representatives: 1962–1996," *American Politics Quarterly* 27, 1 (January 1999); and "Political Cleavage in State Legislative Houses," *Legislative Studies Quarterly* (forthcoming 1999).

MARC A. TRIEBWASSER is Professor of Political Science at Central Connecticut State University. Recent publications include "The End of Mass Society?: A Preface to Telecommunications Politics" in Joseph E. Behar, ed., *Mapping Cyberspace* (1997); and *American Government Interactive Video* (1994), which won an APSA award for Best Instructional Software.

ISBN 0-275-96602-X

90000>

EAN

9 780275 966027

HARDCOVER BAR CODE

DATE DUE